CORNELL
UNIVERSITY
LIBRARY

Date Due

PROBLEMS OF WAR AND OF RECONSTRUCTION
EDITED BY
FRANCIS G. WICKWARE

WAR COSTS AND THEIR FINANCING

PROBLEMS OF WAR
AND OF RECONSTRUCTION

Edited by

Francis G. Wickware

The Redemption of the Disabled
> By Garrard Harris, Research Division, Federal Board for Vocational Education.

The Colleges in War Time and After
> By Parke Rexford Kolbe, President of the Municipal University of Akron, Special Collaborator in the United States Bureau of Education.

The American Air Service
> By Arthur Sweetser, Sometime Captain, Air Service, United States Army.

Commercial Policy in War Time and After
> By William Smith Culbertson, Member of the United States Tariff Commission.

Government Organization in War Time and After
> By William Franklin Willoughby, Director of the Institute for Government Research.

The Strategy of Minerals
> Edited by George Otis Smith, Director of the United States Geological Survey.

War Costs and Their Financing
> By Ernest L. Bogart, Professor of Economics in the University of Illinois.

D. APPLETON AND COMPANY
PUBLISHERS   NEW YORK

T 225 C

PROBLEMS OF WAR AND OF RECONSTRUCTION

WAR COSTS AND THEIR FINANCING

A STUDY OF THE FINANCING OF THE WAR AND THE
AFTER-WAR PROBLEMS OF DEBT AND TAXATION

BY

ERNEST LUDLOW BOGART

PROFESSOR OF ECONOMICS IN THE UNIVERSITY OF
ILLINOIS; SOMETIME ASSISTANT FOREIGN TRADE ADVISER
IN THE UNITED STATES DEPARTMENT OF STATE

WITH AN INTRODUCTION BY
RUSSELL C. LEFFINGWELL
SOMETIME ASSISTANT SECRETARY OF THE TREASURY

D. APPLETON AND COMPANY
NEW YORK   LONDON
1921

COPYRIGHT, 1921, BY
D. APPLETON AND COMPANY

PRINTED IN THE UNITED STATES OF AMERICA

TO
MY ASSOCIATES
ON THE
WAR TRADE BOARD
AND IN THE
DEPARTMENT OF STATE

PREFACE

The effort has been made in this volume to present in broad outline the salient features of war finance and some of the financial problems now confronting the United States and the leading nations of Europe. Although it is still too early to assess accurately the relative importance of various economic and financial measures and events, there is a certain gain in recording them while they are still fresh in mind. Many events were so extraordinary, and the measures taken to cope with them so unprecedented, that much time and study will be required finally to determine their part in the World War. But that they played an important *rôle* in determining the outcome of the struggle is clear. The "silver bullets" were equally decisive with those of lead or steel in deciding the victory. Never before were the differences between a good and a vicious theory of war finance so important and so far-reaching, for never before have war expenditures reached such stupendous figures.

It had been hoped that the wide ramifications of international credit and trade would constitute an effectual guarantee against war, but this hope was rudely dashed. Again, when war actually began, it was confidently predicted that the financial exhaustion of the belligerents would bring it to an end after a few months, but events proved these prophecies also false. A constantly recurrent problem throughout the whole war was the question as to whence came the enormous sums which were expended with such reckless prodigality. The important part played by the banks in financing the war, the enormous loans made by all the belligerents, the unprece-

PREFACE

dented inflation as a result of the increase in note issues and the subtler credit expansion, and the more limited resort to taxation, all presented problems of paramount interest and importance. These are discussed in the following pages.

For us the most significant result of the war is the emergence of the United States as a creditor nation and its present dominating position in foreign trade and international finance. The changes in the movements of foreign trade, and in the commercial, industrial, and financial life of the United States, are briefly described. The final chapters of the book present the problems of financial reconstruction — problems of inflated currency, of staggering debts, of crushing taxation — and of the measures taken by the leading belligerents to meet these problems. In conclusion, the cost of the war, so far as this is reducible to money values, is stated.

With regard to the statistics of war finance a word of explanation is needed. For convenience foreign currencies have been converted into dollars at pre-war rates of exchange, but in round numbers rather than in precise equivalents. Thus, the pound sterling ($4.8665) has been converted at $5; the ruble ($0.5146) and yen ($0.4985), at 50 cents; the florin ($0.402), at 40 cents; the krona ($0.268) and mark ($0.2385), at 25 cents; the krone ($0.2022), the leu and leva ($0.1946), the drachma, lira, and franc ($0.193), at 20 cents. This has resulted in a slight overstatement in the case of some of the countries and a slighter understatement in the case of others, but as many of the figures are themselves still open to correction, it was thought that the convenience of this method more than offset the slight variations involved.

In writing this book the author drew upon material used in the preparation of a companion statistical study, "The Direct and Indirect Costs of the Great World

PREFACE

War''; most of the tables and other statistical data incorporated in Chapters IV, V, VI, and VIII of this volume have been drawn from that source. To the Carnegie Endowment of International Peace, by whom this study was published, the author begs to make acknowledgment for their kindness in permitting the use of this copyrighted material. In other respects the present volume is an independent study.

Friendly counsel and assistance have been received by the author from many quarters, but his obligations are so manifest in certain instances that he desires to make public acknowledgment thereof. To Miss Constance Agnes McHugh his indebtedness is especially great for her untiring and capable assistance in collecting and assembling the material, in preparing most of the tables, and in giving information and advice upon many points. Sincere thanks are also tendered Dr. Constantine E. McGuire for the onerous task of reading the manuscript and for many valuable suggestions. For errors which yet remain and for the views herein expressed on disputable points, the author alone must be held responsible.

ERNEST L. BOGART.

CONTENTS

	PAGE
PREFACE	vii
INTRODUCTION	xv

CHAPTER I

THE BASIS OF NATIONAL AND INTERNATIONAL CREDIT

Industrial development furnishes a supply of capital — Development of credit and financial institutions provide a money market — Political democracy creates a willingness to lend — The growth of public debts — Opportunity for profit in the exploitation of undeveloped countries — Investments in foreign countries — London an international money market and center of credit . 1

CHAPTER II

FINANCIAL READJUSTMENTS AT THE OUTBREAK OF WAR

Germany's preparedness — The Entente Allies caught unaware — Panic and temporary breakdown of credit — Remedial measures — Safeguarding the gold reserves — Issue of additional money — Adjustment to war conditions . 21

CHAPTER III

THE UNITED STATES AS A NEUTRAL

Situation in the United States at the outbreak of the war in Europe — The expansion of foreign trade — How Europe paid its bills — The shipment of gold — Foreign loans placed in the United States — Purchase of American securities held abroad — Is New York to be the financial center of the world? . 54

CHAPTER IV

WAR EXPENDITURES

The cost of past wars — Expenditures in the United States — Expenditures in Great Britain — Expenditures in France, Russia, and Italy — Expenditures in Germany and Austria-Hungary — Comparative estimate of total war expenditures . 82

CONTENTS

CHAPTER V

PAPER MONEY AND BANK CREDIT

Large use of banks in financing the war — Direct issues of paper money in Europe — Services of the Federal Reserve System in the United States — Treatment of gold . 107

CHAPTER VI

LOANS IN EUROPE

General characteristics — British war loans — Use of loans in France, Russia, and Italy — The German theory of war finance — German banks and loan bureaus — Loans in Austria-Hungary, Bulgaria, and Turkey . . . 146

CHAPTER VII

LOANS IN THE UNITED STATES

War-finance program of the United States — The First Liberty Loan — The Second Liberty Loan — The Third Liberty Loan — The Fourth Liberty Loan — The Victory Liberty Loan — War savings and thrift stamps — Advances to the Allies 199

CHAPTER VIII

TAXATION IN EUROPE

Vigorous use of taxation in England — Slight results in France, Russia, and Italy — Reasons therefor — Inadequacy of taxation by the Central Powers . . 234

CHAPTER IX

TAXATION IN THE UNITED STATES

A new era of Federal taxation — Revenue Act of October 3, 1913 — Outbreak of the European War — Emergency Revenue Act of October 22, 1914 — Act of September 8, 1916 — The taxation of wealth — Act of March 3, 1917 — Declaration of war by the United States — War Revenue Act of October 3, 1917 — Income and excess-profits tax provisions — Act of February 24, 1919 — Analysis of the measure 264

CONTENTS

CHAPTER X

HOW SHOULD A WAR BE FINANCED? THE LESSON OF THE CIVIL WAR

The problem of financing the Civil War — Chase's loan policy — Inadequacy of taxation — Issue of legal-tender notes — System of short-term loans — Bond acts — Conclusions — Financial management of the World War — Inability to meet current charges — Loans vs. taxes — Arguments for a loan policy — Disadvantages of heavy taxation — Arguments for a tax policy — Evils of excessive loans 297

CHAPTER XI

FINANCING EUROPE AFTER THE WAR

Foreign trade of the United States as a belligerent — Exports and imports by regions — The balance of trade — Europe's need for capital — Greatest supplies to be found in the United States — How can this be made available? — Machinery by which loans can be advanced to Europe — Proposals for the extension of short-time credit — Long-term credit — Conclusions . 326

CHAPTER XII

AFTER-WAR PROBLEMS OF CURRENCY AND DEBT

Inflation of the currency a world phenomenon — Its effect on prices — Why should inflation have been permitted? — The remedy for inflation — Difficulties — The distribution of gold — Financial situation of the principal countries — Comparison of wealth and debt — Can the burdens be carried? — American and European theories as to debt payment — Problem of funding the floating debts — The capital levy — Problem of refunding — Will the debts be paid? . 351

CHAPTER XIII

AFTER-WAR PROBLEMS OF TAXATION

Economic strength of the leading nations — The financial outlook in the United States — The situation in Great Britain — The situation in France and Italy — Germany's position — Proposed revenues of five leading nations — Probable development of principal taxes . . . 391

CONTENTS

CHAPTER XIV

THE COST OF THE WAR

Who pays for a war? — Material costs — Depletion of capital — The burden on future generations — Direct and indirect costs — Immaterial costs — Diversity of losses — Some factors of advantage — Indefensibility of war . 413

APPENDICES

I. British Moratorium Proclamations	. . .	423
II. French Moratorium Decrees . . .	. . .	429
III. Act Providing for German Loan Offices	. .	432
IV. Liberty Bond Acts	. .	437
V. Taxation in the United States	. . .	473
VI. Public Debt of the United States .	. . .	489
INDEX	. .	493

INTRODUCTION

One who attempts, so soon after the fact, to make a comprehensive survey of the financing of the World War by all the belligerents performs an important service, for he sets men's minds thinking about the war's lessons in finance and economics while they still have current interest. He necessarily labors, however, under great handicaps. Authoritative histories of the financing of the war in each of the countries involved remain to be written. Generally the policies adopted and the results are matters of record, but the reasons for their adoption remain to some extent to be disclosed. In the present volume Professor Bogart has performed a valuable service in bringing together in usable form some of the scattered data relating to war finance and in drawing such conclusions as seemed to him warranted by the evidence in hand. In the performance of this task he has displayed industry, discrimination, and breadth of view.

On the continent of Europe generally, currency inflation moved hand in hand with the war itself, and the demands of Governments for the destructive business of war served to inflate prices. The peoples of the Continental countries had been staggering for generations under the burdens of an armed peace. They were perhaps in no condition, certainly in no mood, to submit to additional taxation when called upon to engage in actual war. The price of physical preparedness, long maintained, was, for them, economic and financial unreadiness for a long war. The inflation stimulant was deemed necessary by their statesmen, and it was injected unsparingly and continuously. On the other hand, thanks to relative immunity from land attack, Great Britain and the

xv

INTRODUCTION

United States, though they had maintained great navies, had escaped the greater economic drain of standing armies, and entered the war with resources relatively unimpaired. So in Great Britain currency inflation was strictly limited, and in the United States it was wholly avoided, as an instrument of war finance, and in these countries a vigorous effort was made to limit inflation of credit, a grave, though lesser, evil. Germany seems to have been enabled to conceal the effects of her inflation policy from her own people, almost to the end of the war, by the Allied blockade, which prevented the German people from making purchases abroad, and thus prevented the depreciation of the mark from being fully registered in foreign exchange, while price-fixing and rationing had a similar effect at home. It is an interesting speculation whether the blockade of Germany, which enforced "war saving" on the German people, was more of a benefit than a detriment to Germany, whether her economic collapse was expedited or delayed by it.

On the European continent then, inflation was accelerated by unsound fiscal expedients, whereas in England and the United States it was retarded by relatively sound ones. But the disease spread by railroad and ship, by cable and wireless, to the uttermost parts of the earth, whithersoever war orders could be transmitted and gold or securities shipped, or credits established under the inducement of war profits. Its ravages seem to have been most severe in Japan, India, and other remote places, which assumed little, if any, of the war's financial burdens and enjoyed to the utmost its apparent benefits; just as in this country price inflation was more rapid before we entered the war and after the armistice than during the intervening period when we were engaged in actual warfare and war laws and regulations and the war spirit made it possible to impose a certain restraint.

Certainly inflation could not have been avoided alto-

INTRODUCTION

gether unless the war itself had been avoided, for it had its source in the war's waste of wealth. When the war ended, though the belligerent Governments had on hand considerable stocks of war supplies, ill adapted or not adapted at all for civilian use, and though there had been enormous increases in plant intended for making tools of war, stocks of goods for civilian use were very low, and the normal programme for the maintenance and extension of civilian plant and equipment, including railroads and housing, had been practically in abeyance for the whole war period. The world's working capital and its fixed capital had been reduced. The world had been living beyond its income, living to some extent upon its accumulation of wealth. This would have meant inflation even if the whole cost of the war had been met from current taxes, for the money to pay taxes could only have been had by expanding credit to the extent that war expenditures exceeded the net income of the people.

If it were possible, every expenditure of government in war and in peace should be met from current taxes. The notion that by borrowing the burden may be passed on to future generations is a delusion and a snare. It is true that by long borrowings future generations are burdened. The present cannot, however, escape the burden. Government expenditures for economically wasteful purposes create it. Government loans diffuse it, by absorbing capital and inflating credit, by increasing prices and interest rates. Thus the burden is shifted, not from one generation to another, but from the taxpayer to the community as a whole. Government debt is always bad. When created for the purposes of war, it should be paid off as promptly as possible after peace. Burdensome as taxes may be, their burden is lighter while war inflation lasts. Taxation for redemption of home debt is never really burdensome except as it is inequitably imposed.

INTRODUCTION

But taxes should be paid from income. They cannot be paid without inflation from any other source. They should accordingly be imposed upon and assessed in proportion to income. If it were possible, they should be imposed upon *available* incomes, that is, upon the part of the income of the taxpayer not required with reasonable economy to support himself and his family, or of the business man for the development of his business. But it is impracticable in tax law and administration to make these nice discriminations, and exemptions below a fixed minimum income and graduated surtaxes upon super-"normal" incomes are but a crude effort in that direction. When the tax gatherer takes more than the available income of a given taxpayer, the excess becomes in effect a capital tax and must be borrowed or provided by the sale of capital assets. If the taxpayer happens not to have available property to an amount sufficient to pay his taxes and provide for the expansion of his business, his activities will be curtailed or put an end to.

The difficulties and injustices involved in any system of taxation become more serious as tax rates increase; and when, as in the World War, the Government's needs exceed the whole free income of the people, after providing for operating and living expenses and the capital expenditures that are necessary to enable business to meet the demands for munitions and supplies thrown upon it by the war, then it is impossible to adopt any system of taxation that will fully meet the Government's needs and at the same time avoid inflation. In a war the Government should levy taxes to as great an amount as it can without jeopardizing the productive business of the country, which is as essential to the successful conduct of the war as fighting men themselves.

For instance, if instead of asking $8,000,000,000 taxes for the fiscal year 1919, the Treasury of the United States had in June, 1918, asked $24,000,000,000, which

INTRODUCTION

was the estimated amount of expenditures on a war basis, and if Congress had withstood the outcry and passed such a tax law, it is not difficult to guess that the consequence would have been a business catastrophe in this country which would have put us effectively out of the war. We should not have been able to spend the $24,000,000,000, because we should not have been able to find solvent business concerns to execute the Government's orders. Whether it would have been safe to go somewhat further than $8,000,000,000, it is, of course, impossible to say. One thing is clear, that if excessive taxes were imposed, the fact might not be known until efficiency was impaired and the harm done. In war time it would be impossible to repair the injury done by a tax levy which in fact was excessive. Panic, depression, lowered efficiency, inactivity, will take place sooner or later as the result of a really serious error on the side of severity in taxation. If they take place in war time, the consequences may be irreparable. The consequences of moderate errors on the side of leniency in taxation, however, though very grave, are not irreparable. After a war is won, the people can, if they will, submit to taxation to an amount adequate to repair the error.

The question is, however, largely academic. One hundred million people are not pawns in a game. They will have no better government and no better economics than they want, and even if they wanted and got the best, they could not escape the evil consequences of bad government and bad economics rampant in the rest of the world. To illustrate again. Our Treasury's programme was to finance from current taxes at least one-third of our total expenditures, including loans to foreign Governments. The first War Revenue Act was supposed to carry $4,000,000,000 in taxes. It did not, however, become law until October 3, 1917, about six months after the declaration of war. A little more than six months

INTRODUCTION

later the Treasury demanded that the tax revenues be doubled, so as to produce $8,000,000,000. The leaders of both parties in Congress had agreed among themselves to adjourn in July, 1918, to enable members of Congress to mend their fences before election, and they protested vigorously against the Treasury's programme. Congressional leaders in the Administration party assured the Secretary of the Treasury, and the President himself, to whom they appealed, that persistence in the Treasury's programme would inevitably mean loss of the House of Representatives to the Administration party at the election in the following November. The Treasury nevertheless did persist, the President sustained it, and the Administration lost not only the House, but the Senate as well. The $8,000,000,000 tax bill passed the House after a protracted delay, but the Senate did not act upon it until after the election and the armistice in November, 1918, when, in the light of altered conditions, the Treasury modified its programme and asked for $6,000,000,000, instead of $8,000,000,000. The second War Revenue Act did not become law until February 24, 1919, more than three months after the fighting stopped and about nine months after the Treasury had demanded the additional revenue. The Secretary of the Treasury and the President knowingly took their political lives in their hands in an effort to finance the war as largely as possible from current taxes, and in the issue lost them.

It is inevitable, then, that the amounts collected in taxes fall far short of Governments' needs in such a war. The difference must be made up by loans. Those loans should be distributed as widely as possible among investors. To the extent that Government expenditures are met from loans placed among investors, who pay for them out of income which would otherwise have been spent or invested in non-essential enterprises, inflation may be avoided for the time being. It was the multitude

INTRODUCTION

who financed the war. Whether with their savings the rich bought Government securities, was not very important. To the extent that the rich do not own Government securities they invest in other securities. It was only the multitude who had a capacity of saving and making investments which they had never utilized.

There are those who say that Governments should have paid the market rate for money throughout the war. The fact is that there was no market rate and there could be none. The supply of Government securities always exceeded the demand. Funds to meet this necessity could be had, not by marking down values of existing securities, but by seeking new savings, and these in turn were to be had by appeals, not to acquisitiveness, but to patriotism. The overwhelming necessities of the war dominated the situation; demand was unlimited, and supply very limited. Governments could not tolerate profiteering, under cover of the law of supply and demand, on the part of those possessed of goods, services, or credit, in the face of the dire necessity of the whole people. So they fixed the prices of commodities, controlled exports and imports and gave priority orders, took control of transportation on land and sea, restricted capital issues, restricted the export of gold and silver and controlled transactions in foreign exchange, sought personal saving in food, fuel and money, and drafted the man power of the nations and sent it to war. And they fixed the price of credit too.

But Government war expenditures put too much money into the pockets of people who were not accustomed to have it. They got it as an inducement to work as hard and fast and effectively as Governments asked them to do. Instantly upon the signing of the armistice many persons abandoned the restraint to which they had subjected themselves during the period of active warfare and indulged themselves in idleness or half-hearted

INTRODUCTION

labor and in loose expenditures. War wages, war profits, and war bonds represented just so much accumulated buying power in the hands, very largely, of those who were unaccustomed to have it. The war being over, we had to have our fling, and the fling being over, we have to take our medicine.

Deflation of prices seems to have started during the early months of 1920 with the Chinese boycott of Japanese goods for political reasons, which pricked the bubble of Japan's war prosperity. Price deflation had made great strides all over the world by the end of 1920, though inflation of currency and credit continued unrestrained on the European continent, and was not prevented, though it was retarded, in England and the United States by the dear-money policy adopted by the Bank of England in November, 1919, and the Federal Reserve Banks in January, 1920.

In Europe after the armistice, while the resumption of business activity and production awaited assurance of peace and political stability, still unhappily withheld, millions of men were kept under arms and more or less desultory warfare continued. Governments kept themselves in power by means of this military activity, by distributing food at less than cost, and by making unemployment allowances, which subsidized idleness, and paid the bills by printing currency because taxes and loans were unpopular. War necessity is the only, though perhaps sufficient, justification for the defiance of economic law. One of the greatest evils left by the war in its train was the habit of mind that looks to government to do all things and tolerates government practices that in times of peace are unsound, if not downright dishonest. Government expenditure is the root of all present economic and social evil. To allay domestic discontent by subsidies and doles from the public treasury involves the disturbance of social and economic laws for political

INTRODUCTION

purposes. The issue of paper money to meet government expenditures is a form of surreptitious taxation, which imposes the burden of government expense most heavily upon those in the community least able to bear it and leads ultimately to bankruptcy. Embargoes upon the exportation of gold, persisted in in time of peace by all the countries of the world except the United States, preserve the basis for internal inflation and amount to the refusal of payment of international indebtedness. Embargoes on the importation of securities by the country of issue amount to their dishonor. Embargoes on the importation of goods, whether frankly so called or masquerading as protective tariffs, retard economic recovery and lay the basis for future wars.

Europe has many overpopulated areas and has great populations, ordinarily employed in making finished products for export from imported materials, and fed in large part from imported foods. She cannot, therefore, have prosperous economic life until her currencies have a reasonably firm value in foreign exchange. It would be better if each of these currencies had a definite gold value, even if it were very much less than the pre-war gold value, than that European Governments should continue to print irredeemable paper to produce foreign exchange or current funds at home. We cannot have free and orderly international commerce without rather stable currencies all over the world. The inability of Great Britain and the European neutrals to resume specie payment grows doubtless out of their fear of being drained of their whole gold supply because their neighbors in Europe, to whom they must sell, cannot pay for what they buy. The problem, therefore, is to find what is necessary to give France, Italy, Belgium, and Central Europe sound currencies and to prepare them to resume specie payment. The war has burdened the continental Allies with very heavy debts to Great Britain and the

INTRODUCTION

United States, and Germany with heavy indemnity payments to the Allies. It has deprived Europe of a large part of her "invisible" exports. Obviously gold cannot be found to meet any balance by which the exports of any of these countries fall below the sum of their imports and such extraordinary war payments. The European world has not gold enough for its own requirements as domestic reserve, let alone for any continuous or permanent drain to meet foreign balances. Gold cannot be used to settle a continuing adverse foreign balance. It is only suitable to settle a seasonal or occasional balance except in a country which is itself a substantial producer of gold. Most of these countries require a certain amount of working capital from abroad to enable them to set their industries going at maximum efficiency.

The reasonably prompt economic rehabilitation of Continental Europe can be had through (1) peace and disarmament; (2) freer trade and the open door; (3) balancing budgets, stopping the printing press, and resuming specie payment both at home and in foreign exchange, currencies being revalued, if necessary, in terms of gold; (4) a composition with foreign government creditors, particularly Great Britain and the United States; and (5) capital issues (not merely bank credits) through private channels to provide working capital in foreign markets. America will be greatly the gainer when Europe, her best customer, recovers true buying power and her own speculatively inclined people no longer have to accept irredeemable currencies and credits in exchange for dollar values. America has everything to gain, and nothing to lose, by accepting the moral leadership imposed upon her by the war, and dealing constructively, even generously, with the economic problems of the European Allies. If she will not, she stands to lose the whole world as well as her own soul.

R. C. LEFFINGWELL.

WAR COSTS AND
THEIR FINANCING

CHAPTER I

THE BASIS OF NATIONAL AND INTERNATIONAL CREDIT

Industrial development furnishes a supply of capital — Development of credit and financial institutions provide a money market — Political democracy creates a willingness to lend — The growth of public debts — Opportunity for profit in the exploitation of undeveloped countries — Investments in foreign countries — London an international money market and center of credit.

The World War which has ravaged Europe and set back by at least a generation the progress of the world is estimated to have cost in direct expenses of the Governments involved not less than $200,000,000,000. Most of this enormous sum was obtained by means of popular loans. It is evident that it was possible to wage war on the scale of the late struggle and with the highly perfected technical appliances so lavishly employed in it, not merely because of the development of military strategy or of engineering and chemical science, but also because of the growth of the art and science of finance. Before the vast sums required could be obtained, a system of national credit must have been developed. In any discussion of war costs the question at once presents itself as to where all the money came from to pay for the war, and how the Governments were able to persuade their peoples to place it at their disposal. This very statement of the problem suggests at least three fundamental conditions for the development of national credit. There must be an adequate supply of disposable capital; there must exist the mechanism and machinery for the collection and distribution of this capital; and, finally, the lenders must have some adequate guarantee that it will be repaid.

Modern industrial society is so thoroughly capitalistic that we often fail to realize how comparatively recent is the existence of capital in large amounts and its utilization for any desired purpose. During the period from the fourth to the sixteenth centuries most of the capital in the world was invested in agriculture. The discovery of the shorter route to India and of the New World called into existence a new category — commercial and mercantile capital. Proof of the existence of considerable amounts of free disposable capital in England may be found in the rapidity with which London was rebuilt after the great fire of 1666 and the large sums that were lost in the speculative manias, or "bubble" companies, of 1720. As a result of the excesses of the latter period corporate organization was repressed for almost a century. It was not until after the industrial revolution in England at the end of the eighteenth century that we can recognize industrial capital. Moreover, down to the very beginning of the nineteenth century capital was almost entirely personal — that is to say, the capitalist went with his capital. Almost every business was carried on with the merchant's or the manufacturer's own funds. If these were insufficient, the additional sum necessary was obtained by forming a partnership with a wealthy man. The nineteenth century, however, saw a tremendous growth in the formation of joint-stock companies and of corporations.

The development of corporations with limited liability of individual shareholders greatly stimulated the investment habit. Capital now became impersonal: it could be invested in enterprises without the necessity of managing or supervising its use. Hitherto the national debt had afforded almost the only investment of this character, and as a consequence the rate of interest on Government bonds was extremely low; the subsequent fall in the price of Consols was the result, not of an impairment of the national credit of Great Britain, but rather of the multiplication of other safe forms of investment. The development of manufactures, of mining, and of railroad and water transportation offered attractive and productive fields of investment, and the growth of capital went on apace during the nineteenth century. An illustration of the amazing expansion which occurred within a century may be found in the growth of the value of manufactures in the principal industrial countries of the world between 1780 and 1888. This is shown in the following table:[1]

VALUE OF MANUFACTURES IN VARIOUS COUNTRIES, 1780-1888

(In millions)

Country	1780	1800	1820	1840	1860	1888
United Kingdom....		$885	$1,150	$1,450	$1,935	$2,885	$4,100
France............	235	950	1,100	1,320	1,900	2,425
Germany...........	250	300	425	750	1,550	2,915
Russia............	50	75	100	200	775	1,815
Austria...........	150	250	900	710	1,000	1,265
Italy.............	50	75	125	200	400	605
Spain.............	50	100	130	225	300	425
Belgium...........					300	450	510
United States.....	75	125	275	480	1,960	7,215
Various...........	155	225	300	450	800	1,815
Total.............	$2,400	$3,250	$4,305	$6,570	$12,020	$23,090

[1]Based on M. G. Mulhall, *Dictionary of Statistics* (London 1892), p. 365.

WAR COSTS AND THEIR FINANCING

The explanation of the enormous growth in manufacturing capacity is to be found primarily in the use of non-human power. A new era in human history was introduced with the invention of the steam engine. Before that event production was limited by the number of human hands available; afterwards the only limit was man's ingenuity in fashioning new machines to do his work. The last thirty years has seen an increase in the mastery of man over nature greater than that of any similar preceding period. Electricity and motor fuels have supplemented and in some cases supplanted the work of steam and have vastly increased production. Science has been called to the assistance of industry, and has not only increased output, but has improved quality and reduced cost. Industry has come more and more to be carried on by the use of capital and less by the direct application of human muscle. The vast increase which has taken place throughout the world in capital available for productive enterprises may be gauged by the statistics of the growth of wealth in the United Kingdom, France, and the United States shown on the following page.

Before national credit can be developed, however, there must exist in the community not merely a fund of disposable capital, but a securities market in which this capital can be disposed of must also have been created. Credit and financial institutions, banks, stock exchanges, brokers, credit instruments, commercial law, and other financial appliances of a highly developed industrial people are essential to the proper functioning of the economic machine known as modern industry. Banks are essential first of all as agencies for collecting the small savings of the people, massing them into larger sums and placing these at the disposal of industrial

NATIONAL AND INTERNATIONAL CREDIT

VALUE OF PROPERTY IN THE UNITED KINGDOM, FRANCE, AND THE UNITED STATES

(*In millions*)

	Year	VALUE OF PROPERTY	
		Total	Per capita
United Kingdom	1822	$12,500	$600
	1845	20,000	715
	1865	30,000	1,000
	1890	50,000	1,350
	1910	72,500	1,560
France	1853	25,000	700
	1878	35,000	930
	1886	40,000	1,050
	1910	59,000	1,475
United States	1850	7,135	308
	1870	30,068	780
	1890	65,037	1,036
	1910	187,739*	2,040

* Estimate of Census Bureau, 1912.

enterprise. Before it can be used, capital must first of all be produced, and then it must be saved and made available for use in further production. But the modern commercial bank does more than this. It transfers the control of industry and of labor to the possessor of credit; in other words, it provides the mechanism and machinery by which the capital of the community is brought under the direction of those who can presumably make the best economic, or possibly social, use of it, who can at least pay the best rate of interest, all things considered.

If capital is a new phenomenon, banks are still more

WAR COSTS AND THEIR FINANCING

recent. Modern banking may be said to date from the Florentine banks of the thirteenth and fourteenth centuries, although the first bank of record, the Bank of Venice, was established in 1171. The seventeenth century saw the establishment of banks in Amsterdam (1609), Hamburg (1619), Sweden (1688), and England (1694). Not until 1800 was the Bank of France established and the great central institutions of Germany, Italy, Russia and other countries were organized at still later dates. The earlier institutions were banks of deposit only, until the Bank of Sweden, in 1790, for the first time issued bank notes. Deposit banking in the modern sense is a development of the nineteenth century; it was not until after 1844 that deposit banking and the use of checks took on large dimensions in England, and in other countries its development was much later. But the growth of deposit banking was important, not merely in providing a market for capital, but also in stimulating the investment habit.

Still more recent in development has been the growth of stock and produce exchanges. This was an evolution of modern business, the stock exchange being a product of the eighteenth century, and the produce and cotton exchanges, of the nineteenth century. The system of option trading was only developed during the latter half of the nineteenth century. The oldest of the modern exchanges, the Paris Bourse, dates from 1726; the London Stock Exchange dates from 1773, and the New York Stock Exchange was not founded until 1817. With the creation of these exchanges and of credit institutions it became possible to trade in the evidences of debts of governments and of private corporations; in other words, a securities market was established.

It is scarcely necessary to establish the fact of a

demand for capital in the modern industrial state, on the part either of private borrowers or of the State itself. The extent of such a public demand is sufficiently evidenced by the growth of public debts. Here the interesting question arises: What forces operate to induce owners of capital to lend it to States or Governments? The answer to this question is political rather than economic, and is found in the existence of some adequate security to the lender that the sum borrowed will be returned. As a sovereign State may repudiate its obligations at its pleasure and cannot be sued or have judgment entered against it, such a guarantee would seem especially difficult to obtain. But in fact the strongest sort of security exists in the control of Government by the propertied class. "It follows from this," writes Professor Adams,[2] "that when property owners lend to the Government, they lend to a corporation controlled by themselves." As they are not likely to repudiate a debt that is owed to themselves, a public debt really rests upon the strongest sort of security.

Public borrowing has therefore accompanied the growth of constitutional government; it has had its greatest development since 1848, when constitutionalism became predominant in Europe. Above all else is needed the guarantee of a stable and honest Government. The mere forms of constitutionalism will not alone maintain the credit of a State, as witness the experience of many a Latin-American republic. On the other hand, there can be no stronger guarantee than that given by a Government resting upon the constitutionally expressed consent of the governed. Political democracy creates a willingness to lend by affording a guarantee against repudiation.

---

[2] Henry C. Adams, *Public Debts*, p. 9.

WAR COSTS AND THEIR FINANCING

The existence of a fund of loanable capital, of a money market, and of an adequate security against loss constitutes, however, only the favoring conditions for the growth of public debts; they do not explain the willingness, nay, the eagerness, of modern States to borrow. The explanation of this universal characteristic may be found in two directions. In the first place, the modern State is an industrial State and is called upon to do many things for its citizens which they did not demand a hundred years ago. From street railways and sewers to public baths and vocational schools, the expenditures of Governments have increased so rapidly that they frequently find it easier to meet their outlays by borrowing than by resort to taxation. But far more important than loans for investment purposes or to meet casual deficits have been those contracted for war. Armament, or preparation for war, and the actual costs of war itself are responsible for most of the indebtedness which burdens the nations of to-day. The following table shows the growth of the aggregate public debts of the civilized governments of the world during the last half-century prior to the World War:[3]

GROWTH OF PUBLIC DEBTS, 1848-1913

1848	$7,627,692,215
1860	10,399,341,688
1870	17,117,640,428
1880	27,421,037,643
1890	27,524,976,915
1908	36,548,455,489
1912	42,000,000,000
1913	42,940,000,000

The larger increases shown in this table were the result of war or of preparation for war. The period between 1848 and 1860 was one of armament, marked

---
[3] C. C. Plehn, *Introduction to Public Finance* (3d edition), p. 367.

NATIONAL AND INTERNATIONAL CREDIT

by several small outbreaks like the Crimean War. Between 1860 and 1870 the American Civil War and the Prussian-Austrian War increased public debts by nearly 70 per cent. The following decade, within which fell the Franco-Prussian War, saw the greatest increase of any period. The longer period from 1890 to 1908 witnessed our own war with Spain, the Boer War, and the Russo-Japanese War. The four years 1908-1912 were years of preparation, of military and naval expansion, and of armament. The only period in this table that did not show a marked increase in the growth of debt (from 1880 to 1890) was the only one that was marked by general peace, although the rapid reduction of the Civil War debt in the United States during this period accounts in part for the smallness of the increase.

But although war has been chiefly responsible for this huge burden of public debt, much of it has been incurred for the purpose of economic development, the other of the two objects for which financiers agree that a funded debt may properly be created. Between these two purposes there are many differences. A war debt is unproductive; it lessens rather than increases the debtor's ability to pay (leaving indemnities out of account); it usually becomes a permanent burden on the nation. An investment loan, on the other hand, is productive; it increases the efficiency of the borrower and creates the fund out of which the debt may be paid; finally, it is usually expunged within the life of the improvement. There is one other significant difference between these two kinds of debt: the war debt is usually a domestic debt, while that for "internal improvements," as they are designated in the United States, has generally been raised by means of foreign loans; in other words, wars may be financed by means of national credit, but the internal development of young countries awaits the growth of international credit.

The principles underlying the development of international credit are essentially the same as those upon which national credit is based. A supply of capital must exist, not merely adequate for the industrial needs of the lending country but sufficient also for export; in other words, there must be surplus capital. The machinery for the collection and distribution of this capital must now be international in scope; there must be international banks and trading companies, international shipping and insurance concerns, etc. Finally, sufficient guarantees must be given that the debts will be repaid. Here lies the most difficult problem of international borrowing, for attempts by the Governments of lenders to enforce payment from the borrowers have not infrequently led to international imbroglios and even to open war. What, then, is the motive that induces the citizens of one country to lend to those of another, or, in other words, what is the basis of international credit? It is, in a word, the hope of large profits.

The borrowing nations in the world economy are in general those with undeveloped resources; they are the countries young or industrially backward, but possessed at the same time of great natural resources the exploitation of which promises rich return. The investment of capital in these countries results in a large increase in production which enables the payment of interest and ultimately the repayment of the borrowed capital. By securing the capital goods of an industrially developed country, the improved agricultural machinery, mining machinery, railroad construction material and rolling stock, etc., the young country is able to avoid the slow and painful process of inventing and producing this equipment. It secures at once the latest devices of man's ingenuity. Equipped with those implements, such a country is able to multiply its productive capacity many fold. Perhaps no other single form of investment of foreign capital shows this result more quickly than expenditure for railways. The natural resources of the new country are thereby brought at once within the reach of a market.

The opportunity for large profits through the development of the resources of an undeveloped country has unhappily led to the exploitation of men as well as of nature and to political intrigue and international misunderstanding. The colonial trader was indeed once the chief cause of wars, but his place has now been taken by the concessionary interest.[4] Fortunes have been accumulated, especially in the tropical and semi-tropical regions, by the exploitation of natural resources, the opening of oil fields and mines, the building of railways and water-power plants, and by other enterprises. Such concessions are a prolific cause of war as they need and demand the support of the home Government.

Here we are concerned, however, with the legitimate investment of the surplus capital of an older State in the undeveloped resources of a younger one. This is immediately reflected in the trade relation between the two countries and continues to affect the balance of trade until the debt is entirely expunged. All the nations of the world may be grouped in one or the other of these classes, the lending and the borrowing countries. The chief countries that have supplied capital to other

---
[4] Foreign investment and concessions are discussed at length in this series in W. S. Culbertson, *Commercial Policy in War Time and After.* Cf. also A. S. Johnson, "The War: By an Economist," *Unpopular Review,* ii (July-December, 1914), p. 411.

lands are Great Britain, Germany, France, The Netherlands, Belgium, and Switzerland. Of these countries Great Britain is by far the most important lender. On the other hand, the important borrowing countries have been the United States, Canada, the Australian colonies of Great Britain, British India, Argentina, Chile, Mexico, China, and Japan.

In these movements of capital Professor Seligman finds the fundamental underlying explanation of the late world conflict. Nations pass through three stages of economic national development. In the first they develop their resources and build up their industries, isolating themselves by means of a protective tariff. In the second stage of economic nationalism they export commodities and seek colonial expansion. In the third stage they supplement the export of commodities with the export of capital, when they find it to their advantage to preach the gospel of cosmopolitanism and the benefits of international trade. Great Britain had already been long in the third stage; Germany, just emerging from the second, found in that country her strongest rival. The export of capital yielded its greatest profits in the economic penetration of backward countries, and in this Germany was determined to participate at all hazards. This was her "place in the sun." The industrial inequality of different countries permitted, and in fact induced, the exploitation of the backward ones by those capitalistically developed. Hence international investment of capital, which should promote international peace and good will, has in fact become the gage of an economic struggle between nations.[5]

---

[5] E. R. A. Seligman, "An Economic Interpretation of the War," in *Problems of Readjustment after the War* (1915), pp. 55, 61.

NATIONAL AND INTERNATIONAL CREDIT

The lending and borrowing of capital takes place by the transfer of commodities, and the extent of this movement is evidenced by statistics of exports and imports. One would therefore expect a lending country to export more than it imported and a borrowing country, on the other hand, to import more than it exported. The movement has gone on so long, however, that the wealthy lending countries now receive interest and other payments in excess of the annual investment of capital in foreign lands; consequently their imports exceed their exports. So, too, the payments on capital already invested exceed the new investments in the case of the more important debtor nations. In some of the borrowing countries, however, the investment of capital is still taking place on a considerable scale, and their imports continue to be larger than their exports. The table on page 15 shows these facts for 1913, the last normal year before the World War.

In a monograph submitted to the National Monetary Commission on "The Trade Balance of the United States,"[6] Sir George Paish, editor of the London *Statist*, estimated the amount of capital invested by various European countries in the United States about 1909. According to this estimate Great Britain possessed about $3,500,000,000 of American securities; French investments amounted to nearly $500,000,000; the amount of German investments was placed at about $1,000,000,000, and that of Dutch capital at $750,000,000. In the aggregate the amount of European capital invested in "permanent" securities in the United States was approximately $6,000,000,000. The net payments of interest upon this capital required the remittance annually by the United States of some $225,000,000. Other

[6] Report of the National Monetary Commission, xx, p. 169.

expenditures, such as tourist travel, remittances by immigrants, freights, insurance, etc., brought the total annual drain on American capital up to $500,000,000 in years of depression and to $600,000,000 in years of normal trade activity.

The export of capital has been an international phenomenon of growing importance during the nineteenth and twentieth centuries. In the extent of her foreign investments Great Britain has led all countries. The amount of these investments has varied from time to time, but on the whole they have shown a fairly steady increase. This was particularly marked in the last few years before the outbreak of the Great War, as is shown by the following annual figures of investments in the colonies and abroad:[7]

BRITISH INVESTMENTS ABROAD, 1907–1912

1907	$701,000,000
1908	649,500.000
1909	550,500,000
1910	754,000,000
1911	961.000.000
1912	1,130,000,000

Although these figures do not measure exactly the export of capital, because of the flow of securities back and forth, they indicate roughly the enormous movement that was taking place. The total amount of British investments abroad at the end of December, 1913, was estimated by Sir George Paish at about $20,000,000,000,[8] about 23 per cent. of the total capital investments of the nation. This sum was almost equally divided between the British colonies and possessions on the one hand and foreign countries on the other. Of the former, Canada was the favorite land of investment, over

[7] C. K. Hobson, *The Export of Capital* (London, 1914), p. 223.
[8] *Statist*, February 14, 1914.

NATIONAL AND INTERNATIONAL CREDIT

FOREIGN TRADE OF LEADING LENDING AND BORROWING
COUNTRIES, 1913

(In millions)

Country	Net imports	Domestic exports	Balance of trade

GROUP I. *Lending Countries which were receiving Net Income from their Investments*

			Excess of imports
Great Britain	$3,840	$3,170	$670
France	1,680	1,260	420
Netherlands	1,567	1,233	334
Germany	2,802	2,549	253
Belgium	917	715	202

GROUP II. *Borrowing Countries whose Payments were Greater than Present Additions of Capital*

			Excess of exports
United States	$1,813	$2,428	$615
Russia	586	759	173
British India	780	850	70
Argentina	420	485	65

GROUP III. *Borrowing Countries in which Continued Investment of Foreign Capital is Still Taking Place*

			Excess of imports
Japan	$765	$315	$450
Canada	650	479	171
China	430	305	125
Turkey	198	108	90

one-eighth of all foreign investments being placed there; in the other group a still larger amount was invested in the United States. Other countries especially favored by British investors were India and Ceylon, South Africa, Australia, Argentina, and Brazil, in the order named. Only about five per cent. was placed in Europe. There was evidenced a wide geographical distribution, a spreading of risks in many countries. The income accruing from these investments at the time of the outbreak of the war was probably about $1,000,000,000 per year.

Very different has been the geographical distribution of French and German foreign investments. Both of these countries had a later industrial development than Great Britain and a smaller foreign trade, and consequently their investments outside of their own borders have not been so large. Those of France were estimated in 1902 by the French Minister of Foreign Affairs at 30,000,000,000 francs. A decade later M. Yves Guyot estimated that they had increased to 40 to 42,000,000,000 francs (8 to 8,400,000,000 dollars), or 37 per cent. of the total amount of French capital invested in personal securities.[9] In 1916 C. K. Hobson made an estimate of $8,766,000,000.[10] At the same time Mr. Hobson estimated the foreign investments of Germany to be about $4,870,000,000, or about 6.6 per cent. of the total investments of the nation. A much higher estimate was given by the Federal Trade Commission, which placed the amount of German foreign investments at the beginning of the late war at between $7,500,000,000 and $8,500,000,0000.[11] The investments of the French tended to concentrate in Europe, especially Russia, Tur-

---

[9] "The Amount, Direction and Nature of French Investments," *Annals of the American Academy of Political and Social Science*, November, 1916, pp. 43, 50.

[10] *Ibid.*, 32.

[11] Report on Coöperation in American Export Trade (1916), Part 1, p. 72.

NATIONAL AND INTERNATIONAL CREDIT

key and Rumania, and in Mexico, while those of Germany were found in the neighboring countries of Austria-Hungary, Italy, Rumania and the Balkans, although both nations had large interests in South America and South Africa.

Belgian foreign investments in 1911 were estimated at about $540,000,000,[12] and those of Switzerland at $520,400,000. The foreign holdings of the Dutch were also considerable. Those of the capitalists of other European countries are much smaller; no country lacks them altogether, but in no other case are they comparable with those already mentioned.

In addition to these loans on the security of bonds, stocks, and other securities, there has been also in some cases direct industrial investment by the citizens of one country in another through the building of plants, branch factories, etc. But the characteristic feature of these international investments was after all their impersonal nature; although the capital itself was exported, the owner remained at home and drew his interest or profits from abroad. So widespread have been these movements that no country has been unaffected by them, either as creditor or debtor. A perfect network of international finance bound the nations of the world together. Although these ties did not prove sufficiently binding to prevent the outbreak of war between the nations thus united, as Norman Angell in his suggestive book *The Great Illusion* hoped they might, yet they had important consequences. It is not possible to establish any connection between the existence of investment relations and the later military alliances. Germany had invested largely in Austria-Hungary and Italy, in Bulgaria and Rumania, but she

---
[12] *Ibid.*

17

had as many enemies as friends among these nations. France was the largest creditor of both Russia and Turkey, but this fact did not determine their allegiance in war. Nevertheless, the existence of these international investments brought serious problems to the front upon the outbreak of the war. On the whole the Central Powers suffered more from the suspension of normal credit relations between the nations than did the members of the Entente. As a basis for credits and for use as collateral the existence of these foreign investments proved of great service, especially for Great Britain and France.

The flow of capital and the movement of foreign trade long ago became so complex and intricate that a sort of international clearing house was needed to care for these transactions. For this purpose London was admirably suited. She had first secured the position as the center of international trade after the sacking of Antwerp in 1567, and although Amsterdam later gained importance as a commercial and financial mart, London soon took the leading place in Europe.

The predominance of London as the world center of international trade was never greater than during the period just before the Great War. Although the direct trade of other nations, as France, Germany, and to a smaller extent Italy and Austria-Hungary, had increased, the share of London in the world's commerce grew steadily. Her central geographical location made her the most convenient depot and trading point for the trade between the Far East, Europe, and America. Great Britain's large mercantile marine, her excellent mail and cable connections, and a comprehensive insurance system gave London special facilities for handling

NATIONAL AND INTERNATIONAL CREDIT

the business, in connection with which an expert trading organization had been developed. Especially important was the highly perfected banking system, which was peculiarly adapted to the granting of the short-term loans called for in financing this world trade. Hence most international payments were made in London and international accounts were cleared there. Foreign banking houses kept deposits in London. Bills of exchange were generally drawn on London. Banks and exporters in South America, India, or Europe were paid in these bills, which were accepted by the English banks. Sterling became the currency of international commerce. Mr. Lloyd George described these operations in a speech in November, 1914, as follows:

I ask anyone to pick up just one little bit of paper, one bill of exchange, to find out what we are doing. Take the cotton trade of the world. The cotton is moved first of all from the plantations, say, to the Mississippi; then it is moved down to New Orleans; then it is moved either to Germany or Great Britain or elsewhere. Every movement there is represented by a paper signed either here in London or Manchester or Liverpool; one signature practically is responsible for the whole of those transactions. Not merely that, but when the United States of America bought silk or tea in China this payment was made through London. By means of these documents accepted in London, New York paid for the tea that was bought from China. We were transacting far more than the whole of our own business; we were transacting half the business of the world as well by means of these paper transactions. What is also important to establish is this: that the paper which was issued from London has become part of the currency of commerce throughout the world.

So intimate and close were the economic and commercial bonds which united nations, and so large was the stream of goods which flowed in every direction between them that it seemed to many that the stage of a world economy had actually been reached. Although nationalism had lost nothing of its strength, a new economic internationalism was developing which gave promise of checking militarism and of securing peace to the world. The war was to show, however, that the program of economic internationalism might not suit the nationalistic ambitions of a vigorous but misguided people.

CHAPTER II

FINANCIAL READJUSTMENTS AT THE OUTBREAK OF WAR

Germany's preparedness — The Entente Allies caught unaware — Panic and temporary breakdown of credit — Remedial measures — Safeguarding the gold reserves — Issue of additional money — Adjustment to war conditions.

In spite of a generation of armament and war talk the actual outbreak of war on August 1, 1914, fell upon an unprepared world. Germany alone of all the combatants was ready. She had made full preparation, not only of a military nature, but also with equal care and thoroughness along financial lines. It is said that at the time of the Morocco episode in 1911 the Kaiser decided that the time was ripe for Germany to strike, but was informed by his Minister of Finance that the financial situation would not permit a declaration of war. Thereupon he told the Minister of Finance to see to it that the next time he asked that question he received a different answer. Whether this story is true or not, it is certain that since the Morocco episode Germany had taken steps to strengthen herself financially in various respects. At that time she owed large sums abroad, and upon the threat of war French capitalists called in large balances due them by German banks and also began to dispose of German securities. This nearly brought on a crisis in Germany and without doubt forced the German militarists to yield their demands.

The difficulty with France in 1911 was used in the following year as an excuse to secure additional military credits and to increase the army. After the Balkan wars in 1913 a further addition was made to the army and munitions and other materials of war were collected.[1] To secure the necessary funds to meet these expenditures the so-called *Wehrbeitrag* was imposed, a special, nonrecurring tax on incomes and real property from which it was expected to realize $250,000,000. This tax was to be paid in three installments in 1913, 1914, and 1915, but these payments were later postponed a year, and after the outbreak of the World War they were hardly distinguishable from other taxes. In the budget of 1913 the revenue from this source was set down at $104,196,750. The total actual yield of the *Wehrbeitrag* during the war was recently stated to have been $241,713,525.

Along with the increases in the military establishment efforts were made to build up the gold reserve in the war chest. The war chest was a peculiarly Prussian institution. Collected in Prussia by Frederick the Great, upon the formation of the Germany Empire it had been turned over to the Imperial Treasury. A part of the French indemnity, amounting to about $30,000,000 in gold coin, had been placed in the war chest in 1871. By an act of July 3, 1913, provision was made for the sale of Imperial Treasury notes for gold to a similar amount and the addition of this gold to that already in the war chest. About $21,000,000 had actually been obtained and placed there at the time the war broke out, so that the war-chest fund contained

---

[1] A study of the imports into Germany of copper and other metals that enter largely into war materials and of cotton, rubber and similar articles essential for war purposes shows that the purchases of all these articles during 1913 and 1914 were far in excess of the normal imports for the preceding decade. For a discussion of German mineral imports immediately before the war see, in this series, George Otis Smith, *The Strategy of Minerals.*

READJUSTMENTS AT OUTBREAK OF WAR

between $50,000,000 and $60,000,000 in gold, in addition to a considerable store of silver.

Efforts were also made to build up the stock of gold in the possession of the Reichsbank. The theory had previously been held that it was a wise financial policy to secure as large a circulation of gold among the people as possible. This saturation of the currency with gold provided a fund which, in an emergency, the Government might utilize by the issuance of paper money. About a decade before this time, however, Germany, in common with some of the other governments of Europe, had embarked upon a new policy with respect to the gold stock of the country. This was that the gold should be accumulated and held by the great central banking institution of the country, which should then issue the necessary media of exchange in the form of bank notes. In accordance with this view an act of 1906 had authorized the issue of notes of the Reichsbank in denominations of 50 and 20 marks, the lowest previous denomination having been fixed at 100 marks. Three years later the bank notes were made full legal tender. Imperial Treasury notes (*Reichskassenscheine*) were also placed in circulation in denominations of ten and five marks. As a result of the issue of these forms of paper, gold tended to accumulate in the Reichsbank, which was able to increase its reserve from $258,000,000 in July, 1911, to $339,000,000 in July, 1914.

It would appear from recent disclosures that Germany was prepared to force the issue in 1913, but was prevented from doing so at that time by the refusal of Italy to join Germany and Austria-Hungary in an offensive war. The burden of the additional military expenditures and the impending exactions of the *Wehrbeitrag* made the Junkers prefer actual war, from which they expected to derive a profit, to the costs of an unproductive armament. The militarists, who could hardly be restrained in 1911 and 1913, were completely out of hand in 1914. The murder of the Archduke Franz Ferdinand at Serajevo on June 28, 1914, afforded the excuse for a premeditated attack.

Strange as it seems to-day, looking back over the years of preparation on the part of Germany, of her sword-rattling and then dimly understood mutterings of world domination, the war undoubtedly came as a surprise to the rest of the world.[2] The signs of the impending conflict were clear, but they were unheeded. The most effective answer to Germany's oft-repeated charge that the war was begun by her enemies and that England especially was responsible for initiating it, is to be found in the financial, as well as in the military unpreparedness of Great Britain. England had given hostages to peace in her great foreign investments. London was the center of a delicately organized mechanism for transacting and financing international trade. Any disturbance of these complicated economic and financial relations would have more serious consequences to Great Britain than to any other country. British investments abroad were estimated at about $20,000,000,000, the annual return upon which amounted to some $1,000,000,000. The investment of British capital in foreign countries was estimated to amount on the

---

[2] "In August, 1914, the shock came upon the world's great financial markets with as complete a violence and suddenness as it is possible, in an event of such immense importance, to imagine . . . it is probable that no other war in modern times — with the possible exception of the Franco-Prussian War of 1870 . . . — has taken the great financial communities so completely off their guard." (A. D. Noyes, *Financial Chapters of the War*, p. 25.)

READJUSTMENTS AT OUTBREAK OF WAR

average to about $800,000,000 annually. As a result of the interest paid to her upon investments abroad and the payments for the services of her ships and banking and insurance institutions, imports into Great Britain greatly exceeded her exports. In the year 1913 the excess of imports over exports amounted to $670,000,000, which represented the payment for capital and services by the rest of the world. As a creditor nation on the vastest scale, it would seem that Britain had more to lose by a world war than any other nation.

France, like England, was also a creditor nation on a large scale and had extensive investments in Russia, the Near East, and South America. The excess of French merchandise imports over exports for the year 1913 amounted to about $420,000,000. During the first six months of 1914 France had loaned large sums to Greece, Turkey, and Serbia. The financial relations between France and most of the other countries of Europe were so intimate and so complicated that any break would be sure to prove disastrous. France had already been hard hit by the two Balkan wars because of her large loans to Balkan states, and she was at this time primarily interested in the restoration of peace and prosperity in that section of Europe. Moreover, the financial situation itself in France was unsatisfactory in the early part of 1914. The settlement of expenses in Morocco, the introduction of the three-year service law in response to Germany's enlargement of her army, and an increase in the navy had imposed new burdens which led to repeated deficits. To meet these deficiencies a new internal loan of $180,000,000 was authorized by an act of June 30, 1914. The issue of this loan should of itself absolve France from suspicion as instigator of the war.

WAR COSTS AND THEIR FINANCING

In Russia the fiscal situation in 1914 was sound. A period of industrial expansion had begun after the war with Japan, especially in oil production, and industrial activity gave a firm foundation for the State finances. For several years the budget had shown a surplus. Not only this, but the Treasury had been able to reduce the Government debt by about $100,000,000 in the years from 1910 to 1913, and had also accumulated an emergency reserve fund of about $250,000,000. In 1914 there had been accumulated in the Bank of Russia the largest supply of gold in the history of that institution, amounting to $800,000,000, which was probably the largest store in any European country. On the other hand, the general economic situation was less encouraging. The large loans made in Europe, particularly in France, had probably not quickened production sufficiently to meet the enhanced interest payments,[3] which by 1914 were not far short of $165,000,000 annually. Manufactures and mining showed some development, but agriculture, the mainstay of the people, made little improvement. In the summer of 1914 the harvest was especially poor, owing to a severe drought. The gross crop of all cereals in all Russia amounted, on the average for the four years 1910-1913, to 58,000,000 metric tons, but in 1914 it was only 53,000,000 metric tons. The banks had financed the producers, and as the war broke out in mid-harvest, they were hard hit by the crop failure.

The financial condition of Austria-Hungary in 1914 was probably worse than that of any other nation in Europe with the possible exception of Turkey. Owing to the heavy costs of armament and preparation for war,

---
[3] H. M. Hyndman, " The Economic Basis in India," *Asia*, June, 1919, p. 534.

READJUSTMENTS AT OUTBREAK OF WAR

the Government had for years faced deficits in the annual budgets. The credit of the Empire was consequently seriously impaired. Nor were private finances in a more flourishing condition. Money was high, bankruptcies were frequent, industries were suffering, and unemployment was common. Moreover, the 1914 Hungarian harvest, like that of Russia, had proved almost a failure. A less propitious time for a declaration of war could hardly have been selected, but it is now apparent that, assured of the support of her stronger ally, Germany, the Dual Monarchy believed that this opportunity of crushing Serbia and supplanting the growing influence of Russia in the Balkans was too favorable to let slip.

Taking the situation in Europe as a whole, it is fairly obvious that in spite of the enormous expenditures on armament and the enlargement of military forces on the part of some of the European nations, the bankers, the merchants, and the man in the street regarded war as but a remote possibility. Unhappily, the internationalism of trade and finance did not act as a deterrent as many had fondly hoped it would. Imperialistic ambition and the complete subordination of government to the machinations of a military clique were sufficiently powerful in Central Europe to override purely commercial or financial considerations. It must not be overlooked, however, that certain economic forces were at work in Germany which impelled her to seek what her writers termed '' a place in the sun.''

The assassination of the Austrian Archduke occurred on June 28, 1914. Within two weeks there was a serious fall of 10 to 20 per cent. in the prices of stocks in Vienna. Upon Austria-Hungary's ultimatum to Serbia,

WAR COSTS AND THEIR FINANCING

which was delivered on July 22 and an answer to which was demanded by the 25th, there was a further break in stocks in Vienna, which this time extended to Berlin and Paris. In both Germany and France the conditions on the stock exchanges became panicky. When Russia announced on July 25 that she would protect Serbia, the panic became general. Heavy selling of securities on foreign account took place in the New York market. So serious did conditions become on the Continent that on July 27 the exchanges at Vienna, Budapest, Brussels, and Antwerp were closed. On the 28th Austria-Hungary declared war against Serbia, and on the same day the exchanges at Montreal, Toronto, and Madrid closed their doors, to be followed the next day by those of Berlin and Petrograd. Events now moved so rapidly that it was impossible for the market to adjust itself. On July 29 Russia mobilized. Two days later Germany sent her ultimatum to France and the next day started on her march toward Paris. On August 4 German troops entered Belgium and that night Great Britain declared war on Germany. It had become evident almost from the first that the conflict could not be localized. The stock exchanges in all South American countries closed on July 30, and in Paris the coulisse was forced to suspend dealings. On Friday morning, July 31, the London Stock Exchange officially closed, and this action was followed a few hours later by an announcement that the New York Stock Exchange would not open for business.

It is evident from this brief chronology that Austria-Hungary's ultimatum to Serbia was correctly interpreted by the stock market, and that her declaration of war, in spite of the semi-official declaration "that she hoped the contest would be localized," was regarded as

READJUSTMENTS AT OUTBREAK OF WAR

the first step in a world conflict. By the end of the month of July all the important markets had succumbed to panic, and there was an almost complete breakdown of that delicate mechanism of international exchange which had been so carefully built during the preceding years. The crisis found its readiest expression in the operations on the stock exchanges, and consequently these institutions were the first to cease to function when steps become necessary to prevent further spread of the panic. The selling of stocks in general was due to the efforts of persons having debts to pay or wishing to place themselves in funds to realize at once upon their securities. If this movement had continued unrestrained, it would of course have resulted in a tremendous fall in the prices of securities. It was felt that it was better to check this tendency than to permit the securing of funds at ruinous discounts.

As London was the world center of international trade and finance, the events in that city assumed greater importance than those in other places and they have consequently received most attention. To carry on this international trade there had grown up in Great Britain a complex credit organization of bill brokers, discount and acceptance houses, and joint-stock banks, with the Bank of England at the head. Exporters of commodities from foreign countries were in the habit of selling their goods for bills of exchange drawn on London. To secure cash immediately the exporter would then sell his draft to a bill broker or acceptance house in London. These in turn would probably borrow from the joint-stock banks, which finally looked for assistance to the Bank of England. The payment of the obligations of one of these agencies to another rested ultimately upon the ability of the buyer of the foreign goods, against whom the draft was drawn, to dispose of his goods and to meet his obligations. If the transaction were interrupted at any point, the credit organization would be, temporarily at least, thrown out of gear. The situation was complicated, moreover, by the fact that the joint-stock banks, which held deposits callable on demand, loaned out a great deal of their money to stock-exchange dealers. When the prices of securities began to fall, they started to call in loans, an act which threatened many of their customers with bankruptcy. To save them the Government arranged with the Bank of England that it should advance to lenders on stock-exchange accounts outstanding on July 29, 60 per cent. of the value of the securities at the prices of that date.

More pregnant of danger, however, was the position of the acceptance houses which had discounted foreign bills with the joint-stock banks or other institutions. The situation that developed has been thus clearly stated by Professor Laughlin:[4]

It suddenly became evident, however, that the drawers of these foreign bills could not remit funds on a very large scale to meet them when due. If the drawers could not pay, the acceptance houses could not; if the acceptance houses could not pay, then these bills, which formed assets in the discount houses and banks, were frozen. It is estimated that the sum total of bills involved amounted to about $1,750,000,000; of these the banks held from $500,000,000 to $625,000,000, constituting perhaps 15 per cent. of their assets.

In such a crisis, when there was an interruption of the shipment of goods and also of gold with which the debts could have been met, the proper thing for the banks to have done was to extend further accommodation

---

[4] J. L. Laughlin, *Credit of the Nations* (New York, 1918), p. 82.

READJUSTMENTS AT OUTBREAK OF WAR

to the acceptance houses and brokers in order to tide them over the period of panic and temporary stoppage of exchange. The banks, however, pursued the opposite policy of protecting their reserves and of calling in funds. In this emergency the borrowing public was forced to turn to the Bank of England, and the consequent great pressure for loans from that institution drove the bank rate as high as 10 per cent. on August 1.

The situation was further complicated by the fact that Monday, August 3, was a regular bank holiday, so that the end of the previous week saw the people who were planning expeditions into the country calling upon the banks for cash. To their surprise they were given only 10 per cent. in gold and 90 per cent. in Bank of England notes, the lowest denomination of which ($25) was inconveniently large for ordinary expenditures. This led to a rush to the Bank of England for redemption of its notes in gold, the demand being so great that long queues of people were formed outside the bank.

As a result of these various demands the Bank of England lost $80,000,000 in gold and notes, its reserves being thereby depleted to less than $138,000,000. In this emergency the first thing to do was to gain time. Three extra bank holidays were declared, which postponed the opening of the bank until Friday morning, August 7, and gave the authorities opporunity to prepare remedial measures. It is probably incorrect to say that there was a panic, but there was need for prompt measures to relieve the money stringency and the breakdown of credit. The measures adopted to remedy the situation will be described hereafter.

In France, because of the invasion of her territory, the shock to public credit was probably greater than in any other country except Belgium. Although France

WAR COSTS AND THEIR FINANCING

did not have the widely scattered and intricately ramified international trade relations which Great Britain possessed, a considerable part of the income of her people was derived from foreign investments. Many of these securities were unsalable, even at panic prices, and the banks that had made loans upon them as collateral were unable to secure payment of their loans. Moreover, the value of these securities as collateral for loans declined greatly. The invasion by the Germans of the northeastern section of France lost her the country's richest coal fields and those districts in which the leading textile and iron industries were carried on. French industry and agriculture were also struck a severe blow by the withdrawal from economic activity of practically all the able-bodied men as a result of the general mobilization order of August 1. It is evident that in circumstances like these it is immaterial whether one describes the resulting conditions as those of panic or not. There was a complete breakdown of the normal organization of industries and the coördinate credit structure. In France also immediate and far-reaching measures were necessary to protect the rights of both debtors and creditors and, so far as possible, to provide means for the continuance of necessary economic activities.

As Russia is primarily an agricultural country, there did not exist there the delicately organized mechanism of credit and foreign trade such as had been developed in England and, to a less degree, in France and Germany. Consequently the disorganization of business in Russia was not so complete or so widespread. The partial failure of the crops had already involved the banks, whose credit was strained before the outbreak of the war. Mobilization came after harvest throughout

READJUSTMENTS AT OUTBREAK OF WAR

a considerable section of the Empire, and it was therefore not so serious as it would have been a month earlier. Still, the problems were similar to those in other countries, differing only in degree, and to meet them similar remedial measures were adopted.

In the field of finance, as in military details, Germany had made all possible preparations for the war, and she had hoped by her carefully planned measures to avoid a shock to her industries and credit such as occurred in the other belligerent countries. But no nation carrying on the far-reaching operations of trade and finance in which Germany was involved before the war could suddenly cut off her relations with the outside world without feeling the shock of such an amputation. Allusion has already been made to the panic on the Berlin Stock Exchange and the closing of that institution on July 29. There occurred in Germany a phase of panic that was not duplicated, at least to the same extent, in other countries; there were runs on the banks by frightened depositors. On a single day, August 3, the Berlin savings banks lost over $230,000,000. Hoarding also took place, not of gold merely, but also of notes and silver. The resulting shortage of money was met by the issuance of Imperial Treasury notes for 10 marks and of loan office notes for one and two marks. As in the other belligerent countries, the calling of the able-bodied men to the colors crippled industry, but the disturbance was probably not so great in Germany as in the others because of her carefully worked-out plans for handling this problem.

The situation in Austria-Hungary was not dissimilar from that in the other warring countries, due allowance being made for differences in conditions. The stock exchanges were closed, a moratorium was declared, and

WAR COSTS AND THEIR FINANCING

specie payments were suspended. The financial, industrial, and commercial world of the Dual Monarchy was disturbed by the same shocks that affected other countries, and it suffered the same effects.

If the foregoing analysis is correct, it is clear that an immediate difficulty brought about by the outbreak of the World War was the breakdown of credit, both national and international. The production and movement of goods having been interrupted, the credit transactions based upon these primary operations were disorganized. There was not so much a distrust of credit as there was a complete stoppage of ordinary transactions. Since the movement of goods was stopped, payments based upon them could not be made when due. In these circumstances the first necessity was the further extension of credit. But more than that was needed. Since the ordinary credit machinery had broken down, a larger amount of the other media of exchange must be at once supplied. At the same time the reserves of the banks, especially the gold holdings of the great central institutions, had to be safeguarded and their dissipation prevented. To meet these various aspects of the situation three different types of remedy were adopted, the emphasis being differently placed in the various countries.

(1) *Moratoria.*— Although the moratorium was unfamiliar to American business men, it was a device which had frequently been made use of in Europe; it was generally adopted in France during the Napoleonic wars. The situation in 1914 was so unparalleled and the derangement of business so universal that the moratorium was adopted by practically all the belliger-

READJUSTMENTS AT OUTBREAK OF WAR

ent nations as well as by a large number of neutrals. By the end of 1913, 19 nations had resorted to this expedient. Briefly defined, the moratorium is an act which postpones the date on which debts have to be met. The principle of the moratoria of 1914 was the same in all cases, though the period of postponement differed from country to country. In Great Britain the original proclamation of August 2, known as the Postponement of Payments Act (4 & 5 Geo. V, Ch. 11), declared a moratorium of one month, which was later extended to October 4. It affected an enormous volume of business and is estimated to have stopped payment on credit instruments having a face value of $2,000,000,000. Referring to this Act, Lloyd George said in a speech in the House of Commons on November 27, 1914: " We first declared a moratorium, a limited moratorium, so as to give us time to look around." There has been much discussion of the wisdom of this course. At the time it was pointed to by the Germans as an evidence of the breakdown of the English credit system. But in view of the general demoralization of foreign trade and exchange the world over, it would have been impossible to have insisted upon the immediate settlement of debts. The postponement of settlement for a reasonable time both enabled the debtor to make satisfactory provision for ultimate payment and tended to restore confidence.

The Government arranged with the Bank of England that it should discount all approved bills of exchange accepted before August 4 and continue them, if unpaid at maturity, until one year after the war at a rate two per cent. higher than the bank rate. At the same time the Bank proceeded boldly to discount new acceptances. This arrangement greatly relieved the exchange market but imposed upon the Bank a heavy burden and exposed it to possible ultimate loss. In this emergency the unprecedented step was taken by the Government of guaranteeing the pre-moratorium bills of exchange, with the expectation that any resultant loss would be charged up to war costs. It has been estimated that the total current liability on pre-moratorium bills of exchange amounted to $3,000,000,000, of which about $2,250,000,-000 was discounted at the Bank of England under this Government guarantee. These bills, however, have been met at maturity, and it is said that the ultimate loss, which can only be determined one year after the conclusion of peace, may not exceed $150,000,000.

The French Government at the outbreak of war postponed for one month the payment of all negotiable instruments maturing between July 31 and August 31 provided they had been endorsed prior to August 4. This was wider in its application than the British Act since it included sight drafts as well as long bills. General use was made of the privilege granted. The moratorium was later extended to other liabilities, and its termination was postponed from time to time, so that in some applications it continued throughout the war.[5] The Bank of France carried most of the burden

---

[5] One of the curious effects of the moratorium in France was observable in the case of house rentals. Under it tenants were absolved from the obligation of paying rent. The absolution was universal; neither rich nor poor had to pay. House property is a favorite form of investment of thrifty Frenchmen, and the anomaly thus introduced by the moratorium cut off the total income of thousands of "house-poor" French, in some cases the owners becoming charwomen to the non-rent-paying tenants. The moratorium also established the obligation of extending the leases, written or unwritten, at the same rental for a period equal to the duration of the war. To offset this burden on the houseowner, however, the Senate and Chamber provided that in communes of less than 10,000 inhabitants, when the income thus cut off did not exceed 5,000 francs, the owner was entitled to an indemnity

READJUSTMENTS AT OUTBREAK OF WAR

of these obligations, although it was not, like the Bank of England, guaranteed against loss by the Government. The total pre-moratorium paper at the Bank of France amounted in August, 1914, to almost $900,000,000. This amount had been reduced by December, 1915, to $367,000,000, and by June, 1919, to $206,000,000. It is reasonable to expect that the final losses of the Bank of France will be reduced to a manageable sum.

The methods adopted in other countries were similar to those already described. In Russia a moratorium was immediately declared for one month, covering bills of exchange falling due after July 30; this was later extended from time to time. Similar measures were taken in Belgium, Italy, Bulgaria, Austria, Turkey, and a number of neutral countries.

Germany boasted that she had avoided the opprobrium of resort to a moratorium. This claim, however, can be admitted only with reservations. By a decree of the Bundesrat of August 6, 1914, the term for the payment of bills and checks was extended one month, and this was later extended from time to time until the following May. The civil courts were also empowered to extend the time for the payment of mortgages, and the pressure of public opinion forced creditors to be lenient in the collection of other debts. It is, therefore, incorrect to say that there was no moratorium in Germany. It is not necessary to press this point, however, for it must be admitted that the measures taken in Germany to relieve the situation were very different from the moratoria adopted in other countries. The evil which the moratorium sought to meet was the locking up of securities, the freezing of hitherto liquid assets. The

---

(from the government) of 50 per cent. of his loss; in communes of over 10,000 inhabitants the maximum indemnity to the owner was 8,000 francs, and in Paris it was 10,000 francs.

policy followed in Germany was to render the assets liquid again by providing institutions which should at once discount not only securities and commercial papers but even merchandise. The Reichsbank was first of all empowered to lend freely. The discounts rose from $200,000,000 on July 23, 1914, to $1,152,000,000 on August 15, although it should be pointed out that this sum included advances to the Government, which amounted for the first two months of the war to about $500,000,000. New credit institutions known as "loan offices" (*Darlehenskassen*) were organized to facilitate loans and extend the credit necessary to continue business. The necessity of postponing the time of payment was removed by making large issues of paper money on the basis of practically any security or commodity that could be pledged at a bank. The provision of means of payment did not work any magic in the ultimate goodness of debts which were met in this fashion. The day of reckoning was postponed as truly as if by moratorium. When one takes into account the effects in Germany of the issue of paper money, the inflation, the rise of prices, and the further derangement of foreign exchange, one must conclude that the method of moratorium was much more scientific and greatly to be preferred.

(2) *Safeguarding gold reserves.*— A second series of measures, which were more or less common to all the belligerents, had to do with the safeguarding of the stock of gold within the country. In most of the Continental countries the major portion of the stock of gold was in the possession of the central bank of issue. Consequently one of the first acts of Government was to relieve the central bank of the necessity of redeeming notes in gold — that is, to suspend specie payment. This was

READJUSTMENTS AT OUTBREAK OF WAR

done in the case of the Bank of France (August 5), of the Reichsbank of Germany (August 1), of the Bank of Russia (July 27/August 9), and of the Imperial Austro-Hungarian Bank (August 5). By this means the dissipation of the gold reserves of the countries was prevented and these were held intact for the period after the war when normal relations among nations would be resumed. In England the suspension of the Bank Act of 1844 was authorized by the decree of August 6, but the Bank of England did not in fact take advantage of the permission to issue its notes without cover beyond the legal reserve. The peculiar position held by England in the world of international trade and finance made it particularly desirable that there should be no interference with the free movement of gold into and out of that country. England was hard put to it before the war was over to maintain specie payments in fact as well as in name, but by one means or another she was able to preserve the form at least until after the war.[6] This was an achievement compared with which the avoidance of a moratorium, real or apparent, in Germany was a mere bagatelle.

The stocks of gold in the central banks of the five principal belligerent countries in July, 1914, and on December 31 of each year following are given below.[7] Not only did these central banks with the exception of that of Austria-Hungary maintain their reserves, but with the same exception they increased them. One of the most unprecedented and unpredictable occurrences of the war was the surrender by the citizens of these

---

[6] An embargo was finally placed on the export of gold by an Order-in-Council of March 29, 1919, to become effective after April 1.

[7] Compiled from bank returns in *Federal Reserve Bulletin*, March, 1920, p. 334.

WAR COSTS AND THEIR FINANCING

GOLD RESERVES IN CENTRAL BANKS OF BELLIGERENTS
(*In millions*)

Year	England	France	Russia	Germany	Austria-Hungary
July, 1914...	$190	$830	$800	$340	$255
Dec. 31, 1914.	338	799	803	499	214
1915........	251	968	831	582	139
1916........	264	653	758	600	59
1917........	284	640	667	573	53
1918........	384	664	....	538	53
1919........	444	695	....	259	....

countries of their hoarded gold to the banks in exchange for bank notes, even in some cases after the latter had begun to depreciate. Appeals were made to the people to exchange their gold for bank notes, and, to prevent the exportation of gold, laws were passed prohibiting it entirely or placing such transactions entirely under the control of the central bank. Germany was the first country to make a systematic and determined effort to increase the gold fund in the Reichsbank. Acts were passed penalizing transactions in gold at a premium and prohibiting its exportation. The publication of rates of foreign exchange was also forbidden. It was not enough, however, to keep the money in the country; it must be brought to the Reichsbank itself. To secure this result a campaign was carried on among the people to induce them to exchange gold or coin or jewelry for bank notes. A good account of this campaign was given by Ambassador Gerard in a speech to the New York Chamber of Commerce:[8]

Signs were hung up in the street cars saying, " He who keeps back a gold piece injures the Fatherland." Soldiers

[8] *New York Times Magazine*, July 15, 1917, p. 14.

READJUSTMENTS AT OUTBREAK OF WAR

were given a two days' leave of absence if they would produce a 20-mark gold piece. For that they were given a 20-mark note, just as good as the gold in Germany. School children if they produced a 10-mark gold piece were given 10 marks in paper and a half holiday. In many of the theatres if a person paid for his ticket in gold he would receive a ticket good for another day.

By February, 1915, the gold reserve of the Reichsbank had been increased to about $540,000,000, and by May, 1917, when the highest point was reached, the reserve had been brought up to about $640,000,000. Part of this, however, was obtained from Belgium and from the banks of Austria-Hungary and Turkey.

A similar procedure was followed in France. Exports of gold except by the Bank of France were forbidden. An appeal was also made to the people in July, 1915, following the example of Germany, to exchange gold for notes at the Bank. By October about $160,000,000 had been added to the gold reserves, and by December, 1915, these amounted to over $1,000,000,000. Over $400,000,000 in gold was shipped abroad by France and used as the basis for credits; title thereto remained with the Bank, however, and the exported gold was carried as " gold held abroad " in its weekly statements. By the end of 1918 its gold reserves at home and abroad totalled over $1,095,000,000.

In Russia even stronger inducements were held out to the people to exchange gold for notes in return for a premium. This resulted in considerable sums being surrendered to the Bank of Russia. Because of Russia's necessity of making payment for munitions to England the Bank shipped gold to London, beginning with $40,000,000 in November, 1914, but this was more than made good again by gathering in gold, so that by the

WAR COSTS AND THEIR FINANCING

end of 1915 the reserves stood higher than they were before the war. The necessity for maintaining foreign exchange by shipments of gold only partly nullified the effect in the case of Russia of the collection from the people.

In contradistinction to most of the other countries, the reserves of the central banks of Austria-Hungary and of Turkey showed a steady, and at first blush an inexplicable, decline. This was said by an angry deputy in the lower house of the Austrian Reichsrath to be causally connected with the increase in the reserves of the German Reichsbank. Certain it is that the two phenomena were synchronous. German Treasury bills were furnished to both Autria-Hungary and Turkey in exchange for gold from their central banks which was transferred to the Reichsbank in spite of their laws against the export of gold. With these Treasury bills Austria-Hungary and Turkey were enabled to purchase the munitions and supplies furnished by Germany. It is evident that the gold reserves would not last long in the face of the enormous expenditures that were necessary; as a matter of fact, they were pretty well exhausted by the end of 1915.

(3) *Issue of additional money.*— Because of the temporary breakdown of the credit system and of the demand for immediate means of payment and media of exchange, it was found necessary in practically every belligerent country immediately after the outbreak of war to provide additional money. In some cases this was issued directly by the Government, but in most instances the duty of providing the needed media of exchange was entrusted to banks of issue. In time of panic, such as then prevailed, there is never enough actual cash to

READJUSTMENTS AT OUTBREAK OF WAR

meet the demands of the people. Failure of the ordinary credit devices and methods throws a large part of the demand for media of payment to actual cash. Add to this the withdrawal of considerable sums, as a result of hoarding by frightened and thoughtless people, and there is created a real money stringency which can be met only by the issue of additional forms of currency.

In England there was a considerable withdrawal of gold from the Bank of England, and the joint-stock banks in order to protect themselves hoarded their own stocks of gold. This bad example was followed by the people, and a difficult situation resulted. In this emergency the Currency and Bank Note Act of August 6, 1914, was passed, which authorized the Treasury to suspend the Bank Act, that is, it provided that banks of issue should be indemnified against any liability on the ground of excess of issues after August 1. As the Bank of England did not take advantage of this permission, it has been claimed by many writers that no formal suspension of the Bank Act in fact took place, but that the machinery only was created. In fact the Bank Act suspension was rendered unnecessary because the Government itself under the Currency and Bank Note Act undertook the issue of paper money direct. The Treasury, acting under its authority, issued one-pound and 10-shilling notes ($5 and $2.50) which were given legal tender quality. Postal money orders were made legal tender by the Act, in order to meet necessities at once in all parts of the Kingdom, but this provision was ended on February 3, 1915. The Government currency notes were issued through the Bank of England as the agent of the Treasury to the banks up to a maximum limit of 20 per cent. of their liabilities on deposits and covered accounts. The Treasury was secured by making the issues a prior lien on the assets of the bank. Interest was charged the banks at the current rate, and when advances were repaid, the sums went to a separate fund in the Bank of England called the Currency Note Redemption Fund. This Fund remained at about $142,000,000. The amounts taken by the banks were comparatively small. Although under the law they could have taken as much as $1,125,000,000, they actually took only $65,000,000.[9] Subsequently, however, the volume of the currency notes expanded greatly by direct issue in payment of war contracts, etc. By August 26, 1915, the amount outstanding was $252,000,000; by November 14, 1917, it had risen to $956,000,000, and by January 1, 1919, to $1,616,200,000.

The issue of these notes marked a new departure in British finance, for it was the first time that the British Government had resorted to an issue of paper money. There seems to be no doubt that in the first panic days after the outbreak of war there was a lack of actual money to meet immediate demands. When it is recalled that the lowest denomination of Bank of England notes is $25 and that there was a disposition to hoard the gold which made up the larger amount of the coin in circulation, a justification can be found for the issue of these currency notes by the Government. The criticism may be made, however, that although they were issued as an emergency measure, they were continued in existence during the whole course of the war. Not only that, but as time went on the Government made increasing use of them to meet emergencies. All the objections that can be urged against government paper money may, of course, be directed against these issues, and as a matter of fact they were urged both in Great Britain and elsewhere. In all fairness, however, it must

---

[9] Hartley Withers, *The War and Lombard Street*, p. 83.

READJUSTMENTS AT OUTBREAK OF WAR

be pointed out that these notes were not ordinary fiat money based purely on the credit of the Government; they were convertible and backed up by a gold reserve, although as the issues increased this became painfully small. As in the case of all excessive issues, whether of government paper money or bank notes or deposit currency, the fact was reflected in higher prices, and so far as these notes contributed to that end, they must be condemned. Had provision been made for the issue of emergency notes of the same denominations by the Bank of England, in response to commercial demands rather than to Treasury needs, resort to government paper money might have been avoided.

In France the paper currency was supplied by the Bank of France, which possessed a monopoly of note issues. These notes were protected by the general assets of the Bank, which held enormous gold reserves amounting generally to 75 per cent. of the outstanding issues and to over 50 per cent. of the note issues and deposits combined. There was a legal limit to the Bank's issues, but as this was always raised whenever the actual issues approached dangerously near to this point, it may safely be said that there was no real limit other than that dictated by good banking. The outstanding bank notes in circulation amounted on July 24, 1914, to $1,800,000,000. By October 1, 1914, they had been raised to $1,859,800,000; by the end of December they had passed $2,000,000,000; during 1915 they gradually increased until they reached $2,800,000,000; and the year 1916 saw the issues amount to $3,400,000,000, 1917, to $4,468,000,000, and 1918, to $6,050,000,000. The first big jump was made in response to the demand for actual cash which arose immediately upon the outbreak of war. The Bank was very liberal in granting loans and also in making advances to the Government. As the Government demand was a non-commercial one, the issue of notes to meet it was not made in response to a legitimate business expansion, and it thus resulted in a real inflation of the currency with its undesirable effects of high prices, etc. The greater part of the issues was made to meet the needs of the situation as they developed. With the suspension of specie payments gold quickly disappeared from circulation, and the resulting lack of currency was met by the issue of bank notes in denominations of 5 and 20 francs which had been prepared to meet such an emergency. The Bank also paid out about half of its silver coin, consisting of five-franc pieces. In the southwestern part of France local chambers of commerce issued one-franc and half-franc notes to meet the need for small change.

Russia pursued much the same policy as had been followed in France. The legal limit upon the note issues of the Bank of Russia was raised on July 27/August 9, 1914, to $600,000,000 from the pre-war limit of $300,000,000. On March 17/30, 1915, it was increased to $1,100,000,000; on August 22/September 4, 1915, it was further increased to $1,750,000,000, and later to $4,250,000,000. The issues, which stood at $817,000,000 on July 8, 1914, were more than doubled a year later, standing at $1,898,500,000 on July 15, 1915; by February 16, 1916, they were $2,903,000,000. The gold reserve, which in 1914 was 50 per cent. of the outstanding issues, had fallen on the last named date to 28 per cent. Gold payments had been suspended at the beginning of the war, however, so the note issues had now all the characteristics of inconvertible paper money.

In the countries thus far described the issues of paper money or of bank notes were made in response to de-

READJUSTMENTS AT OUTBREAK OF WAR

mands for additional media of exchange as they arose. Germany, however, adopted this expedient as part of a prearranged policy for financing the war. Immediately upon the outbreak of war the Reichsbank was relieved of the necessity of redeeming its notes in gold. A currency panic ensued which the Government endeavored to meet by the issue of silver coins. As these too began to be hoarded, Imperial Treasury notes in denomination of 10 marks were issued. The most important agencies which were established for the purpose of supplying the people with the necessary currency were the loan offices (*Darlehenskassen*). These were empowered to make loans on various forms of collateral which were not generally acceptable at banks, for which they gave to the borrower loan-office notes. At first these were issued in denominations of five marks and upwards, but after August 31, 1914, on account of the scarcity of small change, they were put out in denominations of one and two marks.[10] Although they were not full legal tender, they were receivable for all Imperial and State dues. No gold reserve was held for their redemption, but they were based upon the collateral which was pledged for the loans. In addition to the loan offices, there were also municipal loan bureaus which loaned to small merchants and handworkers at rates somewhat higher than the State institutions; finally, there were war credit banks which made loans to small tradesmen on stocks of goods or on personal notes with two endorsements. A perfect network of credit institutions was thus provided which made the desired advances to all who could furnish any sort of security.

Austria-Hungary had much the same experience as the other Continental countries. Immediately upon the

---
[10] J. L. Laughlin, *Credit of the Nations*, p. 215.

WAR COSTS AND THEIR FINANCING

outbreak of war the Currency Act requiring metallic reserves and imposing a tax upon excess issues not thus covered was repealed. There were runs on the Imperial Bank and hoarding of gold which necessitated to a certain extent the issue of bank notes. The issues of the Austro-Hungarian Bank, however, were not determined solely by the needs of commerce, but were utilized also to make advances to the Government. The amount of bank notes in circulation, which stood at $425,800,000 on July 23, 1914, had risen to $1,028,000,000 by the end of December. Excuses were given for these additions to the circulating medium on the ground of the increased activities of the Government and the need for additional notes to take the place of the hoarded gold. It is evident, however, that the increase in the note issues was vastly greater than could be justified by either of these reasons. In fact, this was the beginning of a movement of inflation in the Dual Monarchy which went on at increasing speed throughout the whole course of the war.

The movement of foreign exchange in the first few months after the outbreak of war seemed to follow an erratic course and caused apprehension in many quarters. Looking back upon the events of that period, it is now possible to explain them. The great creditor nations, England and France, and to a lesser degree Germany, made a determined effort to collect the debts due them. As these amounted to hundreds of millions of dollars, exchange rates on other countries immediately went in favor of those nations. Sterling and franc exchange in New York rose to unprecedented heights, as the United States was a debtor to an enormous amount to these countries. In consequence of the high

READJUSTMENTS AT OUTBREAK OF WAR

rate of exchange, far above the gold-shipping point, a heavy movement of gold set in from the debtor to the creditor nations. The net exports of gold from the United States between August 1 and December 31, 1914, amounted to $81,719,000. This movement caused great anxiety not only to the countries which were losing the precious metal, like the United States, but also to those countries, like England, the rate of whose exchange was so violently affected. So great indeed was the anxiety felt in banking circles in London that a special commission was dispatched to the United States to inquire into the desirability of measures to correct the existing situation. The worry was needless, however, for the high rate of sterling exchange was only temporary, and the movement of gold from the United States to Ottawa on English account was, and in the nature of things could be, only temporary. The shipment of gold came to an end when the outstanding indebtedness was liquidated or taken care of in other ways. To judge from the prevailing rates of foreign exchange, this movement would seem to have spent itself by the end of the year 1914. By that time the United States and other neutral countries had taken care of their current obligations, and, on the other hand, the belligerents began to buy largely of war materials and foodstuffs. Sterling exchange, which had steadily declined from the high point reached in August, fell in January below its par of $4.87.

Like any organism upon which a serious wound is inflicted, the industrial, commercial, and financial world suffered a serious shock from the outbreak of war, but, like a living organism, it adjusted itself more or less quickly and with varying success to the new conditions.

WAR COSTS AND THEIR FINANCING

Two periods of adjustment may fairly be distinguished. There was the first short, quick spasm of recovery from utter panic and dismay. This lasted possibly a week, during which the first temporary relief measures described above were perfected. Then followed a slower process of transition from a peace to a war basis. The period required for this larger adjustment was naturally different in different countries. In agricultural countries such as Russia or Austria-Hungary, which may be said to have had one hand on the plow and the other on the sword, the disorganization attendant upon the declaration of a state of war was not so serious. But in a highly industrialized state like England, and to a lesser degree in Germany, the disorganization was severe and far-reaching. France stood about midway between the two extremes, but to industrial disorganization was added in her case military invasion and the seizure of some of her most highly developed provinces. Another factor which differentiated the warring countries was the extent to which the adult male population was mobilized for war and withdrawn from productive industry. Here again France was the most crippled, followed by Germany in the second place, with England last.

Because of these differences between the various belligerents, it is difficult to make any generalization, but it is probably safe to say that the necessary adjustments from peace to war conditions were made within a few weeks in the countries primarily agricultural and in the agricultural sections of the others. As their crops had been for the most part harvested, the work of the season was over and the calling of the men to the colors did not immediately affect production. In the industrial sections, however, industry and commerce

READJUSTMENTS AT OUTBREAK OF WAR

had met with a serious shock. Although commerce was greatly disturbed, it was never seriously imperilled, and within a month the British Navy had practically swept the seas of German cruisers. Insurance rates, which in the first panic days had been run up by Lloyd's as high as 80 per cent. of the value of the hull, were quickly brought down to normal. The importance of shipping was realized as so great by Great Britain that the Government early assumed the burden of granting war insurance on British vessels and later on their cargoes. On August 15, 1914, the rates were fixed at 2½ per cent. on hulls for three months. A couple of weeks later this was reduced to two per cent. This fact in itself is eloquent of the increased safety of Allied and neutral trade on the high seas.

There were two obstacles to a complete and speedy adjustment of peace-time industry to war conditions. One of these was the very general belief that the war would be over in a comparatively short time, and that therefore it would not be necessary or desirable to make radical changes in the industrial or financial organization. In all the countries resort was had at first to bank advances and to short-term credit obligations. Germany was the first to place a long-time loan, and she did not undertake this until September, 1914. The other nations followed at intervals less or greater according to their financial strength. There was a general unwillingness to resort to vigorous and heavy taxation, which went so far in Germany as to lead the Chancellor to declare that no taxes whatever would be levied for carrying on the war. What was the use, since they expected to collect indemnities from a conquered foe? Even in England, the single country among the European belligerents to impose heavy taxation during the

WAR COSTS AND THEIR FINANCING

war, it was not introduced until November, 1914, and then it fell far short of the necessities of the situation. Two factors contributed to this attitude. The first was a general belief that the cost of the war was so great that it could not continue more than a few months; the whole finances of the Governments would break down under the strain if in the meantime a military decision did not end it.[11] Second, there seems to have been a general belief that a military decision would be attained within a comparatively few months, for it did not seem possible that the Central Powers could withstand the combination of nations which was weekly securing new adherents.

The other factor militating against a reorganization of industry so as to make it serve the single purpose of winning the war was the general insistence that there should be no interference with normal business. This belief found expression in the slogan "business as usual." Although it was founded upon a thoroughly fallacious economic analysis as to the nature of production and consumption, it nevertheless exercised a potent influence in the early months and even years of the war. Not until shortened rations, lessened man power, higher prices, and grim necessity had forced the lesson home to the people did they begin to understand that war, especially on the scale of the World War, could not be taken on as an "extra" in addition to carrying on business as usual. When that time arrived, the entire productive energies of the people were directed to the

---

[11] Thus Edgar Crammond thought "economic exhaustion and the exhaustion of men and war materials will render it impossible for some of the principal belligerents to continue the conflict after July next." ("Cost of the War," *Journal of the Royal Statistical Society*, May, 1915, p. 364). See also *L'Economiste français*, January 30, 1915, p. 132, for a statement that the war would not last longer than seven months.

task of winning the war, and non-essential industries were subordinated to this purpose. The length of time required to achieve such a unity of purpose and action differed, of course, in the different countries. Germany, it may be said, was thus organized from the beginning. England required probably the longest time to make her adjustment complete and thoroughgoing, and the other nations took varying rank between these two.

CHAPTER III

THE UNITED STATES AS A NEUTRAL

Situation in the United States at the outbreak of the war in Europe — The expansion of foreign trade — How Europe paid its bills — The shipment of gold — Foreign loans placed in the United States — Purchase of American securities held abroad — Is New York to be the financial center of the world?

The disorganization in the European security market which followed the ultimatum of Austria-Hungary to Serbia was not without its effect on the United States. During the week preceding Friday, July 31, in spite of a deluge of selling orders from Europe, where conditions bordering on panic prevailed, the New York market stood its ground wonderfully. There was, however, a steady decline in prices, which became more violent on July 30. The evidences of an approaching panic began to show themselves, and to avoid serious trouble the New York Stock Exchange was closed on July 31,[1] for the second time in its history, the first having been for ten days in 1873. Fortunately, speculation on the New York market had been for several years at low ebb, so that values were not inflated or long accounts standing. Industry, too, was on a firm basis, for the depression of the previous year had necessitated economy and brought business down to bedrock. The financial and

[1] The Exchange remained closed until November 28, 1914, when it was opened for dealings in a restricted list of bonds. This proved very successful, and on December 11 a further step was taken. Permission was given to trade in a list of stocks which were not international in character at or above prescribed minimum prices. Four days later the Exchange opened entirely under a free market.

business world, therefore, was in a good position to withstand the shock to credit which followed the outbreak of the war in Europe.

The credit situation, however, did not pertain to New York alone, but was international in character. The most serious condition which developed was the breakdown in the international credit mechanism. London was the financial center of the world, and there focused a great mass of debits and credits. The floating indebtedness of the United States to London, which was ascertained by special inquiries, amounted to $580,000,000, and the debts of the rest of the world brought the total up to a much larger figure. In the first excitement and uncertainty of the crisis London demanded immediate payment of these obligations by its debtors. On the other hand, the London banks almost ceased the acceptance of further bills of exchange; indeed, with the complete disruption of foreign trade the supply of these bills fell off rapidly. The result was a veritable *impasse*.

The debts owed to England, France, Germany, and the other nations of Europe by the United States maturing between August 1, 1914, and January 1, 1915, amounted to considerably over a half-billion dollars, of which $200,000,000 was immediately due. The most important single item was a debt of $80,000,000 owing by the City of New York to London and Paris and due between September 1 and January 1. New York City with its enormous budget has always been a large borrower and she had been in the habit of borrowing on her tax warrants in the cheapest market, which happened the previous year to have been in France and England rather than at home. To meet this debt a syndicate was formed of New York bankers to which

WAR COSTS AND THEIR FINANCING

New York City sold $100,000,000 of her six per cent. notes, receiving therefor $80,000,000 in gold or adequate exchange. These and other debts owing to London were liquidated within three months by the transfer of gold or credits. To meet this indebtedness large shipments of gold were necessary, as the paralysis of foreign trade, due to activities of German cruisers, prevented the export of commodities with which normally our foreign balances would have been met. Cotton, grain, and manufactured goods of various kinds piled up on the docks and congested the railways leading to the seaboard.

Since the export of commodities was prevented and the stock exchanges were closed, there was practically only one method by which the balance of international indebtedness could be met, and that was by the shipment of gold. On July 28 some $10,700,000 went out on the *Kronprinzessin-Cecilie,* but the ship was intercepted by wireless and returned to the nearest American port. Congress appropriated funds to be sent abroad on the cruiser *Tennessee* for the relief of American tourists overtaken in almost every European port and unable to secure cash by reason of the foreign moratoria. For this purpose $35,000,000 in gold was shipped from New York in early August and its safe passage guaranteed to the United States Government by the warring powers. Sterling exchange, the normal rate for which is $4.866, soared to the high point of $5.50 by the end of July, and it was reported by the *Commercial and Financial Chronicle* to have climbed to the unprecedented price of $7 on August 1.

The situation became chaotic and so fraught with danger in view of the large transfers that had to be

THE UNITED STATES AS A NEUTRAL

made that the leading banks in New York agreed to fix an arbitrary rate of $5 for sterling exchange. This, of course, was only a temporary arrangement. A more effective method of dealing with the situation was the creation of a "gold pool," as it was called; a fund of $100,000,000 in gold was subscribed by a number of national and state banks and trust companies in the reserve cities to guarantee the payment of American debts in London. Ten per cent. of the sum was collected and sent to the New York Clearing House, and part of this was deposited by the Clearing House at Ottawa to the credit of the Bank of England. Arrangements were made by which this gold fund was to be considered part of the Bank of England's gold reserve, so that the danger of shipping gold abroad would be eliminated. Deposits in the Bank of Ottawa were credited to the depositors' London account at the fixed price of $4.90. These measures relieved the tension in a marked degree, and the end of 1914 saw exchange on London and Paris practically back to normal, the sterling maximum for December being $4.89.

The next difficulty that presented itself was the disposal of an unprecedented cotton crop amounting to fifteen million bales and worth some $700,000,000. The exports declined sharply, owing chiefly to the cutting off of the German demand. This placed the cotton growers and traders in a peculiarly difficult position, as the growing and marketing of the cotton crop is financed largely by means of credit. The South was on the verge of a financial breakdown because of the paralysis of the movement of cotton. Accordingly another pool was formed to lend up to $150,000,000 on cotton. Another movement, more or less sentimental in its inception but ultimately profitable to the participants therein, was

WAR COSTS AND THEIR FINANCING

the "buy-a-bale" campaign, which resulted in the purchase of thousands of bales of cotton by purchasers in this country who stored them until prices reached normal again. Relief to the general situation was also brought by the organization of a Bureau of War Risk Insurance by the Treasury Department, which facili tated the movement of our exports. The speedy assertion by Great Britain of her mastery of the seas soon permitted the resumption of ocean transportation and the export of commodities from the United States.

By these various measures the country was able to meet successfully the difficult and complicated international financial problem. But the United States had its own troubles which it was forced to solve at home. The money markets and banks found themselves embarrassed at the outbreak of the war, as always occurs in any panic, by a shortage of currency. This was met by the distribution through the Treasury of $141,228,000 in emergency currency. Provision had originally been made for such an emergency issue in the Aldrich-Vreeland Act of 1908, and when the Federal Reserve Act was passed in 1913 the provision covering an emergency circulation, which would have expired on June 30, 1913, was extended one year. This currency had never been used, and was intended, as its name implies, simply for use in an emergency. The emergency occurred when the war broke out in Europe, and the Treasury promptly took advantage of the provisions of the Act. By October the total issues of emergency notes amounted to $369,000,000. With the opening of the Federal reserve banks for business in the following month these emergency notes were speedily retired. They had been of great service in the crisis which occurred before the Federal reserve system was put in operation, but after

THE UNITED STATES AS A NEUTRAL

November the power to issue Federal reserve notes rendered this emergency currency of no further importance.

One of the most important and far-reaching effects of the war was the enormous expansion of the foreign trade of the United States. After the first panic and disorganization of our foreign commerce, orders began to pour in from Europe for foodstuffs, for raw material of all kinds, and finally for actual munitions of war. This increased demand was not due to the superior excellence or cheapness of our goods. It was caused rather by the necessities of the allied belligerents in Europe, who in the urgency of immediate action against a shrewd and well prepared foe turned to us for material assistance. The excess of our exports over our imports jumped from $470,653,000 in the year ending June 30, 1914, to $1,094,419,000 for the next 12-month period. The following year saw this figure doubled, the favorable balance of trade for the fiscal year 1916 amounting to $2,135,600,000. Not only was the volume greatly expanded, but the character of our trade also underwent a remarkable change. The expansion took place, as might be expected, primarily in the group of commodities which ministered directly to war needs. A tabulation issued in August, 1915, selected the 14 most important groups of commodities of this nature and compared the exports for the preceding 10 months with those of the corresponding 10 months before the war.[2] The four-fold increase shown in this table gives clear evidence of the relation between war orders and the expansion of our foreign trade, and proves how greatly our favorable balance was due to the sale of supplies to the belligerents.

---
[2] Babson's Report of August 29, 1915.

WAR COSTS AND THEIR FINANCING

UNITED STATES FOREIGN TRADE, WAR AND PRE-WAR

Commodities	10 months to June, 1915	10 pre-war months
Mules and horses	$73,000,000	$3,500,000
Brass, bronze, etc	155,000,000	6,000,000
Automobile parts	116,000,000	20,000,000
Railway cars	21,000,000	10,000,000
Airplanes	6,300,000	195,000
Chemicals	93,000,000	22,000,000
Motorcycles	2,700,000	900,000
Cotton goods	88,000,000	43,000,000
Iron and steel	472,000,000	212,000,000
Shoes and leather	120,000,000	47,000,000
Canned goods, meat, and dairy products	231,000,000	124,000,000
Wool and woolen goods	47,500,000	3,900,000
Zinc, etc	36,800,000	328,000
Explosives	366,000,000	5,000,000
Total	$1,798,300,000	$497,823,000

The meaning of this growth in our foreign trade becomes more apparent with further analysis. The most striking feature was the enormous increase in exports to the five leading nations of the Entente Allies. From $927,000,000 in the fiscal year 1914, exports to these countries grew to $2,432,000,000 in 1915, and to $3,012,000,000 in 1916. On the other hand, the exports to the Central Powers, which in 1914 had been $370,000,000, declined in 1915 to $30,600,000, and in 1916 almost disappeared, amounting then to only half a million. Part of this loss to the Central Powers was made up by indirect trade through the medium of the northern European neutrals, the exports to which more than doubled between 1914 and 1916, increasing from $150,000,000 to $328,000,000. Although the following year saw a decline in this trade to $245,000,000, it was still far in excess of the normal pre-war trade.

THE UNITED STATES AS A NEUTRAL

The imports from the Entente Allies not only did not increase with their enlarged purchases, but even fell off in the two years following the outbreak of the war. Those from the northern European neutrals remained fairly steady. The belligerent countries were in no condition to pay for the commodities which they were taking from the United States by a return of their own raw materials or manufactures. All the energies of these belligerents were being directed into war activities, and normal trade was left to take care of itself as best it could. The result was that these purchases had to be paid for by other means than exchange of commodities. There were only three other ways by which such trade could be financed, namely, the shipment of gold, the sale of securities, and the establishment of credits. As will be seen, each of these methods was used in turn.

The enormous trade balance piled up in favor of the United States was hailed with joy in this country as an index of our prosperity, but in some respects the trade developed as a result of war orders exerted an unfortunate influence upon our economic life. Manufacturing industries were almost revolutionized. Those which could contribute to turning out munitions or war supplies expanded under the beneficent influence of orders which were placed almost regardless of price. With the diversion of labor and capital into war industries, however, other enterprises suffered correspondingly. Building operations were almost at a standstill, and in spite of the rush of war orders, unemployment in many cities and industries was a serious problem. The favorable balance of trade had, indeed, one good aspect, for it indicated that the United States, so long a debtor nation, was now paying off its debts. But the stimulation of American business involved in these war orders was not without danger. The development was a very uneven one, resulting in a relative depression of some industries and an over-development of others. The resulting trade expansion was clearly abnormal, based, as it was, not upon the exchange of commodities, but upon the borrowing capacity of our customers. Moreover, while the war orders were bringing a flood of gold and surface prosperity to the people of the United States, prices and wages, especially in the industries affected, were being driven up to record heights. The prosperity was certainly being very unevenly distributed.

There was another aspect of our foreign-trade expansion which has called forth endless comment. This was the opportunity opened to the United States to capture the foreign markets in South America and the East. The stoppage of German trade with those countries as the result of the driving from the seas of practically all German vessels and the reduction of British trade as the result of the absorption of Great Britain in war activities gave an unrivalled opportunity to the United States, but the people of this country were too occupied with the immediate profits to be made in filling war orders to endeavor to build up a new trade in foreign markets. Exports to South America, in fact, showed a decline from $122,000,000 in 1914 to $97,000,000 in 1915. The following year, however, witnessed a significant increase to $176,000,000. Imports from South American countries, on the other hand, showed a rapid growth. From $221,000,000 in 1914, they increased to $259,000,000 in 1915, and to $390,000,000 in 1916. Much of this increase was in foodstuffs and raw materials which found their way ultimately to Europe, although some of them were consumed in this country.

THE UNITED STATES AS A NEUTRAL

In other words, the expansion of our trade with South America, so far as it showed a growth, resulted from our acting as agent for European belligerents or because we were taking our pay from England and her allies in orders on South American countries for their goods. Great as was the expansion of our foreign trade during the first two years of the war, there was nothing in it to make us boastful of our achievements. Our sales to the belligerents and our capture of neutral markets came to us as one of the incidents of the war, and not because we had surpassed our industrial competitors in open market.

While the people of the United States were enjoying extraordinary prosperity from the flood of war orders which poured in upon them, the Governments of Europe were devising ways and means of meeting these expenditures. As already indicated, there were three ways in which the European nations might pay for their enormous purchases: (1) by shipments of gold to cover the adverse balances of trade against them; (2) by returning American securities held by them and disposing of others in the United States market; and (3) by establishing credits in this country. It is a matter of record that all three methods were used. The adoption of one did not preclude resort to the others; in fact, all three were sometimes used at the same time; but in the main, emphasis was placed on each one in turn.

As has been seen, the movement of gold was strongly from the United States to Europe in the first troubled and uncertain months after the declaration of war. The net loss to this country between August 1 and December 31, 1914, was $81,720,000. By that time, and indeed before, the necessary commercial and financial adjustments from a peace to a war basis had taken place, and England and her allies had turned to the United States to supply them with food, munitions, and other materials. The enormous exportations caused sterling exchange to fall lower and lower, until this finally reached the level of $4.49 on September 4, 1915. At these declining rates gold began to flow into this country in ever increasing quantities, the net imports for the first six months of 1915 amounting to $140,694,000, and those for the next six months to $280,268,000.

It is evident that there was a limit to the extent to which gold could be used to pay European debts. The outflow from England threatened to reduce the gold reserve of the Bank of England to an uncomfortably low point, and the Bank of France, from which some of the gold was drawn, was unwilling to see its stock further reduced. Indeed, beyond a certain point Europe could not spare the gold, and to demand it of her would cripple her banking and financial institutions. Nor, on the other hand, did the United States wish to be paid exclusively in gold; its accumulation would simply mean the heaping up of idle reserves and the raising of prices. Large as were the importations of gold, they were after all only a drop in the bucket when compared with the excess of exports over imports. In 1915 the favorable balance of trade to the credit of the United States amounted to $1,094,420,000 and in 1916 it rose to the still more staggering total of $2,135,600,000. It is evident that the $420,000,000 in gold imported would not go far toward liquidating such a balance as that of even the earlier year. In normal times the charges to be met for foreign travel, interest on American securities held abroad, payments for freight, insurance, etc., would have amounted to some $500.000,000 or $600,000,000

THE UNITED STATES AS A NEUTRAL

annually. Fully half of these payments were no longer being made, but even assuming no diminution in these items, they together with the imports of gold would have paid for only something over half of the net merchandise exports from the United States. It was still necessary for Europe to make payment for the excess of some $700,000,000 which she received during the fiscal year 1915. It was evident that other means than shipment of gold would have to be devised to meet these debts.

The purchase of short-term obligations of foreign Governments was practically unknown to the people of the United States before the Great War. A few loans had been made to Canada, to China, and to some of the Latin-American countries, but they had been of a temporary character, and the securities had been easily parted with. The opportunities for investment had always been so profitable in the United States, and the need for capital so great, that there was very little inducement for an American investor to seek foreign enterprises. The West has been to the American capitalist what the colonies have been to the British — the undeveloped region which offered returns larger than he could secure from his immediate neighborhood. There was, therefore, no necessity for American investors to look abroad for opportunities to place their capital, and there had consequently grown up in this country a prejudice against foreign investment which had to be overcome.

At this time, however, the United States was called upon to finance foreign Governments. Canada and Argentina, which had previously secured the capital they needed in Great Britain, now turned for assistance to this country. Not only these and other countries which had previously been in the habit of borrowing from Great Britain or France, but these two financial giants themselves were compelled to turn to the United States for loans. The foreign loans which were now placed in the United States, however, were not the ordinary offerings of foreign securities for investment. They were rather credits established to pay for commodities purchased in the United Statss. It was necessary to make these loans or to see the war orders greatly curtailed. Goods were sold to the belligerent nations of Europe, and the United States then took its pay in the form in which it could be offered. An illustration of this may be found in the flotation of the famous Anglo-French Loan of $500,000,000 which was negotiated on September 28, 1915. A special clause in the loan agreement stipulated that the proceds were to be used exclusively for purchases in the United States. A large part of the loan was simply allotted to various munitions manufacturers in part payment for their sales to England and France, and in some cases at least these shares were later distributed by these companies as dividends among their stockholders. The loan consisted of five per cent. five-year bonds which were a direct obligation of the British and French Governments. It was underwritten at 96 and sold to the public at 98.

Although this was the largest of the foreign loans placed in this country during the first two years of the war, there were many other loans placed here by other Governments, as well as further loans by the British and French Governments. The following table shows the extent to which American capital was being drawn upon by investment in foreign short-term obligations down to the time of our own entrance into the war:

THE UNITED STATES AS A NEUTRAL

FOREIGN LOANS FLOATED IN THE UNITED STATES, 1915–1917

Great Britain:

Anglo-French Loan of October, 1915	$250,000,000	
Collateral loan of August, 1916	250,000,000	
Collateral loan of October, 1916	300,000,000	
Collateral loan of February, 1917	250,000,000	
Bank credit, renewed	50,000,000	
Treasury bills sold	150,000,000	
		$1,250,000,000

Canada:

August, 1915	$45,000,000	
March, 1916	75,000,000	
July, 1917	100,000,000	
		220,000,000

France:

Anglo-French loan of October, 1915	$250,000,000	
American Foreign Securities loan of July, 1916	100,000,000	
Collateral loan of April 1, 1917	100,000,000	
City of Paris, October, 1916	50,000,000	
City of Bordeaux, Lyons, Marseilles, November, 1916	36,000,000	
Industrial credit through Bonbright & Company	50,000,000	
Treasury bills sold	40,000,000	
Collateral loan through Rothschild on railroad bonds	30,000,000	
Acceptance credits through banks	30,000,000	
		686,000,000

Russia:

December, 1916, Dollar Loan	$50,000,000	
June, 1916, through bank syndicate	20,000,000	
Treasury notes sold	25,000,000	
Banking credits, private	7,000,000	
		107,000,000

Italy, 1916	25,000,000
Germany	10,000,000
Newfoundland	5,000,000
Mexico	500 000
Cuba	10,000 000
Panama	2,911,000
Santo Domingo	12,868,350
Argentina	32,720 000
Bolivia	4,526,000
Peru	1,000 000
Norway	5,000 000
Switzerland	5,000,000

WAR COSTS AND THEIR FINANCING

China	12,500,000
Japan	102,552,000
Municipal and state loans to foreign countries	213,381,262
Corporation, railroad, public-utility, and industrial foreign loans	206,436,675
	$2,912,395,287

The placing of these large credits in the United States rendered less necessary the shipment of gold to this country by European belligerents. The direct influence of the Anglo-French Loan may be seen in the imports of gold into the United States during the first half of 1916. This loan was paid in instalments as needed; by January 3, 1916, some three-quarters of the entire amount had been paid in. While these funds were still available, the gold imports fell off almost completely. This is clearly shown in the following table:

GOLD IMPORTS INTO THE UNITED STATES, 1916

January, 1916	$15,100.000
February, 1916	6,000,000
March, 1916	9,800,000
April, 1916	6,100,000
May, 1916	17,300.000
June, 1916	122,700,000

As long as the credits under the loan were available, importation of gold was unnecessary, but when they were exhausted, gold imports were resumed. Although the inflow of gold steadied the rates of foreign exchange, this method could not be continued for any great length of time, and accordingly further large British and French loans were brought out in July, August, and October, 1916, aggregating $1,000,000,000. As these loans contained some novel features, they are worth recording. The French loan in July was obtained through an organization specially created for this purpose, namely, the American Foreign Securities Com-

THE UNITED STATES AS A NEUTRAL

pany, with a capital of $100,000,000. This corporation obtained from the French Government its obligation to repay the principal in three years, together with collateral amounting to $120,000,000 made up of Government securities of Argentina, Egypt, Spain, Switzerland, Sweden, Denmark, and other Governments, some foreign industrial shares, and about $4,000,000 in American securities. The loan, in the form of three-year five per cent. gold notes, was taken over by the Securities Company at 94.5 and sold to the public at 98. This transaction was interesting as the first case in which a foreign Government placed collateral in order to attract American investors.

This was quickly followed by the flotation of a $250,000,000 British loan in August on much the same terms. A syndicate headed by J. P. Morgan & Company took over two-year five per cent. collateral gold notes of the British Government secured by collateral aggregating in value $300,000,000. It was underwritten by the syndicate at 98 and offered to the public at 99, at which price it was quickly taken up. The securities which were deposited as collateral by the British Government were divided into three classes, each aggregating $100,000,000: the first consisted of stocks, bonds, and other securities of American corporations; the second, of bonds of the Dominion of Canada and the Canadian Pacific Railway Company; and the third, of Government bonds of certain neutral countries, namely, Argentina, Chile, Norway, Sweden, Switzerland, Denmark and Holland. So successful were these collateral loans that in October another British loan of the same general character for $300,000,000 was offered. This consisted half of three-year five per cent. gold notes and half of five-year five per cent. gold notes, secured by

WAR COSTS AND THEIR FINANCING

direct obligation of the British Government and collateral to the amount of $360,000,000. The loan was managed by a syndicate headed by J. P. Morgan & Company, which offered the three-year notes at 99.25 and the five-year notes at 98.5.

French municipal bonds of Paris, Bordeaux, Lyons, and Marseilles were sold in October and November. The first of these issues was very successful, being three times oversubscribed during the first day. But the sales of the subsequent issues were adversely affected by a warning of the Federal Reserve Board to banks against tying up funds in foreign treasury bills, which might not be readily marketable. This was such an unusual and important official utterance that two or three significant sentences deserve to be quoted.[3] After commenting on press reports as to its attitude towards the purchase by banks in this country of Treasury bills of foreign Governments,

> the Board deems it a duty to define its position clearly. . . . It would, therefore, seem, as a consequence, that liquid funds of our banks, which should be available for short credit facilities to our merchants, manufacturers and farmers, would be exposed to the danger of being absorbed for other purposes to a disproportionate degree, especially in view of the fact that many of our banks and trust companies are already carrying substantial amounts of foreign obligations, and of acceptances which they are under obligation to renew. The Board deems it, therefore, its duty to caution the member banks that it does not regard it in the interest of the country at this time that they invest in foreign Treasury bills of this character. . . . In the opinion of the Board it is the duty of banks to remain liquid in order that they may be able to respond to home requirements.

Enormous as were these loans, they were insufficient,

---
[3] *Federal Reserve Bulletin,* December, 1916, p 661.

THE UNITED STATES AS A NEUTRAL

even with the addition of the gold imports, to meet the debts which the European Governments were piling up in the United States through their purchases of munitions and other commodities. For the three years ending June 30, 1917, the excess of exports over imports in the United States amounted to $6,860,500,000. If there be set against this sum the gold imports, the loans which had been granted to foreign Governments, and an allowance for the usual charges against this country for interest, freight, insurance, foreign travel, etc., which might be said to amount in the aggregate to about $3,600,000,000, there would still remain an enormous unliquidated balance. It was evident that some further expedient would have to be devised to balance the accounts and to steady the rates of foreign exchange. This was found in the sale to the United States of its own securities owned by the debtor nations.

The amount of American securities held abroad has been estimated by more than one writer, but probably the most authoritative statement is that of Sir George Paish, who estimated the amount of foreign capital invested in the United States in 1910 at about $6,000,000,000.[4] It is evident that here was an asset of no mean magnitude which might be used to liquidate the debts being created by European purchasers. There is no reason to suppose that any noteworthy change had occurred in these investments in the five years between 1910 and 1914. That we had not paid off any considerable sums in this period is shown by an examination of our trade balances.

The annual payments which must be met by the United States on account of interest and other charges amounted to about $500,000,000, distributed as follows:

[4] See Chapter I for details.

WAR COSTS AND THEIR FINANCING

Interest on securities and other property incomes	$175,000,000
Freight charges	25,000,000
Remittances by alien laborers living in United States	125,000,000
Expenditures of American tourists abroad	150,000,000
Insurance premiums and sundries	25,000,000
	$500,000,000

These payments were met by the excess of our merchandise exports over our imports, supplemented by exports of gold or additional sales of American securities. For the five fiscal years 1910 to 1914 the net merchandise exports of the United States were as follows:

MERCHANDISE EXPORTS AND IMPORTS, 1910 TO 1914
(*In millions*)

	1910	1911	1912	1913	1914
Total exports	$1,744.9	$2,049.3	$2,204.3	$2,465.8	$2,364.5
Total imports	1,556.9	1,527.2	1,653.2	1,813.0	1,893.9
Excess of exports	$188.0	$522.0	$551.1	$652.8	$470.6

As the average for the five years is $476,900,000, it is evident that the excess of exports over imports merely sufficed to meet the current fixed charges against this country for interest and services, and did not go to reduce our foreign indebtedness. We may therefore conclude that this remained in 1914 at practically the same figure at which it stood in 1910.

After the first panic rush to sell American securities in the last days of July, 1914, to which an end was put by the closing of the stock exchanges, there was probably little done in the transfer of foreign-owned securities to American accounts. But with the opening of the exchanges again in November and December some liquidation took place. Unwilling to let their gold go

THE UNITED STATES AS A NEUTRAL

in unlimited quantities, and faced by an inability to market more than comparatively small amounts of their war loans in the United States, it became necessary for the European Governments to effect the transfer of American securities from their foreign owners to the United States. It is difficult to estimate the amount of securities returned to this country. The most extensive, as well as the most reliable, information on this subject is found in four inquiries made by L. F. Loree, President of the Delaware & Hudson Company. His inquiries were limited to railroad securities, but it has been estimated that four-fifths of Europe's holdings were of this class. The figures were obtained from 144 railroads, or from all lines in the United States over 100 miles in length. The results of Mr. Loree's inquiries are shown in the following table:

AMERICAN RAILROAD SECURITIES HELD ABROAD, PAR VALUE
(*In thousands*)

Type	January 31, 1917	July 31, 1916	July 31, 1915	January 31, 1915
Preferred stock..	$91,006	$120,598	$163,130	$204,394
Second preferred stock.........	4,645	4,858	5,609	5,558
Common stock..	258,730	366,762	511,437	573,880
Notes..........	8,475	9,070	24,632	58,254
Debenture bonds	56,752	74,797	160,229	187,508
Collateral trust bonds.........	57,776	85,166	180,591	282,418
Mortgage bonds.	672,969	774,794	1,150,340	1,371,157
Equipment trust bonds........	7,450	7,783	25,253	20,233
Car trusts......	49	836	29	....
Receivers' certificates.........	958	958	2,201	998 ·
Total......	$1,185,811.4	$1,415,623.5	$2,223,450.2	$2,704,402.3

WAR COSTS AND THEIR FINANCING

A study of this table shows that in the half-year ending July 31, 1916, almost $500,000,000 of railroad securities were transferred from foreign to American ownership. The next 12 months saw a further transfer of about $800,000,000, but the ensuing 6 months ending January 31, 1917, saw only $230,000,000 of railroad securities thus transferred. It is evident that the well was running dry.

Large as was the first sum, it was not sufficient to meet the increase in war purchases made by the belligerents from this country, and early in 1916 Government pressure began to be applied to force the liquidation of American securities. The first plan devised was the British mobilization scheme, which was put into effect in January, 1916. This provided for the concentration in the possession of the British Government of American securities owned by British subjects. The owners were given several options: the first provided for the outright sale of the securities to the Government in exchange for British Exchequer bonds; the second provided for the loan of securities by those unwilling to sell them. In the latter case the owner was to deposit them with the Government for a period of five years after March 31, 1917, with an election on the part of the Government to purchase if it so desired, the owner meanwhile to receive the interest or dividends and a payment from the British Government for the loan of one-half of one per cent. on the par value of the securities. If the securities were purchased, the owner received the income and bonus to the end of the loan period, and then either received back the same type of security or its deposit value and a five per cent. bonus.

France also asked its people who held American and

THE UNITED STATES AS A NEUTRAL

other foreign securities to deposit them with the Government on a three-year loan subject to the right of purchase by the Government, in which event the owner would be paid the highest price quoted for his security during the prior three months. The Government secured to the owners the full income from the securities while on loan with it and in addition a bonus of 25 per cent. of the income which the securities earned during that period.

Germany also mobilized the securities of her citizens, both foreign and domestic. Through the agency of the loan-office banks the people were induced to pledge these securities for the purchase of war loans. Because of the British blockade it was never possible for Germany or Austria-Hungary to utilize their holdings of American securities for the liquidation of foreign debts or the establishment of credits in the United States, although some were transferred to Holland and the Scandinavian countries, from which Germany purchased during the early years of the war. Germany during the first and second war loans in the fall of 1914 and spring of 1915 liquidated her foreign securities heavily through Amsterdam.[5]

The securities thus mobilized by the belligerent Governments were used in part as collateral for loans placed in the United States, as in the case of the American Foreign Securities Company loan and the British collateral loans of August and October, 1916. Over $500,000,000 of securities, of which, to be sure,

---

[5] In May, 1918, the Dutch Minister of Finance stated that, according to his best information, foreign securities to the value of 200,000,000 florins ($80,000,000, at the prevailing rate of 2½ florins to the dollar) had been imported into Holland since January 1, 1917 (*Commerce Reports*, July 2, 1918, p. 20). It is probable that the early years of the war saw a similar movement even greater in amount.

only a small part represented investments in the United States, were tied up in this way as collateral. More important was the outright sale of these holdings in the American market and the application of the proceeds to new purchases or the liquidation of debt.

The result of this double movement of gold and securities from Europe to the United States, together with the granting of loans and the sale of our products in enormous amounts at high prices, was the rapid repayment of our net debt to foreign countries. It may be estimated that by the middle of 1917 our net debt to foreign countries was practically extinguished. For the first time in its history the United States became a creditor nation.

The position achieved by the United States as a creditor nation gave rise to statements and hopes that New York would now supplant London as the financial center of the world. A brief statement of the factors necessary to obtain and hold such a position will answer the question whether New York's financial supremacy was simply one of the temporary incidents of the war or whether it is to be permanent.

It is clear that the position of the United States and of New York as its leading financial city was abnormal in 1916. To be sure, the United States had paid off its borrowed indebtedness and was piling up an enormous credit balance against the rest of the world. But to be a creditor nation is a very different thing from being the financial center of the world. To become such a center permanently several conditions must be met. In the first place the American people must invest large sums abroad. To do this they must not only have capital to spare for that purpose, but they must be willing to invest it in other countries. The first question that must be answered, therefore, is whether the United States has any surplus capital which it can spare after meeting the requirements of domestic industries and new enterprises. Five years ago such a query would have been unhesitatingly answered in the negative, but the events of the war have shown that our powers of production are far in excess of our own immediate demands. The Census Bureau estimated the increase in the total wealth of this country at about $80,000,000,000 in the eight years between 1904 and 1912, or from $107,104,193,410 to $187,739,071,090. This was at the rate of about $10,000,000,000 a year; if we exclude the increase in the value of land, the annual gain was about $6,000,000,000. In a recent study David Friday concludes that the annual savings of the American people during the years 1916 and 1917 were about $11,500,000,000.[6] It is evident, if these figures be even approximately correct, that there has been an enormous gain in productive capacity, even after making due allowance for the change in price level, which should furnish a fund with which we can finance not only our own requirements, but out of which we can also make loans to the rest of the world.

At present the United States is in a peculiarly favored position. A large part of the abnormal earnings from war industries has gone into the improvement and enlargement of existing plants. Although the railroads were run down at the beginning of the war they have since been in some measure rehabilitated, and in any case further requirements for equipment will not absorb the total available surplus capital. The

[6] "War and the Supply of Capital," *American Economic Review*, ix, No. 1, Supplement, March, 1919, p. 92.

domestic demand for capital for investment may be indicated by the record of new security issues during the years 1910 to 1916, as shown in the following table:

NEW SECURITIES ISSUED IN THE UNITED STATES
(*In millions*)

	Corporate	Municipal, etc.	Total
1910	$3,486	$320	$3,806
1911	3,577	397	3,974
1912	4,549	386	4,935
1913	3,180	403	3,583
1914	2,331	466	2,797
1915	1,962	488	2,450
1916	3,421	333	3,754

The balance of the $6,000,000,000 which it was estimated above was saved annually by the people of the United States and which did not take the form of corporate and other securities, was invested in farm equipment, new houses and buildings, the establishment of individual businesses, etc. Even allowing for a considerable expansion in each of these items, it seems clear that with the increased production on the part of the people of the United States it would be possible to meet all home needs and yet have a surplus for investment abroad.

The need of further capital for investment in American industry is conditioned in large measure on the available supply of labor. Although the labor force has been increased by the addition of a great many women who formerly were not engaged in gainful occupations or who were employed in domestic service, it is not certain that they will remain permanently in productive work. In this connection too it must not be overlooked

THE UNITED STATES AS A NEUTRAL

that the man power of Europe from which we have drawn so largely in the past has been frightfully reduced by the war, and that we ourselves have erected a barrier against its free immigration by the imposition of a new literacy restriction. It may fairly be admitted in view of all these facts that the United States has the capacity for foreign investment and the ability to finance foreign trade. The further question arises whether its people have the willingness to utilize their resources in this way.

Before New York can aspire to the position of world center, it must, as one writer puts it, "learn to think internationally, and not provincially." Americans had never before the World War been willing to make any considerable investments in foreign countries. If, however, we are to take from England her supremacy in the world's money market, this is the first condition that must be met. The situation has been well described as follows:[7]

In order permanently to fix a new place for ourselves, we must really become a world trade center. Time will show whether we are sufficiently developed for that. To ship to world markets and cultivate them permanently for our manufactures and merchants, we must become lenders of wealth on a big scale. One of the most familiar axioms of international trade is that commerce will flow where the capital flows; one reason for European supremacy in overseas trade has been the tremendous outside investments made by England and France and more recently by Germany. Our people are not yet educated to loan money abroad in large quantities; in spite of our apparently large loans in the past eighteen months, we cannot yet be called in a true sense an international loan market.

---
[7] Report issued by the Mechanics and Metals National Bank of New York, quoted in *Annals of the American Academy of Political and Social Science*, November, 1916, p. 276.

WAR COSTS AND THEIR FINANCING

A third factor that must be considered is the banking and credit machinery for financing foreign trade. In this respect London has an enormous advantage over New York. As has already been pointed out, London banks had for many years furnished banking accommodations to importers and exporters the world over. Sterling exchange was an international currency, and transactions between, let us say, an Argentine exporter of hides and a New York merchant would normally be settled by a draft drawn on London. The same thing was true of European and Oriental countries. Before the war foreigners engaged in import or export trade, even with the United States itself, seldom thought of settling their claims by means of New York drafts. Fortunately the passage of the Federal Reserve Act has made it possible for American banking institutions to utilize their credit in financing export trade. Great progress has also been made in the use of trade acceptances. Moreover, closer connection between the United States and foreign countries, especially with those of Latin America, has been secured by the establishment of branches or agencies of American banks in those countries and by the opening in the United States of accounts by foreign banks or exporters in other countries.

Whether these are mere temporary incidents of the abnormal conditions connected with the war, or are evidences of a permanent shift in international finance can be determined only by time. It may be said, however, that New York has not yet successfully met the essential requisite to supremacy in the world trade, namely, that of developing an active discount market. In this respect London has yielded little to New York even after four years of war. In November, 1918, it was stated that the amount of acceptances of all the

London banks against international business amounted to about $500,000,000, while those of the New York institutions totalled only $210,000,000.[8] Although the United States was able to loan great sums to the European Allies and in large measure to finance the war in its later stages, New York had not been able to wrest from London the business of financing the international trade of the world. The habits and trade connections and specialized training of a century or more were not lightly to be overcome.

A more fundamental factor in determining whether the people of the United States will be willing to lend their capital to Europe permanently and on a large scale remains to be considered. The final test is after all whether larger profits are to be made in Europe or in the United States. Up to this time the returns on investments in this country have always been larger and European capital has flowed here to take advantage of the high rates. It is certain that opportunities for favorable investment have by no means been exhausted; but until they are, or until greater scarcity of capital in Europe causes rates of interest to be higher there than here, no permanent flow of capital seeking investment can be expected to take place from the United States to Europe. As a market for cheap capital it is unlikely that London will yield its place to New York within any brief period of time.

---

[8] Leopold Frederick, quoted in *Federal Reserve Bulletin*, January, 1919, p. 21.

CHAPTER IV

WAR EXPENDITURES

The cost of past wars — Expenditures in the United States — Expenditures in Great Britain — Expenditures in France, Russia, and Italy — Expenditures in Germany and Austria-Hungary — Comparative estimate of total war expenditures.

A discussion of the expenditures of the World War must necessarily deal to a considerable extent with estimates and guesses. Even in peace time the budgets of many of the belligerent countries left much to be desired in clarity and comprehensiveness, and war conditions did not improve this condition. Different methods of accounting in the various countries make comparisons difficult. Nor is it always easy to determine exactly what are war expenditures. In most of the countries certain ordinary expenditures which had previously been carried in the civil budget were transferred to the military side; in others the deficits caused by disorganization of industry and the falling off of revenue were charged up to war costs. Moreover, there have been imposed upon the ordinary budget many additional expenditures which are directly attributable to the war, such as allotments to the families of soldiers and sailors, pensions to families the breadwinners of which have been killed or disabled, the interest on the war debt, and the increasing cost of government itself due to the general inflationist policy of financing the war. Finally, not all of the countries have published complete or veracious statements of their expenditures. Great Britain, France, Italy, and the United States are the

WAR EXPENDITURES

only countries that have published reports at all comprehensive of their war expenditures and of the means adopted to meet them. In the case of the other countries reliance must be placed upon the votes of credit and war loans in estimating war expenditure.

Before describing the actual expenditures made during the World War it will be interesting to note some of the estimates which had been made in advance as to the probable cost of such a conflict. Not a few such estimates were made during the first decade of the twentieth century, usually for the purpose of proving the impossibility of enduring the crushing costs. The average cost per man was usually set down at about $2.50 per day and the daily expenditures were figured out according to the number of men involved. The resulting total depended in considerable measure upon the imagination of the writer and his guess as to the number of participants who would be drawn into the conflict. An Austrian economist figured that a European war involving France, Germany, Russia, and Austria-Hungary would cost about $18,000,000 daily. The French writer, Bloch, estimated the total daily expenditure for these four Powers and Great Britain at about $21,000,000 a day. A Swiss estimate made in September, 1914, after some hint had already been given as to the magnitude of the expenditures, set the total daily cost for the four nations first named at $37,500,000. A computation made at the time of the Balkan wars, with perhaps a more intimate knowledge of the possibilities involved, put the actual expense of a general European conflict at $55,000,000 a day. The expenditures of any one of the five principal belligerents exceeded any of these estimates except the last, and this was outdone by the combined expenditures of any two of these belligerents.

WAR COSTS AND THEIR FINANCING

It is evident that even in the years immediately preceding the outbreak of the World War the frightful financial consequences of a general European conflict were not appreciated. The improvements that had been made in the machinery of destruction, the possibilities of airplanes and submarines, the economic mobilization of whole peoples for war, and the enormous expense involved seem to have been glimpsed but dimly. From the standpoint of costs, as well as from almost every other point of view, the World War established a new record and occupies a unique position. The characteristic feature of the expenditures in this war was the prodigality and even wastefulness with which they were incurred. As it was the first war in which modern technical science pitted machines and the output of factories against the forces of the enemy, the instruments and munitions of warfare were produced and destroyed with a reckless prodigality which ran the costs up to incredible figures. Moreover, the greater the perfection of science, the more enormous became the expenditure. As Professor Seligman wrote after our own entrance into the conflict:[1]

Not only are these munitions infinitely more costly than in former times, but also less durable; the bigger the gun, the shorter its life; the more elaborate the aeroplane, the greater the chance of its destruction; the better the sanitary methods, the more frequent the casting aside of uniforms; the more complete the application of science, the more rapid the ravages of war by both land and sea. Not only are the initial expenses immensely greater, but the sheer waste by destruction grows with every forward step in efficiency. The present war is not only the most expensive of all wars, but also the most wasteful.

[1] E. R. A. Seligman, "Our Fiscal Policy," in *Financial Mobilization for War* (Chicago, 1917), p. 1.

WAR EXPENDITURES

Financial efficiency as well as technical skill was also responsible for the huge outlays. The ease with which money was secured from the banks and from the public engendered a false optimism with regard to fiscal problems and encouraged lavish expenditures. Economy was disregarded, for in matters so vital and so urgent no chances could be taken. The figures soon became so large that all sense of proportion was lost, and men spoke as glibly of billions as they had previously of thousands.

In gauging the magnitude of the costs of the World War a comparison with the costs of the more important wars of the nineteenth century will be enlightening. These are stated in the following table, together with their duration and loss of life:

COSTS OF NINETEENTH CENTURY WARS[2]

Wars	Days	Loss of Life	Direct Monetary Cost
Napoleonic, 1790–1815	9,000	2,100,000	*$3,070,000,000
Crimean, 1854	730	785,000	1,700,000,000
American Civil, 1861-65	1,350	656,000	
North			4,700,000,000
South			2,300,000,000
			7,000,000,000
Franco-Prussian, 1870-71	210	280,000	
France			2,535,000,000
Germany			675,000,000
			3,210,000,000
Boer, 1899–02	995	9,800	1,250,000,000
Russo-Japanese, 1904–05	548	160,000	2,100,000,000

[2] E. Crammond, "Cost of the War," *Journal of the Royal Statistical Society*, May, 1915, p. 361; F. W. Hirst, *Political Economy of War*, pp. 140, 147, 241, 274, 276.
*Increase in debt of Great Britain and France.

WAR COSTS AND THEIR FINANCING

Although we were the last of the major belligerents to enter the war, the expenditures of the United States at once rivalled and soon surpassed in magnitude those of the other countries. Within a month after the declaration of war on April 6, 1917, the war expenditures were reflected in the monthly statements of the Treasury. These are shown for the two years 1917 and 1918 in the following table, excluding advances to the Allies:

MONTHLY EXPENDITURES OF THE UNITED STATES, 1917-1918

Month	1917		1918	
	Monthly	Daily	Monthly	Daily
January....	$79,910,714	$2,577,765	$715,302,039	$23,074,260
February...	75,844,498	$2,708,406	675,209,068	24,114,610
March.....	72,773,903	2,347,545	819,955,367	26,450,173
April......	81,599,598	2,719,986	910,756,758	30,358,558
May.......	114,102,810	3,680,736	1,068,203,026	34,458,163
June.......	134,304,040	4,776,801	1,263,914,905	42,130,497
July.......	208,299,031	6,719,323	1,259,782,599	40,638,310
August.....	277,438,000	8,949,613	1,524,901,777	49,190,380
September..	349,013,305	11,337,768	1,624,583,411	54,152,780
October....	465,045,360	14,904,690	1,174,622,406	37,892,335
November..	512,952,035	17,098,401	1,655,051,004	55,168,366
December..	611,297,425	14,904,690	1,670,890,396	53,899,690

There is seen here the same steady increase that characterized expenditures in other countries, as the administrative and other machinery was created for training men, producing munitions and other war supplies, building ships, and organizing in manifold ways the resources of the nation for the winning of the war. It is not yet possible to tell exactly how this money was

WAR EXPENDITURES

spent, as detailed accounts were not published during the war itself for obvious military reasons, and sufficient time has not elapsed since the signing of the Armistice to permit such publication. An approximate idea may be secured, however, from a statement of the expenditures by main groups for the three fiscal years 1917, 1918, and 1919, together with those of the last peace year. These are given in the following table:

EXPENDITURES OF THE UNITED STATES, 1916 TO 1919

Establishment	1916	1917	1918	1919
Civil....	$204,038,737	$234,649,248	$1,507,367,481	$3,230,890,248
Military	164,635,576	440,276,880	5,684,348,623	9,253,059,384
Naval..	155,029,425	257,166,437	1,368,642,793	2,009,272,389
Pensions, interest, etc.....	200,799,260	215,806,426	406,173,369	872,075,375
	$724,502,998	$1,147,898,991	$8,966,532,266	$15,365,297,396

The expenditures attributable to war may be calculated by subtracting the sum spent during the fiscal year 1915-16, which may be regarded as normal, from the total expenditures of the following years, assuming the difference to be due to the war. This procedure shows war expenditures for the first three months of the war (April 6 to June 30, 1917) to have been $423,405,993; those for the fiscal year 1917-18 would be $8,242,039,268; and those for the fiscal year 1918-19 may be placed at $14,312,821,707 or a total of $22,978,266,968. If to these sums there be added the advances

WAR COSTS AND THEIR FINANCING

to the Allies, the total outlay on account of the war made by the Federal Government for the fiscal years 1917, 1918, and 1919 was $1,308,405,993, $12,981,474,018, and $17,790,386,957 respectively, or a total of $32,080,266,968.[3]

Large as were these sums, they had been exceeded by the plans of the Administration and the appropriations of Congress. The needs of the Government for the fiscal year 1918 were estimated at $18,775,910,955, and the appropriation bills passed in response to these estimates carried a total of $18,879,177,015, to which must be added $2,511,553,925 for contract work authorized. There is a wide discrepancy between these sums and the actual expenditures of $13,705,967,016 which were shown at the end of the year. The overstatement made in the estimates must be attributed to the belief that the resources of the country could be at once mobilized for war purposes. But it soon became evident that considerable time must elapse and much preparatory work be done before such enormous sums could be spent advantageously. Men who had laughed at the idea of

---

[3] The essential correctness of this calculation is shown by the following statement from a letter written by the Secretary of the Treasury, Carter Glass, to Congressman Fordney, Chairman of the House Committee on Ways and Means, on July 9, 1919:

"Expenditures for the war period amounted to $32,427,000,000, and of these more than $9,384,000,000, or about 29 per cent., were met out of the receipts and other revenues than borrowed money, although payment of nearly half of the income and profits taxes for the fiscal year 1919 has not yet been made, such payment being deferred until the fiscal year 1920. In this calculation no deduction is made of expenditures for loans to the Allies, which on June 30 amounted to $9,102,000,000, or for other investments, such as ships, stock of the War Finance Corporation, bonds of the Federal land banks, etc.

"If we assume that the expenditures of the Government on a peace basis would have been at the rate of $1,000,000,000 a year, or for the period under discussion of nearly twenty-seven months would have equaled $2,250,000,000, then we may estimate the gross cost of the war to June 30, 1919, at $30,177,000,000."

WAR EXPENDITURES

"a million men springing to arms between sunrise and sunset" were now to learn that it was equally impossible to spend a billion dollars a month for war purposes without adequate preparation. In fact, a full year was to elapse before the labor and industries of the country were fully mobilized, and the highest pitch of production was probably just being attained when the Armistice put an end to further preparations.

It will be noticed in the table on page 86 that the month of November, 1918, showed the highest daily expenditures chronicled during the war, although December registered a greater absolute sum for the month. This was due to the cancellation of war contracts, which went on rapidly for two months. Thereafter expenditures showed an appreciable and steady decline. But the heavy expenditures of these months may fairly be attributed to the war, as they were caused by the cost of demobilization and similar charges which could not suddenly be discontinued.

One of the striking features of war finance was the almost universal breakdown of constitutional budgetary procedure. Even in England, where the control of the purse by Parliament had been carried furthest, wide discretionary powers were given to the Executive to spend the money voted free from the usual control. Of conditions as they existed just prior to the war a recent careful study says:[4] "The most characteristic feature of the appropriation system of Great Britain is the extent to which discretion is still left to the Executive in respect to the expenditure of the funds granted." The power of Parliament with respect to expenditures

---
[4] W. F. Willoughby, W. W. Willoughby and S. McC. Lindsay, *Financial Administration of Great Britain* (New York, 1917), p. 27.

WAR COSTS AND THEIR FINANCING

was theoretically unlimited, but it had always permitted considerable discretion to the Executive because it was believed that the latter was in a better position to determine the details and to secure efficiency. During the war this principle was stretched to an extent undreamed of, and enormous votes of credit were granted without any determination as to the details of expenditures or control. A vote of credit is a "vote having for its purpose the placing at the disposition of the Ministry of a large sum of money in addition to that provided for the regular conduct of the Government, with which to meet some great emergency."[5] In voting for war expenditures Parliament throughout the whole of the war made use of this method of granting votes of credit. In this way publicity with regard to the purposes and details of the military expenditures was avoided. It is therefore not possible to analyze the British war expenditures in detail.

On the other hand, the gross accounts of the war expenditures were published regularly since the beginning of the war. These are shown below for the fiscal years ending March 31, 1914 to 1919, the expenditures of the last peace year being given by way of comparison:

EXPENDITURES OF GREAT BRITAIN

1913-14	$987,465,000
1914-15	2,802,367,665
1915-16	7,795,791,888
1916-17	10,990,563,550
1917-18	13,481,107,025
1918-19	13,896,505,940

There is evidenced here a steady growth in expenditure which was utterly without precedent in former wars and which was as unexpected as it was unwelcome.

[5] *Ibid.*, p. 128.

WAR EXPENDITURES

Month after month and year after year the reality outran the forecast; never did the budget equal the actual outlay. The imaginations of the Chancellors of the Exchequer did not seem able to cope with the increasing magnitude of the operations and the constant demand for new services. The defect, however, was not peculiar to Great Britain but was shared by all the belligerents. In the case of Great Britain large loans to her allies and to the British Dominions were in part responsible for the progressive increase, but primarily it was due to the putting of larger armies into the field and to increased production of munitions. Toward the end of the war, too, the effect of higher prices was reflected in the increased cost of all war operations. The increase is shown even more strikingly when the daily expenditures are compared. In the following table these are given by quarters for the period of the war:

DAILY WAR EXPENDITURES OF GREAT BRITAIN BY QUARTERS, 1914–1918

Period	Days	EXPENDITURES	
		Quarter	Per day
Aug. 4–Sept. 30, 1914...	58	$351,155,000	$5,975,000
Oct. 1–Dec. 31, 1914...	92	930,490,000	10,115,000
Jan. 1–March 31, 1915...	90	1,202,890,000	13,365,000
April 1–June 30, 1915...	91	1,292,365,000	14,200,000
July 1–Sept. 30, 1915...	92	2,080,120,000	22,610,000
Oct. 1–Dec. 31, 1915...	92	2,127,100,000	23,120,000
Jan. 1–March 31, 1916...	91	2,297,205,000	25,230,000
April 1–June 30, 1916...	91	2,222,800,000	24,425,000
July 1–Sept. 30, 1916...	92	2,301,210,000	25,015,000
Oct. 1–Dec. 31, 1916...	92	3,305,585,000	35,930,000
Jan. 1–March 31, 1917...	90	3,160,970,000	35,620,000
April 1–June 30, 1917...	91	3,356,435,000	36,885,000
July 1–Sept. 30, 1917...	92	3,283,830,000	35,695,000
Oct. 1–Dec. 31, 1917...	92	3,505,905,000	38,105,000
Jan. 1–March 31, 1918...	90	3,333,931,715	37,043,686
April 1–June 30, 1918...	91	3,174,515,000	34,884,780
July 1–Sept. 30, 1918...	92	3,152,794,150	34,269,000

WAR COSTS AND THEIR FINANCING

The end of the first fiscal year, March 31, 1915, saw the daily expenditures doubled, a process which was repeated in the second year. Every effort was made to cut down civil expenditures. The Road Improvement Fund was abandoned and appreciable savings were made in the Consolidated Fund service by suspending the sinking fund. But the remorselessly growing costs of the war quickly wiped out these economies and constituted a demand for ever greater sums. By the end of the fiscal year 1916-17 the daily expenditures were over $35,000,000. The high point was reached in the last quarter of the calendar year 1917, when they averaged $38,100,000 daily. Although the expenditures for the fiscal year 1917-18 ran somewhat higher than those of the previous year, they did not exceed these as much as the rise in the general price level which occurred in the interval would apparently have justified. At this rate the war was costing Great Britain $1,455,000 an hour, or nearly $25,000 a minute.

Such large expenditures could not be made without a certain amount of waste and extravagance, and sharp criticism was made in many of the British journals that a considerable part of them was extravagant, if not needless. The *Spectator* characterized the expenditure of the Government as " lavish "; the *Nation* called attention to the " profligacy of the Government's war finance "; the *Economist* affirmed that " the nation's effort is seriously weakened by the waste and muddling of which new examples appear week by week "; and, finally, Herbert Samuels, Chairman of the Committee on Public Expenditure, in a debate in the House of Commons on June 19, 1918, stated that the matter was approaching a " public scandal." Although allowance may be made for a certain extravagance of language in

WAR EXPENDITURES

these criticisms, the diversity of authorities quoted suggests that there was some basis of fact; indeed, a certain amount of waste and extravagance would seem to have been inevitable in view of the enormous sums involved and the haste and urgency with which they were raised and expended. On the whole, there was probably less real occasion for complaint in England than in most of the other belligerent countries.

There occurred in France the same suspension of constitutional methods of procedure in voting and controlling expenditures as had taken place in England. Votes of credit were granted by the Assembly practically in the amounts asked for by the Government, but no accounting was made in detail as to the purposes for which these sums were expended. Indeed, it may be said that one of the effects of the war was an almost complete disregard of regular budgetary procedure. M. Ribot in a speech in the Chamber of Deputies in 1916 called attention to the fact that, owing to the system of asking for votes of credit at periodic intervals, quarterly budgets had practically superseded the annual budget. A year later he again referred to this point and promised that this would be the last occasion on which provisional credits would be asked, at least for civil expenditures; thereafter, he said, the Government intended to introduce an annual budget which would include all civil expenditures and all payments in connection with the public debt, so that only purely military expenditures would be covered by the quarterly credits. This pledge was carried out by the passage of the civil budget of June 27, 1918, which was the first budget passed as a whole since the beginning of the war.

The disregard of constitutional provisions in the

voting of public money in France finds additional illustration in a statement presented to the Chamber of Deputies by the Chief Public Accountant.[6] This showed that the credits voted for the 13 months ending January 31, 1917, amounted to $6,473,400,000; of this amount the authorized expenditure amounted to $5,122,200,000, and the unauthorized to $1,351,200,000. The large proportion of unauthorized expenditure indicates the effect of war in breaking down constitutional safeguards and the extent to which the Executive exercises its powers in war time in derogation of legislative control. The credits voted from August 1, 1914, to December 31, 1918, are shown in the following table:

CREDITS VOTED IN FRANCE, 1914-1918

Aug. 1 to Dec. 31, 1914	$1,779,717,000
Calendar year 1915	4,560,895,000
Calendar year 1916	6,589,029,000
Calendar year 1917	8,374,185,000
Calendar year 1918	9,217,961,256
	$30,521,787,256

The expenditures of France show the same progressive increase as characterized those of the other belligerents. The average daily outlay remained fairly steady throughout 1914 and 1915 at about $12,300,000; for 1916 the figure increased 66 per cent. to a daily average of $18,275,000; in 1917, an increase of 78 per cent. brought the daily average to $23,290,000; and in 1918, up to November, the daily average was about $28,400,000. The monthly and daily expenditures, averaged on the votes of credit for each year, were as follows:

[6] *Economist*, March 24, 1917, p. 553.

WAR EXPENDITURES

MONTHLY AND DAILY WAR EXPENDITURES OF FRANCE, 1914–1918

Year	Monthly	Daily
Aug.-Dec., 1914	$355,953,400	$11,865,000
1915	380,074,775	12,669,159
1916	548,267,498	18,275,583
1917	697,850,000	23,290,000
1918	768,146,771	28,407,339

These expenditures in France do not include the advances made by her to her allies, which were regarded more as investment than as expenditure, and which amounted to $1,547,200,000 during the period of the war. On the other hand, they include the civil expenditures, which may be estimated, on the basis of those for 1913, at about $5,000,000,000. If these be subtracted, the military costs are found to have been almost $26,000,000,000.

An interesting analysis of the expenditures for the first three and one-half years made by the Budget Committee of the Chamber is as significant for what it fails to disclose as for what it reveals. According to this report, the expenses of the war from its inception on August 1, 1914, to December 31, 1917, totalled $21,305,-000,000 of which sum $17,309,000,000 was used for military and other purposes directly connected with the prosecution of the war. Of this latter sum, some $15,200,000,000 was used for purely military purposes, that is, for waging the war against the Central Powers; the remaining $2,000,000,000 was used for repairing the damage inflicted by the enemy, and to that extent it may be said to have anticipated some of the work of reconstruction and to have lessened the expenditures for

WAR COSTS AND THEIR FINANCING

rehabilitation which will have to be faced after the war. The detailed table is as follows:[7]

CLASSIFICATION OF WAR EXPENDITURES IN FRANCE TO DECEMBER 31, 1917

Military...	$15,200,000,000
Assistance to families of mobilized men...	1,546,000,000
Aid to orphans...	6,000,000
Assistance to invaded departments...	2,000,000
Urgent relief...	25,600.000
Assistance to refugees...	183,800.000
Rehabilitation of invaded regions...	93,507,000
Reconstruction of landed property... $53,480,000	
Reconstruction of industrial property... 20,015,000	
Reconstruction of agricultural property... 20,012,000	
Repair of harbors and construction of means of communication...	65,877,000
Cultivation of abandoned areas...	6,000,000
Credits opened for reparation for damages incurred through the war...	180.000.000
Total...	$17,308.784,000
Extraordinary expenses of civil service...	134.576.345
Total war expense...	$17,443,360,345
Public debt service...	2,139,966,229
Ordinary expenses of civil service...	1,720,255,642
	$21,303,582,216

The increased expenditure for the year 1914 was due almost entirely to mobilization and military operations. The burden of the war in the form of increased debt charges, expenditure for relief of soldiers' families or of refugees from the devastated areas, and other increases indirectly attributable to war were first reflected in the expenditures for 1915. During the rest of the war every item of expenditure in this classification showed a steady and progressive increase. Such a classification

---
[7] *Federal Reserve Bulletin*, April, 1918, p. 275.

WAR EXPENDITURES

is of interest in showing that the burden of war is spread in a multitude of charges over the whole body politic and body social, and is by no means confined to the strictly military outlays.

There were three budgets in Russia, the civil, or ordinary, the extraordinary civil, and the extraordinary military. The first two of these seem to have been continued throughout the war and to have been voted regularly. The third budget was apparently withdrawn from legislative control, as details were never published with regard to military expenditures, nor was authorization asked for votes of credit. The ordinary expenditure did not show any considerable increase until the year 1917, when the expenditure for any one of the previous three years was just about doubled. Slight deficits had been shown every year, but not until 1917 did these assume unmanageable proportions. As these deficits are attributable to the war, they may fairly be counted as war expenditures. The expenditures and deficits on the civil budget are shown in the following table:

CIVIL EXPENDITURES IN RUSSIA, 1914–1917

Year	Expenditures	Deficit
1914	$1,464,000,000	$15,000,000
1915	1,534,000,000	137,000,000
1916	1,587,000,000	130,000,000
1917	3,061,000,000	1,191,000,000

The war expenditures of Russia understate rather than exaggerate the military contribution made by that

WAR COSTS AND THEIR FINANCING

country. This was due to several factors, namely, the very low pay received by the soldiers, the fact that the huge expense of transporting troops, equipment, and materials over the Government-owned railways was left to post-war adjustment, and the low cost of food, although this was in part offset by the higher cost of munitions. The war expenditures to the end of 1917 are given as follows in a review of Russian war finance operations published in the official *Viestnik Finansov:*[8]

WAR EXPENDITURES OF RUSSIA, 1914-1917

Aug. 1 to Dec. 31, 1914	$1,273,000,000
1915	4,687,450,000
1916	7,633,500,000
1917, to Sept. 1	7,102,407,500
	$20,696,357,500

Although Italy delayed her entrance into the war until May 24, 1915, the beginning of her expenditures on war account may be said to have been practically coincident with that of the other belligerents, for the costs of armament and mobilization preparatory to participation were heavy. The war expenditures from August 1, 1914, to October 31, 1918, were as follows:[9]

WAR EXPENDITURES OF ITALY, 1914-1918

Aug. 1, 1914-June 30, 1915	$607,840,000
July 1, 1915-June 30, 1916	1,670,300,000
July 1, 1916-June 30, 1917	2,826,440,000
July 1, 1917-June 30, 1918	3,946,920,000
July 1, 1918-Nov. 1, 1918	1,345,120,000
Interest on debt and outstanding liabilities	2,127,200,000
	$12,523,820,000

The expenditures of Germany have not been published and therefore must be estimated from the votes of credit

[8] Quoted in *Federal Reserve Bulletin*, April, 1918, p. 276.
[9] *Economist*, February 1, 1919, p. 136.

WAR EXPENDITURES

and the popular loans. Because of the secrecy maintained by the German Government regarding its financial operations and the difficulty of securing the few facts that are published, these are practically the only data upon which an estimate may be based.

An attempt was made during the first year of the war to effect a balance between expenditures and receipts by transferring the whole of the military and naval outlay, amounting in the fiscal year 1913 to $344,425,000, from the ordinary civil budget to the extraordinary war budget. In this way not only was a deficit prevented, but Karl Helfferich, the Minister of Finance, was able to announce a surplus for the year of $54,750,000. The following March, however, in presenting the budget for the fiscal year 1916-17, Dr. Helfferich stated that owing to the great increase in the service of the Imperial debt, which was estimated at $575,750,000, as against $317,000,000 in 1915, and $62,500,000 in the last peace budget, even this formal balance could not be maintained. There was an increase in the ordinary budget of over $84,000,000 in expenditure as compared with 1915, and as the receipts had fallen off over $36,000,000, a deficit of $120,000,000 resulted. By the end of the fiscal year the debt charges had risen to $891,500,000, and in his budget speech of February, 1917, the Finance Minister reported a formal deficit in the ordinary budget of $312,500,000 for the year ending March 31, 1918. This was based upon an estimated nominal expenditure of $1,337,500,000.

The expenditures of the Imperial Government for the war are probably best estimated by taking the total credits granted by the Reichstag. As it was constitutionally necessary to have the money even for military expenditures first appropriated by that body, these votes

WAR COSTS AND THEIR FINANCING

are matters of public record and the figures may be accepted as accurate. No details, however, have been made public as to how these sums were distributed among the different services. From the beginning of the war to the signing of the armistice, the Reichstag granted 12 votes of credit as follows:

VOTES OF CREDIT IN GERMANY, 1914-1918

August, 1914	$1,250,000,000
December, 1914	1,250,000,000
March, 1915	2,500,000,000
August, 1915	2,500,000,000
December, 1915	2,500,000,000
June, 1916	3,000,000,000
October, 1916	3,000,000,000
February, 1917	3,750,000,000
July, 1917	3,750,000,000
December, 1917	3,750,000,000
March, 1918	3,750,000,000
July, 1918	3,750,000,000
	$34,750,000,000

The actual expenditures, however, far exceeded the credits which had been granted. This significant fact was announced by Dr. Schiffer, Minister of Finance, in a speech to the German National Assembly at Weimar on February 15, 1919.[10]. According to his statement the expenditures of the war were as follows:

WAR EXPENDITURES OF GERMANY, 1914-1918

1914	$1,875,000,000
1915	5,750,000,000
1916	6,650,000,000
1917	9,875,000,000
1918	12,125,000,000
	$36,275,000,000
Treasury bills	1,500,000,000
Credits to Allies	2,375,000,000
Total	$40,150,000,000

[10] *Vossische-Zeitung*, February 16, 1919.

WAR EXPENDITURES

The existence of these large unauthorized liabilities shows that in Germany, as in most of the other European belligerent countries, the necessities of the war led the Executive to override the constitutional provisions regarding the voting of credits and to disregard the requirements for legislative control. It is significant, however, that the sums thus involved were far larger in Germany than in any other country. The daily expenditures, according to the table just given, ranged from $12,250,000 in 1914 to $33,750,000 in 1918. These sums, however, did not include the unauthorized expenditures which it is not possible to distribute by fiscal years. In a later memorandum presented to the National Assembly,[11] Dr. Schiffer estimated that the total war expenditure of Germany amounted to $42,500,000,000. A still later announcement made the startling disclosure that Germany's floating debt amounted to $18,000,000,000. This statement shows that the actual expenditures made during the war were far in excess of the officially admitted outlays and throws an interesting light upon German financial methods.

In addition to this direct money outlay the war damages inflicted on German property were estimated at $1,124,000,000 and the claims of ship owners at $375,000,000, and $1,240,000,000 were stated to have been spent for the relief of families of dead soldiers by the states and municipalities. This latter expenditure had been defrayed during the course of the war by the local governments, but on the understanding that it would be assumed by the Imperial Government upon its conclusion.

Huge as is the sum stated above, it by no means

---

[11] Copenhagen despatch, March 26, 1919, in *Washington Post*, March 27, 1919.

measures completely the real expenditures made on the war by Germany. In the case of the other nations the money outlay may be accepted as a correct statement of costs. Not so in the case of Germany. For years she had been preparing for this conflict and had collected immense stores of materials, munitions, and supplies of every kind. Part of the real cost, therefore, is represented by outlays made in previous years, though it is impossible to state how much should be credited to these earlier expenditures. During the war, moreover, Germany exacted tribute from occupied territory. This was estimated in October, 1917, at $1,600,000,000 in the case of Belgium alone. The exploitation of the resources of the people of Belgium, Northern France, Poland, Rumania, and parts of Russia must also be counted in any comparison, as such items in other countries were paid for. The total value of supplies and materials and services used by Germany in prosecuting the war must therefore be reckoned at a figure considerably larger than the total votes of credit, huge as these were.

In none of the other major belligerent countries was there greater secrecy concerning financial operations maintained than in Austria-Hungary. The figures for the civil budget, as to both expenditures and revenue, were published, but information regarding military expenditures was jealously guarded. The report of the State Debt Control Commission which was published in November, 1915, showed the war expenditures to the end of 1914. For the first five months of the war the war costs to Austria were about $1,125,000,000, or about $225,000,000 a month. Hungary paid during the same period the sum of $375,000,000, or about $75,000,000 a month.

WAR EXPENDITURES

After that date all is conjecture. There was a complete breakdown of ordinary budgetary procedure and no budget was presented during three years. It was not until July, 1917, that the lower house of the Austrian Parliament was able to secure the observance by the Government of the constitutional provisions concerning the passage of the budget. Then the Chamber of Deputies in passing the provisional budget asked for by the Government insisted on fixing a maximum limit of $1,200,000,000 instead of leaving the amount indefinite. Up to that time the money had been raised and expended by Executive act alone. The Chamber insisted that future estimates must show the war expenditures separately from the civil budget and that a real effort must be made to cover the latter by means of taxes and other revenues. The expenditures of Austria-Hungary, both for the civil and military budgets, so far as they have been published, are given in the following table:

EXPENDITURES OF AUSTRIA-HUNGARY, 1914–1918

Fiscal year ending June 30	EXPENDITURES		
	Civil	Military	Total
1915....	*†$692,200,000	*†$2,164,000,000	$2,856,200,000
1916....	*†651,600,000	*†2,993,000,000	3,644,600,000
1917....	§800,000,000	§3,200,000,000	§4,000,000,000
1918....	§1,000,000,000	§3,400,000,000	*4,433,900,000
1919....	*1,302,000,000	*3,564,400,000	*4,866,400,000
Total..	$4,445,800,000	$15,321,400,000	$19,767,200,000

* Budget estimates.
† Estimates of Copenhagen Society for Study of the War.
§ Writer's estimates.

WAR COSTS AND THEIR FINANCING

There seems to be no doubt that the official figures of expenditures are in all cases too low, both for the military budget and for the civil budget, which includes the interest on the public debt.[12] The Government seems to have published wilfully false statements as to the financial situation in order not to alarm the people unduly; consequently, all of the figures concerning expenditures must be taken with considerable reserve. But although these figures may not be accurate in themselves, they serve to give a fairly correct picture of the progressive course of expenditures during the war. As every effort was made by the Government to conceal the real facts, the admitted increase shown in these figures is all the more impressive.

It has not been possible to secure the expenditures of Austria and of Hungary separately for the period of the war. During the year 1918 the Austrian and Hungarian Parliaments were unable to agree upon the distribution of their common expenditures, and accordingly this was fixed by Imperial rescript at 63.6 per cent. for Austria, and 36.4 per cent. for Hungary. If this proportion be applied to the total joint expenditures in the table just given, it would appear that the expenditures of Austria amounted to $12,571,939,000, and those of Hungary to $7,195,300,000.

It is now possible to bring together the figures for all the belligerent countries and to estimate the total expenditures for the war during the four and one-half years from August 1, 1914, to such dates after the signing of the Armistice as the different belligerents closed their fiscal years.

---

[12] The expenditures of the Empire covered only the three items of war, finance, and foreign affairs. Austria and Hungary each had its own budget in addition to the Imperial budget.

WAR EXPENDITURES

GROSS MONEY WAR EXPENDITURES OF BELLIGERENTS

United States	$32,080,266,968
Great Britain	44,029,011,868
Canada	1,665,576,032
Australia	1,423,208,040
New Zealnd	378,750,000
South African Union	300,000,000
India	601,279,000
Crown colonies and dependencies	125,000,000
France	[13]25,812,782,800
Russia in Europe	22,593,950,000
Italy	12,313,998,000
Belgium	1,154,467,914
Serbia	399,400,000
Rumania	1,600,000,000
Greece	270,000,000
Japan	40,000,000
Other Entente Allie	500,000,000
Total	$145,287,690,622
Germany	$40,150,000,000
Austria-Hungary	20,622,960,600
Turkey	1,430,000,000
Bulgaria	815,200,000
Total	$63,018,160,600
Grand total	$208,305,851,222

It should be noted that these are the gross expenditures and include the loans made to their allies by the United States, Great Britain, France, and Germany, amounting in all to about $22,072,214,125. If this sum be subtracted to avoid duplication, the net expenditures are found to be, in round numbers, $186,000,000,000. The figures given in this table are so stupendous that

---

[13] This is the calculation of the writer, based upon the declared yearly expenditures. In February, 1919, the Chamber of Deputies estimated the costs of the war to France at $36,400,000,000, but these seem to have been the total gross expenditures during the war and not those attributable solely to the war itself. If this estimate were accepted the gross cost of the war would be raised to approximately 219,000,000,000 dollars and the net cost to 197,000,000,000 dollars.

they fail to carry a definite impression. If the annual national incomes of the more important nations be compared with their expenditures for the last year of warfare, the real burden is made more comprehensible. In some cases the war was already costing more in a single year than the estimated pre-war income of the whole people, and in all the others except the United States it was approaching very close to this point. Only in the United States did there remain any appreciable resources which might yet be drawn upon to defray the costs of the economic reconstruction of the belligerent world. The following table gives these figures:

NATIONAL INCOMES AND WAR EXPENDITURES OF THE PRINCIPAL BELLIGERENTS, 1918

	Annual national pre-war income	War expenditure, 1918
United States	$38,000,000,000	$18,000,000,000
Great Britain	10,700,000,000	13,896,505,940
France	7,300,000,000	10,671,000,000
Russia	6,500,000,000	*9,000,000,000
Italy	3,000,000,000	3,946,920,000
Germany	10,500,000,000	12,125,000,000
Austria-Hungary	5,500,000,000	3,560,000,000

* 1917.

In conclusion it should be noted that the costs thus far tabulated are only the direct money outlays of the countries involved. They do not take into account the indirect costs, such as destruction of property, depreciation of capital, loss of production, depletion of producers, interruption to trade, and similar economic losses.[14]

---

[14] For an estimate of the indirect costs see the author's "Direct and Indirect Costs of the Great World War" (Washington: Carnegie Endowment for International Peace, 1919).

CHAPTER V

PAPER MONEY AND BANK CREDIT

Large use of banks in financing the war — Direct issues of paper money in Europe — Services of the Federal Reserve System in the United States — Treatment of gold.

One of the outstanding features of the World War was the large extent to which belligerent Governments availed themselves of the assistance of the banks, directly and indirectly. Almost without exception the Government of each country involved turned to its great central banking institution for immediate advances with which to meet the costs of mobilization and the first military operations. Although these advances were generally paid back, in part at least, after the issue of the first war loans, the Governments continued to ask further advances from the banks, and the end of the war found practically every Government in debt to its banks for very large amounts.

The problem presented to the banks was two-fold: In the first place they must provide the industrial and commercial world with needed accommodations, and in the second place they must give to the Governments all assistance possible for the vigorous prosecution of the war. In general, it must be said that the banks were well prepared for their tremendous task and that they acquitted themselves nobly. Methods differed somewhat in the different countries, but on the whole there is a striking similarity in the use made of the banks and in the way in which they responded to private and Government demands.

WAR COSTS AND THEIR FINANCING

In Great Britain the extension of the bank holiday and the moratorium postponed the necessity for immediate action on the part of the banks in granting the credit necessary to meet the obligations of their customers that were falling due. There was, however, an enormous mass of unliquid bills and acceptances which had to be taken care of, and the great problem confronting the banks, so far as concerned their responsibility to the industrial and commercial world, was to render these securities available as means of payment. Little was done until August 12, when the Government announced that the Bank of England, under Government guarantee against loss, would discount at the existing bank rate without recourse to the holder all approved bills accepted before August 4. By this operation the " frozen " bills were released and great assistance was given to British credit abroad. There was little new business, as the closing of the Stock Exchange, the interruption of ordinary business, and general unwillingness to engage in new enterprises suspended applications for additional credit. The movement of goods having been greatly reduced, there were few new bills of exchange presented for discount. This abnormal condition, however, did not continue long, as the energies of the nation were soon diverted to the production of munitions of war. Purchases of foodstuffs and other supplies from the United States and other countries brought foreign trade up to the pre-war level, so that it was not long before the discounts at the banks exceeded the amount granted before the outbreak of the war.

As Great Britain depended so largely upon foreign sources of supply for food and for many of the materials of war, it was essential that foreign exchange

PAPER MONEY AND BANK CREDIT

be stabilized and that the goods be secured with as small an export of gold as was possible. Imports were increasing to enormous proportions, but exports were necessarily reduced as the productive energies of the nation were directed more and more into war channels; hence the ordinary balancing of exports against imports could no longer be depended upon to maintain the rates of foreign exchange at par. Securities were used in part payment for the purchases abroad; soon after the exchanges were opened in November, 1914, the sale of American securities owned in England began, but this was not in itself sufficient to meet the steadily growing international balance against England and to maintain the normal rates of sterling exchange. The Government endeavored to meet the situation by restricting the importation of unnecessary goods and at the same time encouraging the exportation of British manufactures. But after all these expedients had been exhausted, there was still a balance against England which would have occasioned the exhaustion of the Bank of England's reserve had shipments of gold been permitted to follow their ordinary course. Owing to large purchases of supplies and munitions the rate of exchange began early in 1915 to run against Great Britain. The Bank's gold reserve was used, by redemption of its obligations, to pay exchange from $4.813 in March down to $4.7625 in July, but it was evident that a more far-reaching remedy would have to be taken to stop the decline. This was found in the floating of the Anglo-French Loan in the United States in October, 1915, by which time sterling exchange had fallen to the unprecedented point of $4.49.[1]

In still another way the Bank of England lent its

---
[1] Chapter III.

assistance in financing the war. This was through the direct loan of its credit to the Government by the purchase of short-term Treasury bills. In the first days after the outbreak of the war, when commerce and industry were disorganized, the banks invested largely in Treasury bills at rates of interest as low as 3⅝ per cent. Later, however, as industry became adjusted to war conditions and the demands of business men on the banks for loans became greater, the Government was forced to pay higher rates of interest on its Treasury bills, which were issued in large amounts. When the mass of bills on the market became unwieldy, the Government funded them into long term debts. In all these transactions the assistance of the Bank of England was of the greatest value to the Government. The burdens laid upon the institution were great, but it came through the ordeal of the war with heightened reputation. Although the British credit system has been severely criticized, and by none more than by English writers themselves, it has emerged from the most severe stress ever imposed upon it, not merely unscathed, but with its roots sunk deeper into the fabric of British business and with the increased confidence of the British people.

Perhaps on no other single bank was a greater burden of responsibility laid than upon the Bank of France. The dislocation of industry was greater in France than in any other country except Belgium; at the same time, owing to the very close relations between the Government and the Bank, the appeal of the Government for assistance was more immediate and greater than in most of the other belligerent countries. The demands upon the Bank for discounts by private business began before

PAPER MONEY AND BANK CREDIT

the actual outbreak of hostilities. In the week ending Saturday, August 1, 1914, the amount of commercial paper discounted by the Bank increased to $608,000,000 from $316,000,000 for the preceding week. So great, indeed, was the pressure that the bank rate was raised from three per cent. to six per cent. It is difficult to follow the operations of the Bank of France after this date for the publication of its weekly statement was discontinued and it was not renewed until February 4, 1915. Subsequently, however, this omission was partly corrected by the publication of the Bank's condition on October 1 and 15 and December 10 and 24. The extent of the service of the Bank in meeting the needs of the business community is evidenced by the expansion of the discounts and private advances. By October 1 the discounts amounted to $895,200,000, which was the highest point recorded during the course of the war. Although this figure had fallen by October 15 to $871,800,000, the private advances had increased to $168,200,000, or $19,400,000 more than they were on July 31. Thereafter there was a steady decline in the amount of discounts, while the advances on securities fell off until December, 1915, after which they fluctuated around a considerably higher level. The reason for the decline in the amount of the discounts was the gradual liquidation of the paper affected by the moratorium. As this was reduced, its place was not taken by an equivalent amount of new paper. The prostration of business was too great for normal activities to furnish the usual amount of commercial paper. Probably the service of the Bank to the public is adequately measured by the amount of pre-moratorium paper it carried. This stood at $895,200,000 on October 1, 1914, but thereafter it steadily declined. By October 7, 1915, it was

WAR COSTS AND THEIR FINANCING

$391,100,000, and on October 5, 1916, it had been reduced to $276,600,000. New discounts developed very slowly. On December 10, 1914, they amounted to only $42,600,000, and a year later; on December 9, 1915, they had grown only to $63,400,000. It is clear that the accommodation of the Bank to the public had been greatly lessened as a result of the war.

The Bank did not curtail its loans; it simply changed their character. The advances to the State, which had stood on July 31, 1914, at $41,000,000, increased by leaps and bounds. These stood on October 15, 1914, at $420,000,000; on April 15, 1915, they were $1,000,000,000; by May 31, 1917, $2,100,000,000; and by October 31, 1918, had reached the high mark of $3,430,000,000. It is needless to try to chronicle the successive advances; there was a steady increase as time went on, with occasional temporary decreases after the subscriptions to the national loans were paid in. In contrast to English and American experience, the advances to the State occasioned not an expansion of the credit deposits, but an enlargement of the note circulation. These issues, which amounted on July 24, 1914, to $1,182,200,000, jumped to $1,859,800,000 on October 1, and from that time on continued to increase in a menacing manner. It is evident from what has been said that the increase in notes was not made in response to monetary needs of business, but rather in response to the fiscal needs of the Government. Failure to distinguish between these two needs led to a large and dangerous inflation of the currency in France with consequent depreciation of the money unit and rise in prices. The suspension of specie payments by act of August 5, 1914, and the grant of legal-tender quality to the notes gave to the issues of the Bank of France the character of inconvertible paper

PAPER MONEY AND BANK CREDIT

money. Great as were the services of the Bank of France to the country, the very magnitude of advances to the State has been the measure of the inflation of the French currency. Although a certain addition to the circulation medium was called for in the first days of panic and readjustment the subsequent inflation cannot be explained on the ground of monetary necessities.

The Bank of Russia was closely affiliated with the Government and in that relation served principally the needs of the State. A legal limit was placed upon its note issues, which were permitted to exceed the cash held by the Bank by a fixed amount of $150,000,000. As cash there was counted not only the gold and silver in the vaults of the Bank itself, but also the deposits maintained in the chief financial centers of Europe. The fiduciary issue was unimportant until the outbreak of the war, as the cash generally exceeded the note circulation. The last return before the war, July 21, 1914, showed that the Bank held $824,600,000 in gold and $36,910,000 in silver in its own vaults and $71,975,000 on deposit abroad, a total of $933,485,000 against note issues of $841,600,000. On July 31, 1914, the legal limit of the fiduciary issue was raised to $750,000,000, and after the outbreak of war specie payments were suspended.

The Bank of Russia began almost at once to increase its issue of notes, both for the accommodation of private borrowers and to meet the demands of the State. By the end of the year (December 29, 1914) the note issues amounted to $1,474,900,000 and the Treasury short-term bonds in the portfolio of the Bank to $255,700,000. From that time on there was a steady and rapid increase in both items in practically similar amounts. Represented by lines on a chart, they result in two almost parallel lines running steeply athwart the page in an upward direction.[2] In other words, the additional bank notes were issued almost exclusively for the purpose of discounting Treasury bills, and were used by the Government to defray its own expenditures. The additional issues, therefore, were not made in response to an increased commercial demand. This was as clear a case of inflation as the issue of inconvertible paper money directly by the State would have been. By August 29, 1917, when the Bank ceased to discount further Treasury bills, the account stood as follows:

Gold in vault	$668,400,000
Notes in circulation	7,558,200,000
Treasury short term bonds discounted	6,199,300,000

The last published report by the Bank of Russia, made as of October 29, 1917, showed gold reserves of practically the same amount, $667,000,000, but with note issues swelled to $9,458,500,000, an increase of almost $2,000,000,000 in two months.

The annual reports of the Bank of Italy and of the other Italian banks of issue, those of Naples and of Sicily, segregate the total amount of notes issued to satisfy commercial needs and those issued on account of the State. The following table[3] gives the total classified note circulation of the three banks of issue and of the Bank of Italy separately at the close of each calendar year during the war:

---

[2] See chart in *Federal Reserve Bulletin*, December, 1917, p. 944.

[3] Compiled from tables in *Federal Reserve Bulletin*, April, 1918, p. 278, and in *Economist*, February 1, 1919, p. 136.

PAPER MONEY AND BANK CREDIT

BANK NOTE CIRCULATION IN ITALY
(*In millions*)

	TOTAL			BANK OF ITALY		
December 31	For needs of Commerce	For needs of Government	Total	For needs of Commerce	For needs of Government	Total
1913......	$456.7	....	$456.7	.....	.....	.....
1914......	440.2	$147.0	587.2	$328.7	$103.8	$432.4
1915......	379.7	413.9	793.6	286.3	321.8	608.0
1916......	499.6	510.8	1,010.4	409.2	366.1	775.3
1917......	518.4	1,166.6	1,685.0	442.4	865.4	1,307.8
1918......	916.9	1,433.2	2,350.1	.....	.....	.....

It is evident from this table, condensed as it is, that the expansion of their fiduciary circulation by the Italian banks of issue was made to meet the needs of the State rather than the commercial needs of private borrowers. Indeed, for the first year and a half there was a decline in the discounts of ordinary commercial paper, which, however, was more than made good by the discount of Treasury bills. Thereafter both showed increases, though this was much greater in the latter than in the former.

In Germany the whole practice of war finance had been carefully arranged in advance. The policy followed was no temporary makeshift or hastily devised plan to meet an emergency; it was rather a deliberate, methodical policy. The Reichsbank remained, as it had always been, the central source of credit, but in addition to this institution and the other large banks which supplied the needed loans to the large manufacturing and trading establishments, loan offices (*Darlehenskassen*) were established for the purpose of making loans to small traders, merchants, and others whose security would scarcely be acceptable at a commercial bank.[4] The loan offices were peculiarly a German institution, dating back to experiments made in Prussia in 1848. Based essentially upon the principle of the pawnshop, they were authorized to loan upon merchandise, securities, and other collateral which might not be acceptable at commercial banks, and made loans on five classes of collateral ranging from 40 per cent. of the market value of non-perishable merchandise up to 75 per cent. on the obligations of the Empire or of the German states. The loans were all made in loan-office notes (*Darlehenskassenscheine*), which were made receivable for all public dues although they were not given the legal-tender

---

[4] Although this was the original purpose, these institutions came to serve increasingly the needs of the states and municipalities as the war continued; by the end of the year 1917 loans to these agencies amounted to $1,425,000,000. The following table shows the changes in the classes of borrowers (*Economist*, lxxxvi. p. 979):

Classes of Borrowers	PER CENT	
	1916	1917
Federal states and municipalities	25.0	74.9
Savings banks	23.3	5.6
Banks, etc	4.9	2.1
Official war companies	10.5	3.4
Commerce, transport, and insurance	12.0	4.1
Industry	3.0	1.4
Agriculture	.7	.5
Miscellaneous	20.6	8.0
Total	100.0	100.0

quality. Loans were granted in amounts as small as $25 for periods running from three to six months and were generally renewable. The interest rate was somewhat higher than the bank rate, being about 6½ per cent.

The four private banks of issue were permitted to redeem their notes in those of the Reichsbank. The soundness of the note circulation which was furnished the German people during the war depended, therefore, in the last analysis upon the character of the assets which were behind it.

Before the war one-third of the outstanding notes of the Reichsbank must be covered by cash and the other two-thirds by commercial paper. After the outbreak of the war, however, this provision was modified so that Imperial Treasury notes and loan-office notes were counted as cash, and the term "commercial paper" was extended so as to include both Imperial bonds with a maturity of three months and Imperial Treasury bills with average maturity of about 30 days. In this circle of reserves and security one is forced back finally to the ultimate soundness of the securities held by the Reichsbank and the loan offices, that is, the bonds and bills of the Imperial Treasury and the securities and merchandise placed by private individuals with the loan offices. The former are as good as, and·no better than, the rest of the German debt. The latter, whatever their value at the time they were mortgaged, have undoubtedly shrunk in value with the deterioration of German business concerns. So far as they represent solvent concerns or foreign securities the value of which has not fallen, they have not, of course, lost in value, but such must be much the smallest proportion.

It was the boast of Germany that she was able, prac-

WAR COSTS AND THEIR FINANCING

tically alone of all the belligerent countries, to avoid a moratorium. This was done by the methods indicated, that is, by coining all forms of wealth into cash in order that everyone might have the means immediately of meeting his indebtedness. The appearance of the avoidance of a moratorium may have been secured, but ultimately the liquidation of the securities pledged will become inevitable. There was no difference in principle between the German and the English or French method. There was simply a difference in the period of time at which premoratorium engagements should be finally settled. History has now recorded its verdict as to which method was the better. Like most other phases of German military and financial preparations for the war, the German financial program was adapted to a short and victorious struggle but did not lend itself well to a prolonged war.

The demand for discounts on the part of business houses began earlier in Germany than in England or France. German business houses seemed to sense the coming war or were informed of its approach, and they began in the latter part of July, 1914, to put their affairs in order. The total discounts of the Reichsbank, which, however, included advances to the Government, increased from $200,000,000 on July 23, 1914, to about $700,000,000 on July 31 and to $1,152,000,000 on August 15. The larger part of these early loans were undoubtedly made to meet the needs of industry and commerce, but the Government too called upon the Reichsbank to lend it large amounts. In the first week or two nearly $200,000,000 was required for mobilization purposes, and during the first two months of war it was estimated that the Government received some $500,000,000 for military and naval purposes. On the other

PAPER MONEY AND BANK CREDIT

hand, the Government had turned over to the Reichsbank the war chest of $51,000,000 in gold against which the Bank was authorized to issue three times this amount in notes.

As in the case of the other continental banks, the extension of credit was made by the issue of notes. As the loans of the Reichsbank to the State increased, so the volume of issued notes expanded. At the end of 1914 the discounts stood at $984,142,000 and the note issues at $1,261,474,000; at the end of 1915, they stood at $1,351,475,000 and $1,729,480,000, respectively; at the end of 1916, $2,402,437,000 and $2,013,665,000; at the end of 1917, $3,649,025,000 and $2,866,935,000, with Treasury notes amounting to $326,195,000 on the same date; and at the end of 1918 the discounts and note issues were $4,167,725,000 and $3,122,600,000, respectively. Thus the average note circulation for 1914 was $729,500,000; for 1915, $1,352,250,000; for 1916, $1,171,500,000; and for 1917, $2,500,000,000. At the same time the loan-office notes in circulation showed an equally steady expansion, from $192,000,000 at the end of 1915 to $718,500,000 at the end of 1916, $1,566,500,000 at the end of 1917, and $2,527,000,000 at the end of 1918. The total notes in circulation on July 23 of each year were:

NOTES IN CIRCULATION IN GERMANY

(*In millions*)

July 23	Reichsbank notes	Treasury notes	Loan office notes
1914	$473.0	$34.5	....
1915	1,328.5	72.0	174.5
1916	1,710.0	80.0	318.0
1917	2,157.5	85.0	1,137.0
1918	3,142.5	86.0	1,896.5

WAR COSTS AND THEIR FINANCING

The note issues expanded so greatly that the Government itself was alarmed and sought to restrict the use of paper money by encouraging the habit of settling accounts by means of checks and other credit instruments. The use of postal money orders was agitated and encouraged by financial journals, and the banks sought to educate the people in the use of checks. These efforts bore their fruit, and deposits at the Reichsbank rose from $236,000,000 on July 23, 1914, to $1,977,500,000 on July 6, 1918, these figures, however, including Government deposits as well as private deposits. In estimating the degree of inflation which took place in Germany the increase of the credit currency must be taken into account as well as the issues of circulating notes. The note issues of the private note-issuing banks, on the other hand, remained almost stationary. These increased by only $15,000,000 between July 23, 1914, and June 30, 1918, the change being from $390,000,000 to $405,000,000.

The greatest expansion of the currency in Germany, however, occurred after July, 1918. When the German retreat began, the people began a run on the banks just as they had at the beginning of the war. The events of this period are best described in a report made by Herr Havenstein, the President of the Reichsbank:[5]

There was a run on the bank, September 23-October 23, unparalleled in its history. People feared a moratorium or the insolvency of the banks, and hoarding took place on a large scale. The total circulation increased 2,651.7 million marks [$662,900,000] in the period September 24-October 23, as against 734.0 million marks [$183,500,000] in the same period last year [1917]. In the quarter, July 1-September 30,

[5] Report of Herr Havenstein to the Central Committee of the Reichsbank on lack of instruments of payment, *Frankfurter Zeitung*, Oct. 31, 1918.

PAPER MONEY AND BANK CREDIT

the Reichsbank added 4,325.5 million marks [$1,081,400,000] to the instruments of payment, which far surpassed any preceding quarter. The withdrawals of new currency from the Reichsbank equalled 1,493 million marks [$373,250,000] in the first three weeks of October, 1918. The net addition to the currency for the period, July 1-October 23, was thus 5,484.2 million marks [$1,371,000,000] — the highest amount during any war loan.

Unhappily the official printing press was unequal to the emergency owing to the calling of a number of its workers to the army and the absence of hundreds of others because of grippe. Early in October the towns were asked to prepare immediately notes up to 50 marks [$12.50]. By November 1 over 400 million marks [$100,000,000] of this emergency money had been issued, and during the weeks following a similar amount was put into circulation. The coupons of the five per cent. war loan, due January 2, 1919, were declared by the decree of the Bundesrat to be legal tender. This amounted to 600 million marks [$150,000,000], which will be increased by another 300 million marks [$75,000,000] as soon as the eighth war loan is issued.

The four private banks of issue augmented their output to the legal limit.

It is evident from the operations of the Reichsbank and the loan offices that the assistance granted both to private industry and to the Government by the credit institutions of Germany took the form primarily of the issue of notes. As the Government needs expanded, additional sums were put into circulation without any regard to the monetary demands of the community, but solely in response to the fiscal necessities of the Treasury. This confusion of functions on the part of the note-issuing agencies led to an enormous inflation of the currency with its consequent depreciation and a rise of prices. The result was that the Government was forced to pay more for its supplies and services as the war continued, owing to the steady depreciation in the value of the monetary unit. Germany slid rapidly from a would-be scientific system of credit into the abyss of practically fiat paper money. That this is not too strong a statement may be seen from the ratio of reserves to note issues. On July 23, 1914, the gold reserve amounted to $339,215,000 against notes issued to the amount of $472,720,000 and total liabilities of $718,700,000. On December 23, 1918, the gold reserve had increased to $565,655,000, but the notes had meanwhile expanded to $5,281,080,000 and the total liabilities had grown to $8,536,040,000. The ratio of gold reserves to notes had therefore fallen in the interval from 71.7 per cent. to 10.7 per cent., and the ratio of gold to notes and deposits from 47.8 per cent. to 6.9 per cent.

As Austria-Hungary, the hotbed of the European conflict, declared war on Serbia on July 28, 1914, its banks felt the shock to credit earlier than those in the other countries. There were immediately runs on the Imperial Austro-Hungarian Bank and demands by business houses for accommodation. These were met by the passage of a limited moratorium, which was later made permanent, and by authorizing the banks to refuse to pay more than three per cent. of the checks presented and three per cent. of their customers' current accounts. On August 5 the requirement that the Imperial Bank should hold a metallic reserve against notes issued was suspended, which meant the suspension of specie payments. At the same time the publication of the Bank reports was prohibited. These were not published again until December, 1917, but as statements were then given which covered the earlier years, it is possible to trace in a general way the course of the intervening operations. These are shown in the following table:

PAPER MONEY AND BANK CREDIT

CONDITION OF IMPERIAL AUSTRO-HUNGARIAN BANK, END OF YEAR, 1913–1917[6]
(*In millions*)

	1913	1914	1915	1916	1917
Gold	$248.0	$214.0	$139.0	$59.0	$52.8
Foreign exchange	12.0	2.8	12.0	1.1	12.0
Silver coin and bullion	52.3	25.1	13.2	11.7	11.3
Discounted bills, warrants, etc.	185.2	410.6	595.4	571.3	564.4
Loans on securities	62.1	678.9	658.6	685.6	685.8
Advances to Austrian Government				78.3	735.6	1,808.0
Advances to Hungarian Government			46.8	324.3	831.6
Bank notes in circulation	498.7	1,027.0	1,432.5	2,177.7	3,687.9
Deposits	37.5	285.4	54.6	85.0	391.6

The most striking thing about this table is the almost complete disappearance of the metallic reserve. Much silver coin was paid out in the early days of the war to supply the need for small coins, but these were soon withdrawn from circulation and hoarded by the people. No such dissipation of the gold reserve took place, as the Bank had been relieved of the necessity of redeeming its notes in gold and naturally did not pay it over the counter. Its disappearance was obviously the result of its utilization by the German Reichsbank either directly by being added to its own reserve or indirectly by exportation to neutral countries on Germany's account, though a cleaner sweep could scarcely have been made if the Austro-Hungarian Bank had been looted outright. It is very significant that the gold reserves of the Bank of Turkey dwindled in similar fashion, while the reserves of the German Reichsbank showed a steady and continu-

---
[6] Report of Imperial Austro-Hungarian Bank, December 7, 1917.

WAR COSTS AND THEIR FINANCING

ous increase throughout most of the period of the war. Whatever the explanation, the result was the same. The gold cover of the Austro-Hungarian bank notes, which before the war was fixed by law at 40 per cent., was steadily reduced. A year later it was 22.9 per cent., at the end of 1915 it was 9.4 per cent., of 1916, 2.7 per cent.; and by the end of 1917 it had sunk to the negligible figure of 1.6 per cent. At this point the note issues were practically inconvertible fiat money.

The increase in the issue of bank notes took place at an even more rapid rate than the decline in the metallic reserve. As deposit banking was but slightly developed in the Dual Monarchy, the extension of banking credit took the form almost exclusively of the issue of bank notes. This is shown by the slight increase in deposits as compared with the enormous expansion of note issues. These stood at $425,800,000 on July 23, 1914, just before the outbreak of the war; by the end of 1915 they had risen to $1,432,500,000; of 1916, to $2,177,700,000; and of 1917, to $3,687,900,000. The year 1918 saw the issues increase at an accelerating rate. In April they were $4,060,000,000; in July, $4,600,000,000; and by October 1, $5,400,000,000. On January 23, 1919, the note issues had grown to the enormous total of $6,434,400,000. Excuses were found for these additions to the circulating medium first in the need of notes to take the place of the hoarded gold and in the increased activities of the State. Later it was asserted that more money was needed for circulation in the conquered territories of Poland and Serbia, and still later of Rumania. Finally, the need for a larger circulating medium because of higher prices was urged. Here is seen the real evil of a policy of financing a war by issues of paper money. Over-issue means inflation and a depreciation of the

PAPER MONEY AND BANK CREDIT

paper-money units with consequent higher prices. Not only is the cost of living raised thereby to private individuals, but the Government itself is forced to pay more for all its supplies. At the same time it sells its bonds and other obligations for a cheaper money unit the purchasing power of which is constantly declining. Such a policy is improvident when the Government itself issues inconvertible paper money; when it authorizes a bank to inflate the currency, the policy is suicidal.

The depreciation of the Austro-Hungarian bank money may be shown by a few figures. The decline began almost immediately after the outbreak of the war and continued uninterruptedly; by the end of December, 1915, the krone showed a depreciation in Zurich of 41 per cent.; in New York, of 44 per cent.; and in Amsterdam, of 52 per cent. At the same time the cost of living rose by leaps and bounds. A report of the Vienna Board of Trade showed that in July, 1915, prices were 86 per cent. higher than they had been a year before. The mad dance of inflation went on through the next three years at an even faster pace, and by the end of 1918 prices had reached heights that were reminiscent of the *assignats* during the French Revolution. The following table shows some typical prices as quoted at Budapest for November 12, 1918:

COMMODITIES		WAGES	
Milk, per litre [quart]	$.40	Driver, per day	$6.00
Cabbage, per head	5.67	Coal shoveler, per day	5.00
Steak, per kilo [2.2 pounds]	4.00	Day laborer, per day	4.20
Other meat, per kilo	4.00	Grave digger, per day	8.00-10.00

Incomplete as this table is, it illustrates one unhappy result which always follows the depreciation of a currency through inflation. Although nominal wages showed an enormous increase, reaching undreamed-of heights, they still lagged behind prices, so that there was a steady decline in real wages. By the end of 1918 the political situation had become so desperate that the depreciated bank notes had practically ceased to serve the purpose of money, and trade had become mere barter of commodities. In November, 1918, the Government announced that it would issue temporary bank notes in denominations of 25 and 100 kronen to meet the scarcity of currency which followed the general panic in the country. The frightened people had made runs on the banks to such an extent that the available supply of notes had been completely exhausted and payments were being made in war-loan coupons and Treasury bills. By the end of the year a complete financial collapse had taken place and there was widespread bankruptcy throughout the country. Retail trade in Vienna was ruined and panic permeated all economic activities. Prices were fantastic and trade had become a gamble.

The other items in the bank statement given on page 123 combine to show the complete subordination of the Bank's normal activities to the demands of the Government for aid in financing the war. It is impossible to say how much of the item " Discounted bills, warrants, etc.," were on private account and how much for the Government, but it is safe to say that by the end of the war practically all loans of the Bank were made against Treasury bills. Private commercial paper had virtually disappeared from the market, and in lieu of this the Bank's portfolio was filled with Government obligations. " Loans on security " were doubtless loans made upon war bonds and Treasury bills to permit the borrower to subscribe to new issues of bonds. The Bank loaned up to 75 per cent. of the nominal value of

PAPER MONEY AND BANK CREDIT

the bonds for this purpose at a rate of interest one-half of one per cent. more than the interest on the bonds. The former of these two items showed its greatest increase in 1914 and 1915 and the latter in 1914, after which periods they remained fairly constant. As a result of these operations there was a great expansion in bank credit which played its part in the continuous inflation and consequent rise in prices.

But the most significant feature of the statement is to be found after all in the two items of "Advances to the Government." These did not begin until 1915. In the first part of the war the calls upon the Imperial Bank were indirect. To procure funds to meet its needs the Government entered into an arrangement with the Bank by which it was to advance money in return for Treasury bills, which it agreed to sell to the public on commission. The first call was for $190,000,000. Treasury bills to this amount were issued to the Bank (of which Austria took $120,000,000 and Hungary $70,000,000) which it then sold to a consortium of bankers, which in turn borrowed the requisite cash from the Bank on the security of these same bills. But the needs of the Government were too great to permit it to use the Bank only as a brokerage firm. It soon made direct appeals to the Bank itself for funds, which the Bank granted by discounting Treasury bills freely. These operations are reflected in the doubling of the item "Discounted bills, warrants, etc.," between the end of 1913 and 1914 and the ten-fold increase of the item "Loans on security," though it is not possible to separate the Government operations from those of private borrowers. The magnitude of the Treasury borrowings was so great, however, that most of the increase must be credited to Government operations.

WAR COSTS AND THEIR FINANCING

The year 1916 and the following saw a still more direct utilization of the Bank's resources by direct advances to the Government. By the end of 1917 these amounted to $2,600,000,000.

It is clear from even this brief summary that the normal commercial functions of the Bank were completely subordinated during the course of the war to the financial needs of the Government. It had become simply a manufactory of credit and an issuer of fiat money. The gold reserve, originally back of its notes, had entirely disappeared, and the latter were based, so far as there was any security back of them, upon the Bank's holdings of Government securities. The assets of the Bank were as good as, and no better than, the credit of the Dual Monarchy. The solvency of the former was clearly dependent upon that of the latter. With the collapse of the political structure of the Empire the insolvency of the Imperial Austro-Hungarian Bank became inevitable.

In addition to the vast issues of bank notes which were put out in all the belligerent countries by the central note-issuing institutions, several of the belligerent Governments added to the mass of currency by direct issues of paper money. Great Britain authorized the issue of currency notes in denominations of $5 and $2.50 by the Currency and Bank Note Act of August 6, 1914, and made them unlimited legal tender. This constituted such a marked departure from previous British practice that it has been referred to as "the currency revolution."[7] The issue of these currency notes steadily increased from $192,390,000 on December 30, 1914, to $515,625,000 on December 29, 1915; $2,750,720,000 on

---
[7] H. J. Jennings, *Nineteenth Century and After*, November, 1914.

PAPER MONEY AND BANK CREDIT

December 27, 1916; $1,063,910,000 on December 26, 1917; and $1,616,205,000 on December 31, 1918. As the coin and bullion held in the redemption account remained practically fixed at $142,500,000, the ratio of reserve to notes steadily fell until on the last named date it was only 8.9 per cent.

Canada had issued Dominion notes before the war, amounting on June 30, 1914, to $114,182,100, against which the Treasury held $92,663,375 in gold. During the war these issues were almost trebled, the notes outstanding on March 31, 1919, amounting to $298,058,698. As the amount of Dominion notes issued increased, the security back of them diminished. The regulations covering the issue of Dominion notes had permitted an issue of $30,000,000 of notes against a 25 per cent. gold reserve. Any further issue was to be covered by a 100 per cent. reserve. By the Dominion Notes Act of August, 1914, the amount of notes that could be issued against a 25 per cent. reserve was raised to $50,000,000; under the provisions of the Finance Act of 1914 the Minister of Finance was authorized to issue Dominion notes to banks upon deposit with them of approved securities; and subsequent acts permitted additional issues under different conditions. Of the new notes some $23,000,000 was issued against deposits of gold; over $70,000,000 was issued to banks upon deposit of approved securities; some $16,000,000 was advanced to the railways; $50,000,000 consisted of advances to the British Government on its securities; and the balance was issued without additional security. As a result of this serious dilution of the currency, as well as of other causes, there has occurred in Canada the same rise in prices that has taken place in all the other countries. In view of the excellent banking system of Canada it would seem that a resort to direct issues of paper money by the Government might have been avoided.

In Australia the issuance of the fiduciary money in use in the Commonwealth had been taken over from the banks by the Government; the direct issue of notes by the latter, therefore, stands on a somewhat different footing from similar issues in other countries. In 1910 the Commonwealth Treasurer was empowered to issue notes in denominations of $2.50 and up, which should be legal tender throughout the Commonwealth and redeemable at the seat of the Federal Government. Against these notes the Treasurer was to hold a reserve of gold amounting to 25 per cent. up to $35,000,000 and 100 per cent. of all notes in excess of that amount. At the same time the circulation of state notes was prohibited, and a tax of 10 per cent. per annum was imposed on bank notes issued after the passage of the act. The provision as to reserves was amended in 1911 by providing that the gold reserve need be only 25 per cent. irrespective of the amount of notes issued, and by the end of 1911 the Australian notes were practically the only credit money in circulation in the Commonwealth. Early in the war specie payments were suspended, and the redemption of the notes ceased for the period of the war. The note issues have shown a considerable increase, and as a result the gold reserve has formed a smaller and smaller proportion of the outstanding issues. For the period August to December, 1914, the total note issue amounted to $71,665,040; by December 1915, it was $159,184,250; by December, 1916, it was $221,920,-195; and in December, 1917, it was $239,506,345.[8] At the same time the gold reserve declined from 45.22 per

---

[8] *Official Yearbook of Commonwealth of Australia*, 1916, pp. 706, 742; *Federal Reserve Bulletin*, April, 1918, p. 273.

PAPER MONEY AND BANK CREDIT

cent. on December 27, 1913, to 40.27 per cent. on December 30, 1914; to 36.09 per cent. on June 30, 1916; and to 32.38 per cent. on May 30, 1917.

If any of the countries that resorted to direct issues of paper money by the Government was justified in so doing, it would seem to have been Italy. In that country the taxes had already constituted a grievous burden before the outbreak of the war, and it was difficult to screw them up very much higher. The poverty of the people, moreover, made it impossible to secure the large amounts in popular loans which were obtained in other belligerent countries. The Government accordingly pursued the apparently easy method of issuing its own notes in payment of its expenditures. These issues grew rapidly until by the end of 1917 they amounted to $349,760,000. One year later, on December 31, 1918, they had increased still further to $430,800,000.

Germany, not content with providing for the enlarged issue of bank notes by the Reichsbank noted above and creating a new form of money in the loan-office notes, also increased the issues of Imperial Treasury notes (*Reichskassenscheine*). These notes were obligations of the Imperial Government, payable to bearer on demand, redeemable at the Reichsbank in cash, and acceptable at all public offices for public dues. At the time of the outbreak of the war the authorized issue was $60,000,000. Since these notes circulated as money and were held by the Reichsbank as part of its cash reserve, they may fairly be regarded as constituting direct issues of paper money by the Government. They were issued in denominations of $1.25 and upwards, and on August 4, 1914, were made legal tender. The suspension of specie payments on the same day made them inconvertible. The amount of these notes in circulation was as follows:

WAR COSTS AND THEIR FINANCING

GERMAN TREASURY NOTES IN CIRCULATION, 1914–1918

July 23	In Circulation	In Reichsbank
1914	$34,500,000	$8,360,000
1915	72,000,000	64,347,000
1916	80,000,000	104,020,000
1917	85,000,000	131,310,000
1918	86,000,000	435,905,000

An adequate appreciation of the services rendered by the Federal Reserve System in the United States during the war can be obtained only if American banking methods as they existed prior thereto are fully understood. In 1914 there were some 7,500 national banks with combined capital, surplus, and deposits of about $9,000,000,000, and perhaps 20,000 state banks, private banks, and trust companies with capital, surplus, and deposits of about $14,000,000,000. In spite of their name the national banks were essentially local in their business and independent of each other, being brought together only by the loose association of banks in the clearing houses. The national-bank system had been established at the time of the Civil War to provide a market for war bonds and to supply the country with a uniform currency. These services had been performed efficiently, but in the half century that had elapsed since 1863 the country had outgrown the rigid and defective system then established. The most serious defects of our former national banking system have been summed up by a recent writer[9] under the four heads of decentralization, inelasticity of credit, cumbersome

[9] E. W. Kemmerer, *The ABC of the Federal Reserve System* (Princeton, 1918), p. 2.

PAPER MONEY AND BANK CREDIT

exchange and transfer system, and defective organizations as regards relationship with the Federal Treasury.

The banks of the country were not only scattered geographically, but they were without effective union or leadership. In good weather each sailed on its own course; in storm each had to depend upon itself. If a crisis came and reserves were drawn upon, no banker could look to his neighbor for assistance because the salvation of each depended upon his keeping his own reserve intact. The reserves, moreover, were widely scattered and also immobile, in that they could not be quickly moved and massed at one place in time of need. This was peculiarly wasteful in a country like the United States where the currency demands of trade, commerce, industry, and agriculture alternate and vary from place to place and from time to time. The crops of the West and Middle West drain the eastern money market at one season; the cotton movement of the South demands financing at another; the shipping at seaboard cities makes intermittent and at times coincident demands in the East; and the industrial sections require attention the year around.

The inelasticity of the bank-note circulation was notorious. Based as it was upon the deposit of Government bonds, it was limited by the size of the national debt and fluctuated inversely with the price of the bonds rather than directly according to the needs of commerce. Rigid regulations as to bank reserves had the effect of limiting also the elasticity of bank credit in the form of deposits. The reserve requirement limited banking practically to 75 per cent.; lack of a rediscounting market tied up bank paper until maturity; the necessity of having liquid assets practically confined the extension of bank credits (at least in central reserve cities, where the larger reserves were held) to "call" paper collateraled by stock-exchange securities. This tended to centralize banking in New York and to a less extent in Chicago and St. Louis. Wall Street had bank credit, but the farmer did not; he had no "liquid assets" to offer.

The old banking system possessed also certain defects in the mechanism of domestic and foreign exchange. Although the clearing-house machinery was highly perfected for the settlement of local checks, there was considerable loss of time and expense in caring for checks from distant points or drafts on foreign countries. But perhaps the most obvious defect in the old system was the lack of correlation between the fiscal operations of the Government and the movement of commercial credits. According to the original theory the funds of the Government were to be kept in the independent Treasury and its branches, known as subtreasuries. This theory, however, had been widely departed from, and at the end of June, 1914, the Government's funds were deposited in some 1,584 national banks as well as in the Government's own vaults. Even this dispersion of the Government funds did not altogether remedy the earlier evils of complete periodic withdrawal of cash from circulation, and on the other hand it led the depository banks to rely unduly upon the Secretary of the Treasury for relief in times of financial pressure.

This system had been modified by patchwork legislation, but it remained for the Federal Reserve System to place the American banking system upon an entirely new basis and to reorganize the machinery so as to adapt it more adequately to the needs of the twentieth century. It must be regarded as providential that the

PAPER MONEY AND BANK CREDIT

system was got into running order within three months after the outbreak of the World War.

The Federal Reserve System, which was designed to unify the national and state banks and trust companies throughout the United States into an integrated financial organism, became operative in November, 1914. The country was divided into 12 districts, in each of which was established a Federal Reserve Bank situated in the logical banking center of the district. All national banks were required to become members of the system, and state banks and trust companies were urged to join. The capital of the Federal Reserve Bank in each district was subscribed by the member banks in proportion to their capital and surplus. At the head of the system stands the Federal Reserve Board at Washington. By means of this organization it has been possible to effect a centralization not only of administration, but also of reserves and banking power. The legal reserves of the member banks are kept on deposit in the Federal Reserve Bank of the district, although each bank also keeps a certain amount of " counter cash " on hand, which, however, is not reckoned as a part of the legal reserve. This centralization of reserves permitted such efficient and economical use of them that it became possible very materially to reduce the reserve requirements of the banks. Those in the central reserve cities were permitted to reduce their reserves from 25 to 18 per cent. and finally in 1917 to 13 per cent. Similarly, the reserve city banks were permitted to reduce their reserves from 15 to 10 per cent., and the country banks are now required to maintain a reserve of only seven per cent.

The gold reserve was not only centralized, it was by this very fact also rendered more mobile. Federal Reserve Banks were permitted to rediscount member banks' paper, more liberality was granted in dealing with the outside public, and the greater use of trade acceptances and bank acceptances created a broader discount market for commercial paper, thus permitting a freer flow of funds from bank to bank and from district to district. In this way the localism and lack of coöperation of the old system has been effectually remedied. The final step in the mobilization of the gold reserves was taken by the establishment at Washington in May, 1915, of a Gold Settlement Fund, to which each Federal reserve bank was compelled to contribute and maintain as a balance not less than $1,000,000. Settlement of balances between the Federal Reserve Banks is effected daily by a mere bookkeeping transfer of the gold held in the Fund, thus obviating almost completely the necessity of shipping money between Federal Reserve Banks.

The foremost service of the Federal Reserve System has been the establishment of a real asset currency based on commercial paper created to finance trade and production and protected by a 40 per cent. gold reserve. Further issues are permitted in excess of this reserve in times of emergency, but they are penalized by a graduated tax which ensures their prompt retirement when the need is over. Issues are made in response to a demand evidenced by the creation of commercial paper and are retired upon liquidation of this paper, thus providing a maximum of elasticity.

Other improvements were made which enabled the Federal Reserve System to be of much greater service to the business world than the national banking system could be. Among these were the development of trade acceptances and of "open-market" purchases; the establishment of branch banks in foreign countries, of which there were 70 by July 1, 1919; the establishment

PAPER MONEY AND BANK CREDIT

of a variable discount rate; and the development of "commodity paper" whereby banks may advance loans on staple agricultural products properly warehoused and insured, a form of credit which saved the situation in the South in 1915 when England put cotton on the list of contraband.

The assistance rendered by the Federal Reserve System both to the public and to the Treasury during the two years of war can be stated in briefest fashion. The period of two and one-half years between its organization and the declaration of war by the United States was one of development of the Federal Reserve System to a point of efficiency which enabled it easily to assume and carry through the onerous and responsible tasks of war finance. The banks continued to grant the accommodation necessary to enable business to meet the new and often untested demands upon it. In accordance with the Government's policy of conserving so far as possible the capital resources of the country for purposes that would assist in winning the war, the banks were urged to discourage the production of nonessentials and to limit loans for such purposes. In order better to carry out this principle the Capital Issues Committee of the Federal Reserve Board was created on February 1, 1918, to pass upon applications for the issue of new securities. Although it was without specific legal authority, it was able to effect a considerable stoppage of non-essential security issues. By the War Finance Corporation Act of April 5, 1918, its functions passed to a new committee of the same name.[10] In still other ways the Federal Reserve Banks rendered valuable serv-

---

[10] For a description of the operations of this Committee see, in this series, W. F. Willoughby, *Government Organization in War Time and After*.

WAR COSTS AND THEIR FINANCING

ice in carrying out the program of war finance, as by supervising foreign-exchange transactions.

The work of the banks as fiscal agents of the Government can best be illustrated by stating results. The Government's policy was to meet current expenditure by placing short-time Treasury certificates of indebtedness, funding these later into long-term bonds. It made the Federal Reserve Banks its fiscal agents in their respective districts. Certificates were offered through the Federal Reserve Banks and subscribed by all banking institutions according to fixed quotas, and the credit placed to the account of the Government. When loans were to be marketed, each reserve bank organized loan committees, with interlacing subcommittees throughout its district. Loan quotas were allotted in a predetermined ratio according to resources, population, etc. All banks received applications, accepted payments, distributed bonds. Sometimes they underwrote their respective quotas and remarketed the bonds with subscribers, holding temporarily many bonds sold on the instalment plan. The Federal Reserve Board also facilitated placing loans by adopting the rule of preferential discounts for loans made by member banks to borrowers for the purpose of purchasing bonds, at first at $3\frac{1}{2}$ per cent., then at 4 per cent., and for the Fourth Liberty Loan carrying the borrower at the same discount as the interest of the bonds. Still later member banks became the agents of non-member banks for the rediscounting of such loans as the latter made to their customers to purchase war bonds. The banks rendered invaluable service not merely to the Government by assisting the flotation of the bond issues, but also to business by loaning freely on war paper.

During 1917 the reserve banks as fiscal agents

PAPER MONEY AND BANK CREDIT

distributed Treasury certificates to the amount of $3,338,698,000. During the same year as fiscal agents they marketed two Government loans totalling $5,808,000,000. In 1918 they distributed under a definite plan of the Treasury Department certificates of indebtedness totalling about $9,000,000,000. In July the Treasury submitted a plan calling for the absorption of $6,000,000,000, of these certificates in bi-weekly lots of $750,000,000 between July and November. In anticipation of the Third Loan the banks distributed $3,000,000,000, and in anticipation of the Fourth, $4,518,000,000. During 1918 as fiscal agents they marketed these two loans which resulted in subscriptions of $11,000,000,000. In these various ways the Federal Reserve Banks performed services for the national fisc which were of incalculable value, and carried through transactions which the old national banking system could not have accomplished.

The enormous expansion of transactions as a result of war financing has not been without some deleterious influences upon both public and private finance. Of these the most striking and far-reaching in its effects has been the inflation both of note issues and of deposits. Between March 30, 1917, a week before the entrance of the United States into the war, and December 27, 1918, the increase in Federal reserve notes was $2,328,000,000, and in deposits, $1,017,000,000. On the side of resources there was an increase for the same period of $1,152,000,000 in gold and $1,400,000,000 in war paper and $502,000,000 in commercial discounts and purchase of acceptances. "It will be seen that after making due allowance for the notes which have been exchanged for gold, the net expansion in note issues has been due largely to the discount by the banks of paper secured

WAR COSTS AND THEIR FINANCING

by war obligations of the Government."[11] Not merely were the banks hampered by this mass of undigested war paper in their portfolios, amounting to about eight per cent. of the first four Liberty Loans,[12] but the rates of discount were fixed with regard to Treasury requirements rather than the commercial needs of the country. The real inflation took place through the expansion of bank deposits, rather than through an enlargement of note issues. In so far as the Government loan policy during the war promoted this, it must bear its share of responsibility for the inflation which occurred.

One of the curious incidents of the war was the treatment of gold. Practically every country except England and the United States suspended specie payments and thereby legally handed over the gold stock to the safekeeping of the great central banking institutions. Campaigns were also inaugurated in Germany, France, and Russia to induce the people to deposit their hoarded gold in the banks, so that these central reserves might be strengthened. Between two and three billion dollars in gold were added to the holdings of the great banks of the world during the period of the war, practically all of which was withdrawn from circulation. Indeed, it may be said that more gold was mined out of the pockets of the people during this period than out of the earth. The Federal Reserve Banks of the United States, holding

---

[11] *Fifth Annual Report of the Federal Reserve Board*, 1919, p. 17. The net increase in currency was much less than the issue of Federal reserve notes, since gold and considerable silver were withdrawn from circulation. This is reflected in the increase in the gold reserves.

[12] It may be estimated, upon the basis of holdings by member banks of the Federal Reserve System, that the banks of the country held on July 1, 1919, between $6,000,000,000, and $6,500,000,000 of war paper as security and collateral.

PAPER MONEY AND BANK CREDIT

about one-third of all the gold, possess the greatest store ever brought together in the history of the world.

Practically every country placed an embargo upon gold. In England and the United States, which nominally had not suspended specie payments, it was made very difficult for the ordinary citizen to obtain gold even at the officially designated redemption agencies. There was a general tacit agreement that it was unpatriotic to ask for the redemption of notes in gold. Foreign exchange came to be regulated, not by the shipment of gold, but by the granting of credit or the placing of loans, and so skillfully was this done that in spite of the extraordinary dislocation of trade the rates between the United States and England, for example, were effectively " pegged " or stabilized.

In spite of the enormous stocks of gold which had flowed into the United States during the war (the excess of gold imports over exports from August 1, 1914, to December 10, 1918, was $1,071,669,000), the Treasury Department would not permit the free export of gold even to those countries with which the trade balance of the United States was adverse. It endeavored rather to correct the unfavorable rate of exchange with such countries by encouraging the export of commodities of high value and small bulk; thus, phonographs, typewriters, and similar articles were shipped to South American countries rather than gold, in spite of the fact that such commodities diverted domestic labor from war industries and could in no event have been shipped in sufficient quantities to have influenced materially the rate of exchange. It was possible that exported gold might come into the possession of the enemy, and it was consequently deemed advisable for the Government to control its movement. On September 7, 1917, a

WAR COSTS AND THEIR FINANCING

Presidential proclamation was issued forbidding the export of all bullion, coin, or currency except in accordance with regulations to be prescribed by the Secretary of the Treasury. The administration of these regulations was placed in the hands of the Federal Reserve Board, which established for this purpose a Division of Foreign Exchange.

Under the operation of these regulations the export of gold was permitted only when the foreign-exchange situation imperatively demanded it,[13] and even when such cases arose efforts were made to avoid it. Arrangements were made with Argentina by which funds were to be deposited in the Federal Reserve Bank of New York as a basis for furnishing exchange on that country, and the United States Government agreed to ship gold at the end of the war if the situation then called for it. Similar agreements were made with Bolivia, Peru, and Uruguay, and different arrangements, but with a like result, were made with India, Spain and Switzerland. As a result the discount on the dollar in those countries was reduced or wiped out, and gold exports fell off. The embargo on gold was finally removed on June 9, 1919. The table opposite shows the imports and exports of gold of the United States during the war.

In addition to the movement of gold there were large net exports of silver, chiefly to India. The net exports were as follows: $43,226,368 in the fiscal year 1917; $68,853,246 in 1918; and $222,349,284 in 1919; a total of $334,478,898.

Back of this universal policy of retention by each country of its stock of gold and unwillingness to permit

---

[13] The exports of gold fell from 202.5 million dollars for the first six months of 1917 to 21.5 millions for the corresponding period of 1918.

PAPER MONEY AND BANK CREDIT

UNITED STATES GOLD IMPORTS AND EXPORTS, 1914–1919
(*In thousands*)

Period	Imports	Exports	Excess of imports
Aug. 1–Dec. 31, 1914	$23,253	$104,972	*—$81,719
Jan. 1–Dec. 31, 1915	451,955	31,426	429,529
Jan. 1–Dec. 31, 1916	685,745	155,793	529,952
Jan. 1–Dec. 31, 1917	553,713	372,171	181,542
Jan. 1–Dec. 31, 1918	61,950	40,848	21,102
Jan. 1–June 30, 1919	50,465	97,008	*—46,543
Total	$1,827,081	$802,218	$1,024,863

* Excess of exports over imports.

it to be exported lay the fear that if it were let go it might get into the hands of the enemy. At the basis lay the conviction that large gold reserves were essential to the support of the credit organization upon which the finances of all the belligerents were dependent. Even though specie payments were suspended and existing issues of bank notes or paper money were inconvertible, the psychological reaction of large gold resources upon the public mind undoubtedly inspired the accumulation of the metal. Perhaps even more than this the necessity of redeeming ultimately the large issues of fiduciary money made the Governments unwilling to surrender any of their gold, even though in the interval it was maintained merely as an idle hoard. Manifestly the nation with the largest ratio of gold to paper would be in the best position to resume specie payments.

The logical inference from the experiences in the shipment of gold and the stabilization of exchange during the war was drawn by the Treasury Department as early as 1916. In that year a convention was framed providing for the establishment of an International Gold Clearance Fund, based upon the conclusions of the meeting of the International High Commission held in Buenos Aires in April of that year.[14] There was proposed the establishment of an International Gold Clearance Fund, under a joint or multiple international guaranty, to facilitate financial transactions between nations without actual shipment of gold, similar to the machinery maintained by the Federal Reserve Board to settle balances between banks within the United States. The Federal Reserve Board has expressed its willingness to assist in the inauguration of such a system, which it thought should be confined in the beginning to the United States and the Entente Allies and a few of the leading neutral nations, but which might eventually admit all civilized countries.[15]

One of the interesting and quite unexpected results of the changes wrought by the war has been a fall in the price of gold during the past five years. This was not caused by overproduction, for the production of gold actually declined during the war. The output in the United States fell off from $100,000,000 in 1915 to $84,000,000 in 1917, many of the smaller mines being closed on account of rising wages and increased cost of production. Gold shared the fate of paper currency, to

---

[14] The Convention Providing for the Establishment of an International Gold Clearance Fund. Published by the Central Executive Council of the International High Commission (Washington, 1919).

[15] The successful operation of the Gold Settlement Fund in the United States has suggested the possibilities of avoiding shipments of gold from one country to another in settlement of balances arising out of ordinary commercial transactions, and the Board is ready if authorized to do so, to undertake negotiations looking to the establishment of an International Gold Exchange Fund, or to assist in any way in its power in negotiations which may be begun by a Government department looking to that end. . . . The saving of loss and expense incident to abrasion and transportation charges, and interest on gold transferred, will be enormous, and the advantage to the commerce of the world will be incalculable.— Report, 1918, p. 35.

PAPER MONEY AND BANK CREDIT

which it was tied by a fixed mint price of $20.67 per ounce. The fall in the case of gold to half its former purchasing power was caused by the general rise in prices of commodities and wages of labor which resulted from the increase in the amount of the circulating media in forms other than gold, as well as from scarcity. The situation thus created led to a demand on the part of gold producers for Government assistance by means of a bounty or some other form of aid. No action, however, was taken towards this end. Although it is recognized that the gold-producing interests have suffered severely from the unprecedented fall in the value of gold, it must be regarded as fortunate that no artificial stimulation has been given to its production. Increased gold production would simply have caused a still greater rise in prices, either by entering directly into circulation or by being made the basis for a further expansion of credit.

The price of silver, on the other hand, has risen in common with that of other commodities. This fact has already caused a renewal of the demand, of which little had been heard for twenty years, for bimetallism. It is not unlikely that bimetallism will be urged on the ground that the stock of gold constitutes an inadequate basis for the existing credit superstructure and that the remonetization of silver would strengthen the system But the arguments that previously caused the rejection of bimetallism and the adoption of the gold standard apply now as strongly as ever. The solution of existing currency and banking problems must be sought along lines other than those proposed by the bimetallists.

CHAPTER VI

LOANS IN EUROPE

General characteristics — British war loans — Use of loans in France, Russia, and Italy — The German theory of war finance — German banks and loan bureaus — Loans in Austria-Hungary, Bulgaria, and Turkey.

In any financial study of the World War the subject of loans assumes a preponderant importance, for over four-fifths of the war expenditures were met by borrowing. Not only did this method of raising funds rank first by reason of its magnitude, but also by reason of its universality. Everywhere the method of borrowing was used as a means of securing the necessary money. Although each country financed its war needs according to its power and its national customs, which differed greatly in some respects among the different countries, these often underwent profound changes during the war. Certain distinct features and tendencies developed which were more or less characteristic of all the belligerent countries and which may be briefly summarized.

(1) *Magnitude*.— Whatever else may be said in praise or blame of the financing of the World War, there can be no question of its preëminence with respect to the magnitude of the war loans. Indeed, it has been said that the costs of the late war exceeded those of all other European wars together since the beginning of the Christian era. Not only was the aggregate enormous, but single issues were brought out and successfully floated which a few years earlier would have been

LOANS IN EUROPE

deemed impossible by the best informed financiers. In point of size the first place is held by the Fourth Liberty Loan of the United States, which reached a total of $6,993,000,000, subscribed in three weeks; England ranks second with her third loan, amounting to $4,811,000,000, although the fourth, which took the form of continuous borrowing over a period of almost 15 months, reached a total of $8,461,000,000. The largest French issue was the fourth, amounting to $6,000,000,000 nominally and representing a return to the Treasury of $4,250,000,000. In Germany the largest loan, the eighth, amounted to $3,520,000,000. In other countries the loans were considerably smaller in amount.

(2) *Limitation of Amount*.— Although the ministers of finance were always anxious to secure as large returns as possible from offerings, they sometimes manifested praiseworthy self-restraint by imposing in particular loans a fixed limit upon the amount that would be accepted by the Treasury. In the United States subscriptions to the First and Fifth Liberty loans were limited to the amounts originally asked, while to the Second Loan oversubscriptions of 50 per cent. only were accepted. Canada limited the amount on all loans except the last. France and Italy limited the amounts accepted on their first loans. In all other cases the full amounts subscribed were taken by the Treasury.

A striking characteristic was the fairly steady increase in the amounts of the loans in all the belligerent countries. This was due in part to the growing war spirit and the determination to carry the struggle through to a victorious finish. But more responsible for the increase in the successive loans was the growing cost of the war, which led to unheard-of demands upon the peoples. These increasing costs in turn were caused partly by the scarcity of needed supplies, but primarily by the inflation of the currency and the steady depreciation of the monetary unit, a phenomenon world-wide in its influence. Measured in purchasing power, the later loans did not represent an increase at all comparable with the nominal amounts subscribed.

(3) *Term.*— A general policy of war borrowing seemed to have been developed by common consent in all the belligerent countries. Advances from the central banking institutions and issues of short-term Treasury bills were first made use of, and these were later funded by issues of long-term bonds. Advances from the banks were used to a large extent in France, Russia, Italy, and Austria-Hungary, countries in which a discount market and the practice of deposit banking were not well developed. The issue of short-term Treasury bills in anticipation of loans characterized the financial policy of the United States, Great Britain, and Germany, and France, too, made large use of short term *bons.* In the first-named group of countries the advances from the banks have been taken up only to a slight extent by the issue of long-term obligations, and they remain still a charge against the State. In the second group of countries the Treasury bills have been or are in process of being funded (except in the case of Germany, where an enormous floating debt, estimated at 72,000,000,000 marks, exists) into long-term loans, either at regular intervals, as in Germany, or at irregular intervals determined by the state of the market, as in Great Britain and France. In all the European belligerent countries the war left a considerable floating debt which must be funded by further issues of long-term bonds.

LOANS IN EUROPE

(4) *Maturing or Perpetual Bonds.*— The type of bond issued in the different countries was determined largely by pre-war habits and predilections of the people. As between terminable or perpetual loans the former was much the more preferred. In France, Italy, Germany, and Hungary the *rente* type of loan was used, in which an optional redemption date was fixed by the Government but no date of maturity was named in the bonds. The issues of all the other countries, and some of those of the countries just named, took the form of terminable bonds. A large number of these contained the optional feature, according to which the Government fixed an optional redemption date within a comparatively short period and a due date at which the bonds matured at a considerably later date. Thus, the first British loan was made redeemable in 10 years and payable in 13; the first Russian loan was a 10-40 year bond; the first Italian loan was a 10-25 year bond. On the other hand, all the war bonds of Canada and Australia were straight-term bonds running from five to 20 years. No country made use of annuities.

(5) *Period of Subscription.*— As the costs of the war and the consequent size of the war loans increased, it became necessary in most instances to prolong the period of subscription. Whereas in the earlier loans a week might have sufficed to obtain the sums needed, toward the end of the war the subscription periods would sometimes be left open for two or three months. Unique in this respect was the continuous loan opened by Great Britain on October 1, 1917, and not finally closed until January 18, 1919, thus covering a period of nearly 15 months. In those countries in which war savings certificates were sold an exception might also be made to cover

WAR COSTS AND THEIR FINANCING

them, for the policy of continuous sale was adopted for these also. In certain instances in which the amount of the loan was fixed and the subscriptions did not equal the amount in the period originally set, the time was extended until the requisite sum was forthcoming.

(6) *Date of Issue.*— The fixing of the date of issue was of secondary importance. Except in the case of Germany dates of issue seem to have been determined largely by convenience, if not by chance. Germany's loans were issued at six-months intervals, evidently according to a prearranged schedule, though the choice of a first date was probably determined more or less by the fortuitous date of the outbreak of the war. Once the dates of Germany's loans were fixed, those of Austria-Hungary and of her lesser allies were determined in relation thereto, in order that there might be no competition among them in the loan market. The same thing was true of the Entente Allies. A proposal for a joint loan on the part of the Great Powers was rejected as impracticable,[1] but an understanding was reached by which the European Powers, although borrowing independently, consulted together so that they did not come upon the money market simultaneously and thus compete against each other for capital.

(7) *Rate of Interest.*— The rate of interest varied from $3\frac{1}{2}$ per cent. for the first British loan and the First Liberty Loan of the United States to six per cent. in the case of the Hungarian loans. There was everywhere a gradual, and in some cases a considerable, increase in the rate of interest that had to be offered to attract the necessary capital, even in those countries

---
[1] " Finance of the War," *Spectator*, February 20, 1915, p. 254.

LOANS IN EUROPE

which started with the lowest rates. An apparent exception exists in the case of Germany and Austria-Hungary, where the rate of interest remained unchanged at five or six per cent. throughout the war. But this exception is more apparent than real, for considerable compulsion was used in the flotation of these bonds, especially of the later issues, and contractors and banks were forced to accept them. Moreover, the appearance of a uniform rate of interest was wholly artificial in the case of Germany, for the later loans had attached to them valuable premiums.

According to a computation published a few years before the war, the rate of Government loans for the leading powers of Europe ranged from a little under three per cent. to somewhat over five per cent. The following table indicates the credit of the different European nations before the war:[2]

PRE-WAR CREDIT OF THE LEADING EUROPEAN NATIONS

Country	Name of Loan	Average price, 1907	Value reduced to 3 per cent. base	Real rate of interest
Great Britain	2½ per cent. consol.	94.1	100.6	2.9
France	3 per cent. *rente*	94.8	94.4	3.1
Germany	3½ per cent. *rente*	94.6	81.1	3.7
Austria	4 per cent. bond	97.9	69.9	4.2
Russia	5 per cent. bond	75.2	56.4	5.3
Italy	3¼ per cent. bond free of income tax	102.4	81.1	3 7

It is evident from this showing that the credit of the

[2] F. W. Hirst, "The Credit of Nations," in *Report of National Monetary Commission* (1910), xx, pp. 6-8.

WAR COSTS AND THEIR FINANCING

different European nations was variously rated before the war. These differences persisted and were further magnified during the course of the war. Moreover, the credit of all the nations suffered as a result of their excessive borrowing. The rise in the rates of interest would undoubtedly have been much greater had the appeal been made only to purely commercial motives, but as a matter of fact the appeal to the patriotism of the peoples of the belligerent countries was sufficiently strong to secure the needed funds at rates which, considering the investment features alone, were remarkably moderate.

(8) *Price of Issue.*— From the standpoint of the purchaser the nominal rate of interest was of less moment than the real yield, and this was a function of the two factors of interest rate and issue price. In this latter particular there was considerable diversity. The United States, Australia, and New Zealand sold all their bonds at par; Great Britain issued all of hers except the third (in part) at par; Canada and India issued about half of theirs at par. The Continental European nations without exception followed the plan of issue at a discount, usually at only a slight concession of from two to seven or eight points. The only departure from this rule is found in the case of France, which issued the first two loans at about 88, the third at 68, and the fourth at 60. This was in conformity with French financial practice, which prefers a low rate of interest on a bond sold at a discount to a bond sold at par bearing a high rate of interest. It is scarcely necessary to point out that such a method makes for a perpetual debt, as it practically denies the possibility of redemption.

LOANS IN EUROPE

(9) *Conversion Privileges.*— In order to make the bonds more attractive they often carried the provision of convertibility into subsequent issues bearing higher rates of interest or more advantageous terms of redemption. This provision was made with the double purpose of strengthening public credit and of preventing discrimination against purchasers of earlier issues, and also for the purpose of amalgamating the pre-war debt and the war debt. In France and in England practically the whole of the pre-war debt was successfully converted in the midst of the issue of war loans. As a result of granting conversion privileges to holders of earlier issues, however, the advantage derived from floating these loans at a low rate of interest was lost.

(10) *Freedom from Taxation.*— It may be said that outside of the United States, Great Britain, and the British colonies the loans were issued free of taxation, with respect to either principal or interest or both. The English-speaking countries experimented with both kinds and fixed unhesitatingly upon the issues subject to tax. The United States was the only country that granted tax exemption for small blocks for a certain length of time. The variety and extent of the exemptions granted in the different countries make it difficult to compare the real rates of interest paid, in addition to which the diversity in the rates of taxation in the different countries adds another element of variation.

(11) *Collateral Privileges.*— Other features designed to make the bonds attractive to investors were added in most of the borrowing countries. For example, the right would frequently be given to tender the bonds in payment of customs duties, or excise duties, or estate taxes.

or war-profits taxes, or as security in any judicial proceeding in which security was required, or in payments on Government contracts. In some of the countries the banks were either authorized or were under compulsion to loan on war bonds as collateral at unusually favorable rates of interest.

(12) *Bond-Purchase Funds.*— Several of the countries, notably the United States, Great Britain, and France, established funds which were to be devoted to the purchase of bonds in the open market with a view to sustaining their price. In Germany the same end was achieved by requiring the Reichsbank and other banks to repurchase the war bonds at the issue price from the original subscriber in case of dire need of the owner. So frequent and so large were the issues of bonds, however, that it is doubtful whether the creation of these funds exercised any potent influence in maintaining the price of the bonds on the market. There was an enormous quantity of undigested securities the presence of which exercised a depressing influence.

(13) *Internal or Foreign Loans.*— Because of the fact that practically every civilized country in the world, belligerent or neutral, was forced into the loan market during the war, there was practically no free market for the loans of the belligerents. The only important exception was the United States, where foreign loans to the amount of $3,000,000,000 were placed with bankers, corporations, or private individuals in the two and one-half years following the outbreak of the war in 1914. Each nation consequently was forced to rely upon its own citizens to supply the Government with capital. The long-term bonds were placed almost exclusively

LOANS IN EUROPE

as internal loans in the country issuing them. It was possible to place in foreign markets on any considerable scale only short term Treasury securities. In some cases these were absorbed by private investors, but for the most part they were taken by allied Governments as evidence of the indebtedness created by the purchase of war supplies and foodstuffs in the selling country. Thus, the Governments of the United States, Great Britain, France, and, to a slight extent, Japan, on the one side, and Germany, on the other, made advances to their allies; in fact, it may be said that these countries financed almost wholly the war operations of the other nations with the exception of Russia and Italy. The last two, though receiving substantial financial assistance from their stronger allies, still raised the major part of their own funds.

(14) *Methods of Subscription and Payment.*— In the endeavor to secure large and general subscriptions every effort was made to facilitate subscription to the bonds and to render payment easy. Subscriptions were received not only at the Treasury of the issuing country, but by any bank or post office, and in some cases special selling agencies were established. Payment was very generally permitted on the instalment plan, and this was made still easier for persons of small means by the acceptance at the banks, often as a result of legislation, of war bonds as security for loans at rates of interest equal to or only slightly higher than the rates borne by the war bonds themselves. Germany went furthest in this direction and established the war loan offices already described, which were authorized to loan money on practically any merchantable commodities for the purpose of financing the war loans.

WAR COSTS AND THEIR FINANCING

(15) *Low Denomination of Bonds.*— It may be said without fear of contradiction that never before in the history of Government borrowing have Government loans been so widely distributed. This was due in a large measure to the general appeal to patriotism in all the belligerent countries and to the loyal response on the part of the people, but partly responsible also was the fact that the bonds were put out in low denominations which brought them within the reach of even the humblest buyer. The lowest denomination in any of the countries was 25 cents, which was the price of the thrift stamps in the United States and Canada and the war savings stamps in Great Britain. These, however, did not bear interest but could be exchanged for interest-bearing war savings certificates, the lowest denomination of which was $5 in each of the countries named. In bonds the lowest denominations were those issued in Hungary ($10); France, Italy, and Austria ($20); Russia and Germany ($25); and the United States and Canada ($50). In Great Britain the smallest denomination of war bond was $250, but inscribed stock or instalment allotments were issued for small sums which might be retained until the bonds were fully paid for or exchanged for scrip certificates to bearer. As a result of these methods the loans were widely distributed and were in the truest sense popular.

(16) *Distribution.*— The number of subscribers in every country in which figures on the subject were published was not only large, but showed a very general increase from one issue to the next. In the countries for which these statistics were published (and we may assume that the lack of information from the other countries indicates that the contrary was probably the

LOANS IN EUROPE

case there) a progressive increase in the number of subscribers was observable. In placing the earlier loans foreign Governments resorted, as was their wont, to bank consortiums or large corporations. It soon became evident, however, that the war was not to end as speedily as had at first been anticipated, and consequently plans were devised in all the countries to attract the small investors. Publicity campaigns, well organized drives, social pressure which amounted practically to compulsion were all made use of to secure a general distribution of the bonds. Taking the largest number of subscribers for any one loan in each country, the results were approximately as follows: United States, 21,000,000; Great Britain, 5,000,000;[3] France, 7,000,000; Italy, 490,000; Canada, 1,000,000; Austrialia, 220,000; Germany, 7,000,000. No statistics on this point were published in Russia, New Zealand, India, or Hungary. Austria announced the number of subscribers only in the case of the sixth war loan, when the figure was given as 290,000.

It is, of course, unlikely that the distribution of the bonds is final, and there is no way of determining the extent to which the original subscribers have sold their holdings. This would vary in different countries according to national characteristics and habits. It may be concluded, however, that a remarkably wide distribution of the war loans has been effected, and it may be expected that this fact will be an influential factor in preventing the repudiation of the war debt in any of

---

[3] "In 1914 the British debt was concentrated in the hands of 345,100 holders; at the present time it is divided among more than 16,750,000 large and small holders, of whom 2.228,300 subscribed through the Bank of England to the war loans, 4,000,000 subscribed through the post office, and more than 10,500,000 possessed war savings certificates." *Federal Reserve Bulletin*, November, 1918, p. 1065.

the countries, the present action of Russia to the contrary notwithstanding. Large amounts of the war loans were taken of necessity by the banks, especially the large central institutions. The portfolios of the banks and credit institutions in all the belligerent countries are to-day filled to overflowing with war paper, but the distribution of these holdings cannot be regarded as final, and one of the problems of the future will be the absorption of this paper by the investing public.

(17) *Success of the Loans.*— In view of the enormous sums secured by the Governments and the wide distribution of the bonds there can be no question as to the success of the loans. This was made possible by the complete mobilization of all the financial resources of the belligerents for the single purpose of financing the war. The business of the banks was reorganized, the amount and character of the currency determined, the exchange market regulated, and the exportation of gold, securities, and other forms of capital prohibited — all to this single end. The loan market was reserved at intervals exclusively for Government issues, and at all times the use of credit for non-governmental purposes was discouraged. The production of non-essentials was curtailed, the placing of foreign loans was forbidden or greatly restricted, issues of corporate securities were strictly controlled and were permitted only in case the industry could be shown to be one which would assist in the prosecution of the war. In short, all available capital was requisitioned as far as possible for the needs of the State, and private industry was rationed with regard to capital as thoroughly as individuals were with regard to food. This devotion of all available financial means to war purposes was made

LOANS IN EUROPE

possible by the active and patriotic coöperation of lenders and of the credit institutions.

So much for general considerations. There are revealed here many and important likenesses in the loans of all countries, but it is likewise evident that the financing of each nation was determined in a large measure by national habits and characteristics. A brief survey of the war loans of the principal belligerents is therefore of interest and essential to the present study.

The British Treasury tried many financial devices for securing funds. At the beginning of the war it issued Treasury bills and also secured advances from the Bank of England, which together provided the necessary funds until the first war loan was issued in November, 1914. It also made use of long-dated Exchequer bonds which were used to fund Treasury bills when the amount of the latter outstanding became too large. Later periodic loans were supplanted by a policy of continuous borrowing without fixed subscription periods or limitation to any one type of security. Unlike Germany, the British Government did not follow any prearranged plan but experimented with various devices in conformity with changing conditions and needs. In addition to the more formal loans it resorted also to the sale of war savings and war expenditure certificates.

To secure the funds necessary to finance the first operations of the war the Chancellor of the Exchequer resorted at once to the issue of Treasury bills. Because of the interruption of normal trade the banks had considerable sums of idle money which they were glad to invest by discounting these bills at rates as low as $3\frac{5}{8}$

per cent. Since it could secure money on such easy terms, there was a tendency on the part of the Treasury to rely upon this form of short-term obligation, but as the Treasury bills grew in volume, they became unwieldy and it was necessary to fund them into long-term bonds. During the period from August 1 to December 31, 1914, there were six emissions of Treasury bills of $75,000,000 each. These were met in part by the issue of the first war loan in November. The net issue of Treasury bills for the fiscal year ending March 31, 1915, amounted to $320,750,000.

The first war loan amounted to $1,750,000,000, in 3½ per cent. 1925-1928 bonds at 95. In addition to this popular loan the Treasury also sold three per cent. five-year Exchequer bonds to the amount of $238,500,000. Advances from the Bank of England during this period amounted to $800,000,000. The loans from the beginning of the war to the end of the fiscal year on March 31, 1915, resulted almost in doubling the pre-war debt. They are shown in the following table:

BORROWING IN GREAT BRITAIN, FISCAL YEAR 1915

Pre-war debt $3,538,270,550	
Treasury bills, net	$320,750,000
3 per cent. 1920 Exchequer bonds..............	238,500,000
3½ per cent. 1914 war loan...................	1,480,000.000
Advances from Bank of England..............	802,138,115
Total..	$2,841,438,115

At the beginning of the fiscal year 1915-16 it was realized that the war was not to end as speedily as had been optimistically anticipated at first. The expenditures for the coming year were estimated at $5,633,270,000, and revenue receipts were expected to yield $1,351,660,000, leaving a balance of $4,311,610,000

LOANS IN EUROPE

to be met by loans. The immediate needs of the Treasury were met by the sale of short-term securities. Treasury bills were issued in large amounts at comparatively low rates of interest, and by June 21, 1915, the amount of these bills outstanding was $1,175,000,000. It was felt to be unwise further to swell the floating debt, and accordingly a second war loan was issued. Chancellor McKenna in commenting upon this loan gave three reasons for its issue, namely, that it did not mature for a long period (30 years), that its issue would help the foreign-exchange situation, and that the resort to long-term loans was economical both in rate of interest and in cost of administration. This second loan differed from the first in several respects. The rate of interest was higher, and the loan was unlimited in amount, the latter provision being made in order to enable the conversion of older Government securities into this new loan. As a matter of fact, most of the 1914 $3\frac{1}{2}$s and a considerable part of the consols were converted into this new war stock. In order to attract small investors the Post Office was authorized to sell small denomination bonds of $25 and $125 and also scrip vouchers of $5, $2.50, and $1.25 which could be applied on the purchase of the bonds.

The first loan had been taken principally by the large financial institutions and wealthy subscribers, the total number of subscribers being only 100,000, but the second loan was taken by 1,100,000 subscribers, and at the same time the amount was almost doubled. The proceeds of this loan sufficed to meet the expenditures for but three or four months, so rapidly were they increasing. The Chancellor was consequently forced to make use of every credit device available. In addition to the war loan of June recourse was had also to short-

WAR COSTS AND THEIR FINANCING

term Exchequer bonds, to loans in the United States, to war expenditure and war savings certificates, and at all times to Treasury bills. By the end of the fiscal year 1915-16 a total of some $6,779,297,280 had been secured from all these sources, from which must be deducted $802,138,115 repaid to the Bank of England. The borrowings of the year are shown in the following table:

BORROWING IN GREAT BRITAIN, FISCAL YEAR 1916

Treasury bills, net	$2,464,090,000
3½ per cent. 1914 war loan	178,992,040
3 per cent. Exchequer bonds, 1920	1,211,725
4½ per cent. war loan, 1915	2,961,725,900
5 per cent. Exchequer bonds, 1920	768,445,000
United States Anglo-French loan	254,100,115
Other advances (Bank of England)	99,482,500
	$6,779,297,280
Less repayment to Bank of England	802,138,115
Net debt created by borrowing, 1915-16	$5,977,159,165

Large as were these sums, the needs of the next fiscal year were larger. By the end of the fiscal year 1917 the daily cost was over $35,000,000. Although drastic increases were made in taxation, it was necessary to rely mainly upon loans to secure the $11,000,000,000 which the war cost Great Britain that year. Short term Exchequer bonds to a total amount of over $1,750,000,000 were sold, bearing five and six per cent. interest. Three loans were floated in the United States and one in Japan. War savings and war expenditure certificates were utilized to secure the savings of small investors, and in February, 1917, a third war loan was floated.

This third loan was issued in two forms, (1) five per cent. bonds redeemable 1929-1947, issued at 95, and sub-

LOANS IN EUROPE

ject to taxation and (2) four per cent. income tax-compounded bonds redeemable 1929-1942, issued at par. Subscriptions amounted to $5,001,564,750, but only $3,901,885,000 was covered into the Treasury before the end of the fiscal year. The public showed an unmistakable preference for the taxable bond at the higher rate of interest, as only $110,000,000 was subscribed in the tax-free form. A new type of sinking fund was provided for in this loan, which was to be used in purchasing stock whenever it fell below the issue price; each month one-eighth of one per cent. was to be set aside until the sum of $50,000,000 had accumulated. Most of the 4½ per cent. stock of the previous loan was converted into the new issue, but there were no conversion rights for the consols and the 1914 3½s, both of which, as a result, declined markedly. The total number of subscribers to this loan was 5,289,000, showing a growing determination on the part of the British people to see the war through, and also evidencing the

BORROWING IN GREAT BRITAIN, FISCAL YEAR 1917

Treasury bills	$8,949,774,000
4½ per cent. war loan, 1925-45	2,120
5 per cent. Exchequer bonds (U. S. loans)	904,493,000
6 per cent. Exchequer bonds	804,758,500
War expenditure certificates	149,392,500
War savings certificates	363,750,000
Other debt	1,659,479,405
4 and 5 per cent. war loans	3,901,883,550
Other advances	988,150,000
	$17,721,684,075

Less redemptions of:		
Treasury bills	$9,441,130,000	
War loans and Exchequer bonds	6,428,525	
War expenditure certificates	31,587,500	
Other debt	93,029,925	
		9,572,175,950

Net debt created by borrowing, 1916-17 .... $8,149,508,125

WAR COSTS AND THEIR FINANCING

efficiency of the publicity work which by now had been developed to a high degree.

With the proceeds of this loan it was possible to reduce outstanding Treasury bills, of which nearly $9,000,000,000 had been issued during the fiscal year. The net borrowings of the year ending March 31, 1917, are shown in the table on page 163.

The cost of the war increased somewhat during the next year, but the high-water mark had practically been reached. The daily expenditure amounted to about $37,000,000, but although the increase in cost was slight, the additions to the revenues were equally small, so that greater resort had to be made to borrowing than had been anticipated. The fiscal year 1918 was marked by two notable changes in the loans of the British Government. In the first place the advances from the United States Government furnished a needed and welcome relief to the strain imposed upon the British Treasury. During the fiscal year 1917-18 these advances amounted to $2,390,000,000. Second, in the raising of internal loans a new policy was inaugurated in October, 1917, when the plan of fixed subscription periods for the sale of bonds was superseded by the day-to-day borrowing plan. It was stated by the Chancellor of the Exchequer that a minimum amount of $100,000,000 a week would be needed to make this method a success in meeting war expenditures. In his budget speech of March 13, 1918, he announced that since October 1, 1917, the total sales had amounted to $2,850,000,000, which was slightly more than the prescribed minimum.

The bonds offered for sale under this plan consisted of four issues of different maturities, all of which were sold at par. There was a four per cent. ten-year bond which was exempt from income tax, and three five per

LOANS IN EUROPE

cent. issues due, respectively, in 1922, 1924, and 1927, payable at 102, 103, and 105, respectively. The denominations were made as low as $250, and no limit was placed upon the amount which the Treasury would accept. The bonds under these issues were accepted for death duties, excess-profits taxes, or munitions Exchequer payments on the part of residents of Great Britain. In addition to these, short-term obligations were also used, so that the plan of continuous borrowing combined Treasury bills, short-term Exchequer bonds, and long-term war bonds. By the first immediate necessities were met, which could be funded into the second and disposed of temporarily, and the third funded the debt for a longer period. So successful was this plan that the experiment finally developed into a distinct loan policy. Its success was due in large measure to the efficient publicity methods used and also to the fact that restrictions on the issue of new securities for industrial or local purposes practically reserved the market for Government loans. The day-to-day borrowing plan

BORROWING IN GREAT BRITAIN, FISCAL YEAR 1918

Treasury bills, net	$2,544,425,000
5 per cent. Exchequer bonds, 1922	411,352,000
6 per cent. Exchequer bonds, 1920	220,000
3 per cent. Exchequer bonds, 1930	60,106,000
War savings certificates	311,100,000
Other debt (U. S. Government loans, etc.)	3,707,520,490
4 and 5 per cent. war loans	840,413,100
National war bonds	3,071,075,000
	$10,946,111,590

Less redemptions of:
War loans, Exchequer bonds, etc..	$114,578,185	
War expenditure certificates	3,143,500	
Other debt retired	505,345,165	
Advances repaid	126,275,735	
		749,342,585

Net debt created by borrowing.................. $10,196,769,005

was finally closed on January 18, 1919, having resulted in a yield of $8,002,955,275 during its life.[4]

The net borrowings for the fiscal year 1917-18 are shown in the table on page 165.

Expenditure during the fiscal year 1918-19 remained very steady, and as a result of this and other factors the total borrowings declined somewhat. This was due to two principal causes: first, the Armistice in November ended actual warfare, and second, revenues increased. The day-to-day borrowing continued; advances from the United States Government were steady; war savings certificates brought in $447,500,000, and advances from the Bank of England from time to time made up the deficit in Treasury needs, reaching a total of $1,313,000,000.

In January, 1919, after the discontinuance of the day-to-day national war bonds, the fourth war loan was announced. It consisted of two issues of five per cent. bonds subject to the income tax, with 5- and 10-year maturities, respectively, and four per cent. tax-compounded bonds with a 10-year maturity. The issue price of the 5s was at par, and that of the 4s at 101.5 as before, and the prices at which the bonds were redeemable remained as before, namely, 102 for the five-year 5s, 105 for the 10-year 5s, and par for the four per cents. The new issues differed from the old, however, in that the seven-year maturity bonds were dropped, and the new bonds were given no rights of conversion into past or future war loans. The first official announcement of the total subscriptions to the loan was made by the Chancellor of the Exchequer, Austen Chamberlain, on July 17, 1919.[5] He stated that

---
[4] *Economist*, January 25, 1919, p. 98.
[5] *Commercial and Financial Chronicle*, July 19, 1919, p. 208.

LOANS IN EUROPE

the grand total was $3,540,000,000 of which $2,695,000,-
000 was new money. These figures fell considerably
below the estimates, and the yield was less than had been
hoped for.

Great Britain's borrowings during the fiscal year
1918-19 are shown in the following table:

BORROWING IN GREAT BRITAIN, FISCAL YEAR 1919

5 per cent. Exchequer bonds...................	$20,175
6 per cent. Exchequer bonds, 1920.............	4,185
3 per cent. Exchequer bonds, 1930.............	4,018,000
War savings certificates	447,500,000
United States advances and other debt.........	2,776,123,000
National war bonds	5,332,068,900
Advances from Bank of England..............	1,313,603,235
	$9,873,337,515

Less redemptions of:		
Treasury bills	$82,320,000	
War expenditure certificates	114,661,500	
War loans and Exchequer bonds..	329,795,360	
Foreign debt retired	772,123,795	
		1,298,900,655
Net debt created by borrowing................		$8,574,436,860

The total war borrowings of the British Government,
less redemptions, from August 1, 1914, to March 31,
1919, were as follows:

TOTAL BORROWING IN GREAT BRITAIN, 1914-1919

Treasury bills, net		$4,705,590,000
Anglo-French loan in United States............		254,100,115
United States Government and other foreign loans..		6,873,874,030
Bank of England advances through Ways and Means....................................		2,274,960,000
War savings certificates		1,122,250,000
3, 5 and 6 per cent. Exchequer bonds..	$3,193,308,585	
War loans ....:............	11,483,014,590	
	$13,676,323,175	
Less redemptions	450,802,070	
		13,225,521,105
Total debt created by borrowing		$28,456,295,250

WAR COSTS AND THEIR FINANCING

The history of loans in France begins with the prewar loan which was issued on July 7, 1914. This was for $180,000,000, in 3½ per cent. 25-year bonds issued at 91, and was for the purpose of meeting the deficit occasioned by the expenditures in Morocco and the extension of the army and navy. Although the loan was 37 times oversubscribed, it immediately became a stumbling block which hampered war-time finance in the succeeding months. Two of the four instalments fell due after the war was declared, and it was finally disposed of by being converted into the first war loan.

Following the practice of most of the other Continental countries, the Government on the outbreak of war turned at once to the Bank of France for financial assistance. This institution stands in very close relation to the Government. In return for the renewal of its charter in 1897 for 23 years, it was under obligation to lend to the Government certain agreed sums at the nominal rate of one per cent. In 1911 these compulsory advances had been fixed at $580,000,000, but in September, 1914, they were increased to $1,200,000,000, and in May, 1915, to $1,800,000,000. During the first five months of the war, from August 1 to December 31, 1914, the actual advances of the Bank of France to the Government amounted to $785,000,000, constituting about two-thirds of all the money borrowed.

In addition to the returns from the 3½ per cent. loan and the advances from the Bank of France, an appeal was made direct to the small investor by the offer of short-term Treasury bills known as *bons de la defense nationale*, bearing four per cent. for the three-months' issue and five per cent. when issued for six months or a year. They were sold at 96.60 in denominations as low as 100 francs and were also used to pay contractors for

LOANS IN EUROPE

military supplies. By the end of December, 1914, about $339,600,000 of these *bons* had been issued.

The credit operations of the last five months of 1914 may be summarized as follows:

BORROWING IN FRANCE, 1914

Correspondents of the Treasury	$80,700,000
Ordinary Treasury bills	23,820,000
Bons de la defense nationale	339,460,000
3½ per cent. pre-war loan	43,940,000
Advances from Banks of France and Algeria	785,000,000
	$1,272,920,000

The year 1915 saw little change in the use of credit or credit devices by the French Government. The tax situation was slightly bettered during this year, revenues being only 19 per cent. below normal, whereas in the last five months of 1914 they had been 38 per cent. below normal. On the other hand, expenditures were mounting rapidly and the needs of the Treasury were steadily growing. Further advances were accordingly secured from the Bank of France, which by the end of the year stood at $1,080,000,000. *Bons de la defense nationale* to the amount of about $1,400,000,000 were also issued during the year. These found a ready sale, not merely in France, but also in England and the United States. In February, 1915, a second type of short-term obligation was offered to the public, known as *obligations de la defense nationale*. These were five per cent. 10-year bonds issued at 96.5 without limitation of amount. *Bons* and the pre-war 3½s could both be funded into the new issues, the latter at 91.

The *obligations* had two features which were significant of the difficulties that faced the Treasury, both designed to make the security more attractive to

WAR COSTS AND THEIR FINANCING

investors: they were tax-exempt, and the interest was paid in advance. The former was a decided break in French practice, because all bonds hitherto issued had been taxable. The second feature, payment of interest in advance, was not only without precedent in France, but was probably without parallel in the financial history of modern European states. By the end of the year the issues amounted to about $760,000,000, a large part of which, however, consisted of conversions of existing obligations.

In October, 1915, the Anglo-French Loan was placed in the United States, netting the Government in all about $250,000,000, of which $80,020,000 was paid in during the year 1915. All these sums proved insufficient, however, and in November the first national loan was issued. This, known as the "National Defense Loan," consisted of a five per cent. perpetual *rente* issued at 88. Exemption from taxation was granted as to both principal and interest. This loan proved to be very popular, the number of subscribers being 4,156,000. The total amount subscribed was $2,648,500,000, of which about half represented fresh money and the other half conversions of Treasury bills and bonds. About $2,200,000,000 was paid in before the end of the fiscal year.

The transactions for the year 1915 may be summarized in the following table:

BORROWING IN FRANCE, 1915

Treasury bills (*bons*)	$1,294,600,000
National defense *obligations*	126,400,000
Anglo-French Loan in United States	80,020,000
National War Loan, November, 1915	2,193,400,000
Advances by Bank of France	230,000,000
Miscellaneous	46,800,000
Total	$3,971,220,000

LOANS IN EUROPE

During the year 1916 the same policy was continued. The advances of the Bank of France continued to grow steadily during the year, from $1,060,000,000 on January 6 to $1,760,000,000 on October 19. The Government was then able to reduce this floating indebtedness to the Bank with the proceeds of the second war loan, bringing the amount down to $1,330,000,000 on November 2, 1916, but by the end of the year (December 31) it had increased again to $1,460,000,000.

The chief dependence of the Government, however, was the *bons,* of which over $3,000,000,000 were issued during the year. In February, 1916, a $30,000,000 credit for war munitions purchases was raised in the United States, and in July a $100,000,000 collateral loan was negotiated through the American Foreign Securities Company, consisting of five per cent. three-year gold notes issued at 98. Another collateral loan of $50,000,000 was placed in the United States in September. Foreign credits were also created by the French Government during this year by the shipment of gold to England, and about $80,000,000 was borrowed in Japan, Argentina, Switzerland, Holland, Spain, and other neutral countries. In October, 1916, a second war loan was issued. This was a perpetual *rente* at five per cent. similar to the first loan, issued at 88.75. The subscriptions amounted to $2,272,000,000. The loan transactions of this year are summarized on page 172.

The year 1917, like the two previous years, saw France still financing the war on credit, primarily by the use of short term securities. As the burden of the war became greater, expenditures grew much more rapidly than additions to tax receipts, and accordingly larger amounts had to be raised by means of loans. Over three-quarters of the credits granted for the year

WAR COSTS AND THEIR FINANCING

BORROWING IN FRANCE, 1916

Balance of Anglo-French Loan	$170,000,000
United States collateral loans	150,000,000
Treasury bills sold in England	463,000,000
Bons, unconverted	2,633,200,000
Second loan, 1916, new money	1,136,000,000
Advances from Bank of France	400,000,000
Advances from Bank of Algeria	9,000,000
Obligations	207,400,000
Credits in England by gold shipments	300,000.000
Other foreign credits	80,000,000
Ordinary Treasury bills	28,400,000
Total	$5,577,000,000

1917 was raised by unfunded debt. The Bank of France contributed about $1,020,000,000; *bons de la defense nationale*, the issue of which had been suspended at the time of the second war loan, were resumed in February, 1917, and by the end of the year the total emissions for the year totalled $8,020,000,000. The Treasury also resumed the issue of *obligations* in March, and of these there were some $60,000,000 outstanding just before the November loan. In addition to these two issues a new kind of security was put out, beginning March 1, 1917, which may be called *obligations-bons*, for it united the characteristics of both these securities. They were issued at par, bore five per cent., and were repayable at the end of any six-months' period. If the purchaser held them until the end of the five-year period, however, he received a bonus of half a year's interest. By the end of the year there were outstanding of these securities some $4,000,000,000.

In April of this year another $100,000,000 collateral loan was placed in the United States in the form of 5½ per cent. convertible two-year gold notes offered to the public at 99, yielding slightly over six per cent., and a $15,000,000 industrial credit was also arranged,

LOANS IN EUROPE

covered by French Treasury bills. Treasury bills were sold in England to the amount of $600,000,000.

After the entry of the United States into the war on April 6, 1917, the United States Government became banker for the Allies. The United States Treasury advanced to France during the remainder of the year 1917 the sum of $1,285,000,000.

Large as were these sums, they were yet insufficient to meet the growing needs of the French Treasury, and it became necessary to issue a third war loan in November, 1917. This was a four per cent. perpetual *rente* issued at 68.60. This loan was limited to $2,000,000,000 real capital or $2,600,000,000 nominal capital. The new loan was exempt from the income tax. Various measures were taken at the time of its issue to maintain its price: it was made acceptable at its issue price for the payment of the excess-profits tax, and a fund was constituted for the purchase of these bonds in the open market if they should fall below the price of issue. The results of this loan were very satisfactory, the subscriptions amounting to $2,914,000,000, of which about half represented fresh money and the other half conversions of *bons, obligations,* and other securities.

The total borrowings for the year 1917 were:

BORROWING IN FRANCE, 1917

Advances from Bank of France	$1,020,000,000
Advances from Bank of Algeria	8,000,000
Bons, net	1,667,000,000
Collateral loan in United States, April, 1917	100,000,000
Industrial credit in United States	15,000,000
Obligations-bons, net	2,715,000 000
Advances from United States Government	1,285,000,000
Treasury bills sold in England	600,000,000
1917 war loan, less conversions	1,423,000,000
Total	$8,833,000,000

WAR COSTS AND THEIR FINANCING

The war expenditure, already crushing, was raised during the year 1918 to even greater heights. The total credits granted for the year aggregated $10,671,000,000, to meet which the Government relied for the most part on loans. The advances from the Bank of France still continued, the net for the year being $930,000,000, and the total on December 26 being $3,430,000,000. *Bons de la defense nationale* continued to be extremely popular and represented a steady and dependable reliance of the Government at all times. The sale of these *bons* continued steadily from month to month, by December reaching a maximum of $100,000,000 a week, with a total for the year of $2,614,000,000; in fact, so popular were they that the Government found it possible by the end of the year 1918 to reduce the rate of interest on the one- and three-month *bons* from five to four per cent.

Toward the end of the year the amount of short-term obligations and of the floating debt became so great that it was necessary to fund them into long-term bonds. Accordingly the fourth war loan was announced in October, 1918. This was a four per cent. perpetual *rente,* free from taxation and inconvertible for at least 25 years. It was issued at 60.80, and no limit was placed upon the amount of the loan. Provision was made for acceptance in part payment of *bons, obligations,* 3½ per cent. redeemable *rente* scrip, Treasury bills, and coupons of Russian Government bonds maturing during the year 1918. In spite of the supposed financial exhaustion of France, the subscriptions to this loan reached the total of $6,000,000,000 nominal capital, representing a net yield to the Treasury of $4,300,000,000. In addition to the sums raised at home, France obtained during the year 1918 advances from the United States Government to the amount of $1,151,000,000.

LOANS IN EUROPE

The total borrowings for the year 1918 were:

BORROWING IN FRANCE, 1918

Advances from Bank of France.................	$930,000,000
1918 war loan, less conversions.................	4,300,000,000
Advances from United States Government.......	1,151,000,000
Bons and *obligations*, net	4,483,750,000
Total..	$10,864,750,000

During the progress of the war about one-quarter of the borrowings of the French people were obtained from foreign countries. Three-quarters of the enormous sums expended on the war by France were raised from the French people themselves. Whatever criticism may be urged against the exclusive loan policy followed by France in financing the war, it must be tempered by admiration of the industry and thrift of the French people which made it possible for them to contribute such sums to the defense of their country.

The total government borrowings of France from August 1, 1914, to the end of the year 1918 may be summarized as follows:

TOTAL BORROWING IN FRANCE, 1914 TO 1918

		Nominal	Actual
War Loans:	1915	$3,041,000,000	$2,661,600,000
	1916	2,302,800,000	2,016,400,000
	1917	2,960,600,000	2,034,200,000
	1918	6,000,000,000	4,300,000,000

	$14,304,400,000	$11,012,200,000	$11,012,200,000
Advances from United States Government to Dec. 31, 1918			2,436,427,000
Advances from Great Britain			2,170,000,000
Private loans in United States, collateral and industrial..			686,000,000
Loans in neutral countries			150,000,000
Advances from Bank of France.................			3,430,000,000
Advances from Bank of Algeria			17,000,000
Floating debt (*bons, obligations*, etc.)..........			4,483,750,000
			$24,250,377,000

WAR COSTS AND THEIR FINANCING

The financial policy followed by Russia in the war was similar to that adopted by the other European belligerents. It was stated distinctly by the Minister of Finance in his budget speech of March, 1916; the civil expenditures, he said, were to be defrayed as far as possible out of taxation, but the cost of the war and deficits in the civil budget were to be met by loans and issues of paper money. Taxes were never sufficient to meet the civil budget, so that not only were the entire expenditures of the war met by loans, but also to some extent the civil expenditures. The Treasury consequently resorted to many forms of loans, and when all else failed, as indicated in an earlier chapter, it issued paper money.

During the first few weeks of the war the Government depended for financial assistance upon the Imperial Bank of Russia, from which it received advances through the discounting of Treasury bills averaging about $50,000,000 a week. Short-term Treasury bonds were issued abroad, and Russian Treasury bills were discounted by the Bank of England. By December 31, 1914, about $260,000,000 had been borrowed abroad. In addition to the foreign loans the Government also appealed to the people at home. It first issued short-dated four per cent. Treasury bills in August to the amount of $150,000,000, and in July, October, and December it issued short-term Treasury bonds amounting to $650,000,000. In November the first war loan was announced, consisting of five per cent. 10-50-year bonds, issued at 95; the total subscriptions yielded the Government the sum of $257,000,000. The transactions by loans of the Imperial Russian Government to the end of 1914 were, therefore, as follows:

LOANS IN EUROPE

BORROWING IN RUSSIA, 1914[6]

INTERNAL

Long-dated 5 per cent. 49-year loan, Oct. 3	$257,000,000
Short-dated 4 per cent. Treasury notes, Aug. 22	150,000,000
Treasury bonds, July 23, Oct. 6, Dec. 26	650,000,000

EXTERNAL

Short-dated Treasury bonds, 5 per cent., sold in London, Oct. 6, Dec. 26	260,000,000
Total	$1,310,000,000

The year 1915 saw no change in the financial policy already established. The Government depended upon loans for meeting war expenditures, and in placing these loans relied almost exclusively upon short-term obligations discounted by the Imperial Bank or subscribed by private banks. It was not thought wise or feasible to obtain from the poverty-stricken Russian people any large amount by issuing popular loans. Continued resort was had during this year to the Imperial Bank, which not only discounted Treasury bills, but also helped the flotation of the war loans; indeed, the Bank itself subscribed two-fifths of each internal loan issued in 1915, or a total amount of about $700,000,000.

During 1915 three internal war loans were issued. Russian war finance differed from that of the other belligerents in making use of a series of comparatively small loans instead of large loans at less frequent intervals. The first of the three loans of 1915, that is, the second war loan, issued in March, was a five per cent. 10-50-year bond issued at 94; subscriptions amounted to $257,000,000. Within two months the third loan was issued, which was a 5½ per cent. bond issued at 99. This had two peculiar features which differentiated it

---

[6] The dates given are those of the Gregorian calendar, which is 15 days earlier than the Julian calendar.

WAR COSTS AND THEIR FINANCING

from anything else in Russian finance or in that of any other country: (1) the rate of interest remained at 5½ per cent. for only six years, after which it was reduced to five per cent.; (2) the bonds were redeemable at par in 1921, but if not presented at that time, did not mature until 1996.[7] Whether because these features made the loan particularly attractive or because it was better advertised, the subscriptions were double those of either preceding loan, reaching $515,000,000. This sum, together with other receipts, sufficed the Government until November, when the fourth war loan was issued. This was a 5½ per cent. 10-year bond issued at 95. The amount subscribed was the same as the third loan, $515,000,000.

In addition to these long-term loans the Government also issued during 1915 seven series of short-term Treasury bills to a total of $1,625,000, four per cent. bills in March and August aggregating $275,000,000, and five per cent. bills amounting to $1,350,000. Short-term Treasury bills amounting to $400,000,000 were discounted in Great Britain and France and unspecified credits created abroad during the year amounted to $3,162,500,000.

The result of this exclusive loan policy was practically to double the debt in the year and a half since the beginning of the war. The Russian public debt had stood at $4,412,105,000 on January 1, 1914. A year later it was $5,236,786, but at the end of 1915, during which the Government made full use of its borrowing power, the debt was raised to $9,438,315,500.

The loan transactions of 1915 were as follows:

---

[7] Prospectus of loan given in "Internal War Loans of Belligerent Countries," published by National City Bank, New York, 1918, p. 51.

LOANS IN EUROPE

BORROWING IN RUSSIA, 1915

INTERNAL

Second war loan, 10-50-year, 5 per cent..........	$257,000,000
Third war loan, 5-10-year, 5½ per cent..........	515,000,000
Fourth war loan, 10 year, 5½ per cent..........	515,000,000
4 per cent. Treasury notes, March and August...	275,000,000
5 per cent. Treasury bonds, Feb. 6, March 27, June 18, July 15, Aug. 26	1,350,000,000

EXTERNAL

5 per cent. short-term Treasury bonds, June 10, Sept. 9	400,000,000
Unspecified credits, March 13, April 6, Oct. 9....	3,162,500,000
Total...............................	$6,474,500,000

The loans thus far placed in Russia had been comparatively small, but an effort was made during the next year to secure sums that would contribute measurably toward meeting the war costs. In March the fifth internal loan was issued, consisting of a 5½ per cent. 10-year bond issued at 95. The amount subscribed was $1,029,000,000, which was equal to the proceeds of the two preceding loans. Successful as this was, it was surpassed by the proceeds of the sixth war loan, issued in October on the same terms as the March loan, the yield of which was $1,544,000,000. As the net addition to the debt during the year 1916 was $3,172,103,000, it is clear that most of the money needed for war expenditure was being obtained from long-term bonds. There was left a balance of only about $600,000,000 to be raised by short-term Treasury bills and similar obligations. During 1916 the so-called " dollar loan " of $50,000,000 was floated in New York, and Treasury bills were sold in the United States to the amount of about $35,000,000. Great Britain afforded the chief market during this period for Russian Treasury bills sold abroad, and France took the balance. The borrowings of 1916 are given in the following table:

WAR COSTS AND THEIR FINANCING

BORROWING IN RUSSIA, 1916

Fifth war loan, 10-year, 5½ per cent............	$1,029,000,000
Sixth war loan, 10-year, 5½ per cent............	1,544,000,000
Dollar loan in the United States...............	50,000,000
Treasury bills sold in England and France......	600,000,000
Total...................................	$3,223,000,000

The year 1917 was marked by such kaleidoscopic changes of both a military and a political character that the mere narration of the loan transactions ceases to have any significance. In March the seventh war loan was issued in the form of a five per cent. 10-75-year bond issued at 85. There was here an approach to the French policy of selling a low-interest bond at a discount. Either because this feature made the loan more attractive or because the great inflation in the paper money had provided people with more money than hitherto, the amount subscribed was the largest yet obtained, namely, $2,059,000,000.

In March the revolution took place, and the new Government was forced to raise funds to carry on its activities. For this purpose it offered a so-called Russian Liberty Loan of $1,500,000,000. This was a five per cent. 40-year loan, issued at 85, of which half was secured from bankers and the rest was sold to the public. A credit was also obtained in the United States to a total of $365,000,000, and during the year 1917 $187,729,250 of this was advanced to Russia. A credit of $333,000,000 was obtained in Japan through the sale of Treasury bills, the proceeds of which were used to pay for munitions bought in that country.

Because of the disturbed political situation and the uncertain powers of the Provisional Government, little could be done in the way of securing revenue from taxation; consequently reliance was placed upon loans

LOANS IN EUROPE

not merely for military, but for practically all expenditures of the Government. The public debt of Russia, which on January 1, 1917, amounted to $12,610,468,500, was estimated on September 7, 1917, to have more than doubled, standing then at $28,643,904,349. With the overthrow of the Provisional Government by the Bolshevist *régime* and the repudiation by the latter of all foreign-owned debt, the issue of loans, of course, came to an end. A final survey shows Russian war borrowing to have taken the forms shown in the following table:

TOTAL BORROWING IN RUSSIA, 1914-1917

Seven internal war loans	$6,176,000,000
Advances from Great Britain	2,840,000,000
Advances from France on Treasury bills	1,085,000,000
Advances from United States	187,729,750
Advances from Japan on Treasury bills	333,000,000
Private loans and credits in United States	162,500,000
Advances from Bank of Russia by discount of Treasury bills	7,239,663,000
Total	$18,023,892,750

Loans formed the mainstay of Italy's financial policy, although she made a valiant effort to enlarge her tax revenues. Resort was had both to Treasury bills and to long-term war loans. During the fiscal year ending June 30, 1915, when Italy was busy preparing for the war although she was not actually engaged in it, the Treasury bills issued by the Government amounted to $309,700,000. During the following fiscal year the amount was only about half as great, or $145,000,000. The reason for the lessened resort to temporary borrowing was the flotation of war loans during this latter period. The so-called "mobilization loan" issued in January, 1915, antedated Italy's formal entrance into the war, but it must properly be included in any estimate of war costs. This

WAR COSTS AND THEIR FINANCING

was a 4½ per cent. 10-25-year bond issued at 97. The amount subscribed was $200,000,000 nominal. The real war loans began with that issued in July, 1915, subsequent loans making their appearance with clocklike regularity in each succeeding January. In the flotation of these loans the Government availed itself of the assistance of a syndicate of banks.

The public debt of Italy practically trebled in the four years ending June 30, 1918, while the interest charge quadrupled in the same period. The growth of the debt and interest charges are shown in the following table:

GROWTH IN PUBLIC DEBT OF ITALY, 1914–1918

	Public debt	Interest charge
1914	$2,893,374,032	$98,848,804
1915	3,273,743,460	109,998,237
1916	4,413,046,485	174,258,691
1917	5,992,206,192	254,818,892
1918	8,682,890,299	382,028,327

These figures show only the funded debt, and are exclusive of the floating debt created by advances from banks, short-term Treasury bills, and other similar obligations, although short term obligations never played so prominent a part in Italian war finance as they did in England and France, because of the slighter financial development of Italy. The chief dependence for domestic supplies of capital was from the beginning placed on long-term loans. England and the United States supplemented these internal loans by credits aggregating $3,375,000,000. State note issues and advances from the three Italian banks of issue for Government needs supplied $1,700,000,000, and short-

LOANS IN EUROPE

term Treasury bonds and Exchequer bills amounted to $1,600,000,000. The following table shows the forms taken by Italian borrowing during the war period:

TOTAL BORROWING IN ITALY, 1914-1918

Mobilization loan, Jan., 1915	$200,000,000
First war loan, July, 1915	229,200,000
Second war loan, Jan., 1916	602,800,000
Third war loan, Jan., 1917	797,100,000
Fourth war loan, Jan., 1918	1,224,600,000
	$3,053,700,000
State note issues $339,740,000	
Advances by bank notes issued.... 1,376,500,000	
	1,716,240,000
Advances from Great Britain to April, 1919	2,065,000,000
Advances from United States to April, 1919	1,521,500,000
3-year and 5-year Treasury bonds	650,000,000
3-year and 12-month Exchequer bills	1,950,000,000
Private banking credit in United States	25,000,000
Total	$10,981,440,000

The expenditures of the British Dominions which were met by the flotation of loans offered no distinctive features, and it is sufficient to list them in the general table on pages 184 and 185.

The expenditures of the other active Entente countries were met chiefly by advances from their more powerful associates, Great Britain, France, and later the United States furnishing them with the funds and supplies they needed. Neither Belgium nor Serbia was in a position to float loans of their own, and Rumania seems to have made no attempt to do so. This method of subsidization can hardly be characterized as a loan policy.

The original, carefully planned policy of Germany for financing the war relied chiefly upon loans and extensive use of bank credits. According to the plan announced by Dr. Karl Helfferich, Minister of Finance,

BORROWING IN BRITISH DOMINIONS, 1914-1918

Loan	Date	Interest	Issue price	Subscriptions	Accepted	Maturity	Subscribers
CANADA							
1	Nov., 1915	5	97.5	$103,729,500	$100,000,000	Dec., 1925	24,862
2	Sept., 1916	5	97.5	201,444,800	100,000,000	Oct., 1931	34,526
3	March, 1917	5	96	260,768,000	150,000,000	March, 1937	40,800
4	Nov., 1917	5.5	100	419,289,000	398,000,000	5-10-20 year	820,035
5	Oct., 1918	5.5	100	690,000,000	690,000,000	Oct., 1934	1,080,000
Debenture Stock		5-5.5			16,837,350	1919-20=21	
War Savings certificates					11,820,943		
					$1,466,658,293		
AUSTRALIA							
1	Aug., 1915	4.5	100	$66,947,200		Dec., 1925	$18,748
2	Feb., 1916	4.5	100	103,298,400		Dec., 1925	28,945
3	July, 1916	4.5	100	117,938,250		Dec., 1925	102,042
4	Dec., 1916	4.5	100	107,920,100		Dec., 1925	66,960
5	Sept., 1917	4.5	100	106,068,900		Dec., 1927	216,965
6	Feb., 1918	4.5 tax free taxable		181,625,650		Dec., 1927	
		5 taxable		32,635,000		Dec., 1927	
7	Oct., 1918	5 taxable		217,116,375		Oct., 1923	
				$938,549,875			
War savings certificates				22,700,000	All		
				$961,249,875			

LOANS IN EUROPE

BORROWING IN BRITISH DOMINIONS, 1914-1918—*Continued*

Loan	Date	Interest	Issue Price	Subscriptions	Accepted	Maturity	Subscribers
NEW ZEALAND							
1	Sept., 1916	4.5	100	$38,932,000	.....	Sept., 1941	.....
2	Sept., 1917	4.5	100	58,398,000	.....	Nov., 1938	.....
3	April, 1918	{4 bond / 5 stock}	100 / 100	47,500,000	.....	{April, 1938 / April, 1928}	.....
War savings certificates	.....	.....	.....	65,000,000	All		
INDIA				$209,830,000			
1	March, 1917	{5 bond / 5.5 bond}	95 / 100	}$175,000,000	.....	{1929-47 / 1920-22}	.....
2	June, 1918	5.5	100	100,000,000	All	3-5-7-10 yr.	.....

WAR COSTS AND THEIR FINANCING

taxes were not to be imposed during the period of the war. They would not only be burdensome, but they would be unnecessary, for the German financial policy was based upon the assumption of a speedy victory and the collection of an enormous indemnity from the conquered peoples. In the Reichstag on March 10, 1915, Dr. Helfferich proclaimed his financial policy as follows:

> The means of financing a modern war are substantially the following: first, the issue of loans; second, the use of the printing press for the issue of paper money; third, a reduction of expenses, and war taxation.

The main dependence of the German Government was on the first two. War taxation was not resorted to during the first year and a half of the war because, as Dr. Helfferich said, "we have a firm hope that after the conclusion of peace we shall present to our opponents a bill for the expenses of the war forced upon us." This theory of war finance was further elaborated in his budget speech of August 20, 1915, from which the following significant sentences are taken:

> I explained in March the reason which determined the united Government against the imposition of war taxation during the period of the war. These reasons still stand. We do not desire to increase by taxation the heavy burden which war casts on our people so long as it is not absolutely necessary. . . . As things are, the only method seems to be to leave the settlement of the war bill to the conclusion of peace, and the time after peace has been concluded. And on this I would say: If God grant us victory and with it the possibility of moulding the peace to suit our needs, we neither can nor will forget the question of costs. We owe that to the future of our people. The whole course of the future development of their lives must, if at all possible, be freed

LOANS IN EUROPE

from the appalling burden caused by the war. Those who provoked the war, and not we, deserve to drag through the centuries to come the leaden weight of these milliards. . . .

Moreover, all the country's expenditure on the war, with trifling exception, has remained in the country; it has gone to our soldiers, our agriculture, industry, undertakings, and workmen; it has served as payment to the last loan, and so gone to create new capital, the result of saving.

There is involved in the last sentence the fallacy that if the money is only spent at home, it does not matter how great the debt may be. This theory dates back to the seventeenth century. It has been disproved by innumerable writers from the time of Hume to the present, but it seems to have lived on in Germany and to have influenced the financial policy of the war.

The first needs of the Government were met by the issue of Treasury bills which were discounted by the Reichsbank. For the first two months the war was financed with money obtained from the war chest or from the Reichsbank. By the middle of September, 1914, however, the floating debt had become uncomfortably large, and it was funded by the issue of a loan. This was done in pursuance of a carefully devised policy for financing the war by means of the issue of short-term Treasury bills and other obligations and then funding these at half-year intervals into long-term bonds. Every six months from the beginning of the war the German Treasury regularly issued a popular loan in September and March. Details concerning the war loans were published in great fullness and probably may be accepted as accurate, although no allowance was made in the gross yields of the loans for funding of Treasury bills or other short-term obligations. The table on page 188 shows the nine war loans issued during the war.

GERMAN WAR LOANS, 1914–1918

Loan	Date	Character	Amount	Per cent.	Issue Price	MATURITY Repayable by Drawing	MATURITY Irredeemable before	Subscribers
1	Sept. 10–19, 1914	Imperial loan	$970,250,000	5	97.5		1924	1,177,235
		Treasury bonds	250,000,000	5	97.5	1918–20		
2	Feb. 27–Mar. 19, 1915	Imperial loan	2,082,750,000	5	98.5			2,694,063
		Treasury bonds	193,750,000	5	98.5	1921–22		
3	Sept. 4–22, 1915	Imperial loan	3,040,000,000	5	99		1924	3,966,418
4	Mar. 4–22, 1916	Imperial loan	2,299,000,000	5	98.5		1924	5,279,645
		Treasury bonds	393,000,000	4½	95	1923–32	1924	
5	Sept. 4–Oct. 5, 1916	Imperial loan	2,206,500,000	5	98		1924	3,810,696
		Treasury bonds	468,250,000	4½	95	1923–32		
6	Mar. 4–April 18, 1917	Imperial loan	3,280,515,000	5	98	After Jan. 1, 1918, at 110	1924	7,063,347
7	Sept.–Oct., 1917	Imperial loan	3,156,415,000	5	98	After Jan., 1918, at 110	1924	5,213,373
		Treasury bonds		4½	98			
8	March, 1918	Imperial loan	3,691,500,000	5	98	After Jan., 1918, at 110	1924	6,510,278
		Treasury bonds		4½	98			
9	Sept., 1918	Imperial loan	2,608,489,925	5	98	After Jan., 1918, at 110	1924	2,717,657
		Treasury bonds		4½	98			
			$24,640,419,925					

LOANS IN EUROPE

The first war loan was unquestionably a success and measured the war spirit of the German people. Dr. Helfferich declared that the amount subscribed, which was $1,220,250,000, was twice as large as had been expected, and that the proceeds would meet the needs of the Government to the end of the fiscal year 1915. But war expenditures were increasing so rapidly that after paying off part of the outstanding Treasury bills the proceeds lasted only until December, 1914, when the Government was forced to resort to a new issue of Treasury notes. Although a considerable part of this loan was taken by banks, corporations, and State insurance organizations, there was also a large number of subscriptions from small investors. The participation in the loan had been provided for and facilitated by the creation of "loan offices" which were authorized to make loans on securities and even merchandise that would not be acepted as collateral by commercial banks. The following quotation from a leading German newspaper, which may be regarded as a semi-official spokesman for the Government, explained on the occasion of the third loan how this could be done:[8]

It is not necessary that one should have actual gold or silver, and anyone possessing anything can participate, whether they have ready cash or not. If you have money in the bank, simply withdraw it for the purpose of subscribing. .

If you hold securities you will find it easier still to raise money. It is not necessary to sell them; you simply borrow money against them at any "*Reichs-Darlehenskasse*" or at any large bank. And as you will receive almost as much interest on the war-loan stock, or even more interest than you pay to the lending bank, you will be nothing out of pocket. You must, however, hand over to the bank the

---
[8] *Kölnische Zeitung*, Sept. 2, 1915.

securities against which the money is advanced to you and the bank will retain them until the loan is repaid. No loss can ensue from the above mentioned procedure. Or at the most it could only be one-quarter per cent. per annum in the interest, if, as is the case with the *Reichs-Darlehenskassen*, you pay 5¼ per cent. on the borrowed money whilst you receive five per cent. on the war-loan stock and even this possible loss will subsequently be made good in view of the fact that you pay only 99 marks for each 100 marks of war-loan stock for which 100 marks will be repaid in full. . . .

If you have already subscribed to the first or second war loan and paid in full for the same, you can at once participate in the present issue. All you need to do is take your stock — or, if you have not yet received the stock, the receipt for the amount paid — to a bank, which will advance to you 75 per cent. of the nominal value, so that if you have 400 marks old war loan, you can subscribe 300 marks in the new issue without paying a single pfennig. You can even subscribe four times this amount, i. e., 1,200 marks, if you will also leave with the bank the stock that you take in the new loan, in which case you will have given the bank as security 400 marks of old war loan and 1,200 marks of the new war loan, together 1,600 marks, against a loan of 1,200 marks.

There is here explained in remarkably clear, untechnical language a system of pyramiding. By this arrangement an initial investment of 10,000 marks based in the first instance on the hypothecation with a loan office of possibly unmarketable securities, would enable a total subscription to the nine war loans of 36,997 marks with no additional cash payment. If, as has been abundantly proved by the course of events, a war can be paid for only by the increased production or the saving and self-denial of the people, it is difficult to see how such a policy as that just described could lead to anything except inflation and self-stultification. It was a case of endeavoring to lift one's self by one's own boot straps. The power of the German Government and

LOANS IN EUROPE

the blockade of the Allies forced the German people to practice economy and to finance the war out of their past accumulations and current production. But the theory of war finance here outlined made no appeal to the citizen to curtail nonessential consumption or to save the sums necessary to invest in war loans — in fact, every effort was made to avoid reference to such an unpleasant necessity. It took some time for the peoples of the various belligerent countries to realize that the only effective subscriptions to war loans were those paid for out of savings and not those financed by the easy method of borrowing at a bank. But in Germany the opposite theory was officially promulgated and religiously followed. The increasing yield of the successive war loans thus becomes a measure, not of the effective support of the war in terms of commodities and service, but rather a measure of the progress of inflation and of success in pyramiding.

No change was made in the fiscal policy of the German Government in the year 1916.[9] War expenditures were still to be met by means of loans. The inflation of the currency still continued, and although new taxation was introduced, it was not sufficient to meet even the interest on the new war debt. The easy method of financing the war by means of borrowing and the use of the printing press, however, was by now showing some of its bad

---

[9] Not only was no change made, but adherence to the exclusive loan policy was thus made the occasion of congratulation to the country by Dr. Helfferich:

"Germany is the only belligerent power which has covered her total war expenditure by long-term loans. That a nation of 70,000,000, cut off from the outer world by arbitrary acts in conflict with international law, should have borne for 20 months the heavy burden of the war, and should now again be offering to the Fatherland more than 10,000,000,000 marks, is proof of greatness beyond praise of words." (Quoted in the *Independent*, April 17, 1916, p. 100.)

effects. Whatever might have been urged in its favor as a scientific policy for a short and victorious war lost its force as the war lengthened and the debt piled up. The costs of the war, moreover, were growing steadily. Whereas the monthly costs had been estimated at $500,000,000 in 1916, they had risen by the end of 1917 to $750,000,000.

The year 1917 marked a new departure in the case of the Treasury bills that were offered for sale. These were made redeemable by drawings at 110, which was a high premium to pay the subscriber. The Imperial loans were issued at practically the same price in all the nine issues and bore the fixed rate of interest of five per cent. It was a matter of considerable self-glorification on the part of German writers that they were able to sell successive issues of war bonds practically at par without resorting to higher rates of interest, as in the case of Great Britain, or to reduction in price, as in the case of France. The real explanation of Germany's apparent ability to maintain her credit unaffected by the vast loans she made is to be found in the methods pursued to induce people to purchase bonds with the proceeds of bank loans. As money could be easily borrowed, not only from commercial banks but also from the loan offices especially established for this purpose, and upon every conceivable form of security, no one could offer the excuse of inability to buy. Add to this the social and governmental pressure, amounting in the case of the later loans to practical compulsion, and the flotation of successive loans at nearly par is sufficiently explained. The deception practiced upon the mass of the people as a result of the inflationist policy may have served to maintain the ruling class in power a little longer than would otherwise have been possible,

LOANS IN EUROPE

but it was a terribly expensive way to secure a short reprieve.

By August 1, 1917, after three years of war, the Imperial debt had passed the limit of $25,000,000,000 which Rudolph Havenstein, the President of the Reichsbank, thought was all that Germany could stand and which he was sure would never be reached. If this figure be compared with the modest debt of the Empire before the war, $1,250,000,000, some measure of the financial burden thus far imposed upon the Empire can be realized; and even this figure, large as it is, does not take into account the large and growing debts of the several states and of the municipalities.

The year 1918 saw no change in the fiscal war policy. Loans and the issue of notes still formed the chief dependence of the Treasury, little additional use being made of taxation; in fact, the costs were growing so rapidly that the financial situation was by this time quite out of hand. By March, 1918, the monthly war cost had risen to $937,500,000. The desperate drive of the spring on the western front undoubtedly brought the average for the next few months beyond the $1,000,000,000 mark. The impending collapse of Germany was indicated by the falling off of both the total amount subscribed and the number of subscribers to the ninth war loan, which was issued in September, 1918. Both of these factors had shown, on the whole, a fairly steady progression in the first eight loans, although there were some fluctuations. But the ninth war loan recorded a tremendous fall from the previous high record, particularly in the number of subscribers. This ended the loan policy of the war.

Germany's war borrowings may be summarized as far as disclosed in the table on page 188. The

WAR COSTS AND THEIR FINANCING

TOTAL BORROWING IN GERMANY, 1914-1918, AS DISCLOSED BY THE
IMPERIAL GOVERNMENT

Nine war loans	$24,640,419,925
Treasury bills furnished Turkey, Bulgaria, etc...	1,500,000,000
Treasury bills discounted at Reichsbank	6,776,700,000
Loans in the United States	10,000,000
Total	$32,927,119,925

effectual concealment of the true state of affairs in German finance is indicated by the later startling disclosure of the existence of a floating debt of $18,000,000,000, instead of the $8,277,000,000 set down in the above table. That such an enormous debt of this character should have accumulated is the strongest possible indictment of the loan policy pursued by Germany. In spite of the vaunted success of the popular loans it is now clear that they produced less than 60 per cent. of the amount needed. As no resort was made to taxation during the war for meeting the costs of the war, when the loans failed the Government was forced to issue Treasury bills. That it should have been considered necessary to conceal the existence of this floating debt simply affords additional evidence of the utter breakdown of Germany's loan policy.

In view of this disclosure it becomes necessary to construct a new table of war borrowings of Germany:

TOTAL BORROWING IN GERMANY, 1914-1918, INCLUDING TRUE
FLOATING DEBT

Nine war loans	$24,640,000,000
Floating debt	18,000,000,000
Loan in the United States	10,000,000
Total	$42,650,000,000

The loans made by Austria-Hungary followed a prearranged plan, as did those of Germany. They were

LOANS IN EUROPE

issued at half-year intervals every November and May, following the German loans at an interval of about two months. As in Germany loans constituted the main dependence for meeting the cost of the war. In distinction from the German policy, however, the proceeds of the loans were not used primarily to repay any part of the advances of the Imperial Austro-Hungarian Bank or to fund the outstanding Treasury bills, but were also applied to the payment of contractors and other needs, while the floating debt was renewed. This was the practice at least during the early part of the war. In floating their loans the Austrian and Hungarian Governments relied, as they had done in times of peace, exclusively upon bank consortiums. The war loans in these countries were never so truly popular as they were in other countries, if we may judge by the number of subscriptions. In a large part the issues must have remained in the possession of the banks themselves.

Although the results of the war loans were published in considerable detail by the Government on the occasion of each flotation, no allowance was ever made for the conversion of outstanding short time obligations. As these were received in partial payment of the loans, however, some allowance must be made for this factor, although it is impossible to give exact figures. The totals, therefore, are somewhat misleading. In most of the other nations the amount of "fresh money" obtained was stated; not so in Austria-Hungary. The table on pages 196 and 197 shows the amounts of the various issues with the rates of interest, issue prices, and dates of maturities.

The other Teutonic allies, Turkey and Bulgaria, followed only too willingly the example of their master. Loans were floated by both countries both at home and

AUSTRO-HUNGARIAN WAR LOANS, 1914-1918

Loan	Date	Character	Amount	Interest per cent.	Issue price	Optional redemption date	Maturity
AUSTRIA							
1.......	Nov., 1914	Bonds.......	$440,149,400	5.5	97.5	Any time	1920
2.......	May, 1915	Bonds.......	537,664,400	5.5	95.25	Any time	1925
3.......	Oct., 1915	Bonds.......	840,520,000	5.5	93.60	Any time	1930
4.......	June, 1916	Treasury notes.	904,058,400	5.5	95.50	Any time	1923
		Bonds.......		5.5	93.	1926	1956
5.......	Dec., 1916	Treasury notes.	892,922,000	5.5	96.50	None	1923
		Bonds.......		5.5	92.50	1922	1956
6.......	May, 1917	Treasury notes.	1,073,000,000	5.5	94.00	Any time	1927
	April, 1917	Bonds.......		5.5	92.50	1923	1957
7.......	Nov., 1917	Treasury notes.	1,117,000,000	5.5	93.00	Any time	1926
		Bonds.......		5.5	91.00	1923	1957
8.......	May, 1918	....	1,152,600,000	..	..	....	....
			$6,957,914,200				

LOANS IN EUROPE

Austro-Hungarian War Loans, 1914-1918—*Continued*

Loan	Date	Character	Amount	Interest per cent.	Issue price	Optional redemption date	Maturity
HUNGARY							
1......	Nov., 1914	Bonds......	$235,067,400	6	97.50	1919	Not fixed.
2......	May, 1915	Bonds......	226,507,000	6	98.00	Any time	Not fixed.
	June, 1915	Bonds......		5½	91.20	1925	Not fixed.
3......	Nov., 1915	Bonds......	396,972,000	6	98.	1921	Not fixed.
4......	May, 1916	Bonds......	386,000,000	6	97.20	1921	Not fixed.
5......	Nov., 1916	Bonds......	405,000,000	5½	91.90	None	1926
				6	98.00	None	Not fixed.
6......	May, 1917	Bonds......	506,000,000	5½	96.25	1922	1942
7......	Dec., 1917	Bonds......	738,000,000	6	96.00	1922	Not fixed.
				5½	91.25	1925	Not fixed.
8......	June, 1918	Bonds......	772,000,000	6	96.10	1922	Not fixed.
			$3,665,546,400	.....	.....	.....	.....

abroad, and paper money was freely issued, but the main source of supply of both the Turkish and Bulgarian treasuries was the German Government by which the war in both countries was largely financed. So far as a policy can be discerned in the case of these two countries it was distinctly a loan policy.

CHAPTER VII

LOANS IN THE UNITED STATES

War-finance program of the United States — The First Liberty loan — The Second Liberty loan — The Third Liberty loan — The Fourth Liberty loan — The Victory Liberty loan — War savings and thrift stamps — Advances to the Allies.

During the 33 months between the outbreak of the war in Europe and the entrance of the United States the industries of this country were to a considerable extent adjusted to supplying the war needs of the belligerents. Manufactures, agriculture, mining, and other branches of industry had shown a tremendous expansion; gold flowed into the country; foreign-owned securities were returned and absorbed; trade balances piled up in favor of the United States in foreign and neutral countries; shipping made an advance greater than that of the previous generation. Profits had doubled, tripled, and quadrupled; steel, $19 a ton before the war, had gone to $44; from $9 a ton southern pig iron rose to $17; copper went from 11 cents to 44 cents a pound; flax soared from $400 to $1,300 a ton; and many other commodities reached unprecedented price levels.

The admonition of the Administration to the banks at the end of 1916 not to overload with non-liquid foreign Treasury bills sounded a note of warning, and the financial institutions began to put their houses in order. The loans of the Federal reserve banks were reduced from $222,000,000 at the beginning of the year 1917 to $168,000,000 at the time of our entrance into the war.

WAR COSTS AND THEIR FINANCING

Large numbers of Federal reserve notes were printed and distributed to the subtreasuries throughout the country, so that they would be readily available in the event of need. When war was declared on April 6, 1917, the banking system of the United States was in the strongest possible condition. The production of the country had reached the highest point ever attained; the gold supply was the greatest in the history of the nation. The United States was now a creditor instead of a debtor nation, and the foreign loans made by its citizens to belligerents amounted to over $2,912,000,000. The position of the Treasury was also strong. The tax legislation of the past three or four years had provided it with machinery that permitted an easy and prompt expansion of revenue. The Government debt was small, its credit stood at a high point, and Government expenditures had remained practically stationary.

In spite of all this, however, the world-wide inflation and high prices which now prevailed created problems of war finance for the United States in 1917 that had not presented themselves to the other belligerents in 1914. During this interval there had been a serious fall in the purchasing power of the dollar. This is clearly shown by the changes in the following index numbers:

INCREASES IN INDEX NUMBERS, 1914–1917

Authority	July, 1914	April, 1917
London *Statist*	100	213.0
London *Economist*	100	210.8
Bradstreet	100	174.5
U. S. Bureau of Labor, wholesale prices	100	172.7
U. S. Bureau of Labor, retail prices	100	142.0

LOANS IN THE UNITED STATES

It was necessary for the United States to enter upon its war-finance program on the highest pinnacle of prices and on a rising commodity and labor market. The same measure of achievement, which in 1914 would have cost $10,000,000,000, in 1917 called for practically twice that amount. On the other hand, the United States had the benefit of the three years' experience of the different European exchequers; their mistakes we could avoid and from them we borrowed ideas freely, adapting to our peculiar needs the ways and means worked out by them sometimes at great cost. Advantage was taken of Great Britain's costly experience in handling the conscription problem, especially with respect to the system of deferred classification. So, too, in the framing of revenue legislation the curtailment of credits for non-essential industries, the rationing program, the issue of war savings certificates, and the insistence upon national thrift — these and many other lessons were learned from Europe's experience. The war had developed by this time to a point at which the necessary machinery of finance was definitely established. The best financial methods had been tested out, and the necessity of a complete mobilization of all the economic forces of the nation was realized.

The war-finance program of the United States was definite and well conceived. Heavy taxes were to be imposed at once, and the difference between tax revenue and the cost of the war was to be raised by loans. The end of the fiscal year on June 30, 1917, disclosed that about one-third of the war expenditures had been met out of revenue and the other two-thirds out of loans, and this ratio was adopted by the Secretary of the Treasury the following year as the principle that should govern the distribution of the burden between the two.

WAR COSTS AND THEIR FINANCING

This theory was clearly stated in a letter written by Mr. McAdoo to Claude Kitchin, Chairman of the Ways and Means Committee of the House, on June 5, 1918:[1]

In the fiscal year ending June 30, 1918, our cash disbursements will amount to between $12,500,000,000 and $13,000,000,000. Of this amount about one-third will have been raised by taxes and two-thirds by loans, all of which will be represented by long-time obligations — that is, bonds of the first, second, and third Liberty loans and war savings certificates. We shall thus have completed fifteen months of the war with a financial record unequaled, I believe, by any other nation. . . .

If I may, without impropriety, offer a suggestion as to the proposed revenue measure, I should recommend:

(1) That one-third of the cash expenditures to be made during the fiscal year ending June 30, 1919, be provided by taxation. According to my estimates, this would involve raising eight billion dollars through taxation.

(2) That a real war-profits tax at a high rate be levied on all war profits. . . .

(3) That there should be a substantial increase in the amount of normal income tax upon so-called unearned incomes. . . .

(4) That heavy taxation be imposed upon all ,uxuries.

To secure the necessary loans the Treasury at the beginning adopted a method which later hardened into a definite policy. This was the issuance by the Treasury of short term certificates of indebtedness which were issued in anticipation of the long term loans and later of tax payments, and their subsequent funding by the flotation of long-term loans. The transactions in certificates of indebtedness during the period of the war are recorded in the table on pages 204 and 205. The

---

[1] Annual report of the Secretary of the Treasury, 1918, pp. 47, 49.

LOANS IN THE UNITED STATES

Treasury placed these certificates through the 12 Federal Reserve Banks, which acted as its fiscal agents and which undertook the marketing of the 5 loans. The general plan was for the Treasury to notify the banks in advance of the amounts it would require, and the necessary percentage of resources was then set aside by the banks to take up the Treasury certificates. These when issued were allotted in quotas to the respective banks, the quotas being based upon the total resources of the banks in the system in the different districts. The amounts accruing from the sale of these certificates were placed to the credit of the Government in the purchasing banks, and the Government in turn designated these same banks as its depositaries, drawing on its credit as need arose for the payment of wages, supply bills, and other expenditures. As the Government warrants were in turn deposited, frequently in the same banks, there was involved in this method only a transfer of credits. When the proceeds of the Liberty Loans were paid in, the outstanding certificates were liquidated and additional credits in favor of the Government were established. In this way the process of financing the war was distributed over the whole financial system, certificates being gradually placed, credits being gradually absorbed, and as funds to meet loan subscriptions came in, outstanding certificates being cancelled and surrendered. Transactions involving the turnover of billions of dollars were thus carried through with a minimum of friction and of disorganization of the money market.

Although this method of certificate borrowing enabled the Treasury to secure the needed funds without business derangement, it undoubtedly exercised an unfortunate influence by tending toward inflation. As carried out

WAR COSTS AND THEIR FINANCING

CERTIFICATES OF INDEBTEDNESS ISSUED BY THE TREASURY DEPARTMENT, 1917–1919

Date	Maturity	Interest, per cent.	Amount of issue	Total
Anticipating First Loan:				
1917: April 25	June 30.....	3	$268,205,000	
May 10	July 17.....	3	200,000,000	
May 25	July 30.....	3¼	200,000,000	
June 8	July 30.....	3¼	200,000,000	
				$868,205,000
Anticipating Second Loan:				
1917: Aug. 9	Nov. 15.....	3½	300,000,000	
Aug. 28	Nov. 30.....	3½	250,000,000	
Sept. 17	Dec. 15.....	3½	300,000,000	
Sept. 26	Dec. 15.....	4	400,000,000	
Oct. 18	Nov. 26.....	4	385,197,000	
Oct. 24	Dec. 15.....	4	685,296,000	
				2,320,493,000
Anticipating Third Loan:				
1918: Jan. 22	April 22.....	4	400,000,000	
Feb. 8	May 9.....	4	500,000,000	
Feb. 27	May 28.....	4½	500,000,000	
Mar. 20	June 18.....	4½	543,032,500	
April 10	July 9.....	4½	551,226,500	
April 22	July 18.....	4½	517,826,500	
				3,012,085,500
Anticipating Fourth Loan:				
1918: June 25	Oct. 24.....	4½	$839,646,500	
July 9	Nov. 7.....	4½	753,938,000	
July 23	Nov. 21.....	4½	584,750,500	
Aug. 6	Dec. 5.....	4½	575,706,500	
Sept. 3	Jan. 2, 1919	4½	639,493,000	
Sept. 17	Jan. 16.....	4½	625,216,500	
Oct. 1	Jan. 30.....	4½	641,069,000	
				4,659,820,000
Anticipating Fifth Loan:				
1918: Dec. 5	....	4½	$613,438,000	
Dec. 9	....	4½	572,494,000	
1919: Jan. 2	....	4½	751,684,500	

LOANS IN THE UNITED STATES

CERTIFICATES OF INDEBTEDNESS—*Continued*

Date	Maturity	Interest, per cent.	Amount of issue	Total
Jan. 16	....	4½	600,101,500	
Jan. 30	....	4½	687,381,500	
Feb. 13	....	4½	620,578,500	
Feb. 27	....	4½	532,381,500	
Mar. 13	....	4½	542,197,000	
April 10	....	4½	646,025,000	
May 1	....	4½	591,308,000	
				6,157,589,500
In anticipation of income and profits taxes, 1918...				1,624,403,500
In anticipation of income and profits taxes, 1919...				3,354,787,500
To secure Federal reserve bank notes............				255,475,000
Special issues.................................				7,733,635,903
Total..				$29,986,494,903

in practice, the certificates taken by the banks were paid for largely by the creation of credit Government deposits. Since no reserves must legally be held by the banks against such Government deposits, the restraint upon credit inflation ordinarily imposed by this requirement was lacking. It would be going too far to attribute to the Treasury system of anticipatory borrowing[2] an inflation which took place as a result of a tremendous expansion of business and of Government expenditures far in excess of the savings of the people. But there was a real inflation of the credit currency of the country beyond monetary needs, with a consequent harmful effect upon prices.

---

[2] For a severe criticism of this policy see J. H. Hollander, *War Borrowing: A Study of Treasury Certificates of Indebtedness of the United States* (New York, 1919), ch. v.

WAR COSTS AND THEIR FINANCING

The marketing of the war loans, as already noted, was also handled through the 12 Federal Reserve Banks, and here also the same method of allotting quotas based upon banking resources was followed. A highly perfected selling organization was created in each district, which took subscriptions in three- or four-weeks drives and endeavored to place with the general public the bonds allotted to the district. There were few cases where failure of the people to subscribe their full quota was registered, and every loan was oversubscribed. The banks acted as fiscal agents for the Government, receiving payments and distributing the bonds when paid for.

Advances to allies in a total amount of $10,000,000,000 were authorized by the first four Liberty Loan Acts. This was a new departure in United States Government finance and attracted unusual attention. The machinery by which it was carried through had consequently to be devised to meet the requirements, and was the result of much careful study. The Secretary of the Treasury was authorized to establish credits in favor of allied Governments and to the extent of the credits so established to purchase at par their obligations, which should bear the same rate of interest and contain in essentials the same terms and conditions as the United States bonds issued for this purpose. Short term or demand certificates of indebtedness were received from the foreign Government in exchange for a Treasury warrant of the United States for an equivalent amount. The sum thus received from the United States would then be distributed by the foreign Government among various banks, and the credits thus established would be drawn upon for the purchase of supplies as need arose. In order that purchases by the Allied Governments might be made in the most efficient manner possible without

LOANS IN THE UNITED STATES

bringing them into competition with one another or with the United States Government, a commission called the Inter-Allied Purchasing Commission was created through which all purchases by the Allied Governments in the United States were made. The interest on the demand obligations of the foreign Governments was first fixed at three per cent. per annum, but shortly thereafter it was increased to 3¼ per cent. in order to conform with the rate paid by the United States Treasury on its certificates of indebtedness. Subsequently the rate was raised to 3½, 4¼, and finally five per cent.

The war loans differed in certain essential respects in the successive issues, but all the bonds had several important features in common. They were issued at par. All except those of the Third Loan had an optional date of redemption prior to the date of maturity. Interest was payable semi-annually. Each issue provided for coupon or registered bonds at the option of the subscriber; the coupon bonds were issued in denominations from $50 to $10,000, and the registered bonds in denominations from $50 to $100,000 except in the case of the First Loan, in which the minimum was $100. Both principal and interest were payable in gold coin of the present standard of weight and fineness. The period of subscription for each loan was fixed at practically four weeks. Subscriptions were received by the Treasury, the subtreasuries, the Federal Reserve Banks, the national and state banks and trust companies, and many private banks, firms, corporations and other organizations. Finally, subscriptions were payable, at the election of the subscriber, in full or in installments over a ten-months period. These were the similarities. The differences between the various loans will be noted in the following more detailed descriptions.

WAR COSTS AND THEIR FINANCING

The First Liberty Loan Act of April 24, 1917, authorized a bond issue of $2,000,000,000 and advances to allies of $3,000,000,000. Authority was also given the Secretary of the Treasury to issue certificates of indebtedness to an amount equal to the Liberty Loan at not less than par, at a rate of interest not exceeding 3½ per cent., and running for a period not longer than one year. In order to provide funds to meet the immediate needs of the Government until the proceeds of the First Loan should become available, the Secretary of the Treasury began at once the sale of Treasury certificates, the first issue bearing date of April 25, 1917.[3] Between this date and June 8 four issues were made, aggregating $868,305,000. The maturities of these early issues were limited to 60 days.

Subscriptions to the First Liberty Loan were opened on May 14, 1917, and closed on June 15. The bonds were 3½ per cent. 15-30-year bonds dated June 15, 1917, maturing June 15, 1947, but redeemable after 1932 on three months' notice. They were tax-exempt except for estate and inheritance taxes. The bonds were convertible into similar bonds at higher rates if such bonds were issued in the future. The amount offered was $2,000,000,000. This sum was settled upon by the Treasury Department after careful consultation with experts, of whom "many students of finance and men experienced in large bond operations believed that the first issue should not exceed $1,000,000,000 and some thought that the first loan should not exceed $500,000,000."[4] The controlling consideration, however, was the essential requirements of the Government and the neces-

---
[3] The dates, maturities, interest rates, and amounts of the various issues of certificates of indebtedness will be found in the table on pages 204 and 205.
[4] Report of the Secretary of the Treasury, 1917, p. 6.

LOANS IN THE UNITED STATES

sities of the Allies, which made a large sum imperative. Even this proved insufficient, however, and the Treasury was compelled to resort again to the issue of certificates of indebtedness in August. Expenditures which had averaged $65,000,000 a month for the year prior to the war, were over $750,000,000 for August, 1917, including advances to Allies. Having fallen behind at the beginning, the Treasury was never able to overtake the rapidly growing expenditures, but was forced to anticipate each successive loan by issues of certificates of indebtedness in advance of the actual flotation. Thus, by November 15, 1917, when the Second Liberty Loan was issued, the certificates outstanding amounted to $2,320,493,000.

It was realized that to float so large an issue as the First Loan it would be necessary to make a direct appeal to the people, and a most effective selling organization was built up for this purpose which continued to function with great success throughout the war. The first step was that of the education of the American public on the nature of bonds as an investment and on its duty to subscribe as a matter of patriotism. The bond-holding public in the United States then numbered less than 350,000. Every city, town, or village that boasted a bank now developed a bond-selling organization. For this purpose the 12 Federal Reserve Banks, which are fiscal agents of the Government, were used as the basis. Each of the 12 Reserve banks appointed a committee of representative business men to act as a central Liberty Loan committee in the respective districts, and they in turn appointed subcommittees in each of the larger towns and cities. Extensive publicity and subscription campaigns were inaugurated and carried through by these committees, which received the coöperation of

WAR COSTS AND THEIR FINANCING

existing organizations and of new ones created especially for this purpose. The American Bankers' Association offered its services, and large numbers of experienced bond salesmen were enlisted in the work of selling Liberty bonds.

In the four-weeks drive which ushered in the First Loan, subscriptions amounting to $3,035,236,850 were secured from 4,500,000 subscribers. This oversubscription of 52 per cent. was unexpected, and as the Treasury had announced that it would accept only the amount of the loan asked for, it pro-rated the subscriptions, allotting smaller ones from $50 to $10,000 in full and the larger ones at varying ratios which ran down to 20 per cent. on the largest subscriptions. The First Loan registered the attitude of the American people toward popular loans and gave promise of larger possibilities for the future.

The needs of the Treasury and of the Allied countries were calling for enormous sums even beyond the original estimates of the Treasury. The loans to the Allies were averaging about $450,000,000 a month, and by November 1, 1917, they had reached a total of $2,717,200,000. Domestic requirements for the same period were about $1,635,000,000. These sums were far in excess of the revenue receipts, even supplemented by the proceeds of the First Liberty Loan, and it was necessary to issue large amounts of certificates of indebtedness. By November the amount outstanding was over $2,00,000,000, and accordingly the Second Liberty Loan was authorized to fund this floating debt and to provide additional capital.

The Second Liberty Loan, authorized by the Act of September 24, 1917, consisted of an offering of

LOANS IN THE UNITED STATES

$3,000,000,000 in four per cent. 10-25-year convertible gold bonds dated November 15, 1917. The great difference between this issue and the preceding one lay in the fact that the tax-exempt feature was considerably modified. There was perhaps no other provision of the first issue that had called forth such hostile criticism as the exemption of the bonds from taxation. The classic argument in favor of the exemption of Federal bonds from taxation had always been that a tax-exempt bond would sell at a higher figure and thus yield a larger return to the Government. If, on the other hand, the Government should tax its own securities, it would lose in the interest rate or in the issue price what it would gain from taxation. In either case, so the argument ran, the aggregate sum would be the same, and there was nothing to be gained, therefore, by subjecting Government bonds to taxation. Although this may be true under normal conditions, with proportional taxes, when the rate of taxation remains unchanged, it did not hold at this time when the taxes were progressive and when the rates were being frequently increased. The very heavy surtaxes on incomes introduced in the War Revenue Act of October, 1917, immediately placed a premium on the tax-free bonds of the first issue. They were termed the "rich man's bonds," as they were purchased in large quantities by wealthy persons who desired to evade the income tax by placing their investments in tax-free securities. It has been estimated by an eminent financial authority that investment in 3½ per cent. tax-exempt Liberty bonds was equal to a similar investment in a taxable security yielding the following returns:[5]

---

[5] Letter from Otto H. Kahn in *New Republic*, June 9, 1917, p. 161.

5.02 per cent. in respect of incomes over $100,000 per annum.
5.93 per cent. in respect of incomes over 200,000 per annum.
7.07 per cent. in respect of incomes over 300,000 per annum.
7.82 per cent. in respect of incomes over 500,000 per annum.
8.75 per cent. in respect of incomes over 1,000,000 per annum.
9.21 per cent. in respect of incomes over 2,000,000 per annum.

The possession of tax-exempt bonds accorded an advantage to the large-income taxpayer which was not shared by the recipient of small incomes. But since the loan was purchased by both income groups, the price was not enhanced by the full amount of the exemption granted, and consequently the gain to the Government from the lower interest rate was not as great as the loss in revenue from the income tax. A change, therefore, was deemed essential in the tax-exemption feature in order that the bonds might be of the same value, so far as taxation was concerned, to all investors and in order that they might make the widest possible appeal. For these reasons the new bonds were made subject to the super-income taxes and excess-profits taxes, and by way of compensation the rate of interest was increased to four per cent. The bonds issued under the Second Liberty Loan Act were exempted, principal and interest, from all taxation except (1) estate or inheritance taxes and (2) graduated super-income taxes and excess-profits and war-profits taxes. At the time of the passage of the Act this phrasing of the law was strongly criticized on the ground that these bonds too would be tax-exempt unless, or only so long as these Federal taxes should be retained. The interest on $5,000 principal in this issue was also exempted during the life of the bond from the taxes enumerated under (2) above. The bonds carried a conversion privilege, but only into the next issue of higher-interest war bonds.

The Treasury announced that it would allot additional

LOANS IN THE UNITED STATES

bonds up to one-half of any oversubscription. Subscriptions opened on October 1 and closed on October 27. The campaign, which was similar to that carried on during the first loan, but more widespread and intense, resulted in total subscriptions of $4,617,532,300 from 9,400,000 subscribers, this being 54 per cent. oversubscription. In accordance with the announcement of the Treasury only 50 per cent. of the oversubscription was accepted, and the total amount allotted was $3,808,758,650. All subscriptions between $50 and $50,000 were allotted in full, and the larger subscribers received from 90 to 40 per cent. of their subscriptions.

The loan was in every respect a remarkable success. Its distribution was twice as wide as that of the First Loan, and over 73 per cent. of the loan was paid in full on November 15. It must be said, however, that a larger resort to borrowing at the banks for the purpose of making subscriptions was noticeable during the placing of this loan than had been the case in the first. On November 23, 1917, after the effect of the loan was reflected in the bank returns, the Federal Reserve Banks showed total holdings for member banks and their clients, as assets and as collateral, of $355,392,000, which measured the credit granted for the purchase of war paper. In order to facilitate the operations of member banks in placing the bonds in the hands of actual investors the Federal Reserve Banks established a rate for the rediscount of customers' loans collateraled by Government bonds or Treasury certificates of indebtedness equal to the interest rate on the bonds. The amount of 3½ per cent. bonds of the First Liberty Loan converted into four per cent. bonds was only $568,320,050, showing that the exemption from taxation was regarded by most of the holders as of greater value than the

WAR COSTS AND THEIR FINANCING

increase in the interest rate. The bonds issued upon conversion retained the date of maturity, the terms of redemption, and the interest-payment dates of the 3½s, but otherwise had the provisions of the new issue.

During the next few months the rapidly growing costs of the war, the rising labor market, and the heavy prospective demands both for domestic requirements and for the needs of the Allies all combined to make imperative the curtailment of every unnecessary draft on credit. It was clear by this time that the slogan " business as usual " was both fallacious and dangerous. Business must be readjusted to the war-making function of the nation. Monthly expenditures, including advances to the Allies, were steadily mounting, and for April, 1918, reached the then record total of $1,215,287,119. The proceeds of the Second Loan had long since been exhausted; issues of Treasury certificates in anticipation of a third loan had begun on January 22, and by April 22 had been sold to an amount of $3,012,085,500. In addition to these, certificates of indebtedness in anticipation of the June taxes were sold to the amount of $1,624,403,500. The condition of the Treasury and the approaching maturities of outstanding certificates of indebtedness, $400,000,000 of which fell due on April 22, made it necessary to consider the offering of another Liberty loan.

Acting under authority of the Act of April 4, 1918, the Treasury now issued $3,000,000,000 in 4¼ per cent. 10-year inconvertible gold bonds. In the issue of this Third Liberty Loan the discussion centered about the rate of interest. The bonds of the previous loan were selling below par, and the return on industrial and other bonds was such as to make it doubtful in the

LOANS IN THE UNITED STATES

minds of many whether even a 4½ per cent. Government bond could be floated at par. The Treasury, however, "stood firm in the belief that the rate of interest itself would not maintain bonds at par in the financial market; that the price of Liberty bonds, even though quoted at less than par on the exchanges, would not deter the American people from buying at par the same bonds when offered by their Government to secure the necssary funds to carry on the war; that the patriotism of the American people was not measured by interest rates, nor determined by the fluctuations of Government bonds on stock exchanges."[6] In other words, the patriotism of the American people was to be relied upon rather than the investment merits of the bonds.

It was hoped that the increase in the interest rate to 4¼ per cent. would result in stabilizing the interest rate so far as this was possible, and would permit the elimination of the conversion feature which in itself had a tendency to create a demand for a constantly rising rate of interest on successive issues. Great Britain by her wholesale policy of conversion had thus lost all the advantage of the lower interest rates at which she had placed her earlier issues. The bonds of the third issue, like those of the second, were tax-exempt except as to (1) estate and inheritance taxes and (2) the surtaxes on income, excess-profits, and war-profits taxes; also, as in the second loan, income from $5,000 principal was exempt from these three latter taxes.

The Third Liberty Loan was offered to the public on April 6, 1918, the first anniversary of America's declaration of war, and the selling campaign continued to May 4. A slogan of this campaign was "Borrow

[6] Report of the Secretary of the Treasury, 1918, p. 6.

to buy." The situation was a very complex one; the former issues were quoted on the market below par, and the provision regarding inconvertibility in the new issue proclaimed that no higher rate of interest would be paid. Every effort, therefore, was put forward to ensure the success of the loan. The banks extended credit facilities for 90 days to "borrowers-to-buy" at the same rate of interest as that borne by the bonds. The great selling organization, numbering over 2,000,000 voluntary workers from ex-Secretaries of the Treasury to 10-year-old Boy Scouts, reorganized its work; groups became responsible for their individual members; the whole country was mapped out; the quotas assigned to the Federal reserve districts were reallotted by states, by counties, by municipalities, by wards, by blocks, and even by single buildings. Social forces were so marshalled as to exert pressure upon the laggard; publicity was pitilessly used; buttons and posters given to subscribers as a sort of receipt served to differentiate the slacker from the patriot and at the same time economized the efforts of the sellers and saved the subscriber from repeated solicitation. The great lists of former drives were checked over against ward rosters and precinct and poll lists, and the missing were tabulated and sought out. Four-minute men invaded every form of public entertainment, restaurant, and meeting, and there took subscriptions. As a result nearly every home in the United States numbered at least one subscriber. The total number of subscribers was 18,308,325, with subscriptions of $4,176,516,850.

But the "borrow-to-buy" policy tended to put a severe strain upon the banks. On April 5, the day before the opening of the subscription campaign for the Third Liberty Loan, the war paper in the Federal

LOANS IN THE UNITED STATES

Reserve Banks stood at $304,075,000. By April 26, when the high-water mark in this respect was reached, loans secured by war paper totaled $642,429,000 or 71.2 per cent. of all the bills discounted by the Federal Reserve Banks. This proportion was reduced until the end of July, after which it began to rise again. The financial organs sounded a warning against inflation, and every possible check was used to remedy the situation.

It was evident that retrenchment and personal economy were imperative. To be sure the pressure of war taxation restricted retail purchases, and war loans curtailed consumption by diverting funds from ordinary purchases to war uses. But in addition to all this, the Government officially restricted through its Capital Issues Committee the flotation of new security issues. This Committee's sanction was withheld from industries which neither directly nor indirectly contributed to the general welfare, and in the case of others sought to prevent competition with the war loans of the Government. In order to furnish capital to essential war industries which needed to alter or enlarge existing plants for the purpose of increasing their output, the War Finance Corporation was created. Its procedure was to lend funds to the banks which themselves advanced funds to war industries. This had a two-fold effect: it relieved the banks of the necessity of extending credit to these war industries, an operation which partook more of the nature of investment than of commercial banking on liquid securities; and at the same time it prevented private enterprise from bidding up by competition in the money market rates of interest to a point higher than that fixed by the Liberty Loans.

A certain measure of relief, moreover, was needed by the banks at this time. In the case of the First

WAR COSTS AND THEIR FINANCING

Liberty Loan no oversubscription had been accepted, and in the case of the Second, only 50 per cent. of the oversubscriptions were taken by the Treasury. Hence the financial institutions that had underwritten large blocks of bonds were relieved of the heavier part of the burden by the allocation of the full amounts of their subscriptions to the small subscribers. This had the effect of cutting the subscriptions of the banks to comparatively small amounts. Thus, in the case of the First Loan the total subscriptions of the national banks were $340,000,000, and the allocation on subscriptions was only $180,00,000, of which probably half was passed on to subscribers who purchased their bonds on the instalment plan. In the case of the Third and Fourth Loans, however, no such immunity was possible, as the Government announced that it would accept the full amount of the subscriptions; the banks, consequently, became the owners of large amounts of Government bonds. The effect of the third Liberty Loan on the condition of the banks in this respect is shown by the increase in holdings of Government securities by the national banks from $2,120,649,000 on March 4, 1918, to $2,657,523,000 on May 10.

In one other respect the Third Loan differed from either of the previous ones, namely, in the provision for a bond-purchase fund. This authorized the Secretary of the Treasury until one year after the termination of the war to purchase bonds in the open market not to exceed in any one year one-twentieth of the amount outstanding. The purchase was not limited to the Third Loan but extended also to the bonds of the first and second issues. The purpose of this provision was to prevent the price of the bonds, which were quoted at less than par and showed a further downward tendency,

LOANS IN THE UNITED STATES

from sinking further. During the period between the enactment of the law on April 4, 1918, and October 31 following, bonds to a total amount of $344,036,500 were purchased, cancelled, and retired.[7] This action undoubtedly exercised a beneficial effect on the price of outstanding issues, but the propriety of using the proceeds of the loans for this purpose may be questioned. On this point the language of the author already published in another place may be quoted:[8]

As a measure of debt redemption it may be justified on the ground that the Government, even though it was still in the market as a borrower, was buying its old bonds at a discount while it planned to sell new ones, bearing the same rate of interest, at par. As a method of maintaining, or endeavoring to raise, the market price to an artificially high level it is open to objections. But as a means of preventing a sudden or violent decline, whether accidental or engineered by speculators, an authorization of this sort is probably desirable. The English Exchequer has had the same power conferred upon it by Parliament. Obviously, it ought to be employed with the greatest possible care and the large use made of this expedient by the Treasury is in no small measure due to the low rate of interest of the loans.

A loan policy which should utilize the patriotic fervor of a people, stimulated by the contagious enthusiasm of a loan "drive," and then attempt to maintain an artificial price by manipulating the market, in order to sell bonds at an unduly low rate of interest, would be open to severe criticism. Assuming that such a policy were possible, the bad effects would at once become apparent upon the return of peace when Government support would be withdrawn as no longer necessary. The price of the bonds might then fall to normal levels and an undeserved loss be inflicted upon such holders as might be compelled to sell them before maturity. . . . Such a procedure, if pursued by a Government, would un-

---
[7] Report of the Secretary of the Treasury, 1918, p. 71.
[8] Report of the Committee on War Finance of the American Economic Association, p. 81.

doubtedly affect its credit when it next appeared as borrower upon the money market.[9]

Scarcely had the Third Liberty Loan been completed when the Treasury began preparations for further credit operations. Expenditures had outdistanced revenues by such a wide interval that the proceeds of each succeeding loan yielded a smaller and smaller amount of clear money. Having run behind at the beginning, the Treasury had never been able to catch up, and had been compelled to resort in ever increasing volume to anticipatory borrowing by means of certificates of indebtedness. Expenditures, now running over $1,500,000,000 a month, were estimated by the Secretary of the Treasury at $27,718,128,900 for the fiscal year ending June 30, 1919, whereas ordinary receipts were estimated at $6,846,900,000. A fourth loan was inevitable in the fall, but it was hoped to finance operations during the summer by further issues of short term Treasury certificates. Accordingly the Fourth Liberty Bond Act was passed on July 9, 1918.

The Federal Reserve Banks were notified on June 12 that bi-weekly allotments of $750,000,000 of certificates of indebtedness would be made to a possible total of $6,000,000,000, and they were requested to arrange their

---

[9] Other countries, as Great Britain and France, made similar efforts to maintain the market, but the most effective measure for supporting the price of Government bonds was worked out in Canada. There all dealings in Government war bonds were prohibited except through a Loan Committee formed to deal in them. Commissions were paid to brokers to bring in buying orders, and prices were advanced from time to time until the market was brought up to par. The plan, however, could scarcely be adopted in the United States because its effect was to deny the bonds a free market, which might seriously react on further new loans, or would require the expenditure of such stupendous sums by the Government itself to deal in the self-created market that it would merely result in borrowing to buy.

LOANS IN THE UNITED STATES

$6,000,000,000, and as fiscal agents were "authorized and requested to receive subscriptions up to an aggregate"[10] specified for each district. Member and other banks were notified to this effect, and beginning with June 25 subscribed for themselves or distributed to their clients seven issues, which on October 1 totalled $4,659,820,000.

The Fourth Liberty Loan consisted of $6,000,000,000 in 4¼ per cent. 15-20-year inconvertible bonds, dated October 24, 1918. Conditions in the financial market had changed since the Third Loan, and it was feared that the rate of interest, which at that time the Secretary of the Treasury hoped had been stabilized at 4¼ per cent., would no longer prove sufficiently attractive to secure the enormous sum which it was now proposed to ask. Moreover, the surtaxes to which the interest on bonds was subject had been extended downward to incomes of $5,000 while the rates had been doubled, thus cutting the income from bonds very materially to larger groups of taxpayers. The Bending Revenue Act of 1918 again doubled the surtaxes. The Secretary of the Treasury, in advocating before Congress the imposition of higher normal taxes on incomes, to which the interest on Liberty bonds was not subject, pointed out as an incidental advantage that such a course would undoubtedly make the bonds of the fourth issue attractive to investors without at the same time increasing the interest rate for the life of the bond. As the normal tax rate was now 12 per cent. under the pending Revenue Act, it made the bonds not subject to it a very favored form of investment for people with incomes not subject to surtaxes. The successive increases in the rate of the normal tax therefore had the effect of increasing the

---
[10] Announcement of the Secretary of the Treasury.

value of the bonds for those who desired a tax-exempt investment, and thus of keeping down the rate of interest. As long as the revenue requirements of the Government necessitated the progressive raising of the rate of the normal income tax, the market value of the bonds would probably not fall much below par.

There is no doubt that the exemption of the interest of the Liberty bonds from normal income taxes, together with the block exemptions from surtaxes, helped to maintain the market price of the bonds. Inasmuch as the latter exemption varied somewhat as between the different bond issues there was a certain amount of discrimination. But it may fairly be admitted that constant increases in the interest rates would have introduced still more serious discrimination, unless the privilege of conversion of the law-interest-bearing bonds into those with higher rates had been granted, in which case the advantages of the sale of the earlier issues at lower interest rates would have been lost to the Treasury. This happened in Great Britain, where interest rates were increased to make the later issues more marketable.

But not merely were the bonds to be made attractive for persons with incomes not subject to surtaxes; an effort was also made to prevent holders of blocks of former issues who would naturally be subject to surtaxes from marketing their bonds and to induce them to purchase additional bonds of the Fourth Loan. For this purpose a provision was inserted in the Bond Act of September 24, 1918, exempting until two years after the termination of the war the interest on $30,000 of bonds of the Fourth Liberty Loan in the hands of any taxpayer from surtaxes and excess profits and war profits taxes. The taxpayer who subscribed for $30,000

LOANS IN THE UNITED STATES

of these bonds and still held them at the time of making his tax return would also receive an exemption from such taxes after January 1, 1918, on an aggregate amount of $45,000 of bonds of the two previous loans, and subscribers in lesser amounts would receive proportionate and similar exemptions. These exemptions were in addition to those already granted. The effect of these block exemptions, together with the operation of the bond-purchase fund, had the effect of holding the issues up to a price only slightly below par.

The Fourth Liberty Loan was offered for subscription on September 29, 1918, and the books were closed on October 19. The campaign for this loan was even more highly organized than the third, but it was carried out under the more discouraging handicap of the epidemic of Spanish influenza. Necessarily a campaign of crowds, it suffered from the enforced closing of public places under the orders of various health departments. The efforts of the four-minute men were restricted to street corners, automobile trucks, and such other outdoor platforms as were available. Receipts and badges of honor, besides the usual buttons, were given to subscribers. In lieu of the great public appeals house to house canvasses were made. The organization of over 2,000,000 volunteer workers, in spite of all handicaps, worked tirelessly during the three-weeks drive. In the middle of the campaign the workers, doubting the possibility of raising so huge a sum in the unfavorable circumstances, canvassed their lists again for " plus " subscriptions, asking former subscribers to increase their amounts. The slogan of the campaign was " Give until it hurts." Strong appeals were made by the press, and banks again agreed to furnish the needed credit facilities to enable subscribers to finance their purchases by borrowing. In spite of all handicaps the loan "went over the top," resulting in total subscriptions of $6,993,000,000 from 21,000,000 subscribers.

The effect of this loan on the assets of the banks was noteworthy, as their offer to extend credit to purchasers of bonds was widely accepted. The result was an increase in the so-called war paper held by the Federal Reserve Banks from the then record mark of $685,000,000 on August 2, 1918, to $1,467,322,000 on December 6, after the full adjustment of the loan had taken place in the discounts of the Federal Reserve Banks. It is clear that the banks in the United States played a *rôle* in financing the war not very different from that assumed by the great European banks. Purely commercial banking functions were for the time being subordinated to the necessities of the Government, and although it is impossible to say to what extent the banks passed on this load to permanent investors in Liberty bonds, it must be accounted a weakness in Government finance, as well as a danger to the banks themselves, that their resources should have been drawn upon to such a large extent.

Within a little more than three weeks after the placing of the Fourth Liberty Loan the Armistice was signed and military operations were suspended. The loan yielded sufficient funds to retire the $4,600,000,000 of certificates of indebtedness outstanding and to leave a balance of $2,000,000,000 for further needs. The signing of the Armistice on November 11, however, by no means ended war expenditures; in fact, the cancellation of war contracts under the break clause entailed heavy financing, and the maintenance of two million men in France and their transportation back to the United States caused expenditures to reach their highest peak

LOANS IN THE UNITED STATES

in December, 1918, when they amounted to $2,060,975,-855. By the end of January, 1919, the Secretary of the Treasury estimated in a statement to the House Committee on Ways and Means that the expenditures for the first seven months of the fiscal year amounted to $12,954,498,537; at the end of March they totaled $15,164,224,227. It was evident that in the face of such enormous outlays the balance of the Fourth Loan, supplemented though it was by revenue receipts, would not suffice to meet current expenditure. Financing by certificates of indebtedness in anticipation of the Fifth Liberty Loan had been begun as early as December 5, 1918, and between that date and March 13, 1919, eight issues were made, totaling $4,920,256,500.

The months following the signing of the Armistice saw the first steps taken toward a readjustment of industry and Government finance to a peace basis. Government control of industry was relaxed by the gradual contraction of the activities of the various war boards, the cessation on December 31 of the work of the Capital Issues Committee, and the decision of the Government to discontinue financing foreign Governments beyond the existing credits of $10,000,000,000. Owing, however, to the continuation of the blockade and the lack of shipping and the necessarily slow process of demobilization, it was not possible for the industries of the country immediately to resume their pre-war activities.

The new Revenue bill, which had originally provided for annual revenues of $8,000,000,000, was modified after the signing of the Armistice so as to yield an estimated revenue of $6,000,000,000 for the fiscal year 1919. It became law on February 24, 1919, barely in time to allow the making out of the schedules of the income tax, the first installment of which was due on March 15. This installment amounted to over $1,000,000,000, of which $800,000,000 was absorbed by maturing certificates of indebtedness. It was necessary for the Treasury, therefore, to continue its reliance upon the banks until another loan could be floated. The Federal Reserve Banks had from 70 to 80 per cent. of their total resources invested in war paper, and the necessity for another war loan to fund these short term obligations grew from day to day. It is indeed difficult to overestimate the severe strain placed upon the banks of the country during the early months of 1919 by the fourfold necessity of providing funds to pay taxes, of absorbing the successive issues of certificates of indebtedness, of extending commercial credits necessary to put war industries on a peace basis, and, finally, of placing the new war loan.

The Fifth Liberty Loan, known as the Victory Liberty Loan, was authorized by Congress on March 3, 1919, but practically all details as to interest rate, maturity, and other features were left to the discretion of the Secretary of the Treasury, the amount alone being limited by Congress to a maximum of $7,000,000,000. After a survey of the financial situation and an estimate of the probable demands on the money market for the rehabilitation of peace industries, the Secretary of the Treasury announced that the new loan would be limited to $4,500,000,000, that no oversubscription would be accepted and that no further loan would be asked. This loan was to consist of 3¾ per cent. tax-free bonds or 4¾ per cent. notes, subject, as in the three preceding loans, to the estate and the graduated super-income, excess-profits and war-profits taxes, but with block exemptions as in previous loans, and in addition an

LOANS IN THE UNITED STATES

exemption from the last three taxes of the interest on $20,000 principal of bonds, but not to exceed three times the amount of notes owned at the next tax return.

The 4¾ per cent. taxable notes were convertible into the 3¾ per cent. tax-free notes and these in turn were freely convertible into the other form. The new notes were dated May 20, 1919, and matured May 20, 1923, the interest being payable semiannually in June and December, with the right of redemption in the Government in 1922. A wider market for the new loan was sought to be created by exempting the war-loan obligations of United States from all taxation when in the hands of nonresident aliens, in the hope that neutrals might thereby be induced to invest, especially in those countries where the exchange was adverse to the United States. The Fifth Liberty Bond Act also created a cumulative sinking fund composed of (1) 2½ per cent. of the aggregate amount of bonds and notes outstanding on July 1, 1920, less the amount of foreign obligations due to the United States held by the Treasury, and (2) the amount which would have been payable for interest on such bonds or notes as may have been retired. It was estimated that under the operation of this provision the war debt of the United States would be expunged in 25 years. The expired privilege of conversion of the 4 per cent. bonds into 4¼ per cent. was revived by this Act. Finally, the War Finance Corporation was empowered to issue bonds to the amount of $1,000,000,000 for the purpose of providing credit with which to promote commerce with foreign nations, such credit to be advanced[11] to American

---

[11] Down to May 10, 1920, when further advances were suspended by order of the Secretary of the Treasury, about $31,000,000 had been loaned.

WAR COSTS AND THEIR FINANCING

exporters, or to financial institutions in turn making advances to such exporters, for appropriate periods up to a maximum of five years.

The total subscriptions to the Victory Liberty Loan amounted to $5,249,908,300 — an oversubscription of 16.66 per cent. In accordance with the terms of the issue the oversubscription was rejected and the sum originally asked for, $4,500,000,000, was allotted among the subscribers. Those subscribing up to and including $50,000 received the full amount, and the subscribers to larger sums received from 80 to 42.39 per cent. of their subscriptions. The number of subscribers was 11,903,895, which was 11.3 per cent. of the population. Although this showed a considerable falling off from the high record of the Fourth Liberty Loan, it was regarded as a satisfactory response in view of the fact that hostilities had now ceased and the appeal for funds now rested upon other grounds than those which had prevailed during active war.

The form of Government borrowing known as war savings certificates was authorized by Congress on September 24, 1917, and was put into effect on December 3 of the same year. Although modeled on the English plan of the same name, it marked an improvement over its prototype. In Great Britain the adjustment of interest was controlled by the date of purchase, the variation of maturity resulting therefrom being very cumbersome. According to the plan adopted in the United States, the war savings stamp of a face value of $5 maturing on January 1, 1923, was sold during the month of January, 1917, at $4.12, and the purchase price increased one cent each month thereafter during the year. This made the yield four per cent. per annum, compounded quarterly.

LOANS IN THE UNITED STATES

Under the United States plan there was also issued a thrift stamp which sold for 25 cents but which bore no interest. To the purchaser of these stamps a folder spaced for 16 stamps was given which represented when filled an investment of $4. This could then be exchanged for an interest-bearing certificate by payment of the excess over $4 in the price of the war savings certificate for the current month.

The first Act limited the amount of war savings certificates to $2,000,000,000, the holdings of any one individual to $1,000, the amount purchasable at any one time to $100. This later limitation was repealed by the Act of September 24, 1918. Later the law was amended so as to make the limit of $2,000,000,000 apply to each annual series, a series being issued in 1919 to mature in 1924, and another in 1920 to mature in 1925.

The campaign for the sale of war savings certificates and thrift stamps opened on December 3, 1917, under the supervision of the National War Savings Committee. State, county, city and town committees were organized throughout the country, and a canvass for subscriptions was begun, less feverish than, but equally persistent with, those of the loan drives. Individuals were pledged to buy certain specified amounts weekly or monthly, and a nation-wide campaign in the interest of thrift and economy was inaugurated. The clamor for " business as usual," of which so much had been heard at the beginning of the war, was now opposed by the doctrine of saving and investing. At first progress was slow, but the efforts of the committees were finally effective. This form of Government borrowing reached down to the purses of the smallest wage-earner and even to school children. The financial returns from this source were by no means negligible, as the yield for the calendar

WAR COSTS AND THEIR FINANCING

year 1918 was $962,677,418,[12] but the lessons of personal thrift and economy which were instilled during the progress of this campaign must be regarded as even more valuable. Although evolved as a form of war finance, because of the beneficial social results it has been found desirable to retain the system as a feature of normal Government borrowing.

That economic and financial strength were equally important with military operations in determining the outcome of the war had been fully shown by the time the United States entered the conflict. The drain upon the European nations had been terrific, and although the Entente Allies had borrowed from private sources in the United States the enormous aggregate of $2,912,395,287 down to April, 1917, the European belligerents were perilously near the point of financial exhaustion. The most important immediate contribution made by the United States to the cause of the Allies was the extension of credits by this Government.

After April 6, 1917, the financing of the Allies ceased to be the function of private enterprise and was taken over by the United States Government. The Bond acts authorized the purchase at par from the Allies of the United States of their obligations bearing the same rate of interest (first Act only) and containing the

---

[12] The steady growth in the sale of war savings and thrift stamps is shown by the following table of receipts into the Treasury from this source by months to the end of 1918:

December, 1917	$10,236,451	July, 1918	211,417,942
January, 1918	25,559,722	August, 1918	129,044,200
February, 1918	41,148,244	September, 1918	97,614,581
March, 1918	53,967,864	October, 1919	89,084,097
April, 1918	60,972,984	November, 1918	73,689,846
May, 1918	57,956,640	December, 1918	63,970,813
June, 1918	58,250,485		
		Total	$972,913,869

LOANS IN THE UNITED STATES

same terms and conditions as the obligations of the United States issued under each Act. The method by which these advances were made was to establish credits with the Treasury for specified amounts, which were then applied to the purchase in this country of foodstuffs, raw materials, and munitions of war. The foreign Government would deliver to the Treasury its short-term obligations conforming in amount and maturity with the Treasury certificates issued to provide the funds. As these obligations accumulated, the foreign Government from time to time converted them into its demand notes. The interest was adjusted on the different forms of short- or long-term obligations so as not in any case to be less than the prevailing rate which the United States was paying its citizens for the funds it loaned to the foreign Governments. These credits were finally fixed by the fourth Bond Act at $10,000,000,000, of which $9,711,739,636 had been allotted by June 30, 1920. The distribution of this sum among the various belligerent Governments is shown in the following table:

ADVANCES TO ALLIES BY THE UNITED STATES TO JUNE 30, 1920

Belgium	$350,428.794
Cuba	10,000,000
Czecho Slovakia	4,277,000,000
France	3,047,974,777
Great Britain	4,277,000,000
Greece	48,236,629
Italy	1,666,260,180
Liberia	5,000,000
Rumania	25,000.000
Russia	187,729,750
Serbia	26,780,465
Total	$9,711,739,636

In order to prevent undesirable competition among the different Allied Governments — and between them and

WAR COSTS AND THEIR FINANCING

DISBURSEMENTS OF THE UNITED STATES DURING THE WAR

Month	Foreign loans	Total disbursements
1917: March...............	....	$99,950,799
April.................	$200,000,000	289,893,953
May..................	407,500,000	526,565,555
June.................	277,500,000	412,723,486
July..................	452,500,000	662,310,845
August...............	478,000,000	757,457,364
September............	396,000,000	746,378,285
October..............	480,700,000	944,368,752
November............	471,929,750	986,081,807
December............	492,000,000	1,105,211,859
1918: January..............	370,200,000	1,090,356,045
February.............	325,000,000	1,012,686,985
March................	317,500,000	1,155,793,809
April.................	287,500,000	1,215,287,779
May..................	424,000,000	1,508,195,233
June.................	242,700,000	1,512,572,700
July..................	343,485,000	1,608,282,654
August...............	279,250,000	1,805,512,223
September............	282,150,000	1,557,264,285
October..............	489,100,000	1,664,862,260
November............	278,949,697	1,935,249,308
December............	389,052,000	2,060,975,855
1919: January..............	290,250,000	1,962,350,949
February.............	145,397,302	1,189,913,903
March................	322,350,000	1,379,801,786
April.................	409,608,608	1,428,928,306
May..................	194,911,857	1,112,337,472
June.................	54,750,000	809,389,950

the United States — for supplies produced in this country, a board known as the Inter-Allied Purchasing Commission was constituted in August, 1917, for the purpose of expending the advances made. Through the coöperation of this Commission and the War Industries Board the purchases of the Allies were coördinated with those of the United States.

The extension of these credits to the Allies placed a continuous strain upon the finances of United States.

LOANS IN THE UNITED STATES

During the last nine months of the year 1917 the monthly advances averaged over $400,000,000. This figure declined somewhat during the next year after the direct contributions of the United States in men and supplies became greater, but the average for the year 1918 was well over $300,000,000 per month. The monthly advances, together with the total disbursements of the United States Treasury, are shown in the table on page 232.

Congress having failed to provide for a continuance of Government advances to Allies during the period of reconstruction, further advances of credit to foreign Governments or individual enterprises now becomes the concern of private banking in the United States. During the continuance of the war the Government alone could have met the enormous demands of the Allies, but it was felt that with the termination of actual hostilities further financial assistance might better be left to business interests. During the period of actual war Government control of these advances was necessary as the labor and materials of the United States had to be rationed according to a unified and coördinated program which would take into account the joint needs of all the belligerents, but during the period of economic reconstruction the best interests of industry will probably be served if the granting of credits is placed upon a commercial, rather than a military or political, basis.[13]

---

[13] See Chapter XI for further discussion of the problem of financing Europe after the war.

CHAPTER VIII

TAXATION IN EUROPE

Vigorous use of taxation in England — Slight results in France, Russia, and Italy — Reasons therefor — Inadequacy of taxation by the Central Powers.

The contrast between American and British policy, on the one hand, and that of Germany and her allies, on the other, is more striking in respect of war taxation than in any other aspect of war finance. The United States and Great Britain were the only two nations that raised sufficient funds by taxation to meet even the ordinary civil expenditures and the interest charges on the war debt. These two countries made an earnest effort also to meet at least a part of the war costs by taxation. But even these nations fell short of the high ideal which an able student has defined for the financial management of a war, that it should be a "tax policy assisted by credits, rather than a credit policy assisted by taxes."[1]

Germany, on the other hand, not only made no effort to meet any part of her expenditures out of taxation, but at the very outset of the war announced a definite policy embodying this view. "We do not," declared the Finance Minister, Dr. Helfferich, "desire to increase by taxation the heavy burden which war casts on our people." Other nations have followed this principle in short struggles, but this was the first time that it had been dignified by adoption as a definite policy of war finance. The war was to be fought on credit, and the

---
[1] Henry C. Adams, *Science of Finance*, p. 542.

TAXATION IN EUROPE

settlement of the bills was to be deferred until after the conclusion of peace. The complete breakdown of the loan policy has already been described, but an account of the inadequate and belated tax measures gives further point to that analysis.

The other nations stood between these two extremes, though it must be confessed that most of them conformed rather with the German than with the Anglo-American example. In their case, however, it was not so much the result of conscious policy as of political incapacity or sheer economic inability to raise the necessary taxes. So rapidly and enormously did expenditures increase that even the interest on the new loans outran the war revenues. The efforts of the Continental Entente Treasuries were directed towards meeting in any fashion the augmenting costs. Of principle there is little trace to be found in their operations, for they were simply swept along in a maelstrom of uncontrollable expenditures without ability to direct their course. If they could keep their heads above water, they did well. In the circumstances European war finance was simply a series of hand-to-mouth expedients.

The British policy of financing the war may fairly be described as a tax policy assisted by credits, though at all times the dependence upon loans was far greater than the resort to taxation. In view of the unprecedented expenditures which the Government was called upon to meet, this was inevitable, but on the whole Great Britain followed the time-honored principle that as large a share as possible of the war costs should be met out of taxation. At the time of the Napoleonic and Crimean Wars the proportion of costs thus defrayed out of taxes had run as high as 47 per cent., but during the World War the proportion averaged about 25 per cent. of the total expenditures.

As a result of old-age pensions and other social legislation on behalf of the working classes, the expenditures of Great Britain had grown rapidly during the years preceding the war, and with them her tax revenues. For the fiscal year ending March 31, 1914, the revenues had been $991,214,485, and the expenditures, $987,464,-840. For the following year the budget of May 4, 1914, had proposed new taxes amounting to about $67,995,000 for the purpose of carrying out the program of social reform and of relieving local taxation of some of its burdens. The Finance Act enacting these proposals into law was passed on July 31, 1914, four days before war was declared against Germany. This Act fixed the rate of the income tax at 1s. 2d. in the pound, or 6¼ per cent., at which it had stood for some five years past; imposed a tax of 5d. a pound on tea; and revised and increased the death duties. It was estimated that these changes would bring the total revenue for the fiscal year 1915 up to about $1,035,000,000.

When war broke out, the immediate needs of the Treasury were met by the discount of Treasury bills and a resort to credit, but taxation for war expenditures was not long delayed. On November 17, 1914, the first war budget was presented by David Lloyd-George, the Chancellor of the Exchequer. In his budget speech he laid down certain principles concerning war financing which were to guide Great Britain during the next four years:

It is easier to raise taxes in a period of war and to lower them in a period of peace, than it would be to raise even lower taxes in a period of peace. . . . It is a time of danger when men part willingly with anything in order to

TAXATION IN EUROPE

avert evils impending on the country they love. .... Every twenty millions raised annually by taxation during this period means four or five millions taken off the permanent burdens thereafter imposed on the country.

The tax proposals consisted of a doubling of the rate of the income tax and the imposition of an additional duty on tea of 3d. per pound and of an additional duty of 17s. 3d. per barrel on beer, making a total of 25s. in all on this beverage. The taxes on tea and beer now amounted to about 80 per cent. of their original cost. The new taxes were to run only for the remainder of the fiscal year to March 31, 1915, when a new budget would make more permanent provision for the burdens of war. It was estimated that the additional duty on tea would yield $4,750,000 in that period; the beer duty, $7,500,000; and the increase of the income tax and supertax, $62,500,000; but a reduction of the license fee was made to compensate for the tax on beer, which lessened the revenue from this source by $2,250,000. It is clear that as yet the problem of war taxation had not been seriously attacked and that these taxes could be considered only as a temporary makeshift. Indeed, this first war budget did not include a single new tax; it was simply an expansion of the existing peace budget.

The second war budget was that of May 4, 1915. It was evident by this time that the war was not to end as speedily as had at first been optimistically anticipated. War costs were mounting rapidly. The deficit for the fiscal year 1914-15 had been $2,039,250,000, which was somewhat less than anticipated because of the fact that the increases in taxation introduced by Lloyd-George were yielding rather more than had been expected. The total expenditures for the fiscal year

WAR COSTS AND THEIR FINANCING

1915-16 were estimated at $5,663,270,000, whereas the revenue receipts were calculated at $1,351,660,000, leaving a deficit of $4,311,610,000 to be met by loans. Evidently it was still thought that the war would be of short duration, for no new taxes were proposed, and the only additions to existing taxation were slight increases in the wine and beer duties. The additions made in the previous November were continued.

A vigorous tax policy on the part of the British Government was first introduced by the third war budget of September 21, 1915, when an energetic effort was made to open up new sources of tax revenue. The need of additional revenues was clearly shown by the revised estimates of war expenditures, which were now raised to $7,950,000,000 from the April estimate of $3,663,000,000. To raise this enormous sum real war taxation would have to be resorted to. The most important source of revenue under the scheme proposed by the new Chancellor of the Exchequer, Reginald McKenna, was the income and supertax, in which the normal income-tax rate was raised to 2s. 6d. in the pound, or to 17.5 per cent. Even more important than the increase in the rate was the reduction of the minimum exemption from $800 to $650, so that a great number of taxpayers who had previously escaped direct taxation were now made to contribute. At the same time a distinction was made between earned and unearned income, the latter being somewhat more heavily taxed. The supertax ranged from 10d. to 3s. 6d., being graduated on incomes from $12,500 to $500,000. From these two increases additional revenues of $67,120,000 were estimated, which, together with the sum already collected from this source, would give total income and supertaxes of $582,120,000 for the fiscal year 1915-16.

TAXATION IN EUROPE

The real war tax of this scheme was the excess-profits tax, which was now introduced for the first time. This was a tax of 50 per cent. on the amount by which the profits for the accounting period "exceeded by more than $1,000 the defined pre-war standard of profits." The standard was the average profit during any two of the three years preceding 1914. If no pre-war standard were possible to define, seven per cent. of the capital employed was taken as the basis in the case of individuals and six per cent. in the case of corporations. The accounting period named under this Act was that of August 4, 1914, to July 1, 1915, the intention being to tax profits during later periods by subsequent legislation.[2]

Although the income tax now reached down to the man with an income of $651 or over, it was felt that even those with still smaller incomes must be made to contribute their share of taxation. But as it was manifestly impossible to reach such persons directly through the medium of the income tax, it was planned to exact contribution from them by increasing the indirect taxes. The customs and excise duties were accordingly raised on a number of articles which were generally consumed by the masses of the people, such as tea, coffee, cocoa, chicory, dry fruit, and tobacco, on all of which the duties were raised by 50 per cent.; sugar, the duties on which were more than quadrupled, from 1s. 10d. to 9s. 4d. per hundredweight, at which point they averaged 3½ cents per pound; motor spirits and patent medicines, upon which the duties were doubled; and cinema films, watches, musical instruments, imported motor cars and motor bicycles, hitherto untaxed, were now burdened with an import duty of 33⅓ per cent. Finally, the

[2] *Economist*, November 27, 1915, p. 85.

WAR COSTS AND THEIR FINANCING

postal, telegraph, and telephone rates were raised. From these new sources it was hoped to secure an additional revenue of $57,500,000.

These tax proposals were severely criticized at the time on the ground that they did not tax nonessentials and luxuries more heavily in order to penalize extravagance and waste and possibly to stimulate saving. Although the war brought hardship and suffering to Great Britain, it also brought prosperity to certain elements of the population. Those engaged in the production of munitions, whether as contractors or workers, reaped an unexpectedly bountiful reward, and the same was true of other branches of industry. As a result of the sudden rise in wages, in many cases to unbelievable heights, there was an outburst of extravagance and display which seemed a strange accompaniment to war and called, in the opinion of many, for repressive taxation. The situation was pictured as follows at the beginning of 1916:[3]

> The theatres are thronged; the picture palaces are packed. The country roads are covered with a procession of joy-riding motor-cars, often in charge of a chauffeur assisted by a footman. Many of the shops have had such a Christmas season as never before, and lurid stories are afloat of the diamond rings, furs, and pianos with which the workers are making the most of the first chance they have had of spending a surplus above the necessaries of life. Some few are economizing drastically, but they are nearly all folk whose income has been lessened or remained stationary.

In spite of repeated demands for a tax policy that should penalize such waste, the Government contented itself with raising the duties on spirits and beer and imposing taxes on a few articles of general consumption

---
[3] *Daily Chronicle* (London), January 8, 1916.

and on a short list of luxuries. It was probably restrained from proceeding further along these lines by the fear of political consequences. The result was a concentration on three or four sources of revenue, mostly direct.

The receipts from taxation for the fiscal year 1915-16 proved to be more than Mr. McKenna had estimated in September, and the expenditures were somewhat less. The actual expenditures were $7,795,790,000, and the revenue receipts were $1,683,834,120. Although this was a satisfactory showing from one standpoint, the percentage which revenue represented of total expenses, 21.5 per cent., was much lower than was demanded by British public opinion. Taxes alone contributed only 18.6 per cent. On the other hand, war expenditures were steadily mounting, averaging about $25,000,000 a day for the last quarter of the fiscal year 1916. The interest and sinking fund charges, moreover, now constituted a heavy charge on the civil budget, amounting to $325,000,000 for the year. It was clear that a resort to still more vigorous taxation would have to be made. Accordingly, when Mr. McKenna brought in the fourth war budget on April 4, 1916, making provision for the fiscal year 1916-17, he proposed to increase the tax revenues to $2,511,375,000. In order to raise this enormous sum, he preferred to increase the yield of a comparatively small number of taxes rather than to impose a multiplicity of new duties. In this connection he said: '' There is a limit in practice to the number of new taxes which may be imposed at any one time, and at this moment when the need is so great, revenue must be my first object. Innumerable small taxes which bring in little revenue, cause much inconvenience, and are costly to collect and of little use for my purpose.''

WAR COSTS AND THEIR FINANCING

The budget which Mr. McKenna presented at this time may fairly be regarded as the first one which grappled earnestly with the problem of meeting a considerable share of the war costs out of taxation, and it was really the only effective war budget. To secure the additional revenue the income tax was first of all raised. Where the total income did not exceed $2,500, the rate was fixed at 2s. 4d., and it progressed from this point to 5s. on incomes above $12,500; in other words, the rates ranged from 11¼ per cent. to 25 per cent. These were the rates on earned incomes. On unearned incomes they were higher, progressing from 3s. on incomes not exceeding $2,500 to 5s. on incomes over $10,000, which figure out at 15 per cent. to 25 per cent. The supertax was this time left unchanged. The rate of the excess-profits tax, which had met with popular approval, was raised to 60 per cent. From these three items the Chancellor hoped to secure $963,675,000.

Attention was then given to customs and excise duties. The duty on cocoa was quadrupled; that on coffee and chicory was doubled; that on sugar was raised 50 per cent. New taxes were imposed on table waters, cider, and similar beverages and on matches, and license fees for automobiles and motorcycles were doubled. Amusements of all sorts were also to be taxed, including these sources it was hoped by the Chancellor to raise $309,900,000.

The essential feature of this budget was the recognition of a considerable war prosperity, a part of which was to be diverted into the Treasury. As this war prosperity was temporary and was made at the expense of the nation, it was an eminently fitting object of taxation. So far as it appeared in the form of profits, it was

TAXATION IN EUROPE

levied upon by the war-profits tax; so far as it appeared in the form of higher wages, it was best reached by indirect taxes on articles of general consumption. The greater part of the burden still fell upon the direct taxpayer, although heavier levies on the wage earners were also imposed.

The budget for the fiscal year 1917-18 was not presented until May 2, 1917, by Andrew Bonar Law, the new Chancellor of the Exchequer. His policy was more distinctly a loan policy, making but slight changes in the existing taxes and relying mainly upon loans to finance the war. Expenditures for the coming year were estimated at $11,451,905,000. The total revenue was estimated at $3,183,000,000, an increase over the preceding year of $325,860,000. Few changes were made in existing taxes, the net increase from this source being calculated at only $130,500,000. Indeed, the small addition to taxation was the most striking feature of the budget, and one which called forth adverse criticism. Thus, the London *Economist,* always a staunch advocate of vigorous taxation, commented on the budget as follows: " In the face of extravagance and inflation the only cure was surely taxation or compulsory borrowing, which alone could have taken out of the hands of thoughtless and ignorant people the power to draw the economic energy of the country from the war work upon which it should be concentrated." The new taxes proposed, or rather the extension of old taxes, were the following: an extra 1s. 10d. per pound on tobacco, which was expected to bring in $30,000,000; an increase in the entertainments tax on tickets costing more than 2d., $5,000,000; an increase in the rate of the excess-profits tax to a maximum of 80 per cent., the munitions tax now being consolidated with it, $100,000,000. On the other hand, further rebates were made on liquor-license duties which reduced the yield from this source by $4,500,000.

In the budget for 1918-19 the revenues were estimated by Bonar Law at $4,210,250,000, of which $339,000,000 was to be obtained from new taxation. The income tax was increased from 5s. to 6s. in the pound on incomes over $2,500, and the supertax was raised from 1s. to 4s. 6d. in the pound. From these two increases a yield of $114,750,000, or just one-third of the new taxation, was anticipated. Another third was estimated from increased customs duties, the chief of which were a rise in the tobacco tax of 1s. 2d. per pound, and of that on sugar from 11s. 8d. to 25s. 8d. per hundredweight. A doubling of the tax on spirits, beer and matches was expected to yield $89,250,000 additional; the balance to be obtained from an increase in the stamp duties on cheques and an increase in postal rates. From these estimates it is seen that increasing resort was being had to indirect taxes, as the limit of endurance seemed to have been reached in direct taxation.

A luxury tax was also voted, which was to be levied at the rate of 2d. in the shilling and collected by means of a stamp duty. It was referred to a committee for the purpose of working out the details and was not reported out by them until August. As it was to continue only until the end of the fiscal year and at that time was not renewed, the returns from this source were but slight. For purposes of this tax articles were divided into two groups: In the first were included articles the character of which as luxuries was not open to question and which were taxed irrespective of their price; in the second group the tax was imposed only if the price of the article was above certain specified minima.

TAXATION IN EUROPE

The revenue receipts of Great Britain for the six fiscal years 1914 to 1919 are shown in the following table:

REVENUE OF GREAT BRITAIN, FISCAL YEARS 1914 TO 1919

1914	$991,214,250
1915	1,133,470,000
1916	1,683,835,000
1917	2,867,140,000
1918	3,536,175,000
1919	4,445,105,000

Expenditures in France before the war had already reached a point where it was difficult to provide by taxation the funds necessary to cover her ordinary civil expenditures and the interest on her enormous indebtedness. Indeed, in the very year in which the war began France was obliged to issue an additional loan to cover the peace expenditures. When the German invasion of northern France tore from her 10 of her richest departments and the mobilization of her men denuded industry and agriculture of their best workers, it seemed out of the question to impose new taxes or to raise the rates of existing taxes. The burden of the war itself constituted a crushing tax upon France. For the last five months of the year 1914 the yield from existing taxes fell off 38.6 per cent. from the same period in the preceding year. During the next year, 1915, there was a further slight decline of $24,400,000 below the tax receipts of 1914, but if the last five months of 1915 be compared with the same period in 1914, an encouraging improvement can be noted, as there was a gain of $74,400,000. The taxes, however, were still far below normal. Notwithstanding the disabilities under which France was laboring in the matter of taxation, any resort to heavier burdens was deprecated on the ground that the war would be of short duration. It was urged not only that no taxes be levied, but that not even a definite loan be issued, as the war could easily be financed from the Bank of France and by the issue of Treasury bills.[4]

By the end of 1915 it had become obvious that a speedy termination of the war was not to be hoped for, and that new taxes would have to be levied in order at least to meet the growing interest charges on the new loans. Existing receipts were now not even meeting the civil expenditures and the debt service. The latter charges amounted to $380,000,000 for 1915 and $653,400,000 for 1916. Accordingly, the year 1916 saw for the first time the imposition of new taxes and the expansion of old ones. The important new taxes were the income tax and the war profits tax. The income tax was not a war tax, strictly speaking, for it had been decreed by the law of July 15, 1914, under which it was to go into effect on January 1, 1915. But the outbreak of the war and the disorganization of all business led the Assembly by act of December 26, 1914, to defer the inauguration of the tax to January 1, 1916.

The French income tax was imposed upon all persons having a net income of $1,000 or over. There were various deductions and abatements: An allowance of $400 was made to a married man and an additional $200 for each dependent child up to five in number; beyond that number there was a deduction of $300 for each child. A limited progression was introduced into the tax by a rather complicated method. The tax was calculated by counting at one-fifth the income between $1,000 and $2,000; at two-fifths that between $2,000 and $3,000; at three-fifths that between $3,000 and $4,000; and at four-fifths that between $4,000 and $5,000; all over

---

[4] *L'Economiste Français*, December 26, 1914; January 30, 1915, p. 132.

TAXATION IN EUROPE

$5,000 was to be counted at its full value. The rate of the tax was two per cent. Although it was estimated that this tax would yield revenues of about $12,000,000 to $16,000,000, the actual yield for the first year of its imposition (1916) amounted only to $4,500,000. The liberal exemptions granted, the low rate of the tax, a certain amount of evasion, and the hardships of the French people all helped to produce this low yield.

A more characteristic tax of this period was the war excess profits tax, which was imposed upon exceptional and additional war profits made during the war. As adopted on July 1, 1916, the law taxed profits made during the war and was to continue for 12 months after the cessation of hostilities. The average net profits for the three years prior to August 1, 1914, were taken as the normal base for determining war profits, and upon the excess a tax of 50 per cent. was levied. The rate of taxation was increased after September 30, 1916, to 60 per cent. of the taxable profits over $100,000. Amounts of $1,000 or under were exempt.

Other taxes were imposed by act of July 1, 1916, as follows: (1) an exceptional war tax on all Frenchmen within the military age limit who for one reason or another were not called to the colors; (2) certain so-called "grouped" taxes were doubled, such as those on mines, carriages, horses, clubs, billiard tables, etc.; (3) the existing tax on securities was raised by one per cent.; (4) special taxes were imposed on certain colonial products, such as tea, coffee, cocoa, chocolate, tobacco, etc., in addition to the existing customs duties; (5) a number of other miscellaneous taxes were imposed, such as those on theatres, alcoholic drinks, and special pharmaceutical products; (6) and finally, rates were raised on letters, telegrams, telephone calls, and money orders.

WAR COSTS AND THEIR FINANCING

The effect of these new impositions was seen in an increase in the tax revenues, which were raised for the year 1916 almost to the point at which they had stood in 1913. The yield for 1916 was $933,286,500, but as the interest charges on the growing debt now amounted to $653,400,000, it was clear that additional revenues would have to be raised. The yield from the income tax, moreover, had proved distinctly disappointing, and the deficit from this source would have to be made good. In spite of vigorous opposition, the conviction gradually prevailed that the income tax must be made more lucrative and that other sources of revenue must be tapped. The end of the year 1916, accordingly, saw the introduction of additional tax measures.

An act of December 30, 1916, imposed a number of additional taxes and raised in a drastic manner the rates of those already existing. It was hoped by means of these new levies to raise about $117,200,000 of new revenue. The greatest dependence was placed upon the general income tax, which was now made much heavier, the minimum exemption being reduced from $1,000 to $600 and the rate progressing from one per cent. on the smallest amount to 10 per cent. on the excess over $30,000. Deductions for dependents were the same as under the former law. As a result of the charges and of the sharper control which was exercised, the yield of the tax, which had been estimated at $30,000,000 to $32,000,000, proved to be $36,600,000 for the year 1917.

Although France was still depending principally upon loans to defray the cost of the war, she was nevertheless making an effort to increase the revenues from taxation. The acts of July 1 and December 30, 1916, had broadened the basis of taxation by the addition of a number of new taxes and by increasing the rates of old ones.

TAXATION IN EUROPE

These taxes went into effect on January 1, 1917. The French mind, however, was too logical to permit the existing patched-up system to remain, and in consequence, the next thing to be done was to overhaul the old taxes not yet touched. Early in the year 1917, M. Ribot, the Minister of Finance, proposed that three antiquated and oppressive old taxes be canceled. These were the tax on doors and windows, the business tax (*patentes*), and the inhabited house tax. To compensate for this loss of revenue he proposed two new taxes, namely, a personal tax of $1 on each person with a private income and an increase of 20 per cent. in the general income tax. These proposals were acted upon, and the law of July 31, 1917, which carried them into effect, marked, according to an eminent French authority, the "beginning of a new fiscal era."[5] The abolition of the three taxes mentioned above was carried through, and thus were got rid of some most unequal and vexatious taxes. The new taxes proposed by M. Ribot, however, were not accepted, but other taxes were substituted in their place. A new annual tax was imposed on business profits, the rate of which was 4½ per cent., but it was graduated in characteristic French fashion, with an exemption of $300. A special tax was also imposed on the turnover of retail business when that turnover, after certain deductions, exceeded $200,000. The rate was graduated from one-tenth of one per cent. on this sum to one-half of one per cent. on the excess over $400,000. Other new taxes enacted by this law were a tax on agricultural profits and taxes on salaries and the liberal professions, at a rate of 3¾ per cent. All of the above were to go into effect on January 1, 1918.

---

[5] Gaston Jèze, *Revue de Science et de Législation financière*, xv, p. 448.

WAR COSTS AND THEIR FINANCING

During the year 1918 France continued the same policy of endeavoring to increase her tax revenue. The total estimated receipts from taxation for the year 1918 were $1,501,961,000, or about $800,000,000 more than had been raised in 1913. The greatest increase had taken place not unnaturally in direct taxation, especially in the income and war profits taxes. A new tax which was imposed during this year was the so-called luxury tax, which was to go into effect on April 1, 1918. This was very unpopular and was correspondingly unsuccessful, at least as a revenue producer.[6]

The income tax was revised again during the year 1918. The exemption minimum was fixed at $600 as before, with heavy rebates to married and dependent persons. Between $600 and $1,000 the tax rate was 1.5 per cent.; beyond this point it increased by one centime for each $20 up to $30,000; from $30,000 to $110,000 the tax progressed by one centime for each $200; over $110,000 the rate was fixed at 20 per cent.

The revenue receipts of France during the war were:

REVENUE OF FRANCE, FISCAL YEARS 1914 TO 1918

1914	$796,821.386
1915	776,794,297
1916	963,286,447
1917	1,261,200,000
1918	1,326,800,000

The war affected the revenue of Russia disastrously. The foreign trade was reduced to about 20 per cent. of that existing before the war, with a corresponding reduction of customs revenue amounting to about $250,000,000 annually. A still greater sacrifice of revenue, amounting to almost $450,000,000, or about a

[6] See my article on "Luxury Taxes" in the *Bulletin of the National Tax Association*, June, 1919, pp. 237-239.

TAXATION IN EUROPE

quarter of the total, was made by the abolition of the state spirits monopoly immediately upon the outbreak of the war. To compensate for these losses new taxes were at once proposed. These comprised a freight tax on all commodities transported within Russia by rail or water; taxes on passenger tickets and on cotton; and an increase in the postal and telegraph rates. These taxes, however, were insufficient to make up the deficit occasioned by the loss of the other revenue.

Few new taxes were imposed during the year 1915. The rate on city realty was raised from six per cent. to eight per cent., and the hut tax in the Asiatic provinces was increased from four to eight rubles a hut. Taxes on apartment houses and trade guilds were increased 50 per cent. From these four sources a net revenue of $43,350,000 was expected, and a further yield of $47,400,000 was anticipated from the increase of a number of indirect taxes, such as those on tobacco, cigarette papers, matches, beer, wine, sugar, naphtha, and yeast. Finally, increased rates on a number of Government monopolies, such as higher port and dock dues, post and telegraph charges, and railway rates, were expected to bring in $146,500,000. The total from all these sources was estimated at $250,000,000. By the end of the year, however, the Finance Minister was compelled to announce that the actual receipts had fallen short of the estimate by some $168,000,000. To make up this deficit Government monopolies of tea, sugar, matches, coffee, and wine were proposed, which it was estimated would bring in about $150,000,000 a year.

The year 1916 was marked by the introduction into Russia of two noteworthy taxes. The first of these, the war profits tax, was a real war tax. By a decree of May 16, 1916, a temporary tax for 1916 and 1917 was

WAR COSTS AND THEIR FINANCING

imposed on the excess profits of commercial and industrial undertakings and personal industrial earnings. Profits of less than eight per cent. of the authorized capital were exempt from the tax on excess profits. Those above this rate were subject to a progressive tax which ranged from 20 per cent. to 40 per cent. The earnings from personal industrial vocations were taxed at the rate of 20 per cent. on all profits above $250. The second tax, the introduction of which into Russia was made possible by the war though it was not so distinctly a war tax, was the income tax. This was made law in October, 1916, but was not to come into operation until January 1, 1917. The tax was graduated on all incomes over $425 a year, beginning with one per cent. on that amount and increasing to 12.5 per cent. on incomes of $200,000 or over. It was estimated that the income tax would yield $20,000,000 per annum. These two taxes affected only the well-to-do and the industrial classes. If the revenues from taxation were to be increased largely, it would be necessary to reach the incomes of those in the exempt classes, that is, the peasants in general. Previously they had been reached by means of the vodka monopoly, and now plans were suggested for an increase in the tax on sugar, the consumption of which had increased greatly.

The taxes just described, which were to have gone into effect in 1917, were never really enforced because of the outbreak of the revolution in March of that year. The war profits tax met with serious opposition from business circles, which claimed that because of the increases in the prices of raw material and labor such a tax, if enforced, would destroy industry. It was proposed, therefore, to defer the levy of this tax until the following year and to provide for its payment in installments. In this exigency an emergency income tax was levied in June, 1917, which was to apply only to the year 1917. This was levied on all persons and corporations liable in that year to the ordinary income tax if the taxable income assessed were over $5,000. Owing to the disturbed political situation and the uncertain powers of the Provisional Government little could be done to enforce existing legislation. In the circumstances, therefore, little could be expected from these taxes, and as conditions became more and more unsettled, the revenues from all sources showed a steady decline.

After the November, 1917, revolution there was no further talk of taxation. In lieu of this the Bolsheviki raised the necessary revenues by conscription and by the nationalization of industry. If this were done universally, there would be, of course, no place left for a system of taxation. The Bolsheviki seem, however, to have maintained the Government monopolies. Because of the decentralization of government and of administration the national system of taxation broke into fragments which were taken over by the local communes. The Commissariat of Finance on November 7, 1918, admitted that $15,000,000,000 in credit notes had been issued since January 1. The note issues, which stood at $8,458,500,000 on October 25, 1917, when the Kerensky régime came to an end, had risen by June, 1919, to an amount variously estimated at $35,000,000,000 to $50,000,000,000. New notes were being printed at the rate of about $2,500,000,000 a month, with the avowed purpose, according to a statement attributed to Lenin, of destroying the value of all money by making it worthless. Five hundred and thirteen undertakings were nationalized, checking production and also profits in the non-nationalized undertakings. As State owner-

WAR COSTS AND THEIR FINANCING

ship resulted only in loss, the revenues were badly hit. The tax on industries fell from $62,900,000 in the first half of 1917 to $18,340,000 in the same period in 1918. The budget estimates called for an expenditure in nationalizing industry of $1,000,000,000 for the first half of 1918 and $400,000,000 for the second half. The budget estimated total expenditures from January to June of 1918 at $7,416,000,000, and from July to December, 1918, at $837,452,000. The revenue side of the " budget " showed receipts from State undertakings of $406,541,000, practically all of which came from the nationalized chemical and metallurgical industries; receipts were therefore less than half the expenditures on State undertakings. Outside of these two industries the manufacture and sale of tobacco was apparently the only flourishing activity, receipts from this source for the first half of 1918 being 76 per cent. higher than in the preceding year, and those from cigarettes and cigarette holders being 287 per cent. higher. The budget of the Supreme Council for 1919 placed expenditures at $5,488,000,000 and revenues at $2,937,165,000.[7]

The revenues of Russia during the four years 1914 to 1917 were as follows:

REVENUES OF RUSSIA, FISCAL YEARS 1914 TO 1917

1914	$1,449,000,000
1915	1,397,000,000
1916	1,457,000,000
1917	1,870,000,000

Italy's record in the matter of taxation is an honorable one. Burdened though she was by enormous expenditures for armament, Italy had seemingly de-

[7] These facts are gathered from the Russian correspondence of the *Economist*. See especially January 4, 1919, p. 4; March 1, p. 367; May 3, p. 718; June 28, p. 1175.

TAXATION IN EUROPE

veloped her taxes before her entry into the war to the limit of the ability of her people to bear. After her entry, with the growth of the attendant expenditures, the need of additional revenues began to be insistent. Almost from the beginning provision was made for the enlargement of old taxes and the imposition of new ones. By royal decree in October, 1914, a general program of taxation had been outlined, which was later put into effect under various legislative decrees. The actual entry of Italy into the war in May, 1915, disrupted industry and trade, and the consequent shift to war production made the taxation yield of 1915-16 fall off from the 1914-15 yield; but the decrease was principally in the state monopolies, customs, and land taxes, and as a result of measures enacted to protect the property rights of the vast body of men called to the colors.

The taxation program outlined in December, 1915, increased the price of all commodities of which the State had monopolies; postal, telephone, and telegraph rates were raised, and at the same time new Government monopolies were created and new taxes introduced. These latter fell under two heads, (1) levies that were expected to become permanent and (2) those of a provisional character. In the first group were included income and business taxes, increase in the postal rates, increased taxes on superfluous commodities such as tobacco, spirits, beer, and petroleum, and new taxes on necessaries such as salt, matches, sugar, and bicycles. From all of these taxes the estimated yield was $61,400,000. In the second group, that is the provisional taxes, were included the war-profits tax and one or two minor imposts from which it was hoped to obtain $19,000,000, or a grand total of $80,400,000. As a result of these new taxes, which only came into full

WAR COSTS AND THEIR FINANCING

operation during the year 1916-17, the total revenues were raised by $52,000,000 over the 1915-16 yield.

The character and variety of the new taxes illustrate strikingly the difficulty with which Italy was raising these additional sums. Unhappily the costs of the war were growing so rapidly and the amount of her loans had swelled to such proportions, that the increased receipts, secured with such labor, were insufficient to meet even the growing civil expenditure and interest on the war debt. For the fiscal year 1915-16 the interest charges amounted to $154,000,000 and total revenues fell off $30,641,000 from the last peace year (1914), though the actual increase in taxation from new impositions amounted to $75,000,000.

By decree of November 15, 1916, further taxes were imposed which were expected to bring in some $40,000,000 annually. Under this decree a large number of taxes was levied which affected almost every commodity and business transaction. The variety and detailed nature of the taxes was characteristic, for in Italy, as in France, the Government seemed to prefer to depend upon a large number of small taxes than to concentrate on a few large ones. The tax on war profits was first of all considerably increased and was continued until the middle of 1918. The tax was levied on profits over eight per cent., and the rate progressed from 20 per cent. on the lowest amount to 60 per cent. on profits that exceeded 20 per cent. on the invested capital. Other taxes were imposed on men of military age who were not called to the colors and on proprietary medicines and fancy toilet articles; stamp taxes were also levied on bills of exchange and certain other commercial paper, and the prices of various classes of stamped paper for legal documents were raised. Limited-liability companies, motorcycles, motor cars, motor boats, and house rent were also subjected to special levies. A monopoly was established on playing cards, and finally rates were raised on telegrams and certain postal services. The total revenues for 1916-17 were $653,000,000. If to this sum there be added the profits from public-service utilities of about $120,000,000, the grand total would be $773,000,000. Since much of the new taxation, especially that on war profits, did not become effective until January 1, 1917, the revenues of this fiscal year, large as they were, did not after all represent the full potentialities of the new tax system.

The revenues for the next fiscal year, ending June 30, 1918, were $929,000,000, which was about $168,000,000 above the preceding year. The income and business taxes contributed about one-third of this total, or $292,460,000; the war-profits tax yielded $80,560,000, which was more than had been anticipated. On the other hand, the newly imposed taxes on motion pictures, jewelry, perfumes, etc., showed only meagre results, quite incommensurate with the irritation they caused. Large gains were made in customs revenues, owing in part to the increased importation of munitions and foodstuffs on Government orders. The greatest gain was made from state monopolies, which yielded a total of $223,800,000, the greater part of this, some $184,600,-000, being derived from tobacco; but as a considerable part of this was purchased by the army, the profits were as illusory as the gains from increased customs duties. Still, even after making all allowance for these factors, the increase in revenue was real and impressive.

In spite of all efforts to increase revenue receipts, the growing costs of the war contrived always to mount more rapidly. If the additional expenditures for interest on the debt, for pensions, and similar items were to be met out of revenues rather than loans, it would be necessary to exact even larger sums from the people. Accordingly in the year 1917-18 the sale and supply of the following articles were declared to be State monopolies: coffee and its substitutes, lubricants, distilled spirits, coal produced in Italy, explosives, electric-light bulbs, mining of mercury, tea, sugar, petroleum, paraffin, mineral oils, and quinine. The extension of State monopolies was very unpopular and aroused bitter opposition on the part of business interests, but on account of their productivity the policy was persevered in by the Government. The dictates of necessity were too grave to permit of any compromise. A few additional taxes were also added to the already long list, the most important of which was the supplementary income tax for the fiscal year 1919 only, in addition to the existing tax on incomes. This began with one per cent. on incomes of $2,000 and ran up to eight per cent. on those over $15,000.

Italy's revenues during the war are shown in the following table:

REVENUES OF ITALY, FISCAL YEARS 1915 TO 1919

1914-15	$609,340,000
1915-16	601,405,000
1916-17	761,000,000
1917-18	929,000,000
1918-19	971,000,000

According to the German theory of financing the war, new taxes were not to be imposed except in the event of a deficit. At the end of the fiscal year 1915 (March 31) a surplus of $43,800,000 was announced by Dr. Helfferich, the Minister of Finance. This showing, which on the face of it apparently evidenced great

TAXATION IN EUROPE

financial strength, was secured by transferring the whole of the military and naval outlay from the ordinary civil budget to the extraordinary war budget. As the item thus transferred amounted in the fiscal year 1913-14 to about $344,425,000, it will be seen that the so-called surplus was only nominal and that there was a real deficit of $289,675,000. Moreover, it may be pointed out that although the Imperial Government had not yet resorted to taxation to meet the extraordinary cost of the war, heavier taxation was already being imposed by the local governments and by the separate states. In explanation of this program, if not in its defense, it may be said that owing to the fact that the revenues of the Imperial Government were indirect and that the customs duties had fallen off very largely, the Imperial Government found it very difficult to enlarge its tax revenues. The direct taxes of the states, which could more readily be adjusted to changing needs, were already very generally being raised.

In his budget speech of March 16, 1916, Dr. Helfferich for the first time urged the imposition of new Imperial taxes. These were very slight, however, and were designed to do no more than meet the interest charges on the war debt. He proposed a war-profits tax, the increase of existing taxes on tobacco, cigarettes, bills of lading, and receipts, and additions to existing postal, telephone, and telegraph rates. The yield from these taxes was estimated at $125,000,000, but the actual receipts were kept a secret as was every vital fact connected with German war finance. As finally passed by the Reichstag, the tax measures differed in several respects from those proposed by Dr. Helfferich. The proposals for a universal receipts tax was rejected, and a tax on the yearly sales of goods was substituted therefor. Sales of less than $750 were exempt; above that sum the rate was fixed at one dollar per thousand. The tax was to go into effect on October 1, 1916. The other proposals were accepted with only minor modifications. As a result of these changes the estimated yield was raised from $125,000,000 to $145,000,000.

By the end of another year the enormous increase in the public debt had so increased the charges for interest that additional revenues were imperative if this charge were to be met out of revenue. When the Reichstag met on February 22, 1917, one of the first duties laid before it was that of voting new taxes. The Government proposed a 20 per cent. increase in the war profits tax, a tax on the Reichsbank, and new taxes on coal and on railway travel. The total yield of these new taxes was estimated at $312,500,000, of which the coal tax was estimated to furnish $125,000,000 and the railway-traffic tax $78,500,000, the rest being from the addition to the war profits tax and the tax on the Reichsbank. Both the coal and the railway traffic tax were very unpopular, as they raised the cost of heating and lighting and travel by about 10 per cent. Although this addition to tax revenue marked a considerable increase over the preceding year, it was yet insufficient to meet the growing civil expenditures. If Germany were to avoid continued deficits and the payment of interest on her war debt out of new loans, a policy which until now she had followed, still heavier taxation would be needed. This, however, was becoming increasingly difficult to secure. The people were already war-weary, and the Government hesitated to impose new burdens in addition to those which the war itself had brought.

By 1918 the financial situation had reached such a desperate pass that there could no longer be any tempo-

TAXATION IN EUROPE

rizing. Accordingly, the Government introduced far more extreme proposals for taxation in its 1918-19 budget than it had yet ventured to suggest. No fewer than 11 new revenue measures were proposed, which it was estimated would yield additional revenues of $718,750,000. Taxes were proposed on practically all beverages; they were applied also to exchange and to certain business transactions. A belated luxury tax was introduced, and the rate of the war profits tax was again raised, as were also the postal rates. This enumeration shows the difficulty with which the Imperial Government was confronted by reason of its restriction to indirect taxation. The heavy inheritance and income taxes of England and the United States were wholly lacking, as these belonged in Germany to the separate states. The war profits tax too, brought in less than it should have, owing to the peculiar method of levy.

The estimated budget revenues for new taxation are:

1916-17	$120,000,000
1917-18	312,500,000
1918-19	718,750.000
Total	$1,151,250,000

The only utterance on the actual returns from taxation was the cryptic statement of Count von Roedern in the Reichstag in March, 1918,[8] when he declared that more had been raised by taxation in Germany than was generally supposed. He said that about $2,000,000,000 had been raised, as follows: War profits tax and Reichsbank tax, $1,250,000,000; increases in municipal direct taxes for war relief, $500,000,000; and $250,000,000 from the special defense levy of 1913. No light was

[8] Reported in the *Economist*, March 9, 1918, p. 425.

thrown upon the question as to how far this actual yield had been offset by deficits in normal revenues, the budgeted new taxation being superimposed on the normal peace budget of 1913-14, in which customs alone had yielded $17,000,000, practically all of which must have been lost as a result of the blockade. On the other hand, if the municipalities met out of taxation the $1,124,000,000 expended by them on separation allowances and relief to families of mobilized men, which Dr. Schiffer announced was an Imperial debt to them, Germany must fairly be credited with having raised revenues to meet war expenditures to the extent of that amount, even though this was actually done by the the muncipalities instead of by the Imperial Government.

The estimated revenues of Germany for the fiscal years 1915 to 1919 were as follows:

REVENUES OF GERMANY, FISCAL YEARS 1915 TO 1919

1915	$851,294,600
1916	829,270,125
1917	970,729,732
1918	1,116,134,367
1919	1,533,824,194

The revenue receipts of Austria showed a considerable fall during the first two years of war, but after that they began to increase. Never, however, were they sufficient to meet the necessities of the civil budget and of the growing debt service occasioned by the war. The Government made a fairly determined but unsuccessful effort to secure additional revenue from taxation. In 1915 the rates of court fees and duties on inheritances were raised by royal decree, but as these new rates were not to come into effect until January 1, 1916, the revenues for the year 1915 were not affected. During the year

TAXATION IN EUROPE

1916 many increases in existing taxes were introduced. The main source of direct taxation in Austria had long been a personal tax law, which had been amended in the spring of 1914 so as to increase the scale of the income taxes and introduce a surtax on directors' fees. In spite of the Russian occupation of part of the Empire, the yield for 1914 was only slightly less than that of the preceding year, when it amounted to $86,300,200. In 1915 it actually increased to $87,456,400. In 1916 the rates were considerably increased, in some cases to double the previous ones. It is impossible to state the yield from the various increases, but if they were commensurate with the increase in the rates, there should have resulted a substantial augmentation of the revenues of the Empire. Nothing seems to have been done during the year 1917 in the way of introducing new taxes or raising the rates of existing ones. Popular discontent was now so great that the Government feared to impose new burdens. In spite of the growing needs of the Treasury, a proposal to introduce an Imperial income tax was rejected in 1918. The yield from the other taxes, although increasing in nominal amount, really represented a greatly decreased purchasing power in view of the depreciation of the currency. The following table shows the Imperial revenues during the war:

REVENUES OF AUSTRIA AND HUNGARY, 1915 TO 1918[9]

	Austria	Hungary
1915	$692,145,200	$452,831,400
1916	641,847,600	401,000,000
1917	777,528,600	536,000,000
1918	971,000,000	893,780,000

[9] The budgets for Hungary in 1916 and 1917 were not published, and these figures are estimated according to the proportionate decrease or increase in the Austrian budgets. All other figures are budget estimates, and probably only faintly correspond with the real facts.

CHAPTER IX

TAXATION IN THE UNITED STATES

A new era of Federal taxation — Revenue Act of October 3, 1913
— Outbreak of the European War — Emergency Revenue Act
of October 22, 1914 — Act of September 8, 1916 — The taxation of wealth — Act of March 3, 1917 — Declaration of war
by the United States — War Revenue Act of October 3, 1917
— Income and excess profits tax provisions — Act of February 24, 1919 — Analysis of the measure.

The year 1913 ushered in a new era of Federal taxation in the United States. Prior to that date the chief sources of revenue had been the customs duties, taxes on distilled spirits and tobacco, and since 1909 an excise on corporate incomes. The total yield for 1913, including postal revenues, was slightly over $1,000,000,000, around which figure it had fluctuated for several years. In 1913, however, the tariff was revised and greatly lowered on raw materials necessary to the American manufacturer. As the lowered tariff directly affected the Treasury receipts, it was necessary to make good the loss in revenue, and for this purpose the income tax was introduced as a part of the Underwood-Simmons Revenue Act of October 3, 1913. This had been made possible by the promulgation on February 25, 1913, of the Sixteenth Amendment to the Federal Constitution.

Although the main purpose in the imposition of the income tax was to make good the loss in revenue involved in the reform of the tariff, just as the British income tax had been an integral part of Peel's tax reform in 1842, yet another very definite

TAXATION IN THE UNITED STATES

purpose in the passage of this Act was the imposition of heavier burdens of taxation upon the possessors of large wealth.[1] Mr. Underwood, Chairman of the House Committee on Ways and Means, in reply to a taunt that the income tax was added because otherwise sufficient revenues could not be raised by his tariff measure, answered that the Republicans were blind to the trend of the times; that the Democrats did not propose to pass the bill because they were compelled to, but because " the time has come in this country when the great untaxed wealth of America must and shall bear its fair share of running the Government of the United States. . . . We remove the taxes at the customs house on necessaries purposely to levy a tax on wealth. I wish my friends on the other side clearly to understand this."[2] Cordell Hull of Tennessee, who was the real author of the income tax section of the Act, was even more explicit, and asserted that the income tax was intended to shift the burden to those who are best able to pay.[3] Similarly, Senator Simmons of North Carolina, Chairman of the Senate Finance Committee, stated that " the income section is not framed to supply a deficit in revenue, but, on the contrary, is based on the theory that property should bear its just share of the Federal as well as state taxation, and therefore the rate of this tax should be fixed with a view to requiring the wealth of the country as reflected in the income of the well-to-do to contribute equitably to these expenses."[4] From John Sharp Williams of Mississippi

---

[1] See my article, "The Taxation of Wealth," in the *Bankers' Magazine* (New York), August, 1917, from which the following citations are quoted.
[2] *Congressional Record*, 1, Part III, p. 332.
[3] *Ibid.*, p. 505.
[4] *Ibid.*, p. 2553.

came perhaps the frankest statement of purpose. "This bill," he said, "marked the inauguration of a new philosophy of taxation, and as it is perfected, the taxes upon consumption will dwindle more and more, and the income tax will more and more take their place."

Turning from a statement of purpose to the record of achievement, the broad outlines of the income tax of 1913 may now be noted. The net incomes of all single persons in excess of $3,000 (married persons, $4,000) were subjected to a normal income tax of one per cent on the excess over $3,000 (married persons, $4,000). In addition to this normal tax, there was also an additional tax or surtax upon persons whose incomes exceeded $20,000, which was graduated according to the following scale:

Income	Surtax, per cent.
$20,000 to $50,000	1
50,000 to 75,000	2
75,000 to 100,000	3
100,000 to 250,000	4
250,000 to 500,000	5
500,000 and over	6

The highest rate under this tax was thus seven per cent. (normal and additional upon the largest incomes). The Act was retroactive, applying the first year to income received between March 1 and December 31, 1913, and thereafter to the income received during the calendar year. Tax returns were to be made before March 1 of the ensuing year and the tax paid in June. The yield from the income tax was considerably less during the first year than had been estimated by the Secretary of the Treasury, but with greater experience and a better trained corps of officials, more was secured in subsequent years from this source.

TAXATION IN THE UNITED STATES

In addition to the personal tax on individual incomes, the Revenue Act of 1913 also imposed a corporation income tax. The special excise tax of one per cent. on net profits over $5,000 of corporations, joint-stock companies, and associations organized for profit, which had been first levied in 1909, was extended in 1913 to all the net earnings in excess of $5,000.

For the three fiscal years during which this Act was in force, the yields of the personal and corporation income taxes were as follows

INCOME TAX YIELD, 1914 TO 1916

	Personal	Corporations	Total
1914	$28,253,525	$43,127,740	$71,381,273
1915	41,046,162	39,144,532	80,190,694
1916	67,957,489	56,909,942	128,867,430

The numbers of persons who were assessed for the income tax during these three years were 357,598, 357,515, and 374,652, respectively. In the first year the normal tax of one per cent. on all taxable income of individuals produced $12,728,028, and the surtaxes on incomes over $20,000 a year yielded $15,525,497. Of this group those with incomes over $100,000 a year paid $9,628,381, or about one-third of the total amount paid by individuals. These proportions were not essentially changed in the two subsequent years.

The European War, which broke out in midsummer of 1914, immediately affected the revenues of the Federal Government and necessitated the imposition of additional taxes to make good the decline in customs duties. Accordingly the so-called "emergency revenue" law of October 22, 1914, was enacted, which the Secretary of the Treasury estimated would bring in $54,000,000 in the fiscal year 1915 and $44,000,000 in the following year. This was to run until December 31, 1915, but as it was obvious before that date arrived that the war would continue much longer, it was extended by joint resolution of December 17, 1915, for another year. On the whole, this Act taxed business rather than wealth, for it imposed special taxes on bankers, brokers, commission merchants, proprietors of places of amusement, and tobacco dealers, as well as stamp taxes on certain legal and business documents, on tickets, telephone and telegraph messages, insurance premiums, perfumery and cosmetics, and chewing gum. The rate on fermented liquors was raised 50 per cent., and new taxes were imposed on wines, artificially carbonated waters, and cordials.[5]

By the end of 1915 it was evident that additional revenue would have to be raised, and President Wilson proposed in his message of December 7 that it be secured by extending the list of articles in the Emergency Act and by expanding the internal revenue system. Congress, however, preferred to tax wealth rather than industry and refused to carry out the executive program. The President recommended an increase in the surtaxes on incomes and a lowering of the exemption, and new taxes on gasoline, naphtha, automobiles, internal-combustion engines, fabricated iron and steel products, pig iron, and bank checks. But Congress rejected the whole plan except the increases in the sur-

---

[5] A list of these commodities, together with the rates imposed upon them will be found in the Appendix.

TAXATION IN THE UNITED STATES

taxes on the larger incomes, which were incorporated in the Act of September 8, 1916.

It had become evident to all, however, that the European War would continue longer than had been anticipated and that a more permanent and lucrative tax system must be provided. Moreover, it was clear that reliance could not be placed upon customs duties, which had already shown a considerable falling off, for imports would undoubtedly continue to be restricted for a considerable period, not only during the war, but even after peace was declared. The necessary revenues must therefore be raised by a further development of internal taxation. The answer to the fiscal problem thus presented was given by Congress in the Revenue Act of September 8, 1916, which was designed especially to meet the extensive Army and Navy program of August, 1916.

The debate in Congress on this measure was complicated by the fact that it was a war measure, the larger revenue to be raised being necessitated by the preparedness program. But in spite of that fact there was evidenced in the discussion a determination to impose the added burden upon wealth rather than upon business or upon the mass of the people through consumption taxes. As typical of the different convictions that found expression, three or four speakers may be quoted, both in opposition to, and in defense of, the bill.

Mr. Collier of Mississippi stated the Democratic position as follows:[6]

We have to raise a certain amount of money to provide national defense. Only one question presented itself: How can this be raised so that the burden will fall lightest upon

---

[6] *Congressional Record*, lxiii, p. 12136.

WAR COSTS AND THEIR FINANCING

the American people? We have done this by increasing the income tax, and adding the inheritance tax, and the tax on munitions.

Said Mr. Keating of Colorado:[7]

This bill provides for a total of $225,000,000 of new revenue, and not one dollar of that vast sum will be raised by a tax on the necessaries of life. Every dollar will come from the purses of those who are most capable of making tl e contribution — the very rich men of the country. It was not until the advent of the Wilson Administration that any serious attempt was made to equalize the burden by compelling wealth to bear something like its just share.

Mr. Crisp of Georgia argued for the Act in a similar strain and concluded:[8] "The bill we are now considering raises the entire amount necessary to pay the expenses of preparedness from the wealth of the country."

Perhaps the most radical, not to say vindictive, speech made during the progress of the debate on this measure, was one by Mr. Bailey of Pennsylvania.[9] In spite of mixed metaphor and trite phrases, his view deserves attention as indicating the attitude of some, at least, of the supporters of the Act. According to him, the most important feature of the whole bill was the fact that the burden of the war expenditure was placed on those chiefly responsible for promoting war. This proceeded from Wall Street and from those whose interests centered there.

They have done the dancing, they must pay the piper. . . . Wealth must foot the bill. . . . This is something new

---
[7] *Ibid.*, p. 12485.
[8] *Ibid.*, p. 12109.
[9] *Ibid.*, p. 12151.

TAXATION IN THE UNITED STATES

under the sun. . . . Always the great and powerful neither did the fighting nor paid the bill. Both fell to the poor and lowly. For once the program had been changed. . . . If we are to have something which approximates an evening-up process, there will be occasion for philosophical satisfaction.

Mr. Hill of Connecticut, who opposed the Act, asserted that it was proposed to meet the expenses of defense by

unloading the whole of this additional burden by a doubled income tax upon one-third of one per cent of our population, and in another form upon the graves of the dead, and the surviving widows and orphans . . . and, in still another form, upon carefully selected industries which you think can be safely plundered and with good results. Is it not robbing the few to pay the equitable obligation of the many?[10]

It is evident that there was intended in this Act a definite return to the principle of taxing wealth which had been temporarily superseded by the business taxes of the emergency revenue measure of October 22, 1914. The Act contained six titles, covering the income tax, estate or inheritance tax, munitions-manufacturers' tax, miscellaneous taxes, dyestuffs, and printing paper, of which, however, only the first four were revenue measures.

The income tax clause of the Act of September 8, 1916, practically repealed the former law. The rate of the normal income tax, both upon individuals and upon corporations, was doubled, being increased from one per cent. to two per cent. At the same time the additional tax rates on personal incomes over $20,000 were raised, and a somewhat finer classification of income groups was introduced. The corporation income tax

[10] *Ibid.*, p. 12104.

was doubled, being raised from one per cent. to two per cent. The annexed table shows the rates of the surtaxes on personal incomes under the new law:

Incomes	Surtax, per cent.
$20,000 to $40,000	1
40,000 to 60,000	2
60,000 to 80,000	3
80,000 to 100,000	4
100,000 to 150,000	5
150,000 to 200,000	6
200,000 to 250.000	7
250,000 to 300,000	8
300,000 to 500,000	9
500,000 to 1,000,000	10
1,000 000 to 1,500,000	11
1,500,000 to 2,000,000	12
Over $2,000,000	13

The tax under this new Act began, therefore, with two per cent. on the smaller incomes of individuals, jumped to 3 per cent. on incomes from $20,000 to $40,000, and then progressed by rather uneven increments until it reached a maximum of 15 per cent. (normal and additional) on incomes in excess of $2,000,000 a year, which was the highest rate yet imposed in the United States.

There was one administrative feature common to this Act and the earlier Act of 1913 which should be noted at this point, both because of the discussion which it aroused and because of the fluctuation in policy regarding it which characterized the subsequent income tax legislation. This was the so-called "collection-at-the-source" provision under which the burden was placed upon corporations, associations and employers who should make payments to any taxpayer in excess of the minimum exemption of deducting the amount of the normal tax from such excess and remitting it directly to the

TAXATION IN THE UNITED STATES

Treasury. The collection-at-the-source feature greatly complicated the administrative work.

The section imposing an estate or inheritance tax marked a new departure in Federal taxation. Down to this time inheritance taxes had been reserved exclusively for the use of the separate states and 42 of them were now deriving part of their revenues from this source. The action of the Federal Government in encroaching upon this field was severely criticized,[11] but the need for additional revenue and the desire on the part of Congress to tax accumulated wealth more heavily led to the selection of this source. The Federal inheritance tax established by the Act of September 8, 1916, was levied on the entire value of the net estate, not upon the distributive shares, a method which made the actual rates heavier than they appear at first glance, for there were none of the various deductions allowed under the state inheritance tax laws. On the other hand, such a provision greatly simplified the administration. An exemption of $50,000 might be deducted in estimating the value of the net estate, and various other deductions were allowed for funeral expenses, support of dependents during the settlement of the estate, and similar charges. The tax must be paid within a year or the assets might be sold to pay the tax. The rates established from time to time applied only to estates created by death after that date. The tax was progressive according to amount but not according to kinship, as was usual under the state inheritance tax laws. The accompanying table shows the rates of the Federal estate tax of September 8, 1916, on net estates above the exemption of $50,000:

---

[11] See, for example, the papers on Federal taxation of inheritances read at the annual conferences of the National Tax Association.

WAR COSTS AND THEIR FINANCING

Net Taxable Estate	Rate, per cent.
Not exceeding $50,000	1
$50,000 to 150,000	2
150,000 to 250,000	3
250,000 to 450,000	4
450,000 to 1,000,000	5
1,000,000 to 2,000,000	6
2,000,000 to 3,000,000	7
3,000,000 to 4,000,000	8
4,000,000 to 5,000,000	9
5,000,000 and over	10

Owing to administrative difficulties in checking estates, allowance of claims necessary before net estate could be determined, and other delays, this tax yielded only a comparatively small amount of revenue. For the last three months of the calendar year 1916 the revenue from this source amounted to $6,828,643.

A new feature in American finance introduced by this Act was the imposition of the munitions-manufacturers' tax in addition to the income tax. This was an excise tax upon corporate and individual manufacturers of war munitions of 12½ per cent. of the entire profits from the sale of such articles manufactured within the United States for the calendar year 1916 and thereafter until one year after the proclamation of peace. It was superseded the following year by the Act of October 3, 1917, which reduced the rate to 10 per cent. for the year 1917 and provided that it should cease to be effective on January 1, 1918. This tax was the first application of the war profits tax, which was later to be expanded so as to include profits from all war contracts. For the year 1916 returns were made by 498 firms, of which 269 were found to be taxable. The tax revenue from these amounted to $27,663,929. For the year 1918 the revenue amounted to $13,296,927. The tax was a disappointment as a revenue producer, owing chiefly to the

TAXATION IN THE UNITED STATES

liberal allowances that were made for depreciation. As the duration of the war was uncertain, a large amount of the capital investment for expansion of existing plants or the building of new ones was charged up against costs. This rendered taxable profits much smaller than would have been the case in a normal business and accounts for the large number of exemptions of firms which made returns.

The fourth title of the Act of September 8, 1916, raised the taxes on wines and imposed special excise taxes on manufacturers of tobacco, cigars, and cigarettes, ship brokers, and corporate capitalization. The special corporation excise tax was 50 cents for each $1,000 of the " fair value " of the capital stock, but a deduction of $99,000 of capitalization was allowed. The so-called war revenue taxes levied under the emergency Act of October 22, 1914, were repealed.

Within six months after the Act of September 8, 1916, was passed, it was amended. On February 1, 1917, diplomatic relations with Germany were severed, and it appeared probable that war would follow, if no change were made by Germany in her submarine warfare. It became necessary, therefore, to provide adequate revenues for all eventualities. The Act of March 3, 1917, was accordingly passed, which bore the significant title, " An Act To provide increased revenue to defray the expenses of the increased appropriations for the Army and Navy and the extension of fortifications and for other purposes."

A novel and important feature of this Act was the segregation of the larger part of the revenues to be raised under its provisions for the purposes named in the title and for no other. Preparedness was thus to be financed by the taxes provided for. The first of these was the excess profits tax, which was levied in addition to existing taxes upon the net incomes of all corporations and partnerships having an income of more than $5,000, such tax to be at the rate of eight per cent. per annum upon the profits in excess of eight per cent. As the rate of the existing corporation income tax was two per cent. on the net income, a corporation whose profits exceeded eight per cent. for the year and were not less than $5,000 would be subject to a combined tax of 10 per cent. The Act was made effective from January 1, 1917, but because of the short time intervening between the date of approval of the Act and the end of the fiscal year, the entire amount of revenue collected under its provisions by June 30 amounted to only $2,953. This Act was superseded by that of October 3, 1917, which was made to apply to the whole calendar year 1917

The rates of the estate and inheritance taxes prescribed by the Act of September 8, 1916, were increased 50 per cent. under the Act of March 3, 1917. The rates therefore ran from 1½ per cent. on net estates not exceeding $50,000 up to 15 per cent. on estates in excess of $5,000,000. The revenue collected under this Act for the year 1917 amounted to $47,452,879.

On April 6, 1917, Congress declared that because of repeated acts of aggression on the part of Germany, a state of war existed between that country and the United States. The immediate needs of the Treasury for war purposes were met by issues of certificates of indebtedness and by the flotation of the First Liberty Loan, but Congress at once set to work to frame a revenue measure that would bring in returns adequate

TAXATION IN THE UNITED STATES

to finance the war costs which the United States had assumed. The War Revenue Act of October 3, 1917, which was passed to provide the necessary revenues, was estimated to yield $3,400,000,000 for the fiscal year ending June 30, 1918.[12] The actual yield for the fiscal year in which it was enacted was $3,696,043,485.[13] This Act contained some 12 titles, the most important of which were those dealing with the income and the excess profits taxes, though resort was now had on a considerable scale to internal revenue and excise taxes. On the whole, however, the burden of the new revenue law took the form of direct taxation, rather than of indirect.[14]

The income tax provisions left the Act of September 8, 1916, in full force, and in addition imposed new rates, so that the total tax to which the income taxpayer under the new Act was liable was a combination of two rates. Exemptions under the new law were $1,000 for single persons and $2,000 for married. An additional exemption of $200 was allowed for each dependent child. The normal tax, which applied to all net incomes above the exemption, was two per cent. under the new law, and was in addition to the normal tax under the old law; thus the normal tax on an unmarried person without dependents was two per cent. on income above $1,000 and under $3,000, and four per cent. on all income above $3,000. Considerable unnecessary complications and confusion were occasioned by this superimposition of the war income tax upon the former income tax, instead of combining them into one single tax. The

---
[12] Report of the Secretary of the Treasury, 1917, p. 71.
[13] *Ibid.*, 1918, p. 126.
[14] Indirect taxes yielded the following proportion of total tax revenues: 89 per cent. in the fiscal year 1914, 60 per cent. in 1917, and 24 per cent. in 1918.

reason may possibly have been the belief on the part of Congress that the war income tax was only a temporary measure and that it could later be repealed without disturbing the existing rates.

As a result of much agitation, the so-called method of "information at the source" was substituted for "collection at the source" in cases where payments above the tax-exempt minimum were involved. Collection at the source, however, continued to apply to non-resident aliens.

In addition to the normal tax, surtaxes were imposed upon all net incomes over $5,000, which were levied in addition to those provided for under the Act of September 8, 1916. The combined rates, therefore, ranged from one per cent. on net incomes between $5,000 and $7,500 up to 63 per cent. on incomes over $2,000,000. The rates on the various income groups are shown below:

Surtax on net income between—	Law of September 8, 1916, per cent.	Law of October 3, 1917, per cent.	Total surtax, per cent.
$ 5,000 and $7,500	None	1	1
7,500 and 10,000	None	2	2
10,000 and 12,500	None	3	3
12,500 and 15,000	None	4	4
15,000 and 20,000	None	5	5
20,000 and 40,000	1	7	8
40,000 and 60,000	2	10	12
60,000 and 80,000	3	14	17
80,000 and 100,000	4	18	22
100,000 and 150,000	5	22	27
150,000 and 200,000	6	25	31
200,000 and 250,000	7	30	37
250,000 and 300,000	8	34	42
300,000 and 500,000	9	37	46
500,000 and 750,000	10	40	50
750,000 and 1,000,000	10	45	55
1,000,000 and 1,500,000	11	50	61
1,500,000 and 2,000,000	12	50	62
Over $2,000,000	13	50	63

TAXATION IN THE UNITED STATES

It will be seen that as a result of these changes the minimum exemption limit was considerably reduced, though it still stood far above the minimum exemption permitted under the income tax laws of any other country. At the same time the rate of the normal tax was doubled. But perhaps the most important change, and the one which most affected the revenue producing character of the law, was the changes that were made in the surtaxes. The minimum income subjected to the surtax was reduced from $20,000 to $5,000, which, according to the tax returns of the preceding year, must have subjected something over 200,000 taxpayers to the operation of the surtaxes. These changes constituted a material improvement, for the tax was now no longer confined to a small group of wealthy taxpayers, but reached down into the lower income groups. At the same time, the progression of the rates was tremendously steepened, so that the highest rate on incomes over $2,000,000, which under the old law had been 13 per cent., was now made 50 per cent. under the new law, thus giving a combined rate on the larger incomes of 63 per cent. As a result of these changes, the income tax had become a real war income tax.

The rates of the surtax were now the highest levied in any country in the world, but their severity was greatly mitigated by the exemptions granted under the various Bond Acts and the constitutional provisions controlling the taxation of state and municipal bonds in the United States. The result was that the amount of taxable income that a given individual possessed was determined not merely by its size, but also by its character. The purpose of Congress to have the rates progress according to amount of income was, therefore, partially defeated, or at any rate rendered uncertain.

WAR COSTS AND THEIR FINANCING

Although this was a defect resulting from the exemption of bonds from taxation, the application of the principle of progression was sound from the point of view both of justice and of obtaining the largest possible amount of revenue. If use was to be made primarily of direct taxation for war purposes, it was evident that great reliance would have to be placed upon the income tax.

The war excess profits tax formed, together with the income tax, the bulwark of revenue during the war.[15] The tax imposed by the Act of October 3, 1917, superseded that of the previous law of March 3; it levied a tax upon the income of every corporation, partnership, and individual, and applied to all trades, businesses and occupations with certain specified exceptions. The tax was levied for each taxable year upon the net income in excess of a certain deduction at the following rates:

EXCESS PROFITS TAX (ACT OF OCTOBER 3, 1917)

If profits from invested capital above deductions are	Rate on Taxable Net Income is
Below 15 per cent.	20 per cent.
15 to 20 per cent.	25 per cent.
20 to 25 per cent.	35 per cent.
25 to 33 per cent.	45 per cent.
Over 33 per cent.	60 per cent.

The taxable year was defined to be 12 months ending December 31, 1917, and each calendar year thereafter, or the fiscal year of the taxpayer. The pre-war period included the calendar years 1911 to 1913, or as many of them as the taxpayer was engaged in business. The deduction from net income was carefully defined, and was differentiated for the three cases of (1) a domestic resident taxpayer in business during the whole pre-war

---

[15] The income and excess profits taxes constituted 44.4 per cent. of the entire collections of internal revenue in 1917, and 76.8 per cent. in 1918 (Report of the Secretary of the Treasury, 1918, p. 371).

TAXATION IN THE UNITED STATES

period; (2) one in business during a part only of the pre-war period; and (3) a foreign or non-resident taxpayer. In the first case the deduction consisted of between seven and nine per cent. of the invested capital plus $3,000 in the case of a domestic corporation and $6,000 in the case of a domestic partnership or individual. In the second case the percentage was fixed at eight per cent. and the lump-sum exemption remained the same. In the third case the exemption was the same as for the domestic corporation or individual but without the lump-sum exemption. In the case of a trade or business having no invested capital, or not more than a nominal capital, there was a flat tax of eight per cent. of the net income in excess of $3,000 in the case of a domestic corporation and $6,000 in the case of a domestic partnership or resident of the United States. Net income and invested capital were further defined.

The excess-profits tax proved a great fiscal success, the 1917 yield as shown in the returns for the year ending June 30, 1918, being as follows:

Individual excess profits tax	$88,731,080
Partnership excess profits tax	93,125,653
Corporate excess profits tax	2,045,713.085
Total	$2,227,569,818

In commenting upon this tax the Committee on War Finance of the American Economic Association[16] made the following observation:

At a time when revenue was a paramount consideration, this result is greatly to the credit of the tax, and, considered in a broad way, is ample justification of its enactment. When

---
[16] Report, printed as Supplement No. 2 of the American Economic Review, March, 1919, p. 15.

this is said, however, praise must end, and criticism begin; for it appears certain that the success of the tax was due not so much to the manner in which the law was drawn, as to the skill and good judgment of the internal revenue department in administering the Act and to the loyalty of the taxpayers in complying as best they could with the crude, obscure and, in many ways, harsh and unequal revenue measure.

The criticisms contained in this valuable report were admirably summed up by the chairman of the committee, and from his summary the following brief extract may be quoted:[17]

The law undertook to levy the tax at rates varying with the percentage which the taxable income bears to the invested capital. Statistics show, as might have been expected, that the tax collected bore no necessary relation to war profits, and imposed much heavier rates upon small, than upon large, concerns. . . . Great difficulties have been encountered in administering the present law in defining invested capital, especially in connection with capital invested in nontaxable securities; in the case of borrowed capital in cases where corporations had issued stock for the purchase of tangible property; in connection with value of good will, and in the provision made for patents and copyrights. In the definition of income also, several difficulties have risen, especially in connection with the limitation of deductions, on account of salaries actually paid in the case of profits which fluctuate from year to year; in the case of industry carried on with different degrees of risk and different degrees of stability, and in the case of net income in excess of the specific exemptions. Other great difficulties appeared in connection with the determination of nominal capital. In fact, had it not been for the administrative discretion exercised by the internal revenue department which went to the extreme limit, and perhaps even transcended the limit, in interpreting the law, the results would have been far more unsatisfactory than was actually the case.

[17] *Ibid.*, p. 120.

TAXATION IN THE UNITED STATES

The war estate or inheritance tax was contained in the ninth title of the Act, but may best be described with the two foregoing taxes, as it was a direct tax and fell upon large wealth. It was superimposed upon the estate tax of the Act of September 8, 1916, as amended by the Act of March 3, 1917, in the same way as the income tax was superimposed upon the earlier one. It will be remembered that the original Act had levied a tax ranging from one per cent. on net estates not in excess of $50,000 to 10 per cent. on estates in excess of $5,000,000, and that these rates had been increased 50 per cent. by the Act of March 3, 1917. A similar addition was now decreed by this measure, so that the total rates were double those of the original law. But in addition to this, three new groups were added at the top of the list upon which still higher rates were imposed, so that as the law finally stood, the highest rate was 25 per cent. on estates over $10,000,000. The original exemption of $50,000 was continued in this Act. The combined rates as they stood after the passage of the law of October 3, 1917, were as follows:

INHERITANCE TAX, ACT OF OCTOBER 3, 1917

Net Taxable Estate	Total Rate, per cent.
Under $50,000	2
$50,000 to 150,000	4
150,000 to 250,000	6
250,000 to 450,000	8
450,000 to 1,000,000	10
1,000,000 to 2,000,000	12
2,000,000 to 3,000,000	14
3,000,000 to 4,000,000	16
4,000,000 to 5,000,000	18
5,000,000 to 8,000,000	20
8,000,000 to 10,000,000	22
Over 10,000,000	25

The Act went into effect immediately upon its passage,

WAR COSTS AND THEIR FINANCING

so that the revenues derived during the calendar year 1917 from the Federal estate tax were obtained under three separate enactments. It is not possible to trace the effects of changes in legislation upon the yield, but the total revenues from this source for the year aggregated $47,452,879.

Titles III and IV of the Act provided for increased taxes on beverages and tobacco. The rates on distilled spirits were increased from $1.10 per gallon to $3.20 when used for beverage purposes and $2.20 when used for other purposes. The rates on beer and wine were doubled, and new taxes were laid upon soft drinks. Instead of a flat rate of $3.00 per thousand on cigars, a progressive scale was introduced which was graduated according to the selling price. The rates on cigarettes and manufactured tobacco were also considerably increased. In view of the needs of the Treasury, the advances in the rates on these articles, which had the advantage of being semi-luxuries and of yielding very large returns, must be regarded as very moderate. The result of the increases, as shown in the receipts for the fiscal year ending June 30, 1918, was an increase from $387,000,000 to $600,000,000 in the revenues from liquors and tobacco.

A new set of taxes was provided for in the next section of the Act, namely, war taxes on facilities furnished by public utilities and insurance. These consisted of taxes varying from three to 10 per cent. on freight charges, passenger fares, Pullman tickets, and pipe-line transportation, and of stamp taxes ranging from one cent on express packages to five cents on telegraph and telephone messages. Taxes on fire, marine, and casualty insurance of one cent per $1 of premium, and on life insurance of eight cents per $100 of policy,

TAXATION IN THE UNITED STATES

were also levied. Excise taxes, too, were imposed upon a number of articles of luxury; these paralleled very closely the English procedure along this line, the purpose of which was not merely to fill the Treasury, but also to curtail extravagance and useless expenditure. They covered automobiles, automobile trucks, and motorcycles, musical instruments, motion-picture films, jewelry, sporting goods, patent medicines, perfumes, cosmetics and toilet preparations, chewing gum, cameras, and boats and yachts. These were really excise taxes levied upon the manufacturer or importer; for the most part they amounted to between two and three per cent. of the price.

The growing popularity of motion-picture shows was probably responsible for the inclusion within this Act of a war tax on admissions and dues, both of which were new as Federal taxes in the United States. A tax on admissions of one cent for every 10-cent charge was imposed. Club dues were also taxed 10 per cent. if in excess of $12 a year. The stamp taxes provided for in the Act of October 22, 1914, were practically reënacted. The rate on playing cards, however, was raised from two cents to seven cents, and a new tax of one cent for each 25-cent charge was imposed on parcel-post packages.

The yield from all of the various taxes just enumerated amounted to $952,000,000 for the fiscal year 1918, which was an increase of $311,000,000, or 33 per cent., over the preceding year. This increase was in spite of a fall of $46,000,000 in customs duties. It may be pointed out in this connection that no attempt had as yet been made to impose any taxes upon the more necessary articles of general consumption among the masses, such as tea, coffee, cocoa, sugar, and similar articles.

WAR COSTS AND THEIR FINANCING

The expenditures of the United States for the month of October, 1917, that in which the Revenue Act was passed, amounted to $465,000,000. From this time on, as the military operations expanded, the expenditures increased at an extraordinarily rapid rate and far outran the revenue capacity of the tax measures. By September, 1918, the monthly expenditures were $1,625,000,000, or almost four times as great as they had been a year before. If the Treasury policy of paying a proportion of approximately one-third of the expenditures out of taxes was to be continued, it was evident that new sources of revenues must be tapped and old ones made more lucrative. The tax revenues amounted to no more than $4,173,800,000 for the year ending June 30, 1918.

In May, President Wilson urged the matter upon the attention of Congress, and in June the Secretary of the Treasury, in a letter to Claude Kitchin, Chairman of the House Committee on Ways and Means, stated that the expenditures for the coming fiscal year would probably amount to $24,000,000,000, and suggested that one-third of this amount should be provided for out of revenue. In accordance with this suggestion, a bill was presented to the House of Representatives on September 3, 1918, which it was estimated would raise this amount. The bill was promptly passed by the House, but while it was under consideration by the Senate Committee on Finance, hostilities were brought to an abrupt close by the signing of the Armistice on November 11. As a result of this event, the estimates of expenditures of the Government were reduced from $24,000,000,000 to $18,000,000,000 for the fiscal year, and the taxes provided for under the new Act were therefore cut down from $8,000,000,000 to $6,000,000,-

TAXATION IN THE UNITED STATES

000, still preserving the ratio of one-third. "Taxes which can be easily borne amid the feverish activity and patriotic fervor of war times are neither so welcome nor so easily sustained amid the uncertainties, the depreciating inventories, and the falling market which are apt to mark the approach of peace," said Senator Simmons, the Chairman of the Committee on Finance, in reporting the bill to the Senate on December 6, 1918.

Owing to the military and political changes which occurred while the bill was under consideration and to party differences in the two houses of Congress, the bill did not become law until February 24, 1919. In spite of the date of its final enactment, however, the measure is officially known as the "Revenue Act of 1918." As finally enacted, the law provided for raising about $6,000,000,000, of which about four-fifths was to be derived from income, war excess profits, and estate taxes, and the remainder from indirect taxes which fell for the most part upon luxuries and semi-luxuries. Few new sources of revenue were added to the list comprised in the earlier Acts. The Act of February 24, 1919, practically codified the earlier measures, repealing their revenue sections,[18] and introducing numerous amendments.

The changes made in the income tax were numerous and drastic. The exemptions remained as they had been under the law of October 3, 1917, at $1,000 for a single person and $2,000 for a married person, together with $200 for each dependent person. The rate of the normal tax was fixed at 12 per cent. on the net income in excess of the exemption except that in the case of a citizen or resident of the United States the rate on the first $4,000 of such excess was six per cent. These rates applied

---
[18] Section 1400.

only to the calendar year 1918; for subsequent years the rates were fixed at eight and four per cent. respectively. There was thus provided a certain element of progression in the normal tax which was designed to ease the burden to the small income receivers with less than $5,000 or $6,000. Even with this allowance the new rates represented a notable increase over those of the previous laws.

The changes introduced in the surtaxes provided for a finer classification of income groups and less abrupt jumps in the rates than had existed under the previous Act. The point at which the surtaxes were first applied remained the same, namely, $5,000; from one per cent. on incomes of this size the rates progressed very steadily, at the rate of one per cent. on each additional $2,000, on incomes up to $100,000, after which the progression was less regular, reaching a maximum of 65 per cent. on incomes over $1,000,000. Under the previous rate the highest surtax had been 63 per cent. on incomes over $2,000,000. These changes must be regarded as a great improvement from the point of view of a scientific and equitable adjustment of rates, as well as from the point of view of lucrativeness.[19]

The income tax on corporations was fixed at 12 per cent. for the calendar year 1918 and at 10 per cent. for subsequent years, on the net income in excess of the credits allowed. These credits comprised (1) the amount received as interest upon obligations of the United States; (2) the amount of excess profits taxes imposed under this same Act; and (3) in the case of a domestic corporation, $2,000 additional.

The rates provided for under this Act were made to

---

[19] A table of rates and of income groups will be found in Appendix.

TAXATION IN THE UNITED STATES

apply to incomes received during the year 1918. In consideration of the fact that the rates were so high and that the payments under this law would be so heavy, the Treasury for the first time adopted the sensible procedure of permitting the income tax to be paid in four quarterly installments, of which the first fell due in March and the second in June. Final statistics of the yield from the income and excess profits taxes for 1919 and 1920 have not yet been published, but the following are the preliminary estimates of the Treasury Department for these two years, together with the actual returns from these two sources for the fiscal year 1918:

INCOME AND EXCESS PROFITS TAXES, 1918–1920

	1918	1919*	1920*
Individual income tax............	$615,008,503	$901,000,000	$1,400,000,000
Corporation income tax......	48,175,985	400,000,000	650,000,000
Excess profits tax	....	1,300,000,000	1,700,000,000
	$663,184,488	$2,601,000,000	$3,750,000,000

*The actual receipts of the Treasury were greater than these figures owing to the payment in these years of back taxes.

The 1919 Act greatly changed and distinctly improved the excess profits tax. In this measure it was styled "war profits and excess profits" tax, and a distinction between war profits and excess profits was established. Individuals and partnerships were relieved from the excess profits tax, and the Act also permitted deduction of losses in transactions not directly connected with trade or business and removed the limitation upon the deduction of interest upon indebtedness. As in the former Act, invested capital formed the basis of all computation. More careful definitions were given of such terms as "net income," "invested capital," "tangible and intangible property," "inadmissible assets," and special provision was made for exceptional cases, for reorganizations, and for difficulties in interpreting the law. After invested capital was determined, net incomes must be calculated according to prescribed rules.

Excess profits and war profits were differentiated and subjected to slightly different treatment. In the former, a deduction of $3,000 and eight per cent. net income on invested capital was allowed to the taxpayer before division with the Government. In the latter, a deduction of $3,000 was allowed, and in addition an amount equal to 10 per cent. net income on invested capital, or, average pre-war net income on invested capital and 10 per cent. on any additional invested capital used in the taxable year. Fine distinctions were drawn in the matter of differentiating between pre-war net income and taxable year net income for corporations coming into being since pre-war days, but, broadly speaking, the legislative intent was to declare normal profits due to the taxpayer to be $3,000 and eight per cent. income on his investment, and in war industry, $3,000 and 10 per cent. on his investment. The excess over these deductions was taxed by the Government in the following percentages:

(1) 30 per cent. between exemption and 20 per cent. on invested capital;
(2) 65 per cent. over 20 per cent. on invested capital;

TAXATION IN THE UNITED STATES

(3) 80 per cent. on the excess net income above the exemption, less the sums paid as taxes under (1) and (2).

This rate applied for the calendar year 1918, but for 1919 and thereafter the above 30 per cent. rate is reduced to 20 per cent., and the 65 per cent. rate is reduced to 40 per cent. Profits on United States war contracts were subject to special taxation computations. The severity of these rates, however, was modified by a provision fixing the maximum ratio of the tax to net income. It was provided that the tax imposed should in no case be more than 30 per cent. of the amount of the net income between $3,000 and $20,000 plus 80 per cent. of the net income in excess of $20,000.

The estate or inheritance tax was remodeled by increasing the number of classes, a change which had the effect of reducing the rates on net estates between $750,000 and $2,000,000. In other respects the Act was substantially the same as that of October 3, 1917.[20]

The next seven titles of the Act dealt with taxes on transportation and other facilities and on insurance, beverages, cigars, tobacco, and manufacturers thereof, admissions and dues, excise taxes, special taxes, and stamp taxes. The tax on transportation, on freight and express, and on tickets was unchanged but the rate on Pullman tickets was reduced from 10 to eight per cent. The rate of the tax on telephone, telegraph, and cable messages between 15 and 50 cents remained at five cents, but a new tax of 10 cents was imposed when the charge was over 50 cents. A new tax of 10 per cent. was also imposed for leased wires. It was estimated that with these changes the revenue from the telephone and telegraph taxes would be raised from $6,000,000 to

---

[20] The rates and groups are shown in Appendix.

WAR COSTS AND THEIR FINANCING

$16,000,000. No changes were made in the insurance taxes as provided in the law of October 3, 1917.

The tax on alcoholic liquors possesses only an academic interest in view of the ratification of the prohibition amendment to the Federal Constitution. Originally expected to provide over a billion dollars of revenue, the estimate was later reduced to half this sum. As finally enacted, the rate on distilled spirits was doubled if withdrawn for beverage purposes, being raised from $3.20 to $6.40 a gallon, but on spirits for non-beverage purposes the rate remains at $3.20. On still wines with less than 24 per cent. of alcohol the rates were doubled, as they were on sparkling wines, artificially carbonated waters, cordials, etc.; on still wines with over 24 per cent. of alcohol the rate remained the same. Other changes were made in the taxes on soft drinks and mineral waters. But the most important provision, not so much from the standpoint of revenue as because of the annoyance it has caused, was the tax of one cent on each 10-cent purchase at a soda fountain. The rates of the tax on cigars were raised about 50 per cent., and at the same time a slight reclassification of the retail price was made. A similar increase was imposed upon cigarettes.

The rates of the tax on admissions were practically the same as in the previous Act, though some additional provisions were inserted, which exacted heavier rates from scalpers, from admissions to roof gardens and cabarets, and on purchases of food where no admission was charged. The rate of the tax on club dues remained unchanged at 10 per cent., but it was now imposed on dues over $10 a year.

The excise taxes provided for in Title IX were divided by the Act into three parts; the first covered articles the tax on which was to be paid by the manufacturer or importer; the second, those on which the tax was to be paid by the purchaser; and the third, those on which the tax was to be paid by the dealer. In the first group were included most of the articles that had been taxed under the Act of 1917, such as automobiles, musical instruments, sporting goods, and cameras; but on all of these, except automobile trucks, the rates were considerably raised. A number of other articles was added to this group, such as firearms, hunting knives, electric fans, thermos bottles, slot machines, liveries, hunting and riding habits, fur garments, and toilet soaps.

The taxes on retail sales, which constituted the second group, followed the line of the luxury taxes introduced by France and England.[21] There was included under this head a miscellaneous assortment of excise taxes, some of which had been imposed under the previous Act, but which was now greatly enlarged by the addition of a number of nonessentials and luxuries. There was evidently a double purpose back of this provision of the Act, one to obtain revenue and the other to check extravagance by taking toll of those who spent money on superfluities or on unnecessarily costly articles.

A tax of 10 per cent. was imposed on prices in excess of specified minima, in the case of carpets, rugs, picture frames, trunks, valises, ladies' purses, lamps, umbrellas, fans, smoking jackets, waistcoats, hats, footwear, neckwear, silk stockings, men's shirts, nightgowns, and kimonos. Another small group of articles, evidently regarded as pure luxuries, were taxed a certain percentage irrespective of their price, such as jewelry, precious stones, ivory ornamented articles, watches, etc.

---

[21] See E. L. Bogart, "Luxury Taxes," in *The Bulletin of the National Tax Association*, June, 1919, p. 237.

WAR COSTS AND THEIR FINANCING

Finally, the third group of taxes, to be paid by dealers, included motion picture films, toilet articles, and medicinal compounds.

The luxury tax, like the excess profits tax, has been one of the new fiscal results of the war, but it has not commended itself in the same degree as the latter. Great Britain has already permitted her luxury tax to lapse after about six months of operation; France seems likely to retain hers, as it suits the national genius better than does the same tax in Anglo-Saxon countries. In the United States President Wilson had already urged the repeal of the tax on retail sales in his message to Congress of May 20, 1919. It is unlikely that this tax will be retained very long in our revenue system.

Under the title "Special Taxes" provision was made for an excise tax on corporations, brokers, proprietors of theatres, circuses, bowling alleys, auto carriers, etc. A penal tax of $1,000 was also imposed on brewers, distillers, and liquor dealers carrying on business in prohibition territory. Manufacturers of tobacco, cigars, and cigarettes were also taxed under this section, at rates distinctly higher than those levied under the existing legislation. Finally, the old tax of $1 a year on manufacturers or distributors of opium was superseded by a comprehensive tax on importers, manufacturers and sellers of opium and other habit-forming drugs. An excise tax of $120 per year was imposed on wholesalers; $24 a year on importers, manufacturers, or producers; $6 on retailers; and $3 a year on doctors, dentists, and others who used the drug in their profession. In addition to these excises, a further tax of one cent per ounce was levied upon the drugs themselves. If any criticism is to be made of this tax, it is that the rates were not sufficiently heavy.

TAXATION IN THE UNITED STATES

Stamp taxes were practically the same as provided for under the Act of 1917, though a few increases in existing rates were made.

The revenues of the Government by the main groups of sources, exclusive of postal receipts, have been as follows for the period of the war in Europe:

REVENUES OF THE UNITED STATES, FISCAL YEARS 1914-1919
(In millions)

Source	1914	1915	1916	1917	1918	1919
Customs	$292.3	$209.3	$213.2	$225.7	$182.8	$183.4
Income and profits	71.4	80.2	124.9	359.7	2,838.9	2,600.7
Miscellaneous internal revenue	308.7	335.4	384.7	449.7	857.0	1,239.5
Sales of public lands	2.6	2.2	1.8	1.9	1.9	1.4
Miscellaneous	59.7	70.8	54.8	81.2	293.2	622.5
Total	$734.7	$697.9	$779.4	$1,118.2	$4,173.8	$4,647.5

In addition to the revenue provisions already enumerated, the Act of 1918 included a provision which was designed to prevent the employment of child labor. Under the name of a tax a wholesome penalty in the form of a forfeiture of 10 per cent. of the net profits was imposed on any mine or quarry in which children under 16 are employed; and on any mill, cannery, workshop, factory, or manufacturing establishment in which children under 14 are employed, or children between 14 and 16 are employed more than eight hours a day, or between 7 p. m. and 6 a. m. Heavy penalties were provided for the evasion of this provision. In view of the fate that overtook the previous Federal Child Labor Act, it is doubtful whether this provision will be able to stand the constitutional tests. Already a test case has been brought which is designed to determine the validity of the Act. Appeals have been filed from Federal court decrees in North Carolina which held that section of the statute invalid.[22]

[22] *Washington Post*, May 26, 1919.

CHAPTER X

HOW SHOULD A WAR BE FINANCED? THE LESSON OF THE
CIVIL WAR

The problem of financing the Civil War — Chase's loan policy —
Inadequacy of taxation — Issue of legal tender notes — System of short term loans — Bond acts — Conclusions — Financial management of the World War — Inability to meet current charges — Loans vs. taxes — Arguments for a loan policy — Disadvantages of heavy taxation — Arguments for a tax policy — Evils of excessive loans.

It has been said that each generation learns only from its own experience and frequently repeats the mistakes of past ages. The financial management of the World War inclines one to believe this statement, for it has been necessary to thresh over again many old problems, and in not a few particulars there has been a repetition of earlier mistakes. A common experience in all great wars has been the belief that the particular struggle would be short-lived. It was expected that the Civil War would be over in a few months,[1] and in the late war there were expressions of opinion from various quarters, otherwise well informed, to the same effect.[2] To this belief and the consequent inadequate realization of present needs must be ascribed many of the failures of war finance. Because of this view Secretary Chase developed his insufficient and disastrous loan policy in the Civil War, and in the late war the hope of the speedy collapse of the Central Powers, so assiduously promulgated by a willing press, undoubtedly affected the fisca'

[1] "Report on the Finances," 1861, p. 21.
[2] See ch. ii, *supra; cf.* also A. D. Noyes, *Financial Chapters of the War,* p. 16ff.

policies of the leading Entente belligerents. As the financing of the World War has been overwhelmingly by means of loans, the financial conduct of the Civil War, upon which history has already rendered its verdict, has a peculiar interest and offers some valuable lessons.

The two main problems that were presented in the financing of the Civil War were, first, to determine the proper proportion between loans and taxes, and, second, to decide how best to raise the necessary funds by the method chosen. It is the purpose of the following pages to suggest that on both of these points serious mistakes were made.[3]

The financial management of the Civil War was inspired and directed primarily by Salmon P. Chase, who was Secretary of the Treasury from March, 1861, to July, 1864, and to him must be given the praise or blame for its conduct. The financial situation of the Treasury when Chase assumed office was disheartening.[4] Under Buchanan's administration the debt had been increased by $18,000,000, bringing it up to $74,985,000; the revenues had fallen off, and the public credit was undermined. The last issue of Treasury notes for $5,000,000 had been issued at 12 per cent. interest.[5] It was estimated on January 18, 1861, by John A. Dix, then Secretary of the Treasury, that it would be neces-

---

[3] This account is taken from a paper read at a conference of the Wes'ern Economic Society at Chicago on June 21, 1917, and printed under the title, "Lessons from Our Past: The Financial Management of the Civil War," in *Financial Mobilization for War*, pp. 68-84; it is now reprinted with the permission of the editor.

[4] "A more difficult position than that of Secretary Chase at this moment few men have ever been placed in." (Appleton's *American Annual Cyclopaedia*, 1861, "Finances of the U. S.," p. 395.)

[5] Bolles, *Financial History of the United States*, iii, p. 5.

HOW SHOULD A WAR BE FINANCED

sary to raise $44,077,525 to meet outstanding and accruing dues before the close of the present fiscal year.[6] The Treasury was all but empty, the available funds amounting only to $1,716,000, and until Congress met for new legislation, Chase was forced to rely upon previous loan acts, under which authority existed for negotiating loans and for issuing Treasury notes to a total amount of about $41,000,000. On March 22, Chase advertised a loan of $8,000,000 at six per cent. and received bids aggregating $27,182,000 and ranging from 85 per cent. to 100 per cent. Right here Chase made his initial mistake in the financial conduct of the Civil War, for he refused all offers under 94. By this act he was able to sell only $3,099,000 and was accordingly forced to issue the balance of $4,901,000 in Treasury notes. These Treasury notes were not Government paper money; they were made payable to the order of the person who received them, were transferable by indorsement, bore interest at six per cent., were convertible into bonds, and receivable in payment of all public dues. They were thus short-time notes, like I. O. U.'s of an impecunious debtor, and should have been reserved for pressing emergencies. It was certainly a bad principle to issue them at the beginning of a war, and their use undoubtedly helped to undermine public credit, for they fell due while the Government was borrowing other sums.[7] On April 12, Fort Sumter was fired upon and

---

[6] Sherman, *Recollections*, i, p. 252.

[7] On this point, as on so many connected with this subject, there was difference of opinion among contemporary writers, the press being about equally divided. The *New York Times* urged the issuance of the entire sum in Treasury bills, as during the Mexican War (May 13, 1861). The action of Chase is defended among later writers by Nicholai and Hay (*Life of Lincoln*), by Shuckers (*Life of Chase*, p. 184), McCulloch (*Men and Measures of Half a Century*, p. 411), Bolles, (*op. cit.*, iii, p. 9), and others.

WAR COSTS AND THEIR FINANCING

war had now begun, an event which affected public credit unfavorably at the time. A second call on May 11 for bids for $8,994,000 worth of bonds brought in offers for $7,310,000 at prices ranging from 85 to 93, and this amount of bonds was sold, the balance of $1,684,000 being issued in Treasury notes. A third invitation for proposals for $12,584,550 resulted in only three bids, aggregating $12,000, and these were " made under misapprehension."[8] Accordingly, the whole amount was issued in Treasury notes. In addition to these resources, about $5,500,000 had been received from customs duties and small amounts from several other sources of revenue in the quarter ending June 30, but the fiscal year 1861 closed with a deficit of about $20,000,000.

The financial outlook was certainly very discouraging. The tone of the European, and especially of the English press, which with a single exception was in sympathy with the rebellious states, showed that no money could be borrowed from Europe.[9] Nor did this foreign hostility to the North cease until the war was ended. When bonds could be had at bargain prices, some were sold to German capitalists, but on the whole it was clear that the people of the loyal states would have to assume the burden of financing the war themselves.

Congress convened in special session on July 4, 1861, and Chase now submitted his plan for the conduct of the war. This was a loan policy. Taxes were to be levied sufficient to pay interest on new debt and to establish a sinking fund, but all additional expenditures were to be met by loans or by the issue of Treasury

---
[8] Bolles, *op. cit.*, iii, p. 10.
[9] McCulloch, *op. cit.*, p. 183.

HOW SHOULD A WAR BE FINANCED

notes. This policy was clearly outlined in his first war report:[10]

> To provide the large sums required for ordinary expenditures, and by the existing emergency, it is quite apparent that duties on imports, the chief resource for ordinary disbursements, will not be adequate. The deficiencies of revenue, whether from imports or other sources, must necessarily be supplied from loans and the problem to be solved is that of so proportioning the former to the latter, and so adjusting the details of both, that the whole amount needed may be obtained with certainty, with due economy, with the least possible inconvenience, and with the greatest possible incidental benefit to the people.
>
> The Secretary . . . is of the opinion that not less than eighty millions of dollars should be provided by taxation, and that two hundred and forty millions of dollars should be sought through loans.
>
> It will hardly be disputed that in every sound system of finance, adequate provision by taxation for the prompt discharge of all ordinary demands, for the punctual payment of the interest on loans, and for the creation of a gradually increasing fund for the redemption of the principal, is indispensable. Public credit can only be supported by public faith, and public faith can only be maintained by an economical, energetic and prudent administration of public affairs, by the prompt and punctual fulfillment of every public obligation.

The slight rôle to be played by taxation in the plan is not sufficiently indicated by this statement. Out of the $318,519,582 estimated to be needed, one-quarter or $80,000,000, was to be raised by taxes. Of this, about $66,000,000 would be needed for the ordinary expendi-

---
[10] Report of the Secretary of the Treasury, July 5, 1861, Senate Executive Document No. 2, 37th Congress, 1st Session, p. 2. It is interesting to note that according to this plan one-fourth of the expenditures was to be met by taxation.

301

tures of the peace establishment;[11] $9,000,000 for the payment of interest; and $5,000,000 for a sinking fund. Chase estimated that the existing customs duties would yield about $30,000,000 and that additional duties on tea and coffee, then admitted free, and on sugar, which was lightly taxed, and a slight increase on the general list of dutiable articles, would bring the total from this source up to $57,000,000.[12] Sales of public land and miscellaneous revenue might be counted on to increase this to $60,000,000. The remaining $20,000,000, he suggested, might be raised by " direct taxes, or from internal duties or excises, or from both," but he abstained from making a definite recommendation.[13] He also urged the confiscation of the property of rebels and retrenchment in expenditures by a 10 per cent. reduction upon salaries and wages paid by the Federal Government, the abolition of the franking privilege, and the reduction of postal expenses.[14]

Slight as was the resort to taxation recommended by Chase, Congress fell short even of his modest demands. The duties imposed upon coffee, tea, and sugar were lower than those urged by Chase[15] and the other changes in the tariff were unimportant. No steps were taken toward the establishment of an internal-revenue or excise system, which it will be remembered had not existed in the country since 1817, but a direct tax of $20,000,000 and an income tax were imposed.[16] As the direct tax

---

[11] That this estimate was rather low is shown by the fact that the average annual expenditures for the five years ending June 30, 1861, were $68,092,000, while for the 10 years past they were $61,488.700.

[12] Report of the Secretary of the Treasury, July 5, 1861, Senate Executive Document No. 2, 37th Congress, 1st Session, p. 8.

[13] *Ibid.*, p. 9.

[14] *Ibid.*, p. 10.

[15] " Report on the Finances," December 9, 1861, p. 10.

[16] Act of August 5, 1861, 37th Congress, 1st Session; c.xlv.

HOW SHOULD A WAR BE FINANCED

was apportioned among all the states, it was manifest that only that part of it falling upon the loyal states, to the amount of $14,846,018,[17] could be counted upon; it was, moreover, not due for eight months. The income tax of three per cent. on incomes over $800 was not to become effective for 10 months. It was quite evident, therefore, from this legislation that it was the intention both of Chase and of Congress to finance the war mainly by loans. It has been urged as an excuse for this policy that there was a general belief that the war would be over in a few months,[18] and there was also an unwillingness to create friction and opposition.[19] The duty of the Secretary of the Treasury in such a crisis, however, was to take measures that would place the Government on a sound financial footing if unhappily his optimism should prove to be unfounded.

In the part of his July report relating to the raising of $240,000,000 by loans, Chase recommended that he be authorized to sell four kinds of securities: $100,000,000 in three-year Treasury notes bearing interest at 7.30 per cent., popularly known as " seven-thirties "; $100,-000,000 in 20-year bonds bearing interest at seven per cent.; and $50,000,000 in Treasury notes of small denomination, either bearing interest at 3.65 per cent. or payable on demand in coin. These latter were known as " demand notes." In making these recommendations he added the warning:[20] " The greatest care will, however, be requisite to prevent a degradation of such issues into an irredeemable paper currency, than which no

---

[17] " Report on the Finances," 1861, p. 14.

[18] " It is earnestly hoped, and, in the judgment of the Secretary, not without sufficient grounds, that the present war may be brought to an auspicious termination before midsummer." (" Report on the Finances," 1861, p. 21.)

[19] Blaine, *Twenty Years of Congress*, i, p. 402.

[20] " Report," December 9, 1861, p. 14.

more certainly fatal expedient for impoverishing the masses and discrediting the Government can well be devised.'' In spite of this condemnation of an irredeemable paper currency, he was already laying the foundation for it by his loan policy.

These recommendations were promptly enacted into law by Congress by the Act of July 17,[21] which added a fifth kind of security to the four suggested by Chase, namely, one-year six per cent. Treasury notes in amount not to exceed $20,000,000. No bonds were to be sold under par. On August 5, a supplemental bill was passed, which provided that part of the issue of 20-year bonds might be issued at six per cent. in exchange for seven-thirty Treasury notes; these bonds could be sold below par.[22] The sixth section of this Act suspended the Independent Treasury Act of 1846 to the extent of permitting the Secretary of the Treasury to make deposits with banks.

After the battle of Bull Run on July 21, 1861, the credit of the Government fell and a popular loan was out of the question. Chase hastened to New York City, where he had a conference with the leading bankers of New York, Boston, and Philadelphia, and arranged for a loan from them of $150,000,000. The banks were to receive seven-thirty Treasury notes at par and were to advance the money to the Government in three installments of $50,000,000 each. On the other hand, the Secretary was to negotiate no other bonds or Treasury notes except the demand notes, which were being used to pay salaries.[23] In his negotiation with the banks, Chase displayed a lack of understanding both of finance

---

[21] Act of July 17, 1861, 37th Congress, 1st Session, c. v.
[22] N. A. Bayley, *National Loans of the United States*, p. 78.
[23] Bolles, *op. cit.*, iii, p. 21.

HOW SHOULD A WAR BE FINANCED

and of human nature. His own account of the interview is as follows:[24]

> I was obliged to be very firm, and to say: " Gentlemen, I am sure you wish to do all you can. I hope you will find that you can take the loans required on terms which can be admitted. If not, I must go back to Washington and issue notes for circulation; for, gentlemen, the war must go on until this rebellion is put down, if we have to put out paper until it takes $1,000 to buy a breakfast."

Threats and coercion were certainly not the methods best adapted to secure the coöperation of the banking institutions. Chase did not seem to realize that in borrowing money the Government is essentially upon the same footing as individuals, except as it may appeal to patriotism. It certainly cannot safely resort to force.

The banks accepted the decision of the Secretary and paid over their specie to the Government at the rate of about $5,000,000 a week. So large, however, were the disbursements of the Treasury and so rapid the movements of trade that the coin thus paid out was returned again to the banks for deposit in about a week. All might yet have gone well if Chase had not begun to issue demand notes again. This he had done in August, but because of the protest of the banks, had refrained while the proceeds of the loans were coming in; but now, finding himself in straits again, he resorted to their use very freely in November. As these were redeemable in coin, the banks were expected by their customers to receive them for deposit and then permit them to be drawn against in coin. In this way the coin reserves of the banks would be drained off by notes over the issue of which they could exercise no control.

---
[24] A. B. Hart, *Chase*, p. 222.

WAR COSTS AND THEIR FINANCING

The banks had met the first two payments to the Government of August and October without difficulty. In spite of the fact that they had loaned $100,000,000, their coin reserve had fallen only $5,000,000, or from $63,200,000 on August 17 to $58,100,000 on December 7. On November 16 the third installment of the loan was called for, but the specie advanced by the banks did not return freely to them as it had in the first two cases, as the channels of trade were now choked by the demand notes. During the three weeks following December 7 the New York banks lost $13,000,000 in specie. Depositors became frightened and began to withdraw funds for hoarding. In the circumstances there was no recourse but the suspension of specie payments, which was declared by the banks of the country on December 30 and speedily followed by the Government. To this result the policy of the Secretary of the Treasury contributed largely, if, indeed, was not entirely responsible therefor.

Chase's report of December, 1861, was a disappointment and did nothing to avert the crisis; in fact it injured the credit of the Government.[25] It was generally felt that the plan of borrowing from the banks and of issuing demand notes should be only a temporary makeshift until a permanent and vigorous policy of taxation could be matured. But Chase presented no such program in his report. He was forced to revise his estimates of the previous July as to tax revenues; instead of the $80,000,000 anticipated, he now estimated only $55,000,000,[26] a loss of $25,000,000, practically all of which was due to the falling off of customs duties. He

---

[25] W. C. Mitchell, in *Journal of Political Economy*, June, 1899.
[26] Report of the Secretary of the Treasury, December 9, 1861, p. 11.

HOW SHOULD A WAR BE FINANCED

realized that duties on imports could not be relied upon as a source of revenue, and recommended that the rates on sugar, tea, and coffee be raised, but "that no other alterations of the tariff be made during the present session of Congress."[27] He also urged that the direct tax be increased so as to raise $20,000,000 from the loyal states alone, and that the income tax be modified so as to yield $10,000,000. In addition to these he suggested for the first time the establishment of a system of internal duties to consist of taxes on stills and distilled liquors, on tobacco, on bank notes, on carriages, on legacies, on paper evidences of debt and instruments for conveyance of property, and other like subjects of taxation; from these sources he hoped to secure $20,000,000. Altogether he planned to raise by taxation for the fiscal year 1862 some $90,000,000, and for the fiscal year 1863 some $95,000,000. The Secretary regretted that he must ask for such large sums but felt that they were barely sufficient "to meet even economized disbursements, and pay the interest on the public debt, and provide a sinking fund for the gradual reduction of its principal."[28]

There is here no evidence of the abandonment of the loan policy or of a vigorous resort to taxation. In fact, Chase takes pains to repeat "the principles by which, as he conceives, the proportions of taxation and loans should be determined."[29] Taxes should meet the ordinary peace expenditures, interest on the debt, and a sinking fund, but all extraordinary expenses should be defrayed out of loans. "It will be seen at a glance," continues the report, "that the amount to be derived from taxation forms but a small portion of the sums

[27] *Ibid.*, p. 14.
[28] *Ibid.*, p. 15.
[29] *Ibid.*, p. 13.

307

required for the expenses of the war. For the rest, reliance must be placed on loans."[30]

One reason for Chase's unwillingness to urge heavy taxation was his belief that the people would not stand it. "He has read history to little purpose," he wrote, "who does not know that heavy taxes will excite discontent." In this respect, however, he failed to realize the loyalty and willingness of the people to support a more vigorous policy. This is illustrated by the tone of various memorials presented to Congress by commercial and scientific associations, begging that more adequate taxes be imposed. The New York Chamber of Commerce advocated that $214,000,000 be raised by excise taxes similar to those in vogue in England, and the American Geographical and Statistical Society urged the raising of $268,000,000 from internal revenue duties and $50,000,000 from customs.[31]

Congress understood better the magnitude of the struggle and the temper of the people, and instead of providing the $90,000,000 asked by Chase, passed a comprehensive internal revenue measure on July 1, 1862, which was estimated to produce an annual revenue of $150,000,000. So slow was it, however, in framing this Act that the year had slipped by before action was taken, and Chase was compelled in the interval to rely upon loans and upon issues of the new legal-tender notes. The full effects of the new Act were not felt until the fiscal year 1863-64, when it yielded $110,210,000.

The guiding principle of this measure was "the imposition of moderate duties upon a large number of objects, rather than heavy duties upon a few." It

[30] *Ibid.*, p. 16.
[31] *Ibid.*, p. 18.

was levied upon luxuries, occupations, processes, evidences of wealth, income, and legacies. "The one necessity of the situation," said D. A. Wells,[32] "was revenue, and to obtain it speedily and in large amounts through taxation; the only principle recognized, if it can be called a principle, was akin to that recommended to the traditionary Irishman on his visit to Donnybrook Fair: 'Whenever you see a head, hit it.' Whenever you find an article, a product, a trade, a profession, or a source of income, tax it." At the same time Congress revised the tariff so as to provide temporary compensatory duties in the case of those articles upon which excise taxes were laid.

In order to provide the necessary funds while these tax measures were getting under way, Congress had authorized a loan of $500,000,000 in six per cent. bonds redeemable at the pleasure of the Government after 5 years and payable after 20.[33] They were known as the "five-twenties." They could be sold at the market value, the interest was made payable in gold, and the legal tenders could be funded into them. This last provision would have resulted in an automatic contraction of the greenbacks as these depreciated, but Chase recommended its repeal,[34] which was done. Chase later admitted he had made two mistakes in the financial arrangements of the war: one, in consenting that the United States notes should be made legal tender; the other, in advising the repeal of the clause which made the notes convertible into bonds.[35] One might lengthen the list of mistakes, but no one would disagree with Chase's own characterization of these two acts.

---

[32] Cobden Club Essays, Second Series, p. 479.
[33] Act of February 25, 1862.
[34] "Report on the Finances," 1862, p. 25.
[35] McCulloch, *op. cit.*, p. 186.

WAR COSTS AND THEIR FINANCING

The loan act proved to be of little immediate assistance, for Chase interpreted the phrase " market value " to mean par value, and refused to sell the bonds below par.[36] As other securities bearing a greater rate of interest were on the market, no one would buy the five-twenties, and by December, 1862, only $23,750,000 had been sold. For his attitude on this point Chase may be sharply criticized, for by refusing to sell the bonds at their market value he was compelled to resort to further issues of legal-tender notes and to various makeshift devices. He was averse to the issue of long-time bonds[37] and made use of short-time and temporary loans of every conceivable character — certificates of deposit, certificates of indebtedness, Treasury notes, demand notes, etc.

" The whole system of short loans was an unfortunate makeshift. Since it was impossible to foresee expenses a year ahead, Chase's budgets were all estimates. What he did was to raise all the money he could, in every possible way; to refund his temporary loans into bonds, so far as he could, and then to resort to new short loans for pressing needs. When everything else failed he issued more legal tenders."[38] But Chase was still firm in his advocacy of his loan policy. " The chief reliance, and the safest," he wrote in his annual report of 1862,[39] " must be upon loans." The existing loan and legal-tender acts he thought had worked well and should be

---

[36] " Report on the Finances," 1862, p. 7.
[37] " No prudent legislator at a time when the gold in the world is increasing by a hundred millions a year, and interest must necessarily soon decline, will consent to impose on the labor and business of the people a fixed interest of six per cent. on a great debt, for 20 years, unless the necessity is far more urgent than is now believed to exist." (*Ibid.*, p. 25.)
[38] A. B. Hart, *op. cit.*, p. 242.
[39] " Report on the Finances," 1862, p. 24.

HOW SHOULD A WAR BE FINANCED

extended; he had no suggestions to make concerning further taxation.[40]

When Congress met in December, 1862, it was confronted with a deficit of $276,900,000, together with unpaid requisitions amounting to $46,400,000. Accordingly it authorized the third issue of legal-tender notes of $100,000,000 to provide for immediate needs,[41] while a new Loan Act[42] provided for $900,000,000 of six per cent. bonds redeemable after 10 and payable after 40 years, and a variety of one-year, two-year, and compound interest notes. The National Bank Act was also passed.[43] Vigorous efforts were now made to sell the five-twenty bonds, but instead of applying to the banks, Chase decided to sell them directly to the people. An experienced banker, Jay Cooke, was employed as general agent, receiving a commission of three-eighths of one per cent. on all sales; he in turn employed 2,500 subagents throughout the country, which he flooded with literature setting forth the advantages of Government bonds as investments. By these energetic methods the sales were increased to nearly $400,000,000 by December, 1863.[44] This method, however, was criticized and was not made use of by Chase in the negotiation of the next loan.[45]

In his report for December, 1863, Chase estimated the tax receipts for the fiscal year ending June 30, 1864, at $161,568,500, leaving $594,000,000 to be provided by loans.[46] The internal revenue receipts had proved very disappointing, amounting to only $38,000,000, instead

---
[40] *Ibid.*, p 10.
[41] Act of January 17, 1863.
[42] Act of March 3, 1863.
[43] Act of February 25, 1863.
[44] "Report on the Finances," 1863, p. 14.
[45] David Kinley, *Independent Treasury*, p. 106.
[46] "Report on the Finances," 1863, p. 5.

WAR COSTS AND THEIR FINANCING

of $85,000,000 as estimated, and in these some changes were suggested. It is interesting to note in this report the first intimation that the loan policy was not proving entirely satisfactory. One or two short quotations will make this point clear:[47]

> No one can be more profoundly convinced than himself [he wrote] of the very great importance of providing even a larger amount than is estimated from revenue. To check the increase of debt must be, in our circumstances, a paramount object of patriotic solicitude. The Secretary, therefore, while submitting estimates which require large loans, and while he thinks it not very difficult to negotiate them, feels himself bound, by a prudent regard to possible contingencies, to urge upon Congress efficient measures for the increase of revenue. . . .
>
> Hitherto the expenses of the war have been defrayed by loans to an extent which nothing but the expectation of its speedy termination could fully warrant. . . .
>
> These statements [estimates of receipts and expenditures] illustrate the great importance of providing, beyond all contingencies, for ordinary expenditures and interest on debt, and for the largest possible amount of extraordinary expenditures by taxation. In proportion to the amount raised above the necessary sums for ordinary demands will be the diminution of debt, the diminution of interest, and the improvement of credit. It is hardly too much — perhaps hardly enough — to say that every dollar raised for extraordinary expenditures or reduction of debt is worth two in the increased value of national securities, and increased facilities for the negotiation of indispensable loans.

Had Chase realized and acted upon this truth two years earlier many of the monetary and financial troubles in our later financial history might have been avoided.[48]

---
[47] *Ibid.*, pp. 9, 10, 12.
[48] *Cf.* H. C. Adams, *Public Debts*, p. 130.

HOW SHOULD A WAR BE FINANCED

By this time Congress, too, had come to realize the essential weakness of the loan policy and directed its energies to providing larger revenues from taxation. The great tax bills of the war were those passed in June, 1864, which provided for drastic increases in the internal revenue taxes. The revenue from this source, which was $110,210,000 for the fiscal year 1864, was thus increased to $210,660,000 in 1865 and $311,200,000 in 1866.[49]

In order to meet the immediate needs of the Treasury, Congress had authorized by Act of March 3, 1864, an issue of $200,000,000 of bonds bearing interest at not over six per cent. and redeemable in 10 to 40 years. These were popularly known as the "ten-forties." For some unaccountable reason Chase decided to issue these bonds at five per cent. interest, though the five-twenties bore six per cent. and were selling at a price to yield 5.4 per cent.[50] The result was disastrous, and bond buying nearly ceased, only $73,337,000 of the ten-forties being sold up to June 30, 1864. Expenditures, however, were increasing rapidly, and Chase was consequently forced to resort once more to short-time loans. He issued one-year and two-year notes, compound interest notes, and certificates of indebtedness. Some of these went into circulation and others were absorbed by the banks for reserves, displacing to this extent greenbacks. In either case the currency was inflated and prices raised. By some writers it has even been charged that Chase inflated the currency purposely so that he could market the ten-forties at par and not be compelled to acknowledge that he had made a mistake. His own words on this

[49] F. C. Howe, *Taxation and Taxes in the United States under the Internal Revenue System, 1791-1895*, p. 69.
[50] Hunt's *Merchants' Magazine and Commercial Review*, li (1864), p. 43.

WAR COSTS AND THEIR FINANCING

matter were as follows:[51] "The bonds do not seem to be readily taken as yet by the people. It required the printing and paying out of $400,000,000 of greenbacks before the five-twenty six per cent. bonds could be floated easily at par, and it will probably require the circulating issues of the Government, now amounting to about $625,000,000, to be increased to $650,000,000 or $700,000,000 before the people will be induced to take five per cent. bonds." Whether this allegation is correct or not, there is no doubt that this was Chase's crowning mistake, and possibly the one most costly to the country. Chase resigned as Secretary of the Treasury on June 29, 1864, for political reasons.

It is not necessary to trace the further course of Civil War financing. Under W. P. Fessenden and Hugh McCulloch a more vigorous policy of taxation was enforced, and this, coupled with military victories, had a beneficial effect upon the national finances.[52] The lessons to be derived from this brief study of our past experience may be briefly summarized as follows:

(1) The fundamental error of our Civil War finance was the dependence upon loans for all extraordinary expenditures.

(2) Resulting from this in large measure was the issue of legal-tender notes.

(3) The undue use of short term loans, amounting to 85 per cent. of all loans in the first year, and 60 per cent. for the four years of the war, tended to embarrass each subsequent operation.

---

[51] Quoted by D. R. Dewey, *Financial History of the United States*, p. 279.

[52] The ratio of taxes to loans, which had been 1:8.5 in the fiscal year June 30, 1862, was reduced to 1:3.5 in the second year of the war, to 1:3.4 in the third, and finally to 1:2.9 in the fourth year ending June 30, 1865. (C. J. Bullock, "Financing the War," in *Quarterly Journal of Economics*, xxxi, p. 363.)

HOW SHOULD A WAR BE FINANCED

(4) The attempt to issue the ten-forties at a rate of interest lower than the market.

"It appears, then," concludes H. C. Adams,[53] an able critic of our financial history, "that the history of the war of 1861 . . . bears direct testimony against the sufficiency of the loan policy."

It may be said in passing that the financing of the Spanish War in 1898 offers a refreshing contrast to the policy followed in all similar emergencies up to that time. While a loan of $200,000,000 was authorized for immediate needs, new internal revenue taxes were also imposed by the same Act, which a year later were bringing in additional revenues of $100,000,000.[54] Here we have presented the correct policy for the financial management of a war which, as H. C. Adams[55] says, should be "a tax policy assisted by credits rather than a credit policy assisted by taxes."

The lesson of the Civil War has an immediate practical bearing in the present study, for the same two inquiries may be raised regarding the financing of the World War. What was the proper proportion between loans and taxes, and, after the determination of this question, were the funds raised in the best manner by the method chosen?

There can be no doubt as to the financial policy that was pursued by all the belligerents except Great Britain and the United States. It must be characterized as an exclusive loan policy, in which not enough was raised by revenues to meet the normal budget and the interest charges on the debt. Loans were even used to pay the interest on earlier borrowings. Heavier taxes were

---
[53] *Public Debts*, p. 133.
[54] "Report on the Finances," 1900, p. 44.
[55] *Science of Finance*, p. 542.

levied, to be sure, but in no case except in the two countries named did these increase rapidly enough to meet the growing charges of the debt service and the ordinary budget, let alone make any contribution to meeting the costs of the war. Neither France, Russia, Italy, Germany, or Austria-Hungary of the major belligerents, nor Belgium, Serbia, Rumania, Bulgaria, or Turkey of the minor belligerents was able to pay a single penny toward war expenditures out of taxes. Compared with such a record the inadequacy of Chase's loan policy seems less reprehensible. The statistical facts in support of these statements are given for the six leading European belligerents in the table following.

After such a presentation the question as to whether the European belligerents should have pursued a "tax policy assisted by credits" rather than a loan policy may appear merely academic. In the case of Great Britain alone were the efforts to raise by taxation a part of the costs of the war vigorous and sustained. On the part of the Continental nations the feeling seemed to be general that the war itself constituted a sufficient burden without adding that of taxation. Germany, as has been pointed out, followed a deliberate and premeditated policy in her exclusive reliance upon loans to meet the costs of the war; when she finally began, in the third year of the war, to increase the taxes somewhat, it was too late, and she was hardly able to raise enough even to meet the interest charges on the debt, to say nothing of the civil budget. A discussion of financial policy, therefore, seems to resolve itself into the question of which was better, the British-American policy on the one hand, or that of the European Governments on the other.

Judged by the results, which is the ultimate touch-

HOW SHOULD A WAR BE FINANCED

TABLE SHOWING THE INABILITY OF EUROPEAN TAXATION TO MEET THE CIVIL BUDGET AND INTEREST CHARGES

Fiscal Year	Interest charges	Total revenues
GREAT BRITAIN		
1915.....................	$113,344,480	$1,133,470,000
1916.....................	301,246,555	1,683,835,000
1917.....................	636,252,470	2,867,140,000
1918.....................	949,255,300	3,536,175,000
1919.....................	1,332,668,000	4,445,105,000
Total.................	$3,332,766,805	$13,665,725,000
Five years' civil budget (1914, $987,464,845)....		4,937,324,225
Surplus revenue over pre-war normal expenditure		$8,728,401,775
Five years' interest charges..................		3,332,766,805
Surplus revenues over normal expenditure and interest.................................		$5,395,634,970
FRANCE		
1914.....................	$273,242,000	$796,821,386
1915.....................	379,879,000	776,794,297
1916.....................	666,603,000	963,286,447
1917.....................	972,677,000	1,261,200,000
1918.....................	1,113,570,000	1,326,800,000
Total.................	$3,405,971,000	$5,126,902,130
Five years' civil budget (1913, $1,013,386,240)...		5,066,931,200
Surplus revenue over pre-war normal expenditure		$59,970,930
Five years' interest charges..................		3,405,971,000
Deficit...................................		$3,346,000,070
RUSSIA		
1914.....................	$226,449,000	$1,449,000,000
1915.....................	240,000,000	1,397,000,000
1916.....................	298,866,000	1,457,000,000
1917.....................	371,209,000	1,870,000,000
Total.................	$1,136,524,000	$6,173,000,000
Four years' civil budget (1913, $1,547,124,000)..		6,188,496,000
Deficit of revenue to meet pre-war normal expenditure...............................		$15,496,000
Plus interest...........................		1,136,524,000
Total deficit.............................		$1,142,020,000

WAR COSTS AND THEIR FINANCING

Budgets of Principal European Nations—*Continued.*

Fiscal Year	Interest charges	Total
ITALY		
1915	$109,998,237	$609,340,114
1916	174,258,691	601,405,400
1917	254,818,892	761,000,000
1918	382,022,327	929,000,000
1919	577,000,000	971,000,000
Total	$1,498,098,147	$3,871,745,514
Five years' civil budget (1914, $632,046,000)		3,160,230,000
Surplus revenue over pre-war normal expenditure		$711,515,514
Five years' interest charges		1,498,098,147
Deficit		$786,582,633
GERMANY		
1915	$317,000,000	$851,294,375
1916	575,000,000	829,270,125
1917	890,250,000	970,729,732
1918	1,467,750,000	1,116,134,367
1919	1,975,000,000	1,533,824,194
Total	$5,225,000,000	$5,301,253,193
Five years' normal civil budget (1914, $851,294,600)		4,256,463,000
Surplus revenue over pre-war normal expenditure		$1,044,790,193
Interest charges as above		5,225,000,000
Deficit on basis of estimated revenues		$4,180,209,807
AUSTRIA-HUNGARY		
1915		$1,144,976,400
1916		1,042,847,600
1917		1,313,528,600
1918		1,732,596,400
Total		$5,233,949,000
Four years' civil budget, 1913:		
Austria	$625,811,000	
Hungary	444,360,000	
	$1,060,171,000	4,240,684,000
Surplus revenue over pre-war normal expenditure		$993,265,000
Four years' interest charges (estimated)		1,394,000,000
Deficit		$400,735,000

stone, the matter does not seem open to doubt. An exclusive loan policy might be permissible in a short and victorious struggle, especially when an indemnity was collected to meet the costs, but no financier has a right to make the success of financial measures contingent upon military strategy. The only safe plan is to prepare for a long struggle, or at least to adopt a plan that can be modified to meet new conditions as they develop. It may safely be asserted that the finances of the European Entente Allies would have broken down completely had it not been for the timely aid rendered by the United States, and that the utter financial collapse of the Central Powers was a powerful factor in their final defeat. The shortsightedness and inadequacy of the exclusive loan policy is sufficiently evidenced by these facts, and it does not seem necessary to pursue this phase of the inquiry further.

In Great Britain and the United States, however, there was a very lively controversy as to the proportion in which loans and taxes should be made to contribute to the costs of the war. Although there were a few extremists who advocated a taxation-only or loan-only program, neither of these extreme policies found any serious support. In fact, in view of the gigantic expenditures of the war, it is hardly correct to say that there was a choice between these two. It was necessary at the outset to make use of credit on a hitherto unknown scale. But at the same time, in accordance with the most approved financial practice of providing a sound basis for public credit, the scope of taxation was greatly extended. Both means of providing the necessary revenues were used. The only question open to discussion was that of the proportion in which loans and taxes should be employed. As a matter of fact, revenues

WAR COSTS AND THEIR FINANCING

provided about one-fourth of the receipts in Great Britain and about one-third in the United States. Was this enough, or should a still higher proportion have been secured from taxation? Without attempting to give a categorical answer to these questions, it will suffice to state briefly some of the arguments for and against a heavier taxation policy.

The arguments used in defense of a large use of loans were of two kinds, positive, consisting of advantages accruing from the issuance of loans, and negative, consisting of evils arising from the imposition of too heavy taxes. Perhaps the foremost argument in favor of loans, implicit if not always expressed, was that this method works; the machinery has been well developed, loans cause little resentment, are more easily obtained than an equal amount of taxes, yield large sums with a minimum of delay, and are almost indefinitely expansible.

It was also urged that since posterity will share the benefits of the war, it should also bear some of the burdens. Without discussing at this time[56] the question as to whether a nation can shift to future generations the costs of the war, it may be pointed out that if the loans can be placed abroad such a shifting may undoubtedly be effected by the borrowing nation. But if all the loans are domestic, it is impossible for the nation as a whole to shift the burden. There is no difference in effect if the Government takes savings of $1,000 by taxation or borrows it at five per cent. and then adds five per cent. in taxes, assuming that the added taxes fall upon the bondholders.

This, however, does not always prove true, and in this fact, it was said, is found another reason why loans are favored by those who determine the policy and

[56] See Chapter XI.

HOW SHOULD A WAR BE FINANCED

advance the major portion of the funds. If the taxes to meet interest charges and redeem the principal fall upon the bondholders in exact proportion to their holdings, it can make no real difference to them whether they advance the money to the Government in the first place in the form of a loan or as taxes. But the incidence of the taxes levied to amortize the loans is seldom so exact. "Experience has never yet revealed a tax system anything like as strongly graduated for increasing incomes as loan subscriptions are normally found to be, at all events when the loan required is large. Hence the rich think rightly that a loan hits them much less severely than an equivalent levy would do."[57]

To the bondholder, however, there is an advantage in buying a bond, even though his future taxes may be higher, over selling securities and paying a lump sum in taxation, for the bond is collateral and may be used for borrowing at a bank. But this so-called advantage is a two-edged sword, for by the advocate of a heavy taxation policy it is cited as a disadvantage since it leads to inflation.

The advocates of a loan policy have, on the whole, devoted most attention to attacking the proposals for heavier taxation. Of the many objections to that program perhaps the one entitled to most serious consideration was the contention that too heavy taxation would impair the incentive to effort. As the main consideration in war is the stimulation of the production of war necessities, and this is secured under our price and profit system by allowing generous rewards to the producers, financiers hesitate to impose tax burdens that

---

[57] A. C. Pigou, "The Burden of War and Future Generations," in *Quarterly Journal of Economics*, February, 1919, p. 248.

may tend to lessen production. They prefer to "play safe." Moreover, a sudden imposition of very heavy taxes seriously dislocates existing arrangements, prevents the meeting of commitments already made, and forces the abandonment of contracts.

In addition to these main arguments, but distinctly subordinate to them, the following objections were made: Heavy taxation will deplete the surplus available for investment; will cause popular resentment; will diminish the funds available for charity, education, and similar purposes; will lead to the expatriation of capital or its withdrawal from productive use; and, finally, such a program is a new and radical departure.

Turning now to the arguments of those who advocated a policy of immediate and vigorous taxation in order to raise from this source a considerable portion of the current costs of the war, it is found that they run the gamut from proposals to pay the entire cost by taxes, or to conscript all incomes over $100,000, to an insistence upon a "reasonably" heavy policy of taxation. Here again the arguments were two-fold, positive, in the advocacy of taxation, and negative, in attacks upon the loan policy.

In favor of the immediate imposition of heavy taxes that should "cut to the bone" it was urged that such a policy will check undesirable consumption; if properly framed it will discourage extravagance and the production of nonessentials, compel economy, and drive out labor from undesirable industries. As an immediate and complete mobilization of the human and material resources of a country is essential to the successful prosecution of war, a policy of heavy taxation is desirable not only for the sake of revenue but also as a war measure.

HOW SHOULD A WAR BE FINANCED

Moreover, a program of heavy taxation can best be introduced at the beginning of a war, when the demand for new capital investment has fallen off as the result of the curtailment of normal productive industry, and when, on the other hand, the immense gains from war contracts and similar activities tend to make the burden relatively less. Translating these abstract considerations into a concrete tax program, the advocates of heavy taxation approved of highly progressive income and estate taxes, excess and war profits taxes running as high as 80 and 90 per cent., and heavy consumption or excise taxes upon all nonessentials.

It was against an excessive loan policy, however, that the advocates of vigorous taxation directed most of their attacks. The major danger was recognized as inflation, and this aspect of the situation received most attention. Said A. C. Miller of the Federal Reserve Board:[58]

> The danger of the loan policy is that by deluding itself with a notion that it is putting the burden onto the future it will, through resort to fatuous and easy expedients, put the burden both on the present and the future. This will happen if the loan policy, failing to induce a commensurate increase in the savings fund of the nation, degenerates through the abuse of banking credit, into inflation — raising prices against the great body of consumers as well as against the Government, thus needlessly augmenting the public debt and increasing the cost of living just as taxes would. The policy of financing war by loans, therefore, will be but a fragile and deceptive and costly support unless every dollar obtained by the Government is matched by a dollar of spending power relinquished by the community — in other words, will fail and will develop into inflation unless the dollars which are subscribed to the bonds of the Government are real dollars, the result of real savings and of real retrenchment.

[58] "War Finance and the Federal Reserve Banks," in *Financial Mobilization for War*, p. 145.

WAR COSTS AND THEIR FINANCING

There were many who denied that the loan policy of the belligerents was responsible for the inflation and high prices that have accompanied the war; these were due, they said, to the increase of money, to scarcity of goods, or to other causes. It may be admitted that if private expenditures were cut down by an amount equal to the bonds issued for war purposes, there would be no inflation; that if the total amount of bank credit in existence were not increased, that used for the payment of bonds being offset by equivalent economies on the part of the public, there would result no inflationary effects. But this is to suppose what did not happen. The expenditures financed by the issue of bonds in fact represented an addition, and were taken up by the creation of bank credit which represented an addition, to normal transactions.

As a result of inflation, it was further argued, the Government competed with its citizens for supplies, prices were raised, the purchasing power of each successive issue of bonds was reduced, extravagance was invited, variations in incomes were caused, much unnecessary hardship was brought about, and the cost of the war was increased. It has been estimated that the cost of the Civil War was enhanced by $600,000,000 because of the issue of greenbacks. The cost of the World War must have been augmented by billions of dollars as a result of the inflation in the form both of bank notes and bank credit which has accompanied the enormous issues of bonds.

Finally, it was urged that an undue dependence upon loans complicates after-war problems; if war costs were paid out of taxes, there would be no such difficulties; that bonds are rarely bought from voluntary savings; that these must be enforced by heavy taxation; that a loan policy simply represents the mortgage of the masses to the classes, as the future taxes to redeem the bonds will almost certainly fall relatively more heavily upon the former.

The conclusion to be drawn from these opposing counsels seems to be that loans and taxes are both necessary; that the best system is the one that secures the funds from savings rather than from bank borrowings; that this is better secured by taxation than by loans; and finally, that the actual practice of the European belligerents was distinctly inflationary and inadequate. The policy of this country was to finance the war as far as seemed practicable by increased taxation and to raise the rest of the needed funds by loans. Larger sums could undoubtedly have been raised by heavier taxation, and changes in particular taxes might have been made with advantage, but conceived as a war-finance policy, that of the United States must, on the whole, be commended. The weakness lay in the enormous sums that had to be raised by means of loans and the methods pursued in securing these sums, with the attendant inflation of bank credit and rise in prices. In view of the fact that the expenditures far outran the customary annual savings of the people, it would have been impossible under any system to have paid for the war out of current savings. The best system, therefore, was that which would promote the maximum amount of saving on the part of the people while at the same time it developed the greatest possible military and economic effort toward winning the war. This end was well achieved in the United States.[59]

---

[59] For a fuller discussion of this latter point, see an article by the writer, "Economic Organization for War," in the *American Political Science Review*, November, 1920.

CHAPTER XI

FINANCING EUROPE AFTER THE WAR

Foreign trade of the United States as a belligerent — Exports and imports by regions — The balance of trade — Europe's need for capital — Greatest supplies to be found in the United States — How can this be made available — Machinery by which loans can be advanced to Europe — Proposals for the extension of short time credit — Long term credit — Conclusions.

After the entry of the United States into the war, her foreign trade was increasingly regulated and controlled for the single purpose of making it contribute to the winning of the war. Imports were restricted to commodities that were needed for war purposes, either on our own or on our allies' account. Because of the shortage of shipping they were taken for the most part from the nearest available market. Exports to non-belligerent countries, moreover, were cut down to the very minimum. Their shipment to any particular country was determined by the necessity of paying for goods purchased from that country or of securing to a friendly neutral the minimum necessary for it to maintain its customary economic activities, and towards the end of the struggle by the necessity of exerting a favorable influence upon the exchange situation. All the supplies and all the available tonnage that could be spared from domestic use and from the most pressing needs of neutral countries were diverted to the service of the Allies and our own army in Europe.

There was done in the World War what probably was never accomplished before: The foreign trade of whole

FINANCING EUROPE AFTER THE WAR

nations was used as a huge economic weapon against enemy countries and was diverted hither and yon as to serve best the Allied cause. It is not possible to describe the financing of the war without taking account of the way in which foreign trade was made to contribute directly to the success of our arms. The payment of money and the use of credit constituted, after all, only the machinery by which the title to goods and services was transferred. The basic fact was the movement of ships and supplies, of food and men as expeditiously and in as large volume as possible to points where they were needed. How successful this movement was is indicated roughly by the statistics of our foreign trade, and yet these by no means measure the whole service, for they do not include the shipments on Government account to the American Expeditionary Force abroad.

Because of our enormous sales to belligerent Europe, our exports showed a steady growth during the war, reaching a climax in the year ending June 30, 1917, when they reached the stupendous total of $6,290,048,-394. During the next year there was a slight decline, to $5,919,711,371, but a new high record of exports was set for 12 months ending June 30, 1919, with a total of $7,225,084,257. The imports showed a similar movement except that the maximum was reached in 1918. Both of these records, however, were far surpassed by the unprecedented exports and imports for 1920. As the latter increased more than the former, the excess of exports over imports was considerably reduced below that of the previous year. The following table shows the actual figures for the four years, 1917 to 1920, together with the resulting favorable balance of trade:

WAR COSTS AND THEIR FINANCING

EXPORTS, IMPORTS, AND BALANCE OF TRADE, 1917–1920

Year ending June 30	Total exports	Total imports	Excess of exports over imports
1917	$6,290,048,394	$2,659,355,185	$3,630,693,209
1918	5,919,711,371	2,945,655,403	2,974,055,968
1919	7,225,084,257	3,095,876,582	4,129,207,675
1920	8,111,176,131	5,238,746,580	2,872,429,551

Owing to the depreciation of money which was taking place, this growth in the value of foreign trade is confusing and may easily lead to false conclusions. The increase in the value of domestic exports during 1918 was 150 per cent. over that of 1914, the last pre-war year, but if the values of 1918 be reduced to the pre-war standard, the actual increase is found to be only 35.5 per cent.[1] The total figures, however, do not tell the story. It is necessary to analyze them still further and to classify our foreign trade by groups of countries. This is attempted in the following table:

DOMESTIC EXPORTS FROM THE UNITED STATES BY GEOGRAPHICAL DIVISIONS
(In millions)

	1914	1915	1916	1917	1918	1919
Europe:						
Allied	$ 922.7	$1,544.8	$2,666.1	$3,929.4	$3,605.6	$4,131.0
Enemy	367.0	30.0	.5	2.2	0.3	28.2
Neutral	181.5	369.5	305.7	392.9	126.3	475.6
Total	$1,471.2	$1,944.3	$2,972.3	$4,324.5	$3,732.2	$4,634.8
North America	509.9	455.2	702.7	1,163.8	1,236.4	1,291.9
South America	124.0	97.5	177.6	259.5	314.5	400.9
Asia	113.1	113.2	277.8	380.2	447.4	603.9
Oceania	83.3	77.4	98.2	109.3	134.9	208.4
Africa	27.8	28.4	43.4	52.7	54.3	85.2
Total	$2,329.7	$2,716.2	$4,272.2	$6,290.0	$5,919.7	$7,225.1

[1] This calculation was made by assuming a price index number of 185 for 1918, as compared with 100 for 1914.

FINANCING EUROPE AFTER THE WAR

It is clear from this table that the increase in domestic exports from the United States was due in large measure to the growth of our trade with belligerent Europe. Two-thirds of the increase that took place in the period 1914 to 1918 went to that section of the world. Between these two years the trade with the neutral countries of Europe, from which it was feared that Germany would be able to draw supplies, actually declined some 30 per cent. The growth of exports to other countries was due largely to the fact of the withdrawal of European belligerents from their customary trade, which left to this country the obligation of furnishing them with their needed supplies. If values were reduced to the 1914 basis for the year 1918, there would be recorded in most cases, not an increase, but an actual falling off in trade.

The following table shows the imports into the United States from the principal regions of the world:

IMPORTS INTO THE UNITED STATES BY GEOGRAPHICAL DIVISIONS
(*In millions*)

	1914	1915	1916	1917	1918	1919
Europe.........	$895.6	$614.3	$616.2	$610.5	$411.6	$372.9
North America.	427.4	473.1	591.9	766.1	918.3	1,052.6
South America.	222.7	261.5	391.5	542.2	567.4	568.4
Asia...........	286.9	247.8	437.2	615.2	826.2	830.9
Oceania.......	42.1	52.5	96.2	65.3	146.2	190.0
Africa.........	19.1	24.9	64.7	60.0	75.9	81.1
Total.......	$1,893.9	$1,674.2	$2,197.9	$2,659.3	$2,945.6	$3,095.9

The significant feature of the import statistics is the great falling off in imports from Europe. After the

WAR COSTS AND THEIR FINANCING

tightening of the British blockade, and especially after the entry of the United States into the war, shipments from the enemy powers ceased almost entirely, while those from the European Allies shrank to almost half of their pre-war amounts, owing to the absorption of industry in war activities and the consequent decline in exportable surplus.

It has already been pointed out (Chapter III) that as a result of the enormous sales of our commodities to Europe, by means of which we had bought back American securities held abroad, the United States had reached the position of creditor nation by the middle of the year 1917. Since that time, however, still larger trade balances have piled up. Europe and the rest of the world have now become debtor to the United States to an amount which has been estimated at about $9,000,000,000. The annual interest charge on this sum will amount to about $450,000,000. As a result of the upbuilding of our merchant marine, the sums that were previously paid to foreign shipowners for freight service will be saved. Assuming that other charges, such as tourists' expenses abroad, remittances of emigrants, commissions and insurance charges, and similar items, remain at the same level as they were before the war, though it is altogether probable that they will be lessened, the net result of the changes will be that instead of the United States being under the necessity of remitting annually to Europe some $500,000,000 to meet these various charges, we shall ourselves be in receipt of perhaps $200,000,000 to $300,000,000 a year. The United States is in fact at the present moment a creditor nation to this extent, and only the abnormal economic situation in Europe could prevent the full effects of this change from being felt. Any further

FINANCING EUROPE AFTER THE WAR

movement of trade balances in favor of the United States will still further increase the amount due annually from other countries.

If this balance were sent us at the present time, it would create an embarrassing situation in the United States, for it is desirable to maintain our exports at the present level in order to provide employment for the demobilized soldiers and to take up the slack of the after-war period. Most of the European countries, however, are taking steps to reduce their imports to the lowest possible level, so as to assist the revival of their own domestic industries, as well as to correct the unfavorable rates of exchange which are handicapping them in their purchase of needed supplies. Practically every country has prohibited the importation of luxuries and is limiting its other purchases to raw materials and machinery and equipment. But it will be necessary for Europe to continue to purchase from the United States during the next few years large quantities of foodstuffs and cotton, lumber, hides, copper, petroleum, and some coal, and also manufactured goods such as railroad equipment, agricultural machinery, and some consumable commodities.

In return for these purchases it is unlikely that Europe will be able to export any considerable amount of merchandise or goods. Some increase of exports of raw materials or semimanufactured articles may be expected from some of the European countries, and a not inconsiderable part of their indebtedness may be canceled by an increase of our imports of jute and tea from India, of tin and rubber from the Straits Settlements, of coffee from Java, of wool from Australia, and of other articles from the dependencies of European nations, the value of which might be set against our claims upon those nations themselves. There is a limit, however, to the amount of such commodities that can be spared by Europe or absorbed by our own industries or people. For the immediate future the United States must content itself with further promises to pay in the future in the form of securities of one sort or another.

Ultimately the balance in our favor will have to be liquidated by larger imports of goods. By some this is regarded as a wholly undesirable outcome, and the fear is expressed that American workmen will to that extent be deprived of an opportunity to work. The fear is an idle one. The large so-called favorable balances of trade of the two years following the entry of the United States into the war were to some extent at least the result of self-denial on the part of the American people. We denied ourselves luxuries and comforts and voluntarily imposed restrictions upon our consumption of certain foodstuffs in order that these or other supplies might be furnished the Allies in Europe. It is quite clear that this program should be continued and that the next few years must be marked by a lower standard of comfort than would be necessary if we are to attempt to help supply Europe with consumable goods for immediate use and with capital for reconstruction purposes. When this period of abstinence shall have ended, it will surely not be a matter of regret if we shall begin to collect some of the debt owing us in the form of larger imports of commodities. The national income of the American people will then be increased beyond the amount of their own production by the excess of the merchandise imports over exports.

For the immediate present, however, the United States, instead of collecting the sums due, is under the necessity of advancing still further amounts to aid in

WAR COSTS AND THEIR FINANCING

the rehabilitation and reconstruction of Europe. During the war the purchases by the Allies from this country were financed with money advanced by the United States Government. For this purpose the sum of $10,000,000,-000 was appropriated, of which some $9,700,000,000 has been lent. So long as any part of this fund remained available, no special pressure was felt by the European Governments to whom it was being loaned, as it was expected that pressing European claims could be offset against the credits in this country. But now that this fund is used up, the question presents itself as to how further exports to Europe are to be financed. The fall in the rates of foreign exchange in the European countries, which showed itself as this fund approached exhaustion, indicates the extent to which reliance had been placed upon it.

So far as the non-European countries of the world are concerned, those which were not directly affected by the war, no special problem seems to be presented, as they should be able, with the normal product of their unimpaired industries, to purchase the needed supplies. So far as they are borrowers their needs to-day differ in no essential respect from those existing before the war, while their credit is probably improved. The discussion may therefore be confined to the European countries.

The present need of Europe is undoubted. Food and other consumable commodities, raw materials, machinery, tools, and capital in all forms are necessary for the economic rehabilitation and reconstruction of the belligerent and, to a lesser extent, of the neutral countries. An estimate in the *New York Times*[2] placed the European financial requirements for the coming 12

---
[2] July 11, 1919. See also *Journal of Commerce*, July 12, 1919.

months at about $2,000,000,000. This sum "probably will cover the more pressing needs and in all likelihood will suffice to start European industry and carry it for the coming year." On the other hand, the Federal Reserve Board announced[3] that considerably more than $3,000,000,000 must be raised here by private initiative if the export trade of the United States is to be kept at its present level. The conclusion was reached that "means must be found during 1919 for the financing of about $3,000,000,000 of new obligations, and for the renewal of perhaps $600,000,000 of old ones. This makes a gigantic, probably an unprecedented, financial problem." No statistics exist which show exactly how much credit actually has been granted to Europe during the last twelve months, but the excess of exports over imports may be accepted as a fair measure of such financing. During the fiscal year ending June 30, 1920, the United States exported to Europe $4,864,155,166 and received in return $1,179,460,699, the difference of $3,684,694,467 having been in large measure sold on credit.

This capital is needed for the reconversion of factories which had been devoting themselves to war production. It has been necessary to alter the machinery so as to make it suitable for peacetime production, and in some cases completely to reëquip the factories and works. Moreover, in the case of such establishments, larger capital is now required for the sake of purchasing raw materials, of replenishing exhausted stocks, and of meeting charges until the new output can be sold. In many cases repairs have been neglected, and these will now have to be made at higher prices. In the devastated areas the demand for capital comprises materials for the

---

[3] *Bulletin*, June, 1919.

FINANCING EUROPE AFTER THE WAR

complete reconstruction of destroyed buildings or the entire equipment òf industries of which the machinery has been destroyed, the stocks of raw material have been carried away, and the markets have been lost. Loans will have to be made to these areas for periods long enough to enable them to reconstruct their establishments and regain their trade connections. On the whole, the demand now consists very largely of investment loans for constructional work, which will be secured by mortgages upon fixed capital, rather than, as has usually been the case, by short term credit upon the security of consumable goods to be met out of the sale of these goods. As the needs are different, so the character of the credit will have to be different.

It is clear that under existing conditions the energies of Europe, especially of the devastated regions, will be fully absorbed in the work of reconstruction and of restoring industries to a normal footing. For this task the belligerents will need all the help that they can secure. For an indefinite period, which may be one year or five years, Europe will be compelled to borrow large amounts of capital. During this period it will scarcely be possible for the borrowing countries to attempt to repay their foreign indebtedness. Not only will they probably be unable to produce enough for their own requirements and to meet the interest charges abroad, but they will even be under the necessity of borrowing further sums.

During the period of reconstruction the peoples of Europe will, on the whole, be too poor to indulge in the purchase of any consumable commodities except to meet their most urgent necessities. On the other hand, as has just been pointed out, their needs for capital goods will be great. We may therefore expect the character of our foreign trade to be determined in part by this fact. Fewer luxuries and high priced consumable commodities will be bought, but on the other hand, we may expect to see an increase in the purchase by Europe of construction material, machinery, implements, tools, and capital goods of various kinds as well as raw materials.

A complication in the normal movement of foreign trade exists in the state of the foreign exchanges. These are highly unfavorable in the case of all the leading belligerent countries of Europe which are likely to borrow most largely of the United States in the next few years. Such a situation acts in itself as an obstacle to the importation into those countries of American goods. On the other hand, there is given thereby a stimulus to exports to the United States. Not content with the normal effect of rates upon the movement of foreign trade, several of the European nations have continued their war embargoes upon imports or have added new ones, which, however, are directed for the most part against the importation of luxuries or nonessentials. The present situation gives point to the movement for the larger use of dollar exchange. If exporters from the United States to-day take their pay in sterling exchange or other foreign currencies, they are exposed to loss through fluctuations in sterling or other rates. Credits should therefore be drawn in dollar exchange.

To meet the demands of the war-swept countries of Europe will require enormous supplies of capital. From what quarters can these be drawn? The United States will probably have to furnish the major share, but other nations may be relied upon to supply no inconsiderable part. The European neutrals, Japan and possibly some of the South American countries, as well as Great Britain and the British colonies will be able to advance

FINANCING EUROPE AFTER THE WAR

part of the sum required. In some of these countries large profits were made during the course of the war, and it is not unreasonable to expect that some of these war profits will be devoted to the work of reconstruction. After all this is said, however, it remains true that the main dependence must be the United States. The needs of Europe will be for raw materials, railway equipment, agricultural machinery, and similar forms of capital; of some of these, as cotton, petroleum, and copper, this country is the main source of supply, while of others it is the largest producer.

Has the United States an available surplus? It is necessary to answer this question in order to determine whether the needs of Europe can be taken care of by this country. On this point the answer must be an undoubted affirmative. The investment in Liberty loans, which averaged about $10,000,000,000 per year during the two years 1917-1919, may be taken as a partial measure of the savings possible for the American people. The normal needs of domestic industries for new capital has been estimated at about five billion dollars per annum. Even if it be granted that the savings will be less and the domestic demands greater, there would still be left a sum sufficient to meet the more pressing needs of Europe for reconstruction purposes. And such a calculation does not take into account our changed position from a debtor to a creditor nation, which has set free funds for foreign investment which formerly went to pay foreign charges for interest and services.

The expenditure during the past year in this country of enormous sums for oil speculation, for pleasure automobiles, and for other extravagances, is sufficient evidence that a surplus over real needs exists.

Granting that funds exist in the United States that

may be loaned to Europe, the further question arises as to how these funds are to be made available for this purpose. By what machinery or methods is this capital to be collected and placed at the disposition of European borrowers? During the period when the United States was in the war, this question was solved by the Government's itself loaning money to the Allies and accepting therefor their promises to pay. The $10,000,000,000 appropriated for this purpose, however, is now exhausted, and Congress has expressed an unwillingness to continue this method. It is clear that an end has come to direct loans by the United States Government. Indirectly, however, there remained authority for the issue by the War Finance Corporation of bonds to the amount of $1,000,000,000. This fund was to be loaned to exporters or to banks and other institutions that finance exporters for the purpose of promoting American trade. The War Finance Corporation, however, made little use of the authority granted it and down to May 10, 1920, when further advances were suspended at the request of the Secretary of the Treasury, it had loaned only about $31,000,000.[4]

Private sources and not the Government, it is evident, must furnish the requisite capital for the reconstruction of Europe. On this point the conclusions of Herbert C. Hoover, based upon a thorough study of the needs of Europe, are of great weight:[5]

In my personal view the largest part of the credits required from the United States should be provided by private credits and we should, except for certain limited purposes, stop the lending of the money of our Government. Credits next year

---
[4] Press despatches of May 11, 1920.
[5] Associated Press despatch from Paris, in *Washington Post*, June 10, 1919.

FINANCING EUROPE AFTER THE WAR

are required for business operation, and when Governments are engaged in business, they always overspread and the years to come must be years of economy. . . . . The credit of private individuals and firms of even the most wrecked states of Europe is still worth something, and what is needed is to reëstablish confidence in such credits.

If we undertake to give credits we should undertake it in a definite, organized manner. We should have consolidated, organized control of the assistance we give, in such a way that it should be used only if economy in imports is maintained and if the definite rehabilitation of industry is undertaken — if the people return to work, if orderly government is preserved, if fighting is stopped, disarmament is undertaken and there is no discrimination against the United States in favor of other countries.

If these things are not done, Europe will starve in spite of all we can do. The surplus of our productivity could not support a Europe of to-day's idleness, if every man of us worked 15 hours daily.

It is one thing to say that capital must be loaned to Europe and that it must be done by private initiative; it is quite another thing to work out the machinery by which credit may safely be extended. The problem is complicated because the amount of capital available for investment purposes is inadequate to meet the enormous demands which are being made and which in all probability will continue to be made for the next three to five years. It has been suggested that some sort of rationing principle may have to be applied, and that if the work of reconstruction in the belligerent countries is to be advanced, credit and raw materials may have to be apportioned to them in accordance with their needs, rather than in strict accord with the security that can be offered.[6] In the devastated areas of Europe industry

---
[6] *New York Times*, June 16, 1919; F. A. Vanderlip, *What Happened to Europe*, p. 184.

is prostrate, and credit is insecure. The people in general are unable to pay for supplies, either with goods or with gold, and accordingly they must be permitted to pay with the only thing that they can offer, namely, their promises. Their position is like that of an insolvent debtor whose creditors advance him new loans in order that he may rehabilitate himself, or like that of a bankrupt corporation that is temporarily financed by means of receivers' certificates.

Such a method of relief is obviously only of temporary value. The peoples of Europe alone can save themselves by their own industry, but they must be furnished with the raw materials and tools with which to work, and in some cases even with the food to support them until the first products of their toil are harvested. It is necessary to reëstablish the industrial cycle as promptly as possible. The present situation is an emergency one, but the period of the emergency may easily run to two or three years. For handling such a problem, Government machinery is too slow, too rigid, too much influenced by political considerations, and too lavish. Many plans have been formulated in Europe calling for large expenditures for public works, frequently for unproductive and extravagant undertakings, for which there is strong pressure on the ground that they are needed to give employment. But as the amount of capital is limited, it must be granted with care, and all requests for loans must be carefully scrutinized, and if improper firmly rejected.

The demands for loans range from short-term accommodation to long-time credits running into permanent investments. For the purchase of food and of other consumable commodities cash payments or short credits will usually be demanded. For productive capital, such

FINANCING EUROPE AFTER THE WAR

as agricultural and industrial machinery, which is used for further production and will normally provide the means of payment, longer credits are necessary, which may run from a year to 18 months. And finally, loans for the purpose of rebuilding plants which have been destroyed or of constructing new ones may be regarded as a permanent investment of capital. It is obvious that the machinery to care for these different forms of credit will be very diverse.

Some of the devices that have been suggested for meeting the problems involved in short term credit may be briefly stated. Early in 1919 a group of American bankers arranged to grant an acceptance credit for Belgium banking institutions of $50,000,000 for the purchase of commodities in the United States, and a group of British banks and acceptance houses likewise arranged a credit for purchases in Europe to the amount of $20,000,000, in three-months bills renewable three times, making a total period for the bills of 12 months.[7] Industrial credits have also been arranged with Germany, France, and Italy, and similar arrangements will continue until those countries rehabilitate their industries and reduce their adverse trade balances.[8] The continued exports to those countries from the United States, far in excess of the imports, evidence the extent to which such credit is being utilized.

A suggestion put forward by Henry P. Davison, of the firm of J. P. Morgan & Company, is that of coördinating the resources of the entire banking and industrial community, both in this country and abroad, rather than of the extension of individual credits by particular institutions. Credits would be established in

---

[7] *Times* (London) Trade Supplement, May 17, 1919.
[8] *New York Times*, June 8, 1919.

Europe secured by everything given against the shipment and further secured by the guarantee of the Government. Against these, debentures would be issued by the banking group in this country and distributed as widely as possible among the investing public.[9]

Another plan is the formation of group export corporations to handle the foreign sales of single commodities like cotton, copper, steel, tobacco, and other American products. Such group corporation would have the backing of a central securities corporation which would sell its debentures to the investing public. An attempt was made to organize the International Cotton Corporation along these lines but it was abandoned because of lack of support. The formation of discount houses has also been suggested, which would be organized for the purpose of dealing in foreign acceptances; such a company has been incorporated under the laws of New York State, to be known as the Foreign Trade Corporation.[10]

Still another method which aims at the facilitating of grants of credit by American producers and manufacturers who are without experience or established connections in foreign trade is the establishment of credit insurance. Companies organized for this purpose would, for a moderate charge, insure the exporter against loss due to the insolvency of the drawee of the bill. Such companies have already been organized in London, New York, and Chicago.[11] Similarly, the National Association of Credit Men has organized a foreign-credit interchange bureau, the object being a reciprocal exchange of knowledge and experiences in foreign trade. The

---

[9] *New York Times*, June 14, 1919.
[10] *New York Times*, August 15, 1919.
[11] *The Americas*, May, 1919, p. 21.

FINANCING EUROPE AFTER THE WAR

plan is based on the domestic interchange system which has worked so well in this country.[12] Finally, legislation has been passed by Congress granting permission to national banks until 1921 to invest not more than five per cent. of their capital and surplus in corporations organized to finance foreign trade.[13]

Many of the demands for credit on the part of Europe, however, will not be for short time accommodation, but will consist rather of long credits and even of permanent investments. To meet this need several other methods have been suggested. A thorough-going scheme has been outlined by Mr. Vanderlip[14] in the form of an international loan between a group of lending nations on the one hand and of borrowing nations on the other. Credits would be allocated and would be secured by first liens on the customs revenues; the bonds would be floated in the loaning countries. The bonds might run for, say, 15 years, but could be liquidated in advance if desired. The obstacles to this plan, however, are probably insurmountable.

For the long term demand good results may be obtained by the investment-trust method. These investment trusts work on the insurance-company plan, selecting securities from all parts of the world and thus spreading the risks by the diversification of their holdings. Successful organizations of this kind exist in England, Scotland, France, Belgium, Switzerland, and, in fact, in all the creditor nations.[15] Such a method seems to lend itself peculiarly well to the present situation between the United States and Europe. A longer step in the direction of permanent investment in Euro-

---
[12] *Journal of Commerce*, July 5, 1919.
[13] Act of September 17, 1919.
[14] *Op. cit.*, p. 183.
[15] *Journal of Commerce*, April 16, 1919.

pean countries is the investment of American capital in foreign manufacturing, mining, and lumbering properties. In view of the strong nationalistic tendencies and the heavy taxation now evident in Europe, however, it is doubtful how far such an invasion of American capital would be successful.

The latest plan suggested is contained in the Edge act approved by the President December 24, 1919.[16] The purpose of this measure is to promote American export trade by providing a method for foreign purchasers to obtain goods on credit backed by collateral, but at the same time provide cash for the American exporters. Private corporations for international banking or financial operations with a capital of not less than $2,000,000 are authorized, subject to the control of the Federal Reserve Board. These have power to deal in all foreign exchange operations and to issue debentures to ten times the amount of their capital and surplus. Branches may be established in foreign countries, and combinations are permitted in the United States which would ordinarily be forbidden under the anti-trust laws. Under the Federal Reserve Act national banks are not allowed to rediscount long term paper, but the Edge corporations will be permitted to accept foreign securities in lieu of cash and then obtain ready money by the sale of their debentures to American investors, or they may use such securities as collateral for loans. Such a corporation would correspond to the investment trust as this has been developed in Great Britain and various European countries. Thus far only one corporation has been organized under the Edge act.

An ambitious and far-reaching scheme was proposed by Senator Owen, who drew up a bill to create a power-

---
[16] S. 2472, 66th Congress, 1st Session.

ful Foreign Finance Corporation to operate under Government supervision.[17] The capital would be subscribed by the Government, by the national banks, and by the public, and the Corporation would be chartered to engage in the business of stabilizing foreign exchange and extending long-time credits to foreign nations. The Corporation would have authority to sell its bonds, secured by foreign bonds or other securities. Little, however, has been heard of this plan since its proposal; indeed, it may be said that this, like many of the other suggestions put forward, has served its most useful purpose in provoking discussion, and leading to a more careful study of the situation. Conditions have changed so rapidly that plans have necessarily been altered to meet the changes in the situation, and it is even yet too soon to say what the final outcome will be. The only thing certain in the discussion is the need of Europe and the certainty that some practicable method will finally be devised for advancing the necessary funds. That a large movement of American capital to Europe is actually taking place is evidenced by the estimate of Werner Wintermantel, Director of the American Department of the Deutsche Bank in Berlin, that since the Treaty of Versailles rather more than 15,000,000,000 marks of American capital had been invested in Germany.[18]

Another phase of the situation which must be taken into account is the need of educating the American investor to buy foreign securities. Until the war the American investor knew little of and cared less for foreign investments. Domestic issues offered, on the whole, larger returns and had the advantage of being

---
[17] *New York Sun*, May 28, 1919.
[18] *New York Times*, July 9, 1920.

familiar and put out by domestic corporations or governmental bodies. Except for some Japanese and Canadian Government bonds and Mexican and Argentine railway bonds, there were few holdings of foreign securities in this country. Much was done during the war toward interesting American investors in foreign government securities, and the present listing of Canadian, French, and British Government and French municipal bonds shows the esteem in which they are held. The total amount of private investment in the securities of foreign Governments during the first three years of the war amounted to about $3,000,000,000. If the program is carried out of having the sums needed for the reconstruction of Europe supplied by private initiative in the United States, it will be necessary for something like this sum or an even greater amount to be advanced again in a similar period. To market foreign securities, however well secured, on such a scale as this will require a campaign of education. It will also call for the continued exercise of thrift and saving, for such sums cannot be subtracted from the amount at present annually invested in American productive industry: it must be provided out of the savings of the people.

Such a campaign to promote a larger investment in foreign securities is justifiable. The idea that the long-term paper representing European loans shall be taken out of the portfolios of the banks and placed in the strong boxes of investors is a sound one. If this can be done, further inflation will be avoided and real savings effected. From this standpoint a series of issues distributed as widely as possible throughout the country is greatly to be preferred to a single great operation which is likely to lead to financial congestion.

A beginning in this direction has already been made

FINANCING EUROPE AFTER THE WAR

by the recent flotation of a Belgium 7½ per cent. 25 year loan for $50,000,000, and of a Swiss 8 per cent. 20 year loan for $25,000,000. Both of these were subscribed at once by investors.

If the investment habits of the American people are to be altered and they are to be persuaded to invest in foreign securities, there must be no question as to the soundness of these securities. Failure in such a program, or even serious mistakes, might jeopardize the whole movement. The securities offered must be unquestionably good as to safety, interest rate, conditions of repayment, and other terms. It has been suggested that the loans made might be secured by a first lien on the revenues of the borrowing countries;[19] but such a proposal, although it might add to the security of the bond, can scarcely be entertained as a practicable method. Although investors may be appealed to on broad-minded grounds to aid in the work of reconstruction in Europe by lending their savings, such loans should be for constructive purposes and must be adequately secured. Capital cannot be withdrawn from domestic investment beyond a certain point without impairing our own ability to render further assistance. The development of American industries must be maintained and expanded coincidently with the restoration of European enterprise.

In conclusion, certain principles which emerge from the foregoing discussion may be briefly stated.

1. The European situation must be treated as a whole, for economic breakdown at any one point would inevitably have a disastrous effect upon the rest of the world. This means the absence of discrimination.

2. Every effort must be made to avoid further infla-

---
[19] F. A. Vanderlip, *op. cit.*, p. 185.

tion. If long term securities are used as the basis of future financing, these must be got as quickly as possible into the hands of permanent investors. It is highly undesirable to throw additional burdens upon the banks in the way of long time investments.

3. The best method of handling the credit situation is probably by having group credits arranged by financial, commercial, and industrial interests in a certain region, or by a single industry for a wider district. Such credits could then be granted by groups of, say, American bankers who stand in close touch with the producers and exporters of the commodities to be purchased with these credits.

4. Short term credits on the whole are preferable to long term bonds, for every effort must be made to restore business to a normal basis as promptly as possible.

5. When this time arrives larger imports must be expected, and ultimately our so-called "favorable" balance of trade will be reversed and an excess of imports over exports become a normal phenomenon. This is the inevitable result of our present position as a creditor nation and may be expected to persist unless we continue to invest the balances due us in additional foreign securities or in permanent investments abroad. This, however, would only postpone the change and make it more far-reaching in the end. For the immediate future it is the duty, as it is the interest, of the people of the United States to loan their available savings to aid in the reconstruction of Europe and to accept pay in the promises of that war-swept continent.

While these and other plans for a broad scheme of economic reconstruction and financial assistance have been under consideration, the actual movement of goods has not been delayed. There has been much individual effort on the part of single branches of trade and industry, even though coördination on a national scale is as yet lacking. This is clearly shown in the volume of exports, the monthly totals of which show an increase, intermittent but real. Although part of this increase is due to advancing prices, there is still, after deduction for this factor, a remarkable growth. The following table gives the merchandise imports and exports of the United States by months for the year 1919:

UNITED STATES IMPORTS AND EXPORTS OF MERCHANDISE, BY MONTHS, 1919

	Imports	Exports	Excess exports over imports
January........	$212,992,644	$622,552,783	$409,560,139
February......	235,124,274	585,097,012	349,972,738
March........	267,596,289	603,141,648	335,545,359
April..........	272,956,949	714,500,137	441,543,188
May..........	328,924,393	606,379,599	277,455,206
June..........	293,069,779	918,212,671	625,142,892
July..........	343,746,070	568,687,515	224,941,445
August........	307,293,078	646,054,425	338,761,347
September.....	435,448,747	595,214,266	159,765,519
October........	401,845,150	631,618,449	229,773,299
November.....	424,824,073	740,033,585	315,209,512
December......	380,710,323	681,649,999	300,939,676
Total........	$3,904,378,733	$7,921,196,047	$4,016,818,314

The larger part of these exports and the group which shows the most marked increase, consists of foodstuffs and raw materials. The need in Europe for these supplies is so desperate and so immediate that they must be had on almost any terms. Whether our exports will continue on the same high level after the most urgent demands are satisfied is a question open to much doubt. The adverse exchange situation raises the cost of American exports to most European countries and to that extent reduces their willingness to purchase our goods. Moreover, because of their enormous indebtedness to the United States, incurred during the war, they are unwilling to add to that burden. Import restrictions have been imposed, an apparent indisposition to arrange credits and make known their needs has been manifested,[20] and a low exchange rate has apparently been regarded with favor as tending to limit foreign purchases. It is too soon to speak with certainty as to the future, but it must not be forgotten that in international, as in domestic, commerce the purchaser, in the final analysis, determines the volume and character of the trade.

---

[20] *Cf.* statement of F. I. Kent, director of the War Finance Corporation, in an interview after his return from Europe, *New York Times*, July 19, 1919.

CHAPTER XII

AFTER-WAR PROBLEMS OF CURRENCY AND DEBT

Inflation of the currency a world phenomenon — Its effect on prices — Why should inflation have been permitted? — The remedy for inflation — Difficulties — The distribution of gold — Financial situation of the principal countries — Comparison of wealth and debt — Can the burdens be carried? — American and European theories as to debt payment — Problem of funding the floating debts — The capital levy — Problem of refunding — Will the debts be paid?

One of the most urgent problems left by the war is the reduction of the enormous inflation now existing in money and credit throughout the world. With an all but universal suspension of specie payment, the expansion of currency issues and of banking credits went on practically unchecked throughout the war. The result is that to-day the note and deposit liabilities of the European banks are altogther out of proportion to the metallic reserves upon which they are supposed to rest. The same is true also of the smaller amounts of direct Government issues. This expansion in the volume of currency was caused by the urgent needs of the Governments during the war, which forced them to rely upon advances from the central note-issuing institutions. In ordinary commercial transactions an issue of bank notes or the creation of a credit deposit is based upon commercial paper, and the expansion of the means of payment is limited by the amount of legitimate business requiring to be financed. During the war, however, no such checks were placed upon inflation. The only limit was the need of the Govern-

GOLD RESERVES AND NOTE CIRCULATION
(In millions)

	JUNE, 1914			DECEMBER, 1918			Paper circulation per capita	
	Gold	Notes	Percentage ratio gold to notes	Gold	Notes	Percentage ratio gold to notes	1914	1918
BELLIGERENTS:								
Great Britain[1]	$200.4	$148.9	134.6	$539.3	$2,105.2	25.6	$3.50	$50.00
France[2]	811.5	1,210.2	67.0	688.1	6,049.9	11.4	30.00	151.50
Russia[4]	799.9	815.2	98.1	667.0	40,000.0	1.7	6.00[4]	286.00[4]
Japan	109.3	163.6	66.8	360.0	437.4[5]	82.3	3.00	7.50
Germany[3]	326.5	601.6	54.3	565.5	8,074.2	7.0	9.00	119.00
Austria-Hungary	261.5	484.4	53.9	55.0	7,400.0	0.7	9.50	144.50
Italy	303.4	510.7	59.4	218.6	2,755.3[6]	7.9	10.3	45.81
United States	1,023.0	1,056.0	99.6	2,248.3	4,810.5[7]	46.8	26.00	47.00
Finland	8.3	22.2	36.9	8.4	228.0[6]	3.7	7.00	69.50
	$3,843.8	$5,013.4	70.2	$5,350.2	$71,860.5	7.3	$12.50	$133.50

352

GOLD RESERVES AND NOTE CIRCULATION—Continued

(In millions)

	JUNE, 1914			DECEMBER, 1918			Paper circulation per capita	
	Gold	Notes	Percentage ratio gold to notes	Gold	Notes	Percentage ratio gold to notes	1914	1918
NEUTRALS:								
Spain	$106.3	$378.4	28.1	$445.7	$663.2	67.2	18.00	$32.00
Denmark	22.8	44.4	51.4	54.0	125.0	43.2	15.00	43.00
Holland	66.9	126.5	52.8	287.3	445.4	64.5	20.00	67.50
Norway	13.5	32.1	42.0	33.6	120.1	28.0	14.00	50.00
Sweden	29.1	60.4	48.1	79.3	219.7	36.1	10.50	38.00
Switzerland	35.1	57.0	61.6	82.9	190.1	42.5	14.50	50.00
Argentina	240.9	339.4	71.0	389.0	570.9	76.6	39.50	59.00
	$514.8	$1,038.4	49.6	$1,371.8	$2,276.6	60.3	$20.50	$44.50

[1] Currency notes included, but exclusive of deposits with Bank of England. [2] Gold in hand. [3] Inclusive of notes of war credit institutions. [4] European Russia. [5] December 7. [6] Beginning of November. [7] November 30.

ment, and issues were made in response to the demands, not of commerce, but of war's necessity. The problem that now presents itself is that of the deflation of the paper money in circulation and the restoration of the gold standard, if this is possible.

The changes that took place in the gold reserves and note circulation of the central banking institutions of the leading European countries and of the United States during the war are shown in the accompanying table. Not all of the increases in the note issues can be counted as net additions to the media of exchange, for a certain proportion simply took the place of gold and silver which formerly circulated as coins but which have now entirely disappeared from circulation. On the other hand this table does not show the direct issues of paper money by the Governments, such as were made in Italy, Germany, and other countries. It has been estimated that this increase of nearly 30,000,000,000 dollars in the money of the world is more than the value of all the gold and silver produced by all the mines of the world since the discovery of the New World.

The inflation which began during the war unfortunately continued after its cessation at an accelerated rate. It was impossible for the belligerent countries suddenly to reduce their expenditures or to increase their revenues and they continued to resort to loans and the issue of paper money in order to meet the deficits. In the thirteen months between the Armistice and the end of 1919 it is estimated that the paper money in circulation in the principal countries of the world increased about 35 per cent.[1] The table on pages 352 and 353 shows the gold reserves and note circulation in 1914 and 1918

---
[1] See table compiled by O. P. Austin in *The Americas*, January, 1920, p. 27.

PROBLEMS OF CURRENCY AND DEBT

In addition to note issues there was a considerable increase in the credit currency of the world in the form of bank deposits, which are a more volatile and inflationary form of currency than circulating notes. There was, moreover, a considerable increase in the use of checks during the war in such countries as France and Germany, where formerly little resort was had to deposit banking. The following table shows the bank deposits of the principal countries at the beginning and the end of the war:

BANK DEPOSTIS
(*In thousands*)

	1913	1918
Great Britain	$5,521,645	$11,250,000
France	1,327,770	2,172,875
United States	10,503,695	[1] 30,000,000
Canada	1,166,180	2,085,060
Italy	407,135	1,795,080
Japan	926,880	[1] 2,600,000
Argentina	684,190	1,207,135
Spain	262,245	[1] 516,000
Switzerland	397,585	[1] 955,000
Sweden	402,905	953,770
Germany	2,715,785	[1] 9,913,000
	$24,316,015	$63,447,920

Increase—$39,131,905, or 162 per cent.

Without going into the vexed question as to what constitutes inflation, this statistical presentation of the facts would seem to indicate that inflation has taken place as a world movement by reason of the enormous

[1] Estimates based on exact figures so far as available and supplemented by estimates based on 1917 figures where those for 1918 are lacking.

addition to the circulating media of the belligerent and even of the neutral countries. If inflation be defined as a more rapid increase in the means of payment than in the volume of business, there seems to be little doubt that it has occurred on such a scale as to have affected all price relations in every country of the globe, no matter how remote from the war. Inflation has resulted, not because the ratio between gold and credits has been changed, for the gold base is probably still sufficient in most countries to maintain the redeemability of the credits based upon it, but because the ratio between money and purchasable commodities has been distorted.

It is impossible to trace the exact effects of this increase in money upon prices, and it is equally impossible to tell what part was played in the general rise of prices throughout the world by this factor and to what extent this was due to other price-raising factors at work, such as government loans, scarcity of commodities, etc. In the report of the Committee on War Finance of the American Economic Association[2] a very careful analysis of the various factors entering into the situation in the United States was made, the chief findings of which are here summarized. The growth of business, which may be said to constitute the demand for money, increased about 13 per cent. between 1913 and 1918. On the other hand, the supply of money in the form of actual money in circulation increased 60 per cent. and the bank deposits 94 per cent. in the same period. In other words, the means of payment increased more rapidly than the business transactions for the conduct of which they were needed. The result would normally be an increase of prices and this is shown actually to

---

[2] Published as Supplement No. 2 of the *American Economic Review*, March, 1919.

PROBLEMS OF CURRENCY AND DEBT

have taken place. Wholesale prices increased 96 per cent. and wages 69 per cent. The following table shows the essential facts in tabular form:[3]

MOVEMENTS OF MONEY, PRICES AND WAGES IN THE UNITED STATES, 1913-1918

Year	Growth of business	Monetary circulation	Growth of bank deposits	Wholesale prices	WAGES	
					N. Y. State	Union scale
1913	100	100	100	100	...	100
1914	99	103	106	99	100	102
1915	103	109	114	100	103	103
1916	107	123	141	123	115	107
1917	112	145	168	175	131	114
1918	113	160	(194)	196	169	...

It would be going too far to say that monetary changes alone have brought about the great rise in prices. The curtailment in the supply of commodities, the difficulty and cost of shipment, and the changes in demand have all been so great that their combined influence has probably been greater than that of changes in the supply of money. The number of nations at war and the extent to which they mobilized their economic resources for military purposes enormously intensified the demand for articles needed in the prosecution of the war, while, on the other hand, articles not so needed were designated as non-essentials and often ruthlessly suppressed. The general and continued demand on the part of so many

---

[3] *Ibid.*, pp. 94, 107. Explanation and limitations as to the manner in which these figures were obtained are given in the report, to which the reader is referred. The statistics are reproduced here without these notes simply to present a picture, believed to be wholly accurate, of the changes which have taken place in the circulating media, prices, and wages.

WAR COSTS AND THEIR FINANCING

countries for articles needed in the war immediately drove up the prices of those articles, while the mobilization of vast armies, the expansion of governmental functions, and the general disorganization of credit all combined to create a demand for more money. But in many cases the issues were made, as has been indicated, without reference to purely monetary needs, and indeed far exceeded these. This brought about a further rise in prices, and so the vicious, never-ending circle was introduced.

If responsibility for this world-wide phenomenon could be fixed, it would undoubtedly be found that the impetus toward higher prices came from Europe. The rise in prices occurred in England and France before it did in the United States. So far as prices rose in the United States in 1915 and 1916, the increase was principally due to the European demand for our commodities. After that, the addition to our circulating medium and bank reserves of a steady stream of gold and later our own currency and credit expansion combined to contribute to this end. It was a movement which could not be isolated, and by the end of the war no country, however remote from the seat of the conflict, had been able to escape the general upward movement of prices. Owing to the existence of enormous issues of fiduciary money, much of which will probably remain for years as inconvertible paper money, it is probably safe to say that the world has entered upon a higher level of prices which will endure for at least a generation.

It will be impracticable here to trace in detail the evil effects of inflation. The most obvious one, and that of the most far-reaching consequence, has been the rise in the prices of commodities, but this has already been sufficiently described. As is usual in situations of this

PROBLEMS OF CURRENCY AND DEBT

sort, wages did not adjust themselves as rapidly as did prices of commodities, and consequently the purchasing power of earnings was greatly diminished and a heavy load placed upon certain classes of workers whose earnings did not increase proportionately and also upon persons with fixed incomes. Another effect of the excessive currency issues was seen in the derangement of foreign exchanges. This was due in a measure to the disorganization of trade movements and to the shift in trade balances, but in part it must be attributed to the uneven depreciation of the currency in the different countries which resulted from their different degrees of resort to inflation. The position of the banks, too, has been greatly affected by the changes which have taken place in bankable paper. Their assets have been very largely transformed from the short term paper of manufacturers and merchants to Government obligations of one kind or another. The solvency of the banks is linked very closely with the credit of the states. It would seem, therefore, that the problem of the retirement of the bank circulation cannot be solved until that of the payment of the debts themselves has been met.

Why should inflation have been permitted? The lesson of history on this point was clear and well understood. The experiences of France during the Revolution, of England during the Napoleonic wars, and of the United States during the Civil War were all matters of record and offered sufficient warning against repeating the mistakes of these periods. There was not in the World War, it is true, a repetition of the grosser form of inflation by the issue of irredeemable government paper money; it took the subtler form this time of the expansion of bank notes and of bank credits. It may be that in some quarters there was a hope that for this

WAR COSTS AND THEIR FINANCING

reason the obvious results of inflation might be avoided. But a more likely and sufficient explanation is the urgent necessity that all Governments were under, of raising money at once in the easiest way.

In some cases, notably in Germany, the view was held and acted upon that a plentiful supply of money would ease the transition from peace to war economy, and this notion doubtless had its influence in other countries. It is not difficult to find expressions of satisfaction during the earlier years of the war that war financing had been accomplished so easily and without violently affecting rates in the money markets. This was avoided by the issuance of paper money and also by the elimination of industrial issues which might compete with Government loans. In other words, the stand was taken that the flotation of loans was aided by the debasement of the currency. Once entered upon, this policy doubtless received further encouragement from the desire of the Ministers of Finance to keep down the rate of interest on the enormous loans which followed one another in such rapid succession.

From another standpoint the inflation of the currency with the consequent rise of prices aided the policy of the Governments in financing the war by curtailing the consumption of nonessentials, thereby setting free for war purposes labor and capital that would otherwise have gone to other lines of production. Later it was sought to secure this end by rationing, by thrift campaigns, and finally by taxation. It may fairly be argued that an earlier and more drastic resort to this last method would have rendered the policy of inflation with all its attendant evils necessary in a much less degree. It may well be doubted whether a war of such magnitude could have been carried on without some degree of

PROBLEMS OF CURRENCY AND DEBT

inflation, but that it could have been greatly minimized is hardly open to doubt.

The evil effect of inflation on the Treasury, not to mention other results, lies in the fact that the Government receives in taxes or from the sale of its bonds money which is constantly declining in purchasing power. After the war, with the return of more normal conditions and the gradual contraction of the currency, these bonds will be redeemed in dollars of higher purchasing power. The loss to the Government is measured by the difference between the two measures of value. But this loss is accompanied by a social cost which is infinitely greater and more widespread, and may carry with it serious social and industrial disorganizations and readjustments, leading possibly to revolution and in extreme instances to complete anarchy. It is going too far to claim any causal connection between the two, but it is noteworthy that Bolshevism should have proceeded furthest in Russia, where the debasement of the currency far exceeded that in any other nation. Moreover, industrial unrest is probably greatest in the other countries that have most closely followed Russia in this direction.

The remedy for the evils of inflation is contraction. But when this is said, the problem has merely been stated in another form, for the question at once presents itself as to how and when such contraction is to be effected. In the case of direct Government issues, the inability of the Government in the majority of cases to meet present budget requirements out of revenue will effectually prevent any retirement of the noninterest bearing debt. However bad may be the effects of an inflated currency, it is not to be expected that any considerable part of the proceeds of taxation will be devoted to its reduction. The most that can be hoped for is the accumulation by the issuing country of a sufficient metallic reserve to deprive the issues of the character of fiat money.

The expansion of note circulation and of credit deposits on the part of the banks would under normal conditions automatically correct itself; as loans fell due, the credit would be cancelled, and as the notes were presented for redemption, they would be retired. In circumstances as they exist in Europe, however, neither of these things is necessarily true. Since the notes represent for the most part compulsory advances to the State and bear little or no relation to the metallic reserve, it may be impossible for the banks to resume specie payments and thus to permit the working out of the principles of supply and demand. The huge deposits of the banks, too, are in large part public deposits and will not be immediately reduced, since the obligations upon which they rest will presumably be renewed many times. Ultimately, however, this debt of the State will be funded and the banks permitted to resume their commercial functions. But even then a reduction in the media of exchange cannot be looked for. The issues of enormous quantities of bonds have afforded unexcelled collateral for bank credit, and with a better knowledge of the advantages of deposit banking in Europe, further expansions of bank currency, rather than its reduction, may be expected. This is even more true of the United States, where the people are already thoroughly habituated to the use of checks, and where the presence of an enormous gold reserve, which is not likely to leave the country, except in inconsiderable quantities, as long as the present favorable trade balances persist, will permit a still further expansion of credit.

Another difficulty connected with the resumption of specie payments by the banks is the uneven distribution of gold among the nations of the world. The United States possesses a gold reserve which constitutes probably the largest store of gold ever brought together since the beginning of recorded history. The holdings of the Federal Reserve Banks amounted on June 25, 1920, to $1,971,696,000. The Bank of Russia stands second on the basis of the last published report of that institution, October 20, 1917, but it is scarcely conceivable that this reserve has remained intact. The Bank of France, which comes next, may therefore be given second place with a total stock on June 24, 1920, of $1,116,000,000, including that held abroad. The Imperial Bank of Germany holds, or held, the fourth largest amount of gold. On October 7, 1918, it held $620,000,000, the greatest reserve of any time during the war, but this amount steadily declined after that time, partly as a result of the restitution of the gold taken from Belgium and from Russia and partly as a result of payments for food and raw materials. By March, 1919, the gold held by the Reichsbank had declined to about $456,000,000, and by June 24, 1920, it had sunk to $272,000,000. At that time, therefore, Germany was surpassed by both Great Britain and Japan. The total gold holdings of the Bank of England, including the coin and bullion held against the currency notes, amounted on June 24, 1920, to $589,000,000. The gold held by the Bank of Japan amounted on March 27, 1920, to $461,000,000. The Bank of Italy reported its total " cash " at $298,000,000 on May 20, 1919, but this included items other than gold; by June 24, 1920, the gold reserve had shrunk to $160,900,000.

The reserves of the banks of the neutral countries have all been greatly strengthened, but a few of the former belligerents lost practically all the gold they formerly held. The reserves of the Bank of Rumania have probably been lost as a result of their removal to Moscow. The gold reserves formerly held by the Austro-Hungarian Bank and the Ottoman Bank were drained off in payments to the Reichsbank, and now the reserves of the latter are being depleted by the payments for food supplies. Before the belligerent nations of Europe can resume specie payments, it is evident that some of them must purchase gold, and that all of them will have to reduce their outstanding issues and bring the notes into a more correct relation to the metallic reserves.

A reference to the table on pages 352-3 will show the percentage which the gold reserves constitute of the note issues in the countries there listed. The warning should be given at this point that the sums of gold thus listed are not held against the note issues, but constitute the total gold reserve of the bank against all liabilities. Even assuming that they were available exclusively for note-redemption purposes, it is evident that it will be impossible for the banks of Russia, Germany, Austria-Hungary, Italy, and Finland, and probably France, to attempt redemption of the outstanding issues without materially strengthening their reserves. If this program is carried out, years must elapse before specie payments can be resumed. The more radical method of deflation by devaluation may be adopted by some of the countries as the quickest solution of the difficulty

The production of gold in the world fell off during the very period when these enormous additions were being made to the note issues. Partly as a result of the rising cost of production, which affected gold mining as well as other activities, and partly because of other factors, such as the cutting off of the Russian supply and the exhaustion of the Australian mines, the output of gold has shown a steady decrease since 1915. The following table shows the annual gold production of the world for the six years 1914-1919 :[4]

1914............................$439,078,260
1915............................ 470,466,214
1916............................ 454,176,500
1917............................ 423,950,200
1918............................ 380,924,700
1919............................ 365,166,000

The problem of the restoration of the gold standard is complicated by the falling off in production at the very time when the need for larger gold reserves is greatest. It would seem, therefore, that the adjustment of note issues to reserves must be made by the diminution of the former rather than by the increase of the latter. As any other method would result in a further addition of money to a supply already too large, this process must be commended. It may be noted at this point that such a process of reducing the outstanding note issues has been initiated in Hungary, Italy, and France during the first half of 1920.

A further complication arises from the unwillingness of those countries possessing considerable stocks of gold to part with it. None of the European nations has as yet removed its embargo upon the export of gold on private account, and Great Britain prohibited exports after April 1, 1919. On the other hand, the prohibition of the export of gold from the United States, which was imposed shortly after this country entered the war, was removed in June, 1919. Since the movement of gold is toward, rather than away from, the United States, however, except to a few Latin-American and Oriental countries, there does not exist to-day such a thing as a free

[4] *Federal Reserve Bulletin*, January, 1919, p. 19.

world movement of gold as a corrective of unfavorable rates of exchange.

Not merely are the note issues excessive in amount and subject to varying degrees of depreciation; they have also but a limited currency, as they are in many cases so thoroughly distrusted by neighboring countries as to be refused acceptance. As a result of the fluctuations in the value of the currency and consequently in the rates of foreign exchange, a highly speculative feature has in many cases been introduced into trade which acts as a retarding influence. In certain sections monetary transactions have all but broken down and trade has reverted to barter. Among certain of the States that formerly made up the Austrian-Hungarian Empire and among the Balkan States, the attitude of each State toward its neighbor is so hostile that exchange has almost ceased. The following condensed account taken from an Austrian paper illustrates this point vividly:[5]

Permission to place any amount to the credit of a German-Austrian or a Vienna bank with a Bohemian branch is as a rule only granted by the bank-note clearing house, in cases of the import from German Austria of goods urgently needed in Bohemia and which come for the most part under compensation traffic and cover only a part of the debts which German Austria should collect for supplies of sugar, coal, and other necessities from Bohemia. German-Austrians, too, can be given credit grants only with the approval of the clearing house. . . . Matters are further complicated by the absence of a note bank in Czecho-Slovakia at which commercial bills and loans on effects could be mobilized. . . . Monetary transactions with Poland are, of course, quite at a standstill, since, in addition to the prohibition upon import of *kronen*, all postal and telegraphic traffic is suppressed. German-

[5] *Oesterreichische Volkswirt*, May 10, 1919, quoted in "Reconstruction Supplement" to the [British] *Review of the Foreign Press*, London, June 18, 1919.

PROBLEMS OF CURRENCY AND DEBT

Austrian banks only receive news of their branches from time to time by courier, and orders for payment can only be passed through the same channels. . . . The Ukraine has introduced a compulsory rate of exchange of one-half *karbovonez* for the *krone*. There are practically no money transactions with the Ukraine, and it is only through the few couriers that the payments can be made. . . . Jugo-Slavia has taken the most stringent measures against money transactions with German Austria. In addition to the note stamping and the prohibition of import and export of currency, it has applied to German Austria the old Serbian law forbidding payments to the enemy, so that German Austria can no longer use its possessions in Jugo-Slavia. Exchanges between Jugo-Slav *kronen* and German-Austrian currency are as rare as between Czech and German-Austrian *kronen*.

So far as the immediate future is concerned, there seems little evidence that a diminution of the European notes now issued will be effected or that the expanded bank credits will be reduced. On the contrary, there is every reason to believe that these will be further increased. New credits are being asked for the rehabilitation and reconstruction of Europe. Further loans are being floated by the European countries, neutral as well as belligerent, for the most part in the United States, but sometimes also at home. Until these new securities are "digested," they will serve as the basis of further expansion of deposits and to that extent will increase the existing inflation.

In addition to these sums, German indemnity bonds will probably soon appear on the market. Although the method of their distribution is not clear, it is altogether probable that they will be made the basis of further borrowings and credit expansion and thus still further increase the existing inflation. It is improbable, in view of these conditions, that deflation will occur soon or on

WAR COSTS AND THEIR FINANCING

any appreciable scale. On the contrary, we may rather look forward to a continuation of present high prices in most nations. So far as these are due to scarcity of goods, this factor will gradually be corrected by the resumption of normal activities throughout the world. But so far as they are attributable to currency and credit inflation, no decided change can be expected for several years. It may be assumed that the world has entered upon a more or less permanent higher price level. The necessary adjustments can be made most quickly and easily in the United States, but even here a complete return to pre-war conditions need not be expected for some time.

Difficult as are the problems raised by the currency and banking situation, those connected with the public debt are even more grave. The growth of the debt in most of the belligerent countries proceeded more rapidly than the enlargement of the tax system, so that the revenue in these countries is insufficient to meet the ordinary expenditures of government and the interest on the public debt. Indeed, for the European belligerents the revenues barely sufficed to meet either one of these items alone. If the debts were completely expunged, the financial situation would still present difficulties; and with the charges for debt service unchanged and ever increasing, the problem is serious in the extreme. The ordinary civil expenditures have increased greatly from those of the pre-war period, though not in the same proportion as the interest charges. The following table shows for the leading countries the amounts that it was necessary to raise for the civil budget and for interest charges on the debt, and the revenues, for the fiscal year following the Armistice:

PROBLEMS OF CURRENCY AND DEBT

CIVIL BUDGETS, REVENUES, AND INTEREST CHARGES OF LEADING BELLIGERENTS
(*In millions*)

	Year ended	Pre-war civil budget	Interest charge last fiscal year	Revenue last fiscal year
United States...	June 30, 1919	$702.2	$615.9	$4,647.6
United Kingdom	March 31, 1919	987.4	1,332.6	4,444.1
France.........	Dec. 31, 1918	1,013.3	1,113.5	1,642.5
Russia..........	Dec. 31, 1917	1,547.1	371.2	1,870.0
Italy...........	June 30, 1919	625.8	800.0	1,492.0
Germany.......	March 31, 1919	851.3	1,975.0	1,533.8

It is evident from this table that in none of these countries except the first two were revenues sufficient to meet the pre-war charges for the civil budget and those for interest on the debt during the last year of the war. Both of these items, however, will be in the future much higher than the figures here given. It is a commonplace of financial history that after every great war the expenditures of government, the functions of which have been expanded as a result of the struggle, never return to their former amount but remain upon a permanently higher level. This will undoubtedly be true of the countries whose budgets are here shown. In fact, for the next few years it may be predicted that they will be several times as much as the last pre-war budget. In the second place, the interest charges given in this table are considerably below the actual payments that will have to be met, since these do not include the interest on the floating debt, which in some cases is extremely large, or the interest on new loans now being issued which will swell the charges to still greater sums.

WAR COSTS AND THEIR FINANCING

And, finally, the revenues will with difficulty be increased now that the war is over, and in some cases may be expected to diminish as a result of the termination of the war-profits taxes and other strictly war levies.

A more adequate picture of the enormity of the debts that have been incurred as a result of the war will be furnished by a statement of the amounts of the debts rather than of the interest payments. If the population, the national wealth, and national income be also presented, some notion will be gained of the ability of the various countries to cope with their existing debts. Such a statement is given in the following table:

POPULATION, WEALTH, AND DEBTS OF BELLIGERENTS
(In millions of dollars)

	Pre-war population	Pre-war wealth	Pre-war income	Total debt*
United States......	102,826,000	$220,000	$38,000	$24,648
United Kingdom...	46,499,000	72,500	11,250	40,385
France............	39,948,000	59,000	7,300	46,025
Russia............	141,679,000	60,160	6,500	25,000
Italy..............	35,097,000	25,200	4,000	18,758
Germany..........	68,442,000	83,250	10,500	†49,250
Austria-Hungary...	51,080,000	40,000	5,500	†27,000

* As of March 31, 1920, except for Russia, in which the debt is of October 1, 1917.   † Exclusive of indemnities.

These figures are so stupendous that they fail to convey a definite impression. The mind refuses to grasp a figure running into a dozen digits. A more comprehensible view of the burden is obtained from a statement of *per capita* debt, and such figures indicate also more clearly the relative burdens borne by the different nations. But a *per capita* distribution of debt alone

PROBLEMS OF CURRENCY AND DEBT

tells, after all, very little as to the ability of the different nations to meet their obligations. Clearer light is thrown on this problem by comparing the *per capita* debt and interest charges with the *per capita* national wealth and national income, which are shown in the following table:

PER CAPITA WEALTH, INCOME, AND DEBTS OF BELLIGERENTS

	Pre-war wealth	Pre-war income	Present debt	Present interest charge
United States.........	$2,120	$360	$240	$10
United Kingdom......	1,590	250	869	37
France...............	1,515	190	1150	63
Russia...............	425	46	177	3
Italy................	720	115	536	26
Germany*............	1,220	150	720	45
Austria-Hungary*.....	784	105	530	32

* Exclusive of indemnities.

Conclusions based upon these tables, however, must be used with caution, for the statistics of population, wealth, and income are based upon pre-war computations, and in practically every instance there has been a decline in the population while the real wealth and income are less to-day than they were before the war, although their nominal amounts have increased as a result of the higher price level. The debts are steadily growing and are in almost every instance greater to-day than they were when these tables were compiled. So far as the tables err, therefore, it is in the direction of a more favorable showing than the present facts warrant.

But favorable though it may be, the facts shown are ominous in the extreme. Will it be possible for the nations of Europe to carry successfully these staggering

WAR COSTS AND THEIR FINANCING

burdens? Although it is not possible to give a categorical answer to such a question, some light may be thrown upon it by a study of the probable revenues of the different countries. This is attempted in the following chapter. The ability to meet the current charges for debt service depends, after all, upon the revenue-producing capacity of the different countries.

Although not of such immediate importance, the question of the ultimate disposition of the principal of the debt is intimately bound up with that of payment of the interest. Assuming that the interest charges will be met, are the debts likely to be paid off or will they remain as a permanent legacy of the war? In spite of the accepted policy of the United States on this point, the principle of debt payment is not universally accepted. The European and the American theories on the desirability of the payment of a public debt are in broad contrast. In general, the European theory favors a perpetual debt, whereas the British and American theory provides for the repayment of the debt. This distinction is clearly indicated by the maturities shown in the bonds issued by the different countries. Those for the United States and Great Britain and her colonies are without exception terminable at a fixed date, the longest maturity being 30 years. In France, Italy, Germany, and Hungary, on the other hand, the larger part of the debt was thrown into the form of a perpetual debt, that is, one without a fixed date of maturity. Russia and Austria are apparent exceptions to the rule, for their war debts were in every case given fixed maturities.

In favor of the European theory of a perpetual indebtedness it is argued that the growth in population and wealth of a country gradually lessens the burden of a debt, which is measured by the annual interest charge, even though no reduction take place in the principal. Thus it has been computed that the pressure of the English debt in 1815 was equivalent to nine per cent. of the yearly national income. In 1880, as a result of the growth of national wealth, it was less than three per cent. although the debt had remained nearly stationary in the interval. In France the capitalized sum of the debt increased more than threefold between 1840 and 1870, but the pressure of the annual payments demanded by the debt was 0.022 and 0.023 of the national income for the two periods; that is to say, the increase in the debt was not felt as an additional burden because of the concomitant growth in national wealth.[6] These and similar facts have often been cited as arguments to prove that the best as well as the easiest method of dealing with the public debt is to let the nation grow up to it.

Another argument in favor of a perpetual debt is based upon the assumed burdenlessness of a domestic debt. If the bonds are entirely owned at home, as is the case in most of the war debts, the raising of taxes to pay interest charges, it is said, imposes no real burden upon the people, as the money is simply taken out of one pocket and put into another. This might be true up to a certain point if the persons who paid the taxes and those who received the interest payments were identical. But as they seldom are, there is involved in any such process an actual redistribution of the national income. Such redistribution may be beneficial, but it is more likely, if the lessons of history may be accepted as a guide, to have undesirable consequences.

---
[6] H. C. Adams, *Public Debts*, p. 243.

WAR COSTS AND THEIR FINANCING

Whatever weight such arguments may have possessed for European countries, they have been without effect in this country, where from the beginning of our history a policy of rapid debt payment has been traditional and has been carried out in practice. The population and wealth of the country have grown so rapidly that this policy has been carried through with comparatively little effort. It has been regarded as desirable that the way should be cleared for new tasks by the removal as speedily as possible of burdens handed down from the past. Such a policy seems to be called for even more urgently at the present time because of the growing demands that will undoubtedly be made upon the Federal Government in the future. There has long been evident in the United States a centralization of administrative functions in the Federal Government which has been greatly hastened by the events of the war. A vast growth of expenditures may be expected in the near future, especially as a result of the larger demands for social insurance, old-age pensions, improvement of internal navigation, government aid to railroads, and similar measures. It is desirable, therefore, to expunge the war debt as rapidly as possible, and leave the Government financially unhampered and able to undertake fresh duties.

Moreover, the period immediately after the war is favorable for the payment of the war debt, unless the losses have proved excessively severe, for taxes have been expanded, industries are adjusted to the new taxation requirements, and business is prospering as a result of higher prices. Where such conditions prevail, little resistance will be made to a policy of debt payment, and this on the whole is true of the United States.

It is not surprising, consequently, to find a policy of

PROBLEMS OF CURRENCY AND DEBT

rapid debt payment proposed for this country by the Secretary of the Treasury soon after the cessation of hostilities. Provision was made for the retirement of the war debt in the Victory Liberty Loan Act of March 3, 1919, by the creation of a cumulative sinking fund. There is to be applied to the payment of the debt for the fiscal year beginning July 1, 1920, and for each fiscal year thereafter an amount equal to the sum of (1) 2½ per cent. of the aggregate amount of bonds and notes outstanding on July 1, 1920, less the par value of any obligations of foreign Governments held by the United States on that date, and (2) the interest that would have been payable during the fiscal year for which the appropriation was made on all bonds and notes redeemed out of the sinking fund. Under this scheme an average of about $1,500,000,000 would be called for annually as payment into the sinking fund. If these payments were maintained inviolably the debt would be expunged in about 25 years.[7] If the American people will submit to the continuation of taxation for debt purposes in such an amount, the debt could be expunged by 1947, when the last bonds fall due. This would be an achievement unparalleled in the financial history of the world. It is earnestly to be hoped that the policy of debt payment may be vigorously prosecuted and the process brought to as speedy a conclusion as possible.

In turning from the debt situation in the United States to that in the various European countries, one is impressed with the fact that the problem there is not so much one of repayment of the debt as of funding the floating debt and of maintaining the interest pay-

---
[7] Hearings before the Committee on Ways and Means on the Fifth Liberty Bond bill, February 13 and 14, 1919, p. 59.

ments on the outstanding principal. Civil expenditures and systems of taxation must be adjusted to meet the burdens presented by the existence of this overwhelming indebtedness. The question is not of payment, but of how to avoid repudiation. Not unnaturally in the circumstances, many proposals have been made for adjusting the debt, some of which may be briefly outlined.

The first and most pressing problem is that of funding the floating debts. Practically every belligerent nation emerged from the war with a troublesome, and in some cases an almost unmanageable, floating debt. That of the United States is the smallest of the major powers, amounting on June 30, 1920, to $3,597,667,202, of which $2,768,927,500 represented certificates of indebtedness and $828,739,702 consisted of war savings certificates. This is a reduction of $603,471,848 from the high point of $4,201,139,050, which it reached on August 31, 1919. It was not until January, 1920, that the Treasury was able to reduce the floating debt to manageable amount and maturities.[7-a]

After that time it was able to pay off the loan certificates and issue in their place tax certificates of indebtedness which are arranged to mature at the dates of payment of the income and excess profits taxes. Assuming that Congress neither authorizes large new expenditures nor reduces existing taxes, it should be possible to clear away most of this floating debt out of surplus revenues by 1922 when the first Victory Notes fall due.

Great Britain has various short-term obligations which

[7-a] R. C. Leffingwell, "Treasury Methods of Financing the War in Relation to Inflation." In *Proceedings of the Academy of Political Science in the City of New York*, June, 1920, vol. ix, p. 17.

PROBLEMS OF CURRENCY AND DEBT

amount to over $6,500,000,000. Some of these are payable at once and others fall due within the present year, but all will have to be funded into long time bonds as the Government cannot hope to pay them in the immediate future. Indeed, equilibrium in the budget will be secured with difficulty even with the present high rates of taxation, and no surplus can be counted upon for retiring the floating debt. This consists of the following items:[8]

Ways and Means advances...................	$1,174,335,000
Treasury bills	5,354,935,000
	$6,529,270,000

In addition to these debts "immediately due," there are also obligations maturing between April, 1920, and March, 1924, amounting to $7,340,000,000. Evidently the advances by the United States Government to Great Britain are included in this sum, but as this Government has the right to extend final maturity to 1938, this debt will probably be prolonged to that time.

France had a floating debt of $6,600,000,000 in short time *bons*, treasury bills, *obligations*, etc., most of which consisted of three- and six-months bills. This debt was of the most liquid type, as it fell due from month to month and therefore presented a problem of the first magnitude, especially in view of the fact that France was still borrowing to meet current expenditures. In January, 1920, a new loan was floated partly to fund this indebtedness and partly to raise needed money. Subscriptions amounted to $3,140,000,000, of which $1,600,000,000 was received in cash, $1,712,000,000 in *bons* and other forms of floating debt, and the remainder in

[8] *Economist*, June 12, 1920, p. 1281.

other securities. The floating debt of Italy amounts to $4,000,000,000 in short maturities.

Germany has a truly staggering floating debt, amounting to $26,250,000,000 (105,000,000,000 marks). No intimation of the existence of this enormous indebtedness had been given under the monarchical *régime*, and it was not until July, 1919, that the unwelcome news was finally broken to the German people of the accumulation of a floating debt of $18,000,000,000; since then it has grown steadily until on March 31, 1920, it amounted to the sum just named. That a floating debt of such magnitude could have accumulated is the strongest possible indictment of the German loan policy of financing the war that could be framed. Its amount is a measure of the insufficiency of the loans and shows how weak a reliance they proved themselves to be in the face of serious demands. This floating debt indicates clearly the complete breakdown of the vaunted German loan policy. Its funding presents an almost insoluble problem.[8a] Equally sinister are the floating

---

8-a The total debt of Germany, on March 31, 1920, was as follows:

Funded:

3 % Imperial loan (pre-war)		$400,000,000
3½% Imperial loan (pre-war)		500,000,000
4 % Imperial loan (pre-war)		250,000,000
5 % War loans		18,100,000,000
4½% Treasury Notes (war)		2,250,000,000
5 % Treasury Notes (war)		500,000,000
Savings and premium loan (since Armistice)		1,000,000,000
Total		$23,000,000,000

Floating:

Discounted Treasury bills	$22,875,000,000
Other debts and obligations	3,375,000,000
Total	$26,250,000,000
Grand Total	$49,250,000,000

The floating debt is reported to be increasing at the rate of about $750,000,000 a month.

PROBLEMS OF CURRENCY AND DEBT

debts reported for Austria ($5,700,000,000), and Hungary ($3,780,000,000). In view of the utter financial collapse of these states it is difficult to see how a satisfactory disposition can be made of this indebtedness, except by some *tour de force*.

In this connection it should be pointed out that the issues of paper money are not included in these sums, which are, therefore, more favorable than the reality. But inasmuch as the paper money issues do not bear interest, they present a problem of a somewhat different character and need not be considered at this point.

The most extreme and the least general method of facing the difficulty is that of outright repudiation. This has been announced by the Soviet Governments of both Russia and Hungary. But it is by no means certain that these pronouncements have finally disposed of the debts of those countries. With the return of stable government it may reasonably be expected that they will recognize the validity of the national debt. No other country has suggested the repudiation of the debt.

Although the ugly word " repudiation " has everywhere been scrupulously avoided, proposals that have looked to a scaling down of the existing indebtedness have not been lacking. Of these the most discussed has been the plan for a capital levy. This proposal has been discussed in Great Britain, France, Italy, Germany, Austria, Holland, and Switzerland. In Great Britain it has been the subject of discussion for a year or more and was taken up in Parliament by the Chancellor of the Exchequer, but the plan was rejected by the Government as impracticable. Subsequently, however, a proposal for a levy on wealth gained during the war wrung " a guarded and apparently reluctant assent " from a Parliamentary Committee on Increases of Wealth, and

WAR COSTS AND THEIR FINANCING

is even now the subject of lively debate.[8-b] In France it was accorded a less sympathetic hearing, in spite of its advocacy by Mr. Klotz, Minister of Finance, and was later declared by M. Ribot to be dead. From Italy came the suggestion that "an extraordinary tax should be levied, divided in a few installments, and equalling the half of private patrimonies; and in a short period the war debt will be liquidated without causing any harmful disturbance of values, salaries or profits, or the whole organization of the national economy."[9] On July 10, 1919, Minister of Finance Schanzer proposed to the Italian Chamber a levy on wealth of 15 per cent. to reduce the internal debt. This plan was discarded, however, in favor of a heavy graduated tax on war profits. In Switzerland the capital levy was endorsed by the legislative bodies but defeated on a referendum by the people; the Geneva State Council, however, has under consideration a bill providing for a levy on capital. The Czecho-Slovak National Assembly has passed a bill providing for a levy on capital according to which net capital will be taxed from three per cent. on $40,000 to 20 per cent. on $4,600,000, payable in six installments; the announced purpose of the tax is to raise the value of the currency. The Budget Committee of the Austrian National Assembly has under consideration a bill which proposes a capital levy, payable partly in cash and partly in securities, in 20 annual installments. The currency stamping act of Hungary, according to which half of the notes presented were funded into four per cent. nontransferable bonds which are available

---
[8-b] *Economist*, May 22, 1920, p. 1039.
[9] Achille Loria, "Italy's After-War Problems," translated from *Nuovo Antologia* in *The Americas*, November, 1918.

"for payment of a capital levy," presages clearly the next step in the deflation and debt-reduction policy of that country. Only in Germany, apparently, has the system actually been put in force. A tax has been introduced in that country providing for a heavy capital levy under the title of "The State Exigency Tribute."[10] It is imposed upon all subjects of the state, individual and corporate, and on foreign individuals and companies residing or doing business in Germany, and is levied on assets of 5,000 marks ($1,250) and above at rates which progress from 10 per cent. on this amount to 65 per cent. on amounts in excess of 100,000,000 marks ($25,000,000). The act provided that declarations were to be made on December 31, 1919. Various allowances are made, and payments are spread over 30 years.

The capital levy is a plan for the conscription of wealth and involves a heavy imposition made once for all either upon all kinds of capital or upon certain specified kinds, as, for instance, the war bonds themselves. The plans actually proposed have generally involved a levy upon all capital, and in some cases the proposal has been made that it should also be imposed upon the capitalized value of large unearned incomes. Payment of the tax would presumably be permitted, not only in money, but in Government bonds, which would then be cancelled. If the capital levy were made equal in amount to the entire public debt, the slate would be wiped clean by one single transaction, and further taxation to meet interest charges or redeem the principal would be unnecessary. A levy smaller in amount would realize these results in smaller measure.

---

[10] J. Jastrow, "The German Capital Levy Tax," in *Quarterly Journal of Economics*, May, 1920.

WAR COSTS AND THEIR FINANCING

As a purely fiscal problem, the strongest argument in favor of the capital levy is that it offers a country a method of escape from an intolerable burden without the necessity of repudiation of its national debt. If a choice must be made between these two methods, there seems to be no doubt as to which is the better. Repudiation places the whole burden upon the holders of the national bonds. In countries where subscribers have been appealed to on grounds of patriotism, such an act would be especially abhorrent. The capital levy, on the other hand, will place the burden upon all owners of capital of whatever form and would thus distribute the payment equitably, on the assumption that property affords a measure of ability. Other arguments have been advanced in favor of the capital levy, but into these it is not possible to enter here.[11] Its advantages are stated thus in Pethick-Lawrence's book:

> The effect of a levy on capital will be to wipe out the whole or part of the debt and to give the state a financial interest in certain national enterprises. It will bring about partial deflation. It will not change the total aggregate of the wealth of the country as a whole, but will change its distribution. It will make it possible to balance the budget and reduce direct taxation. In this way business men with moderate incomes will find the levy much less hindrance to their business than the heavy income tax which will otherwise have to be imposed. The persons who will feel the weight of the levy most heavily will be the men of great wealth and those living without personal exertion on the proceeds of their investments.

---

[11] See Report of the Committee on War Finance of the American Economic Association, Supplement No. 2 of the *American Economic Review*, March, 1919, p. 69; F. W. Pethick-Lawrence, *A Levy on Capital*, London, 1918; A. C. Pigou, *The Economy and Finance of the War*, London, 1916. A very extensive literature on this subject has grown up in France and Germany during the past year.

PROBLEMS OF CURRENCY AND DEBT

Although such a plan for scaling down the debt need not be seriously contemplated in the United States, where the war debt can be easily carried, the problem is quite otherwise in many of the European countries. With the possibility of a complete breakdown of national credit impending, it may even yet happen that other Governments will follow the lead of Germany and resort to this method of reducing their national burdens. The only alternative is heavy taxation over a long period of years.

Another method of scaling down the debt would be by means of a compulsory reduction or postponement of the interest charges. Thus, Dr. Rasin, Minister of Finance in Czecho-Slovakia, suggested that the Austrian war debt bearing $5\frac{1}{2}$ per cent. interest should be transformed into low-interest bearing bonds, say at one or two per cent. interest. This could easily be done, in his opinion, and would avert the otherwise probable bankruptcy of the State. As the $5\frac{1}{2}$ per cent. bonds are now selling at about 60 and a new two per cent. bond would bring about 40, the loss to the bondholder would be less serious than the gain to the State.

Still another method of reducing, in part at least, the indebtedness of practically every European participant in the war on the side of the Entente Allies is for the United States Government to forgive the foreign Governments the sums advanced them during the war. This would mean a reduction of some $10,000,000,000 in the aggregate European war debt, distributed among the different belligerents roughly in proportion to their respective total indebtedness. This suggestion has awakened great enthusiasm wherever it has been made in Europe, but as yet no official notice has been taken of the suggestion either by foreign Governments or by the United States.[12] The Treasury Department has, however, arranged to postpone for three years the collection of interest on the Allied debt, and to spread the accumulated interest charges over a series of years. This arrangement provides a breathing spell during which the Allied governments may adjust their most pressing financial problems.

In the case of nations engaged in the war, a reduction in their debt may be effected by the transfer of German indemnity bonds. Thus, Belgium is to have her war debt, incurred by borrowing from other Governments, liquidated by having German bonds substituted for Belgian bonds. Other nations in similar manner will be able to reduce their indebtedness by the substitution of German bonds for their own. This process, however, is not to take place at once, and the amount that will be received from Germany as an indemnity is as yet indeterminate. The payments to be made by Germany other than payment in kind, surrender of territory,

---

[12] This idea has been endorsed by George W. Wickersham in the United States (*Washington Post*, October 21, 1918), while Senator Kenyon carried it to the point of offering a resolution in Congress that the United States should cancel the financial obligations owed this Government by France (*New York Times*, May 8, 1919). It has also been sponsored by Sir George Paish in England. Sir George Paish in a copyrighted interview sent to the *New York Tribune* of July 20, 1919, by its London correspondent, said he had come to conclusion that "a collapse of world credit is not only possible but imminent. . . . I see only one way out and that is by capital levies, both national and international. I have made the suggestion that America and England each agree to wipe out, say, a thousand million [pounds sterling] of the debts owed them by Continental countries and pool an international credit in the League of Nations. My suggestion is based on the principle that it is better to forego part, thus making the rest good than to force bankruptcy and thereby receive, say, only 50 cents on the dollar." The proposal has also been endorsed by J. M. Keynes in his able and influential book, *The Economic Consequences of the Peace* (pp. 260-282).

PROBLEMS OF CURRENCY AND DEBT

ships, and other forms of restitution, are shown in the following schedule of reparations:[13]

1. To be issued forthwith, 20,000,000,000 marks gold bearer bonds, payable not later than May 1, 1921, without interest.
2. To be issued forthwith, further 40,000,000,000 marks gold bearer bonds, bearing interest at 2½ per cent. per annum between 1921 and 1926, and thereafter at five per cent. per annum with an additional one per cent. for amortization beginning in 1926 on the whole amount of the issue.
3. To be delivered forthwith, a covering undertaking in writing to issue when, but not until, the Commission is satisfied that Germany can meet such interest and sinking fund obligations, a further instalment of 40,000,000,000 marks gold five per cent. bearer bonds, the time and mode of payment of principal and interest to be determined by the Commission.

It is, of course, obvious that even if these indemnity bonds could be substituted by the Governments receiving them for their own obligations, there would be no reduction in the aggregate debt, but merely a shifting from the Entente to the Central Powers. To the extent that the finances of the former Governments would be benefited, those of Germany would be injured.

Evidently a consideration of the methods thus far proposed do not lead very far in the direction of the actual payment of the debt. It remains, therefore, to take up some of the problems that present themselves in connection with real debt payment. The first question that may be raised is whether the debt is of a type that lends itself to repayment. About one-fifth of the war debts are of the *rente* type, that is, in the form of bonds running at the pleasure of the Government with no specified date of maturity. A debt thrown into such a

[13] Peace Treaty, Part VIII, Annex II, Section 12(c).

form may fairly be spoken of as a perpetual debt, as there is no obligation on the part of the Government to redeem it, and history has yet failed to record a single instance of a debt of this type having been paid off. Moreover, bonds of this type are usually sold at a discount, and this was true of the French and Italian *rentes*. Since they are issued under par at low rates in order to save interest, the Government is unwilling to redeem them at par. With the exception of the United States, Australian, and New Zealand loans and most of the loans of Great Britain and Canada, every belligerent country issued its bonds below par.

On the whole, it may be concluded that the debts of most of the countries are thrown into a form convenient for refunding or for payment. Terminable annuities, of which numbers were issued by Great Britain during the Napoleonic wars, were not used at all to finance the World War. Serial bonds were resorted to only in the case of part of four of the German loans. Both of these forms of obligations are objectionable during a struggle in which borrowing is going on continuously and on a large scale, since provision must be made for fixed annual payments from the very beginning. They thus impose an additional expenditure upon the Government at the very time when it is borrowing and when it may be most inconvenient to make payments. Furthermore, they are open to the objection that they preclude a refunding by which advantage may be taken of a possible fall in the rate of interest. They are, therefore, unsuited for use in time of war. Still further objections may be made to the use of serial bonds by a national Government. A Power which may have to finance a war cannot afford to be hampered by the existence of a debt of which payment is compulsory. In

PROBLEMS OF CURRENCY AND DEBT

this respect the effect of the serial bond is like that of the much over-rated sinking-fund policy in that it compels payment of the debt even when the Government is borrowing. And on the other hand, the serial bond prevents more rapid payment if happily larger surplus revenues make such action possible.

The British colonies almost without exception issued their war loans in the form of straight-term bonds. Bonds of this kind have certain advantages, such as simplicity and the possibility of arranging their terms so as to have them mature like bankers' paper at dates convenient for repayment or refunding. On the other hand, they have the disadvantage that the bonds of each issue fall due in a large block which may necessitate refunding. The accumulation of a fund in advance to provide for their payment either by a sinking fund or by some other device, is neither advisable nor likely, and an attempt on the part of the Treasury to purchase them in the open market on any large scale would probably have the effect of driving up their price.

The " optional " or redeemable bond has been preferred in financing the World War, considerably over two-thirds of the debts now outstanding having been thrown into this form. The optional bond is an American device, introduced at the time of the Civil War. Although such a bond introduces a certain element of complexity into the national debt, it has certain decided merits. Perhaps the most important of these is the fact that it furnishes an earnest of the intention of the Government to attack the payment or refunding of the debt as promptly as possible, a provision that has a beneficial effect upon the credit of the Government. It also gives an earlier control over the debt than would be secured by the issue of a straight long term bond.

WAR COSTS AND THEIR FINANCING

The latter has probably been the factor that has led to the selection of this type by most of the belligerent Governments. With one exception (the third French war loan) the latest optional redemption date named is 1931, and the great bulk of the debt is brought by this device within the control of the respective Governments within the next decade. What use they will make of this opportunity it will remain for the future to show. It is possible, of course, that, if market conditions prove favorable, the interest charges may be reduced by refunding the floating or maturing debt at lower rates of interest, but it is unlikely that any considerable savings can be effected by this method for a number of years. At the present writing (July, 1920) the movement of interest rates is still upward.

One other feature of the obligations issued during this war may be mentioned. The United States and Canada were the only countries that specified in the contract that the principal and interest of the bonds must be paid in gold. In every other country, consequently, the service of the debt and its eventual payment may be discharged in the currency of that country, however depreciated that may be. Although no obstacle has been interposed in the way of the payment of the debt by reason of the necessity of securing gold, the absence of this provision may tend to prevent an early return to a gold basis and might even lead some Governments to favor further inflation with a view to making payment easier.

The somewhat belated question may be raised at this point as to whether the Governments of the world have given any indication that they wish to redeem their debts. In candor it must be confessed that the evidence

PROBLEMS OF CURRENCY AND DEBT

is slight. The United States is the only country that has as yet established a sinking fund for the amortization of its entire war debt. Great Britain has provided a sinking fund for the payment of her last loan, which will finally be expunged by its operation in 1990. The French Government entered into an agreement with the Bank of France at the time of the extension of the latter's charter by which the advances of the Bank to the Treasury should be redeemed at the rate of two per cent. per annum. Some of the Governments provided in the laws authorizing the bond issues that the bonds might be used in payment of certain taxes to the Government. To the extent to which bonds are utilized for this purpose a retirement of the debt would be effected.

The all important question involved in a discussion of the payment of the war debt is, after all, the question, *can* the Governments of Europe pay their present debts? If the history of their past record in the matter of debt payment be accepted as a guide to their probable action in the future, it may safely be asserted that they will not pay off the principal of these debts. They will prefer to let them run. The United States and Great Britain alone of modern nations have ever been willing to reduce their national indebtedness, and they alone of the belligerent states have made a beginning in the payment of the debts resulting from the war. The peak of the United States gross debt was reached on August 31, 1919, when it stood at $26,596,701,648; by June 30, 1920, it had been brought down to $24,299,321,467. This reduction of $2,297,380,181 was due in part to the application of a huge Treasury balance of over $1,000,000,000 which had been maintained at a high figure during the war, and in part to the sale of military supplies in an amount which totaled $760,708,222 by April 9, 1920. The high point of the British debt seems to have been attained on December 31, 1919, when it stood at $40,395,000,000; on June 30, 1920, it was $39,225,000,000, or a reduction of $1,170,000,000, due, as in the United States, to the transfer of a Treasury balance, to the sale of military supplies, and to the use of surplus revenue.

The payment of a debt can be effected only by having a clear surplus over expenditures. It is unlikely that any of the European Governments will be able for many years to show a surplus. They will be fortunate if by the strictest economy they can avoid deficits. Moreover, if the budgets can be brought into equilibrium and a surplus established, a double pressure will at once be manifested to prevent the application of this surplus to debt payment. On the one hand there will be a demand from the industrial classes to be relieved from burdensome taxation, and on the other there will be a steady pressure for the expansion of governmental functions and activities. It is altogether unlikely that any effort will be made to apply the revenues of the state to a reduction of the principal of the debt.

In conclusion it may safely be asserted that no reduction in the aggregate sum of European indebtedness will be effected within the next generation or two except by means of partial repudiation or by a capital levy or other methods of scaling down the debt. Repudiation by name will undoubtedly be avoided, but substantially the same result may be achieved under some other guise. There is, therefore, little likelihood of any real payment of the debts of the European countries.

CHAPTER XIII

AFTER-WAR PROBLEMS OF TAXATION

Economic strength of the leading nations — The financial outlook in the United States — The situation in Great Britain — The situation in France and Italy — Germany's position — Proposed revenues of five leading nations — Probable development of principal taxes.

The nations of Europe are faced with a gigantic and almost insuperable problem in raising the necessary revenues to meet the financial burdens that have come to them as a legacy of the World War. In estimating the abilities of the different countries to provide the necessary revenues, they must be differentiated sharply, for some of the countries have large reserve strength and will undoubtedly be able to meet their obligations, whereas others have probably reached the limit of their capacity, or possibly even exceeded it. Any estimate of the ability of the different nations to bring their budgets into equilibrium and to maintain them there must take into account not merely the national wealth of the country, but also the productivity, energy, and thrift of the people. The most important factors in such an estimate are the extent of the undeveloped resources of a country and the degree of industrial intelligence possessed by the population.[1] The United States has both in large measure; the people of Great Britain and Germany are intelligent and well-trained, but few undeveloped resources exist in either of these countries; the same is true of France and Italy, though

---
[1] See H. C. Adams, *The Science of Finance*, p. 89.

WAR COSTS AND THEIR FINANCING

their workmen must be rated lower in industrial capacity than those of the countries just named; Russia has vast natural wealth, but her population possesses a low grade of industrial intelligence; the states of the former Austro-Hungarian Empire have neither of these elements of industrial progress. The actual situation in the United States and the leading European countries as shown in the budgets for the fiscal year ending in 1920 may be analyzed with due consideration of these differences.

The expenditures of the United States Government for the fiscal year ending June 30, 1919, exclusive of disbursements for the Post Office, amounted to $15,365,-362,742, and the revenue receipts to $4,647,603,852. The expenditures for the following year, exclusive of public debt transactions, and on the basis of preliminary estimates were placed by Secretary Glass in his annual report of December, 1919, at $6,812,522,729,[2] while the receipts were estimated as follows:

Internal revenue	$4,990,000,000
Customs	275,000,000
Sale of public land	1,250,000
Miscellaneous	841,000,000
Total ordinary receipts	$6,107,450,000
Public debt receipts	1,210,556,634
Total	$7,318,006,634

"In the absence of a budget system or of any Treasury control of governmental expenditure it is even more difficult to foretell the expenditures than the receipts of the Government." The receipts from taxation, from the final instalments of the Victory Liberty Loan, and from further issues of Treasury certificates

---
[2] Report, p. 202.

AFTER-WAR PROBLEMS OF TAXATION

of indebtedness would probably suffice, he thought, to meet the needs of the coming year. He added:[3]

> I need scarcely say that the realization of these sanguine expectations is contingent upon the practice of the most rigid economy by the Government and the continuance of ample revenues from taxation. Such a course, accompanied by the practice of sober economy and wise investment by our people and strict avoidance of waste and speculation, will make it possible for the American people to respond to the demands to be made upon them privately for capital and credit by the nations of Europe.

The actual transactions of the Treasury for the fiscal year ending June 30, 1920, as shown by the Treasury statement of that date, were receipts of $6,694,565,389 and expenditures of $6,766,444,461, with a resulting deficit of $71,879,072. For the year 1921 the total receipts, excluding public-debt receipts, were estimated by Secretary Glass[4] in his annual report of 1919 at $5,420,000,000 and the expenditures at $3,535,997,985. As these estimates were made eight months before the beginning of the fiscal year to which they apply and do not include such items as the Government's payments to the railroads, little dependence can be placed upon them, especially on the side of expenditures. It is altogether probable, however, that, unless unforeseen appropriations should be made, the Government will hereafter be able to meet its current expenditures out of its current income and even to apply a surplus to the reduction of the floating debt.

In the case of Great Britain it will probably suffice to contrast the last peace budget for the year ending

---
[3] Letter of July 25 to banks and trust companies, quoted in *Federal Reserve Bulletin*, August, 1919, p. 726.
[4] Report, p. 204.

WAR COSTS AND THEIR FINANCING

March 31, 1914, with the budget passed for the year ending March 31, 1920. In the former the civil budget amounted to $864,964,845 and interest payments, including sinking-fund payments, to $122,500,000, giving total expenditures of $987,464,845. Against this the revenues amounted to $991,214,250, yielding a surplus of almost $4,000,000. The budget for 1920 stands in striking contrast to this. The total expenditures proved to be some $8,328,865,000, of which the interest on the debt accounts for $1,800,-000,000. The remaining $6,500,000,000 was about equally divided between civil and war expenditures. Against this enormous total there were received revenues amounting to $5,697,855,000, to which an additional $1,000,000,000 was added from the sale of assets. This left a deficit of $1,631,010,000, which it was proposed to meet by further borrowing. For this purpose a new loan of $1,250,000,000 was voted by Parliament. It will be noticed that the interest payments now amount to more than double the total civil budget before the war, in addition to which the civil budget itself has been enormously swollen by pensions and added costs, such as the civil service bonus (of $20,000,000), the loans to Allies ($140,000,000), liabilities " in respect of coal " ($100,000,000), unemployment benefit ($40,000,000), etc. Even if it could be assumed that as a result of universal disarmament all military and naval expenditures would be at once discontinued, Great Britain would be left with a heavy burden as a result of the war. To meet these growing expenditures taxes have been imposed which before the war would have been regarded as unbearable. They rest now with oppressive weight on wealth and large incomes, the latter being taxed in certain circumstances as high as 67 per cent.

AFTER-WAR PROBLEMS OF TAXATION

The budget for 1920-21 makes a much better showing and evidences the extent of Great Britain's financial recovery within the previous year. Expenditures are estimated at $5,920,510,000 and revenues at $7,091,500,000, which is a distinct improvement over 1920 on both sides of the budget. If this plan is carried through there will be available for reduction of the debt the sum of $1,170,990,000. To obtain this favorable balance Mr. Chamberlain proposed to increase the postal and telephone rates, to raise the duties on spirits, beer, and wines, and on cigars, and to double the stamp duties on transfers and bearer securities, and on ordinary receipts. The income tax was left unchanged at 6s. in the pound, but the excess profits tax was raised from 40 to 60 per cent., although its abolition had been hoped for. The Chancellor offered, however, to leave the tax at its old figure if Parliament would impose a special levy on war wealth.[5] From all these sources additional revenues of $383,250,000 might be expected.

This will constitute a heavy burden, but not necessarily an unbearable one. New powers of productive efficiency have been developed among the British people during the war, and the ability to produce certain kinds of goods and to meet foreign competition in competitive markets has probably been heightened. Much depends upon the solution of labor difficulties, but it may be assumed that proper steps will be taken to meet the legitimate demands of the working classes. If the morale and spirit of the nation is sustained, there is no reason to doubt the ability of the British people to carry the present load of charges on the foreign debt and of expanded governmental activities.

It is difficult to present an accurate statement of the

---

[5] *The Round Table*, June, 1920, p. 626.

WAR COSTS AND THEIR FINANCING

French situation since matters are in flux to such a degree that estimates change almost from day to day. The total ordinary expenditures for the year 1919 were about $3,700,000,000.[6] More than half of this amount represents the interest charge on the debt, which it is estimated will amount to $2,000,000,000 yearly, including $100,000,000 for payments to the Bank of France for the redemption of the redundant bank notes. The Government expressed the hope that these payments might soon be raised to $150,000,000 a year. The debt, however, is steadily increasing, owing to the delay in imposing adequate taxation; it amounted on February 1, 1919, to $35,000,000,000, and has now reached over $46,000,000,000 with no certainty that its growth has been finally checked.

The budget for 1920 as adopted amounts to $9,764,200,000, but the expenditure is divided into three sections: (1) the ordinary budget comprising the normal expenditure of the state of $3,864,200,000; (2) the extraordinary budget, consisting of exceptional expenditure resulting from the war of $700,000,000; (3) a budget comprising the expenditure recoverable from the enemy under the Peace Treaty, amounting to $5,200,000,000. Existing taxes and other revenue receipts are expected to yield $2,144,800,000, leaving a deficit of $7,619,400,000. But to this must be added additional expenses for special services of $900,000,000, and a further sum of $750,000,000 for repaying short time foreign loans falling due, notably the Anglo-French loan in the United States. Thus the total deficit is brought up to over $9,000,000,000. This sum must

[6] See M. Ribot's speech before the Chamber of Deputies, *Journal Officiel*, May 30-31, 1919, and the tax proposals of M. Klotz as reported in the *Economist* (London) June 7, 1919.

AFTER-WAR PROBLEMS OF TAXATION

come from fresh taxes, new loans, liquidation of war stocks, and payment of indemnities by Germany and her allies.[7]

From new taxes it is hoped to obtain $1,719,400,000 and from the sale of army supplies $700,000,000, which together with existing revenues, will produce total receipts of $4,564,200,000. It is also hoped to effect additional economies in expenditure amounting to $1,600,000,000. But even if all these proposals are realized, there will still remain a deficit of more than $3,600,000,000 to be met out of further loans and German indemnity payments. It is evident from this exposition how dependent French finances are upon this last named source.

The new taxes introduced in 1919 consisted of increased duties on wines, coffee, sugar, mineral water, and taxes on gas and electricity; increases were also made in the taxes on tobacco, matches, succession duties, registration duties, and special taxes were imposed on incomes and war profits. A state monopoly of petrol and petroleum was also established. For 1920 the Finance Committee of the Chamber of Deputies propose to increase the rate of the *impots cedulaires* on income and industrial profits, to raise the maximum rate of the general income tax from 20 to 40 per cent., and to establish a super tax of 10 per cent. for bachelors; but on the other hand, they plan to raise the exemption minimum of the general income tax from $600 to $1200 and to increase the exemptions for children. The total yield from direct taxes is estimated at $276,000,-000. Increases are recommended in the stamp duty on sales, shooting licenses, etc., in the taxes on alcohol, liquors, beer, cider, and wines, on playing cards and

---
[7] *Economic World*, July 24, 1920, p. 127.

WAR COSTS AND THEIR FINANCING

public amusements, and new duties are levied on public conveyances and private motors, coffee, tea, chocolate, chicory, glucose etc. The aggregate yield of these increases in indirect taxes is given as $407,600,000. The balance of $1,000,000,000, to make up the total of $1,700,000,000 from new taxation, it is hoped to obtain from a tax on turnover at the rate of one per cent. on ordinary transactions and of 10 per cent. on articles of luxury. This program thus calls for loans amounting to about $3,000,000,000. Subscriptions to the recent loan totaled $3,126,000,000, of which, however, only $1,360,000,000 was in new money, the balance being in Government securities.[8]

One of the weaknesses of the French revenue system has been a disinclination on the part of the French people to submit to direct taxes. Even during the war most of the taxes were indirect, the income tax not being levied until 1916, and then only at very low rates and with very high exemptions. Moreover, after the introduction of the income tax, there was considerable delay and evasion.[9] Before revenues can be made to equal expenditures it will be necessary to apply a drastic and far-reaching system of direct taxation.

---

[8] *Federal Reserve Bulletin*, May, 1920, p. 491.

[9] The following sentences from M. Ribot's speech of May 30, 1919, already alluded to, throw a vivid light upon the situation: "Why does not the Minister ask more of the direct tax? The cause of this is sad enough . . . the cause is that the administration for direct taxation is not capable of filling the part which events have imposed upon it. . . . The disorder is excessive; the treasury losses billions. Note also the delay. In March and April we received bills for the general income tax founded on the basis of the 1917 income. We are late by a year. The question of exemption must also be settled and workmen made to pay their income taxes. . . . Agricultural profits are not taxed — it is scandalous. . . . The Minister of Finance hesitates to increase direct taxes, but taxes on wealth and income must be increased."

AFTER-WAR PROBLEMS OF TAXATION

Assuming that the increase in the debt measures the destruction and waste of capital during the war, it is clear that the enormous revenues required by the present budget must be obtained from a smaller taxable base. The destruction of property in France has been estimated at $10,000,000,000, to which may be added another $4,000,000,000 for shipping and cargoes.[10] Large investments in Russia and Turkey, amounting possibly to $5,000,000,000, are temporarily nonproductive and probably worthless, and those in Rumania and Mexico have lost considerably in value.[11] To replace the wasted capital and provide for further needs, both private and governmental, will require the sacrifice of everything nonessential and possibly even a reduction in the standard of living. The question of national solvency seems to be reduced to one of willingness to submit to heavier taxation.

According to a statement by S. Nitti, the Italian Prime Minister,[12] the total Italian debt now amounts to $18,758,000,000, on which the annual interest charge may be placed at not less than $900,000,000. The expenditures for the civil service have trebled and are estimated for the year 1920 at $1,000,000,000. Other expenditures, including $150,000,000 for war liquidation purposes, are expected to bring up the total annual outlay to about $2,000,000,000. Against these expenditures the total receipts of the year 1920 were estimated at $1,800,000,000. For the fiscal year 1921 the expenditures are estimated at $1,900,000,000, exclusive of interest on the foreign debt or wage increases, while receipts

---

[10] See my "Direct and Indirect Costs of the Great World War" (Washington, 1919), pp. 285, 289, 290.
[11] Most of the foreign investments of French citizens have been made in these four countries.
[12] *Federal Reserve Bulletin*, May, 1920, p. 489.

are put at $1,500,000,000, thus leaving a deficit of $400,000,000 on incomplete returns.

The wide discrepancy between receipts and expenditures existing in 1919 and 1920 showed the need of radical tax reform. Accordingly a series of Royal decrees dated November, 1919, put a new system of taxation into effet from January 1, 1920. Formerly taxes were levied mainly upon land, buildings, and private incomes, but according to the new law capital, both normal and due to war profits, is also taxed. The original plan was to impose a capital levy, but in view of the stormy opposition which this aroused, it was modified to a compulsory loan at a nominal rate of interest. This in turn gave place to the present scheme of a five per cent. voluntary loan and a tax on capital. The loan has already brought in some $4,000,000,000, which is to be applied immediately to the refunding of the floating debt and the retirement of some of the bank notes issued on account of the state.

The taxes provided for under the new system consist of the following: (1) an extraordinary tax on capital, which again is made up of (a) a tax on the increase in wealth due to the war, and (b) a tax on the original fortune existing prior to the war. Both of these are progressive, the rates of the first ranging from 10 per cent. on $4,000 to 60 per cent. on the largest fortunes, while the rates of the second run from 4.5 per cent. on $10,000 to 50 per cent. on $20,000,000; in the latter case the tax may be paid in annual installments over a period of 20 years. (2) By decree of November 24, 1919, the taxes on land and buildings, the special war tax on incomes, the personal war tax, etc., were abolished and in their place were established a normal tax on incomes and a supplementary tax on total income,

AFTER-WAR PROBLEMS OF TAXATION

the latter applying only to individuals with incomes above $900, at rates ranging from 1 to 25 per cent. These two taxes do not go into effect until January 1, 1921. (3) Supplementary taxes are revised so as to make them more productive, the rates being raised in case of taxes on registration, mortgages, government concessions, mortmain, insurance policies, bicycles, automobiles, and inheritances. New taxes are imposed upon the sales of articles of luxury and of common use, and upon mineral waters.[13]

During the course of the war taxes and other revenues in Italy were gradually screwed up to the top notch and now rest upon every conceivable commodity, transaction, and form of realized wealth. Some of these are purely war measures and temporary in their nature and will disappear, while the desire to protect native industries will act to keep down or reduce customs revenues. A difficult, if not insoluble, problem is presented to Italy of bringing her swollen expenditures and her revenues into equilibrium. The burden of taxation upon the Italian people is already crushing, and it is scarcely conceivable that much more can be raised from this source. The fiscal situation is aggravated by a greatly depreciated currency and unfavorable rates of foreign exchange, both of which impose an additional burden upon Italy in meeting her foreign obligations. At the same time the stoppage of the tourist traffic and the decline of remittances from emigrants, of whom about 1,200,000 were recalled as reservists, as well as the falling off of the export trade, reduced the national income at the very time that expenditures were growing.

---

[13] *The Great Fiscal Reform and Rehabilitation of Italian Finances*, 1920. Issued by the Office of Italian Minister Plenipotentiary, 291 Broadway, New York City.

WAR COSTS AND THEIR FINANCING

A considerable period will elapse before any one of these factors will reach pre-war proportions, and in the interval it is difficult to see how the Government can maintain its normal functions and carry the burden of the interest on the war debt, war pensions, and other charges incidental to the war without continued resort to credit.

The financial situation of Germany was set forth candidly and in detail for the first time since the outbreak of the war by Dr. Schiffer, Minister of Finance, in a memorandum presented to the National Assembly at Weimar in February, 1919.[13] Dr. Schiffer estimated that the national annual expenditures for the future civil budget and debt charges would be $2,500,000,000, as compared with $900,000,000 before the war. The annual expenditures of the states and the communes would be about $1,250,000,000, as compared with $750,-000,000 before the war, the difference measuring the war burden imposed upon the local units. The total amount of revenue to be raised by taxation in the future would therefore be $3,750,000,000, as against $1,650,000,000 before the war. In July, 1919, Mathias Erzberger, the new Minister of Finance, raised these estimates considerably, and at the same time vigorously attacked the problem of raising the necessary revenues. Tax proposals of the most drastic and thorough-going character were submitted by him and finally adopted by the National Assembly. Some of these went into effect at once and others did not become effective until 1920; some were permanent and others non-recurrent, so that it is difficult to estimate their revenue-producing character. The following were the principal new taxes:[14]

---
[13] *Vossische Zeitung*, February 16, 1919.
[14] *Berliner Tageblatt*, April 25, 1920.

AFTER-WAR PROBLEMS OF TAXATION

(1) A war tax on the increase of wealth during the war, at rates ranging from 10 per cent. on $2,500 to 100 per cent. on the excess over $100,000, with an initial exemption of $2,500 and various deductions, effective September 26, 1919.

(2) An extraordinary war tax for the year 1919 on the excess of income in 1919 over that of 1914, at rates varying from 5 per cent. on the first $2,500 to 80 per cent. on $750,000. Effective September 10, 1919.

Either of these taxes may be paid with government bonds.

(3) The inheritance tax is made more severe, being levied both upon inheritances and upon donations to living persons, but fairly liberal exemptions exist. The rates progress according to both size of fortune and degree of relationship, ranging from 1 per cent. on small estates to near relatives to 90 per cent. on large fortunes to distant heirs. Effective September 1, 1919.

(4) Emergency sacrifice tax. This is a heavy non-recurring tax upon the total real and personal property of all persons and corporations according to their assessment of December 31, 1919. Exemption is made of $1,250 for a man and in the case of a married man of an equal additional sum for wife and each child after the first. The rates progress from 10 to 65 per cent., but payment may be spread by annual installments over a period of 32 to 50 years. Effective January 14, 1920.[15]

(5) Imperial income tax, which now replaces all former state and municipal income taxes, these latter governments sharing in the revenues. Effective April 14, 1920.

---

[15] It is estimated that there is in Germany from $67,500,000,000 to $70,000,000,000 worth of property which will be subject to this tax; and it is calculated that the Government will realize from this source in 1920 about $562,500,000.

(6) Corporation tax. This is the income tax applied to corporations. Effective April 15, 1920.

(7) Tax of 10 per cent. on the proceeds of capital, that is upon returns from foreign investments, and on domestic dividends, interest, royalties, etc. Effective March 31, 1920.

(8) A property tax on the increase of wealth, calculated at intervals of three years. The rates are from 1 to 10 per cent., with exemptions of a present fortune of less than $5,000 and an increment of less than $1,250. Effective April 21, 1920.

From these various sources it is hoped to obtain for the present fiscal year revenues amounting to $3,450,000,000; the customs duties are relied upon for $2,275,000,000, while $250,000,000 are expected from tobacco taxes and as much more from the new export duties. Altogether total revenues of about $6,250,000,000 are estimated. Against this the expenditures are reckoned at $6,987,500,000, of which interest on the public debt makes up almost half or $3,100,000,000. But this is only the ordinary budget. In addition Dr. Wirth, the Minister of Finance, has submitted an extraordinary budget of $2,900,000,000, which, however, does not include the deficit of $3,225,000,000 attributable to the postal and railway administration. It does include a sum of $1,000,000,000 for the execution of the Peace Treaty, but any amounts in excess of this which Germany may be compelled to pay will call for the raising of additional revenues.[16]

Drastic as are these levies, it is clear that they will have to be not only continued but increased if budgetary equilibrium is to be at all maintained. In spite of the enormous burden which will thereby be imposed

[16] *Industrie und Handelszeitung*, April 21, 1920.

upon the German people, there is reason to believe that their industrial intelligence, their habits of industry and thrift, and their national tenacity will enable them to assume and carry this burden. It will involve a sacrifice of all nonessentials, a probable virtual confiscation of all large fortunes, and possibly a temporary suspension of the interest payments to holders of the domestic debt, but ultimately even these charges will probably be met.

An effort is made in the following table to present for the leading nations the relation of present revenues and expenditures to pre-war revenues and expenditures, their relative increase, and the *per capita* burden they constitute:

PRE-WAR AND POST-WAR REVENUES AND EXPENDITURES

	Per cent. growth of present over pre-war revenue	Per cent. growth of present over pre-war expenditures	Per cent. which present revenues are of present expenditures	Present revenue per capita
United States....	540	547	99	$65
United Kingdom.	474	743	68	120
France..........	158	801	22	51
Italy...........	185	539	45	51
Germany........	684	1,601	63	91

* By pre-war is meant the fiscal year 1914, and by present the year 1920.

The United States, Germany, and Great Britain have increased their revenues over those of the pre-war period the most, but the increase in the last-named country has involved the greatest effort and has absorbed the largest proportion of the national income, amounting, indeed, to two-fifths of the pre-war income. How heavy this burden is, and how much greater than that of any other country, is shown by the column of *per capita* revenues. Although the United States shows the greatest relative increase in taxes, they constitute a relatively lighter burden upon the people than do those of Great Britain by whatever standard they are measured. There is still considerable financial power that could be taken up in further Government exactions or that may be devoted by private initiative to the rehabilitation and reconstruction of the European countries.

France succeeded in increasing her taxes over those of the pre-war revenues less than any other country, and the *per capita* charge to-day is the least of those shown in the table. The record of Italy is only slightly better than that of France, judged by this standard. If, however, the third column, showing the percentage growth of present over pre-war expenditures be made the basis of comparison, it is evident that the growth of expenditures in all countries has proceeded much more rapidly than that of revenue. The explanation of the present deficits is to be found in this fact. Until those swollen outlays can be reduced, there is little likelihood of securing equilibrium in the budgets. The insufficiency of the existing revenues to meet expenditures for the year 1920 is clearly shown in the fourth column, though this has already been corrected in the case of the two first countries for the budget of 1921.

Germany, in spite of her misguided financial policy during the war, has applied herself seriously to the task in hand and is proposing greatly to increase her taxation. Judged by what Great Britain has done, she has by no means reached the limit of her capacity as yet,

AFTER-WAR PROBLEMS OF TAXATION

and should be able to carry still heavier burdens. In fact, the taxes could be made about 30 per cent. heavier than they now are before the *per capita* burden would be as heavy as that borne by the British.

That taxation will necessarily be heavier and that these charges will continue for many years, is evident. The character and incidence of the taxes to be levied is therefore a question of paramount importance. Although it is too early to say definitely just how the different countries will order their systems of taxation, certain general principles stand out with sufficient definiteness to permit their statement.

Those countries that made the greatest use of taxation during the war were the ones that were able to develop direct taxes quickly and effectively. Great Britain was the only country that in 1914 had a well organized system of direct taxation. There the income tax was normally used to meet new demands and was easily expanded. During the war this tax, together with the inheritance and excess profits taxes, formed the sheet-anchor of the Exchequer, about two-thirds of the total revenue being derived from these sources. The United States was saved by a hair's breadth from the fate that befell the other countries that relied chiefly upon indirect taxes for their revenues. Only in 1913 was the income tax made a constitutional possibility. It is difficult to think how the Federal Government would have financed its enormous war expenditures without the income tax and its twin, the excess profits tax. There was a rapid development in these two taxes and in the inheritance tax, even in the years preceding the entrance of the United States into the war, and after that event they became the very backbone of the revenue system. There is no reason to suppose that these taxes, which proved so lucrative and, on the whole, equitable during the war will not continue for a time to be used to supply the tax revenues, scarcely less in amount, that peace demands in these two countries, though the opposition to the excess profits tax will probably result in its gradual modification if not elimination.

The other countries depended for the most part on indirect taxes. In France there has always been a disinclination on the part of the taxpayers to submit to direct taxes. The income tax itself was first introduced during the war. Although Italy had an income tax before the war, it relied for the additional revenues during the struggle upon a multitude of indirect exactions. In Germany the income tax, as well as other direct taxes, belonged to the separate states, and the revenues of the Imperial Government were derived for the most part from customs duties and other indirect taxes. The disadvantages of this system were recognized, and it would undoubtedly have been reorganized in a few years; but this distribution of the sources of revenue was a decided weakness in a military state like Germany and was responsible for some of the weaknesses of her excessive loan policy during the war. As foreign trade was disorganized in all the European countries, but little dependence could be placed upon the returns from customs, and to make good this deficit the Governments were forced to resort to a multitude of excise and consumption taxes. One of the striking features of war finance was the slight importance of customs duties as a source of governmental revenue; in those countries where they increased, as in France, the growth was of no fiscal significance, for it resulted from the enlarged purchase of war supplies on Government account.

AFTER-WAR PROBLEMS OF TAXATION

Certain marked tendencies in direct taxation were developed during the war. In the first place, heavier burdens were placed upon realized wealth than had ever been dreamed of before. There was also a great development of the principle of progression, and rates were raised to unheard-of heights. The rates of the income tax reached 77 per cent. in the United States; and in Great Britain 47½ per cent. The highest rates, however, were levied not unnaturally in the war profits and excess profits taxes, these reaching 80 per cent. in the United States and Great Britain and 60 per cent. in France and Italy. This tax was remarkable not only for the height of the rates and the large yields obtained, but also for its universality. By the end of the war it was to be found in practically every European country, neutral as well as belligerent.

The inheritance tax was the third of the three important instruments of direct taxation. A moderate use of this tax had been made before the war, but it remained for the necessities of the great struggle to bring about its real development. Before the war the highest rate imposed in any country in the world was 25 per cent., but Germany in her recent tax proposals has shown the extent to which this method can be developed; according to these a tax of 90 per cent. will be imposed upon large amounts going to distant heirs. There is every reason to expect that large use will be made in other countries of this source of revenue in post-war finance. Indeed, as a tax for the payment of the debt the inheritance tax has much to recommend it.

Taxes on business have also become increasingly important and may be expected to be developed still further. These existed in one form or another in most European countries before the war. As Federal taxes, however, they were new in the United States until the introduction of the corporation excise and excess profits taxes. The productive possibilities of these taxes have been shown during the war, and now, when revenue is needed so urgently in all the foreign belligerent States, so lucrative a source will not lightly be given up. It is not improbable that the excess profits tax in a modified form will persist. At any rate, the taxation of business profits will undoubtedly constitute an important source of revenue for most countries in the immediate future.

Consumption taxes are undergoing a transformation. The internal excise taxes are being shifted from the necessities of the poor to the luxuries of the more well-to-do. In addition to whiskey, beer, and tobacco, which have always been favorite objects of taxation, other articles of luxurious expenditure are now being drawn into the net. The luxury tax, which was introduced into Great Britain, France, and the United States at the very end of the war, was belated and poorly organized. This tax has already been abolished in Great Britain, and the tax on retail sales in the United States will probably soon go, but the principle of taxing luxurious expenditure will be applied in other ways. Prohibition and the consequent loss of revenue from that source forced a solution of the difficulty in the United States. By this act revenues were sacrificed which in 1918 amounted to about $350,000,000. Whether this deficiency will be made up by the introduction of new consumption taxes on what are commonly designated "food luxuries," such as tea, coffee, cocoa, and sugar, which might be made to yield about $250,000,000 annually, or by a continuance and expansion of taxes on such articles of luxury as automobiles, musical instruments, sporting goods, toilet articles, etc., is as yet not clear. Certain

AFTER-WAR PROBLEMS OF TAXATION

it is that large revenues can be obtained only from articles of large, general consumption.

Customs duties are almost certain to increase. One of the striking results of the war has been the growth in nationalistic feelings and aspirations, the economic consequence of which is a strong recrudesence of protectionism. The demand for protection is emphasized in Europe at present by the unfavorable condition of exchange, which has led to the complete prohibition of certain articles or the limitation of imports by several European nations. This movement, which even in free-trade England finds expression in Imperial preference, is likely to persist indefinitely. Much heavier duties on imports may therefore be expected, but as these will be levied to a considerable extent for purposes of protection, their revenue-producing character will be rendered uncertain.

Another striking financial result of the war has been the growth in the resort to fiscal monopolies. These had existed in most European countries before 1914 in one form or another, as tobacco in France, alcohol in Russia, salt in Switzerland, etc. But during the war there was an enormous extension of Government control over industry, partly for military, partly for social, and partly for fiscal, reasons. Although the first reason has disappeared, the other two still persist, especially the third. Governments are now reorganizing the old fiscal monopolies or establishing new ones in practically all the European countries. For this purpose the favorite articles are alcohol, tobacco, petroleum, matches, sugar, salt, and other articles of general consumption the sale of which can be easily controlled. Although they are protested by the interests whose business is interfered with, they are defended on the double ground of the desirability of governmental control of industry and of the fiscal needs of the Treasury.

In conclusion, it may be said that the framing of the revenue systems of the European States will be guided primarily by the urgent necessity of securing revenue, but the new taxes to be developed will have important industrial and social consequences. The burdens upon wealth and large incomes, whether in the form of returns from property or from large earning power, will undoubtedly be greater than they were before the war; indeed, it is not improbable that they will be carried to such a point as to bring about a slow but steady redistribution of wealth. In the United States these taxes should serve as the incentive to greater exertion, but in more than one of the European States there is danger that the burden may be so great as to repress initiative and thrift, and even, if they are carried to the extreme called for by the present budgets, to partial repudiation or confiscation under the guise of taxation.

CHAPTER XIV

THE COST OF THE WAR

Who pays for a war — Material costs — Depletion of capital — The burden on future generations — Direct and indirect costs — Immaterial costs — Diversity of losses — Some factors of advantage — Indefensibility of war.

The question has frequently been raised as to who pays for a war, and whether it is possible to transfer a part of the burdens to future generations.

The material cost of a war is measured by the resources used up in the prosecution of the war, whether they are devoted to this end by the war-waging countries themselves or whether they are destroyed by the enemy. It is true that food must be consumed and shells exploded to-day and not in future years. A war must be fought with goods produced at the time. But to say this does not imply that the burden of war may not be shared by future generations. If all the war expenditures were met out of current production, either by enlarging the national output, or by economies in personal consumption, or by non-investment of capital in industries not contributing to the prosecution of the war, or by all three methods, then the whole cost of the war would be borne by the people who waged it. At the end of the struggle all the bills would have been paid. But such a pay-as-you-go policy was manifestly impossible in the World War. The costs equalled the total annual national pre-war income of many of the belligerents, and in some cases even exceeded it.

WAR COSTS AND THEIR FINANCING

In cases where the money cost of the war exceeded the surplus beyond the minimum needs of the people for subsistence, it is evident that it was necessary to resort to the savings of the nation and to use up accumulated capital itself. To the extent to which existing capital was reduced, either directly by being used for war purposes or indirectly through lack of provision for depreciation and obsolescence, and the usual savings thereby prevented, the economic position of the nation was rendered worse than before the war. As a result of the impairment of the capital fund, the ability to produce is lessened. Future generations will in such a case receive a depleted heritage of capital. Until this is made good, if indeed it can be, future generations will share the burden of the war and will as a result have a lower standard of living than they otherwise would have enjoyed. In addition to this indirect cost, they will also be saddled with an enormous load of pensions, interest on the foreign debt, and other charges which result directly from the war. In these two ways they will feel and share its burden.

The issue of bonds which mature at a date more or less remote does not alter the essential facts. This is simply the method by which the Government secures title to goods and command over services. A war might be financed by bond issues and yet be borne entirely by the generation that waged the war if they increased the national income by an amount equal to the cost of the war or saved it out of nonessential expenditure. Bond issues constitute a device for distributing the burden among the people of the warring countries. Since, however, the issue of bonds does not exercise the same pressure to save as does the imposition of taxation, or stimulate in the same degree to greater exertion, there

THE COST OF THE WAR

is apt to be a greater using up of capital if large resort is had to this method. By as much as the existing capital fund is reduced, succeeding generations will suffer an economic loss, and to that extent may be said to pay for the war.

In this connection there is a certain analogy between the situation of an individual and that of a nation. An unusual and unexpected expenditure in a family, caused, let us say, by a sudden accident to one of its members, may be met by the extra effort of the breadwinner, by overtime work, or by unusual personal economies. Or, on the other hand, no change may be made in the ordinary expenditures of the family, but the whole of the extra sum to meet the new financial burden may be borrowed. In the former case the end of the convalesence of the injured one finds the family in the same economic position as it enjoyed before the accident, although for a time they have endured extraordinary sacrifices. In the latter case they will have to devote their energies for many years in the future to paying off the debt.

It is impossible to say to what extent the burden of the war has been thrown on future generations. The amount must be very large, for practically every nation has emerged from the struggle with impaired resources. Later in this chapter an attempt is made to estimate in very general terms the amount of damage and loss which was suffered by all the belligerent nations and by those neutral countries that were most directly affected by the war. Speculative as any such estimate must be, it is equally difficult to ascertain the extent to which the war was paid for out of current savings and enlarged production. In general it may fairly be concluded that this can be measured by the amount of taxation collected

WAR COSTS AND THEIR FINANCING

in each country. Such a conclusion would have to be modified in the case of the devastated countries, where the diversion of wealth to war purposes would be measured by the amount of destruction inflicted by the enemy, rather than by taxation. In those regions enforced economies which went to the extent of dire privation were practiced. But unhappily the destruction of their capital prevented the residents of these districts from putting forth any extra efforts towards production.

The payment of the debt does not mean a loss to the nation if the debt is held internally. The real loss occurred when the money was spent. Debt payment is a problem in distribution. The war has indeed been paid for, but a subsequent reassessment of expenses is made by taxation. If this assessment is just, that is, if the system of post-war taxation is equitable as between income groups, then no evil effects in the distribution of the national income will follow. But if the system is so arranged as to transfer wealth from the less well-to-do to the rich, bonanolaing class, serious injustice may result. It is all-important that there should be a fair apportionment of taxation as between the richer and the poorer classes.

An attempt has been made in the earlier chapters of this volume to estimate the direct money cost of the war, and the conclusion was reached that this amounted in round numbers to $186,000,000,000. This estimate did not take into account the indirect costs, such as the loss of human life, the destruction of property, the depreciation of capital, the loss of production, the interruption to trade, and similar items. Another study by the present writer attempts to estimate these varied factors and to reduce them to a common money

THE COST OF THE WAR

standard. The following summary statement is taken from that book:[1]

In conclusion, an attempt may be made to bring together the scattered data of this study into one final comprehensive picture which shall show the total cost of the war. The direct costs were estimated at $186,333,637,097. The indirect costs are now seen to have amounted to almost as much more. The combined direct and indirect costs are set forth by the principal items in the following table:

DIRECT AND INDIRECT COSTS OF THE WORLD WAR

Total direct costs, net		$186,333,637,097
Indirect costs:		
Capitalized value of human life:		
Soldiers*	$33,551,276,280	
Civilian	33,551,276,280	
Property losses:		
On land	29,960,000,000	
Shipping and cargo	6,800,000,000	
Loss of production	45,000,000,000	
War relief	1,000,000,000	
Loss to neutrals	1,750,000,000	
	$151,612,542,560	
Total indirect costs		151,612,542,560
Grand total		$337,946,179,657

* No attempt has been made to place a money value on the injuries done to crippled soldiers and the invalided and devitalized army and civilian population. If this were included the totals would be considerably increased.

Stupendous as are the figures just given, they fail properly to set forth all the losses involved in war. The losses of human life and the sufferings and privations represented by the destruction of property and loss of production cannot be reduced to a money standard without losing their real meaning. Nor do statistics of war debts measure accurately the burdens of the future.

[1] "Direct and Indirect Costs of the Great World War" (Carnegie Endowment for International Peace, 1919), p. 299.

WAR COSTS AND THEIR FINANCING

The really serious burdens of the war cannot be reduced to statistics or presented in tabular form. Material resources can be replaced in a comparatively short space of time,[2] but the immaterial intangible losses and burdens may persist for generations. The physical deterioration in the population as a result of the death of the fittest males has been attested for past wars by more than one writer,[3] and since the loss of life was so enormous in the World War, amounting to about 13,000,000 for soldiers and as many more for civilians, there is every reason to expect a serious lowering of racial vitality and of personal vigor throughout the major part of Europe.

It is almost impossible to enumerate all of the other manifold items which constitute the real burden of the war, but a rough analysis of the principal losses and burdens may be given. Such a classification would cover the following points: (1) the loss of men through death and disablement; (2) the reduction of national physical vitality as a result of privation, overwork, anxiety, strain, etc.; (3) the loss of capital and resources through actual destruction, diversion to war purposes, deterioration, depreciation, etc.; (4) the loss

---

[2] John Stuart Mill, speaking of the recuperative power of a country after war, says: " What the enemy has destroyed would have been consumed in a little time by the inhabitants themselves. . . . Nothing is changed, except that during the period of reproduction they have not now the advantage of consuming what had been produced previously The possibility of a rapid repair of their disasters mainly depends upon whether the country has been depopulated." *Principles of Political Economy.* Book I, v, Sec. 7, Ashley's ed., p. 74.

[3] D. S. Jordan, *The Blood of the Nation: a Study of the Decay of Races through the Survival of the Unfit* (Boston, 1910) and *War and the Breed: the Relation of War to the Downfall of Nations* (Boston, 1915); V. L. Kellogg, *Eugenics and Militarism* (London, 1912) and *Military Selection and Race Deterioration* (Oxford, 1916).

THE COST OF THE WAR

of production through the withdrawal of men from normal production, lowered efficiency, poorer tools, scarcity of raw materials, unemployment; (5) the extent to which the country has mortgaged the future by borrowing abroad. And even this list does not include the imponderable evils such as the lowering of ethical standards, the destruction of approved social *mores,* and in some instances, it would seem, from events of recent history, the very undermining of modern industrial institutions.

On the other hand, certain offsets may be mentioned which reduce to a certain extent the evil effects of the factors just described. Just as a fire sometimes sweeps away ramshackle buildings or clears out a slum district which inertia or ignorance has maintained, so a war jostles people out of old habits, calls for new methods of production and organization, and teaches lessons of coöperation and common social purposes. The productive capacity of a nation may even be increased, in spite of loss of life and material resources, as a result of changes wrought by war. Lloyd-George is responsible for the statement, made, to be sure, comparatively early in the struggle (1916), that improvements in industry and the more effective control of the liquor industry resulting from the war, would compensate for all economic losses. An almost invariable economic accompaniment and aftermath of previous wars, moreover, has been a quickening of inventive genius. Labor-saving machinery and more efficient methods of production have been substituted in many parts of Europe for antiquated and inefficient processes. The movement toward the greater democratization of industry, which, like most popular movements, has at first revealed its most radical and even dangerous possibilities, will probably in the long run be counted as a step forward in the slow march toward social justice.

But after all allowances have been made, the net result is one of indescribably heavy burdens and losses. No more serious indictment of war can be made than the impartial cataloguing of its costs. The economic and financial indefensibility of war has been abundantly set forth, it is hoped, in the previous pages of this book. For one who has studied its effects there can be no more fervent prayer than that a repetition of similar events may be rendered unlikely, if not impossible, for all time. It may not be possible wholly to abolish war, but it is unlikely that the nations of the world will ever again be plunged into a world struggle except in defense of some common ideal of international justice. To the principle of international arbitration, administered by some such organization as a League of Nations, as distinguished from the appeal to force in the settlement of international difficulties, all thinking men must subscribe. War, as a method of determining international rivalries, stands condemned on many counts, but on none more decisively than on that of cost.

APPENDICES

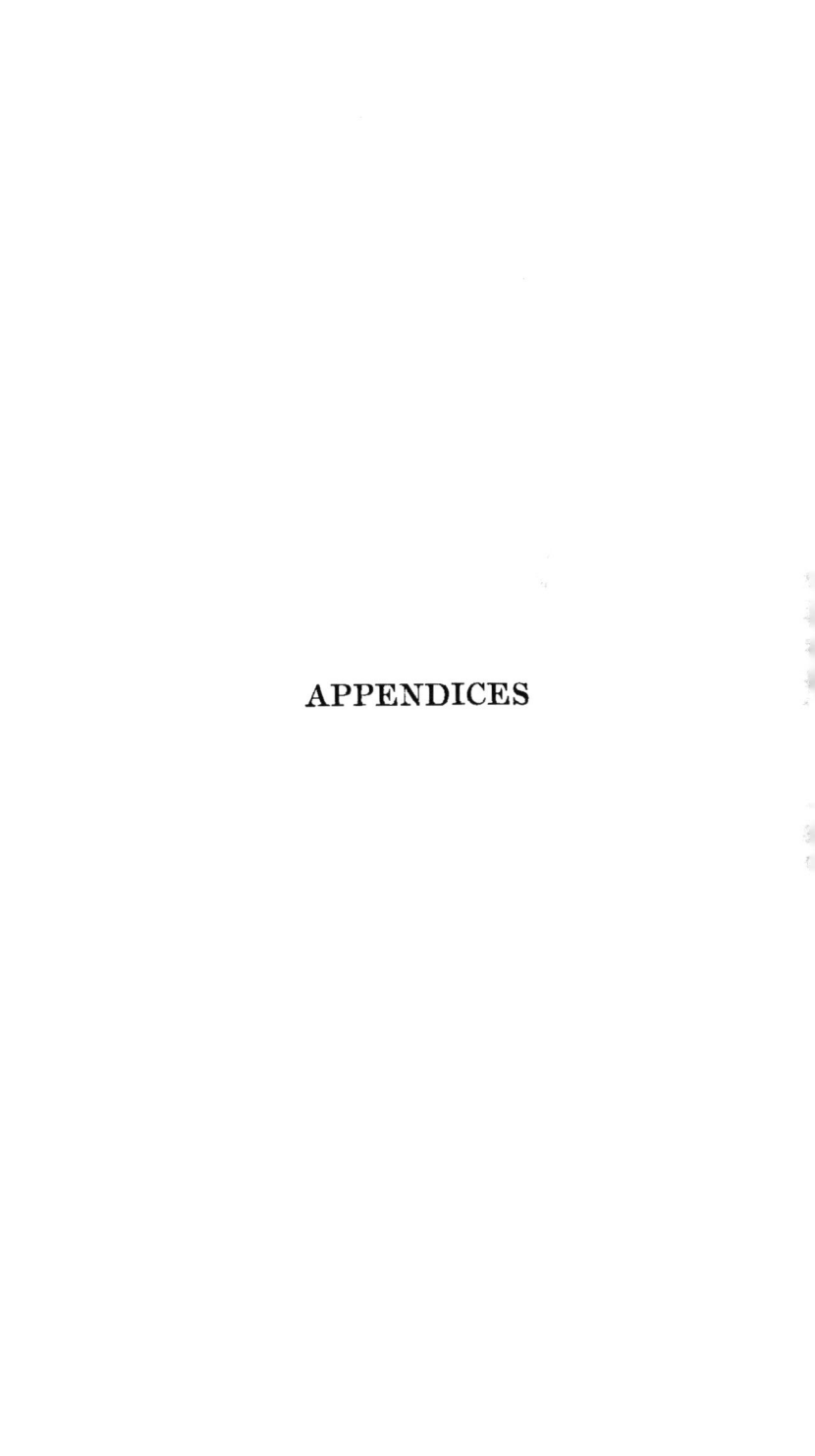

APPENDIX I

BRITISH MORATORIUM PROCLAMATIONS

1. PROCLAMATION POSTPONING PAYMENT OF BILLS OF EXCHANGE, AUGUST 2, 1914

. . . If on the presentation for payment of a bill of exchange, other than a cheque or bill on demand, which has been accepted before the beginning of the fourth day of August, nineteen hundred and fourteen, the acceptor re-accepts the bill by a declaration on the face of the bill in the form set out hereunder, that bill shall, for all purposes, including the liability of any drawer or indorser or any party thereto, be deemed to be due and be payable on a date one calendar month after the date of its original maturity, and to be a bill for the original amount thereof increased by the amount of interest thereon calculated from the date of re-acceptance to the new date of payment at the Bank of England rate current on the date of re-acceptance of the Bill.

Form: Re-accepted under Proclamation for £..........
(insert increased sum).

Signature............................

Date...............................

2. PROCLAMATION OF AUGUST 6, 1914

Save as hereinafter provided, all payments which have become due and payable before the date of this Proclamation, or which will become due and payable on any day before the beginning of the Fourth day of September, nineteen hundred and fourteen, in respect of any bill of exchange (being a cheque or bill on demand) which was drawn before the beginning of the Fourth day of Augusst, nineteen hundred and fourteen, or in respect of any negotiable instrument (not being a bill of exchange) dated before that time or in respect of any contract made before that time, shall be deemed to be due and payable on a day one calendar month after the day on which the payment originally became due and payable, or on the Fourth day of September, nineteen hundred and fourteen, whichever is the later date, instead of on the day on which the payment originally became due; but payments so postponed shall, if not otherwise carrying interest, and if specific demand is made for payment and payment is refused, carry interest until payment as from the Fourth day of August, nineteen hundred and fourteen, if they become due and payable before that day, and as from the date on which they become due and payable if they become due and payable on or after that day, at the Bank of England rate current on the Seventh day of August, nineteen hundred and fourteen; but nothing in this Proclamation shall prevent payments being made before the expiration of the month for which they are so postponed.

This proclamation shall not apply to:

(1) any payment in respect of wages or salary;
(2) any payment in respect of a liability which when incurred did not exceed five pounds in amount;
(3) Any payment in respect of rates or taxes
(4) any payment in respect of maritime freight;
(5) any payment in respect of any debt from any person resident outside the British Islands, or from any firm, company or institution whose principal place of business is outside the British Islands not being a debt incurred in the British Islands by a person, firm, company, or institution having a business establishment or branch business establishment in the British Islands;
(6) any payment in respect of any dividend or interest payable in respect of any stocks, funds, or securities (other than real or heritable securities in which trustees, are, under Section One of the Trustee Act, 1893, or any other Act for the time being in force, authorized to invest;
(7) any liability of a bank of issue in respect of bank notes issued by that bank;
(8) any payment to be made by or on behalf of His Majesty or any Government Department, including the payment of old age pensions;
(9) any payment to be made by any person or society in pursuance of the National Insurance Act, 1911, or any

BRITISH MORATORIUM PROCLAMATIONS

Act amending that Act (whether in the nature of contributions, benefits, or otherwise);
(10) any payment under the Workmen's Compensation Act, 1906, or any Act amending the same;
(11) any payment in respect of the withdrawal of a deposit by a depositor in a trustee savings bank.

Nothing in this Proclamation shall affect any bills of exchange to which Our Proclamation dated the Second day of August, nineteen hundred and fourteen, relating to the postponement of payment of certain bills of exchange applies.

3. PROCLAMATION OF AUGUST 12, 1914

Nothwithstanding anything contained in the Proclamation, dated the sixth day of August, nineteen hundred and fourteen relating to the postponement of payments), that Proclamation shall apply, and shall be deemed always to have applied:

(a) to any bill of exchange which has not been re-accepted under Our Proclamation, dated the second day of August, nineteen hundred and fourteen, as it applies to a bill of exchange, being a cheque or bill on demand, unless on the presentation of the bill the acceptor has expressly refused re-acceptance thereof, but with the substitution, as respects rate of interest, of the date of the presentation of the bill for the seventh day of August, nineteen hundred and fourteen; and

(b) also to payments in respect of any debt from any bank whose principal place of business is in any part of His Majesty's Dominions or any British Protectorate, although the debt was not incurred in the British Islands and the bank had not a business establishment or branch business establishment in the British Islands.

4. PROCLAMATION OF SEPTEMBER 3, 1914

1. If on the presentation for payment of a bill of exchange which has before the fourth day of September, nineteen hundred and fourteen, been re-accepted under the terms of Our said Proclamation, dated the second day of August, nineteen hundred and fourteen, the bill is not paid, then, the said Proclamation shall, in its application to that bill, have effect as if the period of two calendar months had been

in the Proclamation substituted for the period of one calendar month, and the sum mentioned in the form of re-acceptance under the said Proclamation shall be deemed to be increased by the amount of interest on the original amount of the bill for one calendar month calculated at the Bank of England rate current on the date when the bill is so presented for payment as aforesaid.

2. Our said Proclamation, dated the sixth day of August, nineteen hundred and fourteen, as extended by Our said Proclamation, dated the twelfth day of August, nineteen hundred and fourteen, shall apply to payments which become due and payable on or after the fourth day of September and before the fourth day of October, nineteen hundred and fourteen (whether they become so due and payable by virtue of the said Proclamations or otherwise) in like manner as it applies to payments which became due and payable after the date of the said first mentioned Proclamation and before the beginning of the fourth day of September, nineteen hundred and fourteen.

3. Nothing in this Proclamation shall effect the payment of interest under the Proclamation extended thereby, or prevent payments being made before the expiration of the period for which they are postponed.

5. PROCLAMATION OF SEPTEMBER 30, 1919

1. The first General Proclamation as extended by paragraph (b) of the Second General Proclamation shall, subject to the limitations of this Proclamation, apply to payments which become due and payable on or after the fourth day of October and before the fourth day of November, nineteen hundred and fourteen (whether they so become due and payable by virtue of the said Proclamations or the third General Proclamation or otherwise), in like manner as it applies to payments which become due and payable after the date of the first General Proclamation and before the beginning of the fourth day of September, nineteen hundred and fourteen.

Provided that, if the payment is one the date whereof has been postponed by virtue of any of the said General Proclamations, and is one which carries interest either by virtue of the terms of the contract or instrument under which it is due and payable or by virtue of the said General Proclamations, then

BRITISH MORATORIUM PROCLAMATIONS

the person from whom the payment is due shall not be entitled to claim the benefit of this Article unless, within three days after the date to which the payment has been postponed by virtue of the said General Proclamations, all interest thereon up to that date is paid.

This Article shall not apply to:
(a) Any payment in respect to rent;
(b) Any payment due and payable to or by a retail trader in respect to his business as such trader.

2. The Bills (Re-acceptance) Proclamation shall continue to apply to bills of exchange (other than cheques and bills on demand) accepted before the beginning of the fourth day of August nineteen hundred and fourteen, the date of the original maturity whereof is after the third day of October.

If on the presentation for payment of any such bill the bill is not paid and is not reaccepted under the said Proclamation, then, unless on such presentation the acceptor has expressly refused re-acceptance thereof, the bill shall for all purposes, including the liability of any drawer and indorser or any other party thereto, be deemed to be due and payable on a date one calendar month after the date of its original maturity instead of on the date of its original maturity, and to be a bill for the original amount thereof increased by the amount of interest thereon, calculated from the date of the original maturity to the date of payment at the Bank of England rate current on the date of its original maturity, and paragraph (a) of the second General Proclamation shall not apply to any such bill.

3. If on the presentation for payment of a bill of exchange, the date of maturity of which has before the fourth day of October nineteen hundred and fourteen become postponed either by virtue of the Bills (Re-acceptance) Proclamation or paragraph (a) of the second General Proclamation (whether or not the date of maturity has been further postponed by virtue of the third General Proclamation), the bill is not paid, then the date of maturity shall be deemed to be further postponed for fourteen days from the date of such presentation for payment, and the original amount of the bill shall be deemed to be further increased by the amount of interest on the original amount of the bill for fourteen days, calculated

at the Bank of England rate current on the date of such presentation for payment.

4. Save as otherwise expressly provided, nothing in this Proclamation shall affect the application of the General Proclamations to payments to which those Proclamations apply, and nothing in this Proclamation shall prevent payments to which this Proclamation applies being made before the expiration of the period for which they are postponed thereunder.

APPENDIX II

FRENCH MORATORIUM DECREES[1]

On July 29, 1914, the first moratorium was decreed. The maturity of obligations entered into before August 1, 1914, and falling due after that date or before August 15, 1914, was postponed 30 days.

On August 2, 1914, the above decree was applied to deposits in banks and institutions of credit: if less than 250 francs, the whole could be drawn; if more than that sum, only five per cent. of the excess, in addition to 250 francs; commercial or industrial employers of labor could draw the whole for wages; and the decree was applied to savings and insurance contracts.

These two early decrees were completed by that of August 9, 1914, which follows:

DECREE OF AUGUST 9, 1914

Art. 1. For all negotiable instruments falling due after July 31, 1914, inclusively, or maturing before September 1, 1914, the date of payment is delayed thirty days, on condition that they were underwritten previous to August 4, 1914.

The negotiable instruments in the view of the present article are: bills of exchange; notes to order, or to bearer; checks, with the exception of those presented by the drawer himself; orders and warrants.

Not falling under the application of the present article are negotiable instruments issued upon the public Treasury.

Art. 2. [Applies to commitments for merchandise entered into before August 4, 1914.]

Art. 3. [Applies likewise to advances on movables.]

Art. 4. [Applies to demands for deposits, except up to 250 francs, plus five per cent., etc.; not to demands for

[1] Printed in J. L. Laughlin, *Credit of the Nations* (1918), p. 369.

WAR COSTS AND THEIR FINANCING

paying labor; not to those whose establishments have been requisitioned, etc.]

Art. 5. The postponement of thirty days dating from August 1, 1914, is applicable to the redemption of obligations or contracts of insurance, of capitalisation or savings for fixed terms, or those stipulated to be redeemable at the will of the owner or bearer.

On August 10, 1914, all prescriptions and limitations, civil, commercial, or administrative were suspended until the end of the war. They were further treated by the decree of December 16, 1914, and modified by that of May 12, 1915.

The main moratorium of August 9 was given more in detail on August 29, 1914, and extended until October 1, 1914. On the same day, a decree suspended payments on obligations of departments, communes, etc., until the end of the war.

From time to time the moratorium was extended by many decrees as follows:

```
September 27, 1914, 30 days to November 1, 1914
October   27, 1914, 60 days to January   1, 1915
December  15, 1914, 60 days to March     1, 1915
February  25, 1915, 60 days to May       1, 1915
April     15, 1915, 90 days to August    1, 1915
June      24, 1915, 90 days to November  1, 1915
October   16, 1915, 60 days to January   1, 1916
December  23, 1915, 90 days to April     1, 1916
March     18, 1916, 90 days to July      1, 1916
June      24, 1916, 90 days to October   1, 1916
September 20, 1916, 90 days to January   1, 1917
```

Out of a total of 4,480 million francs in August, 1914, postponed at the Bank of France (from which should be deducted 800 millions for those under the colors or in territory occupied by the enemy) the amount remaining December 14, 1916, was only 1,346 millions. Successful efforts had been made to have postponed debts paid up, and in December, 1916, practically no delay

FRENCH MORATORIUM DECREES

was granted unless good cause could be shown to a magistrate. Thereafter moratorium decrees ceased.

DECREE OF SEPTEMBER 27, 1914, CONCERNING TRANSACTIONS
IN SECURITIES

Art. 1. Provisionally suspended are all demands for payments and all judicial actions relative to the sale and purchase in the period previous to August 4, 1914, of *rentes,* public securities, and other transferable instruments, as well as the dealings for carrying them forward.

The sums due by reason of these sales, purchases, and carrying charges should be increased by interest for the time of postponement at the rate of five per cent. per annum.

This decree was modified by that of September 14, 1915, which brought pressure on all not under the colors or in occupied territory to make payment of 10 per cent. of differences due in settlements, and 6 per cent. on delayed payments.

APPENDIX III

ACT PROVIDING FOR GERMAN LOAN OFFICES[1]

DARLEHNSKASSEN ACT (REICHSGESETZBL., P. 340) AUGUST 4, 1914

1. In Berlin and those places within the Empire, in which there is a branch or agency of the Reichsbank, shall be established wherever necessary, on the order of the Imperial Chancellor, according to the report of the Committee on Trade and Commerce of the Federal Council (*Bundesrath*), Loan Bureaus (*Darlehnskassen*) for the purpose of making loans on security to meet the need of credit, especially in the interest of trade and industry.

Subsidiary branches of the *Darlehnskassen* may be estabtablished in other than the designated places to aid in the work of lending and of building up depots.

2. For the full amount of the loan granted shall be paid out of a special form of money known as "*Darlehnskassenscheine.*" These notes shall be received at their full face value in payment at all the Imperial offices as well as at all the public offices of the States of the Empire; in private transactions they shall not be a compulsory means of payment.

In the meaning of paragraphs 9, 17 and 44 of the Bank Act of March 14, 1875, the notes of the Loan Bureaus stand on the same footing as the *Reichskassenscheine* (Imperial Treasury notes).

The total amount of the notes of the Loan Bureaus shall not exceed 1500 million marks. The Federal Council is empowered in case of necessity to raise the amount of notes outstanding.

No notes of Loan Bureaus shall be issued by the management of the Loan Bureaus (paragraph 13) for which sufficient security, as fixed by paragraphs 4 and 6, shall not be provided.

---

[1] Printed in J. L. Laughlin, *Credit of the Nations* (1918), p. 384.

ACT PROVIDING FOR GERMAN LOAN OFFICES

Before their issue, an exact description of the notes shall be made public by the management of the Loan Bureau.

3. Loans can be given for not less than 100 marks, and shall not run as a rule for a longer term than three, and only in exceptional circumstances for six, months.

4. The security may consist of:

(a) The pledge of industrial, agricultural and mineral products and non-perishable merchandise, stored within the limits of the Empire, as a rule, for one-half, or in exceptional cases, for two-thirds of their value, according to differences of circumstances and salability.

(b) The pledge of securities issued by the Empire, or by the government of a German State, or those conforming to legal requirements issued by corporations, joint-stock companies, or limited partnerships, which are located within the Empire, at a reduction from their current or market price. Paper not running in the name of the bearer must be transferred to the Loan Bureaus.

(c) The pledge of other securities which the management (paragraph 13) declare to be satisfactory.

For the fulfillment of the pledge of articles mentioned in (a) it suffices, instead of actual delivery, to indicate the pledge clearly by some external mark, such as a tablet or the like.

5. Commodities which are subject to serious changes of price will be accepted as pledge only if a third solvent person guarantees the payment of the loan.

6. A loan may also be protected by the pledge of claims, which have been entered in the Imperial Debt Records (*Reichsschuldbuch*) or in that of a German State, at a reduction from the current value determined according to the face value and the rate of interest of the obligations corresponding to the pledged claims.

In case a mortgage on a claim of the sort mentioned in the first paragraph be inscribed on the records in favor of the Loan Bureau, it is sufficient to have the attestation of two members of the Board of Directors.

As to the attestation, the regulations of paragraph 183 of the Act concerning matters of voluntary jurisdiction have like application.

7. If a mortgage to a Loan Bureau has been entered on the records (paragraph 6), the Bureau thereby acquires a

right, even if a third person has a claim on it, prior to the rights of that third person unless the right of the third person had been entered at the time of the inscription of the mortgage on the records; or was known at that time to the Bureau; or was not known because of gross negligence.

If the debtor has delayed meeting the obligation secured by the pledge, the Administration of Debt Records is thereby empowered and obliged, on a written request of the Loan Bureau, without requiring any proof of the delay, to issue obligations payable to bearer to liquidate the whole or a corresponding part of the claim; unless an order of the court intervenes which forbids the payment to the Loan Bureau; or unless some right of a third person, or a limitation of the mortgage in favor of the third person has been recorded, which was entered earlier than the pledge in favor of the Loan Bureau.

The Administration of the Records must inform the Loan Bureau of later entries affecting the adequacy of the obligation.

As to the satisfaction of the Loan Bureau regarding the obligations discharged by the Administration of the Debt Records, the regulations of paragraphs 10, 11 have corresponding application.

8. The rate of interest on a loan granted shall as a rule not be higher than the published rate at which the Reichsbank buys bills of exchange.

9. The security should suffice for the principal, interest, and expenses; these secondary claims should be deducted from the sum of the loan.

10. If payment is not made at maturity, the Loan Bureau may sell the security through one of its officials or a broker and reimburse itself out of the proceeds. The Loan Bureau shall dispose of the security only to the highest bidder in the open market.

11. Also, if the debtor should go into bankruptcy, the Loan Bureau retains the right to sell the security without an order of the Court. (Paragraph 127, Sec. 2, of the Bankruptcy Act of May 20, 1898, does not apply.)

12. The Loan Bureaus form independent institutions with the attributes and rights of a legal persona. Their business enjoys freedom from stamps and duties.

ACT PROVIDING FOR GERMAN LOAN OFFICES

13. The Reichsbank assumes the management of the Loan Bureaus under the direction of the Imperial Chancellor in the interest of the Empire, but quite apart from its other business. The general administration shall be established in Berlin in a special bank department known as the "*Hauptverwaltung der Darlehnskassen*" according to more detailed directions given by the Imperial Chancellor. In addition, there shall be appointed for each Loan Bureau a Special Board of Directors subordinate to the *Hauptverwaltung*, to which shall be appointed by the Imperial Chancellor a representative of the Empire as well as members from the commercial or industrial classes. The Imperial Chancellor issues instructions for the conduct of the business of the Loan Bureaus.

14. The opening of the Loan Bureaus is to be brought to general attention over the names of the Imperial representative and the members of the Board of Directors through the journals designated for official notices.

15. Two of the members of the Board of Directors chosen from the commercial or industrial classes shall, in alternate weeks, manage the business of the Loan Bureaus and see that the provisions of this Act are observed.

16. The Imperial representative must keep informed of the whole business of the Bureau and has a right of veto upon all applications for loans. The determination of the reduction to be made from the current or market price of the securities pledged, within the limits set by the regulations of the business, rests with the imperial representatives after receiving the advice of the Board of Directors.

17. The profits of the Loan Bureaus, after deducting the expenses of administration, shall be applied to covering any possible losses and to the future redemption of the notes of the Bureaus. Any possible surplus goes to the Imperial Treasury.

18. The notes of the Loan Bureaus shall be issued in denominations of 5, 10, 20, and 50 marks. The issue of larger denominations of the notes, and the proportions in which the various denominations are to be used, will be determined by the regulations of the Imperial Chancellor. [Under this provision, and by Act of August 31, 1914, denominations of 1 and 2 marks were issued.]

WAR COSTS AND THEIR FINANCING

The notes of the Loan Bureaus shall be issued by the Administration of the Imperial Debt (*Reichsschuldenverwaltung*), within the maximum limits (paragraph 2, part 3), according to the orders of the Imperial Chancellor given to the Administration-in-Chief of the Loan Bureaus, which assumes the responsibility for the issue.

The control over the preparation and issue of the notes of the Loan Bureaus is exercised by the Commission on the Imperial Debt.

The Imperial Chancellor is to make public monthly the amount of the notes of the Loan Bureaus outstanding.

19. As soon as the need for a Loan Bureau no longer exists, the Imperial Chancellor is to close it up and make public the fact.

On the return of peace, the notes of the Loan Bureaus, issued by virtue of this Act, shall be withdrawn according to the detailed instructions of the Federal Council.

20. [Paragraphs 146-149, 151, 152 and 360, Numbers 4-6, of the criminal law apply to these notes.]

21. The advances on securities (Lombards) granted by the Reichsbank, in the period from August 3, 1914, to the establishment of the Loan Bureaus, on other securities than those mentioned in paragraph 13, No. 3, of the Bank Act (March 14, 1875), are hereby ratified.

22. This law goes into effect on the day of its promulgation.

APPENDIX IV

LIBERTY BOND ACTS

FIRST LIBERTY BOND ACT

AN ACT To authorize an issue of bonds to meet expenditures for the national security and defense, and, for the purpose of assisting in the prosecution of the war, to extend credit to foreign governments, and for other purposes.

Be it enacted by the Senate and House of Representatives of the United States of America in Congress assembled, That the Secretary of the Treasury, with the approval of the President, is hereby authorized to borrow, from time to time, on the credit of the United States for the purposes of this Act, and to meet expenditures authorized for the national security and defense and other public purposes authorized by law not exceeding in the aggregate $5,000,000,000, exclusive of the sums authorized by section four of this Act, and to issue therefor bonds of the United States.

The bonds herein authorized shall be in such form and subject to such terms and conditions of issue, conversion, redemption, maturities, payment, and rate and time of payment of interest, not exceeding three and one-half per centum per annum, as the Secretary of the Treasury may prescribe. The principal and interest thereof shall be payable in United States gold coin of the present standard of value and shall be exempt, both as to principal and interest, from all taxation, except estate or inheritance taxes, imposed by authority of the United States, or its possessions, or by any State or local taxing authority; but such bonds shall not bear the circulation privilege.

The bonds herein authorized shall first be offered at not less than par as a popular loan, under such regulations prescribed by the Secretary of the Treasury as will give all citizens of the United States an equal opportunity to participate therein; and any portion of the bonds so offered and not subscribed for may be otherwise disposed of at not less than par by the Secretary of the Treasury; but no commissions shall be allowed or paid on any bonds issued under authority of this Act.

SEC. 2. That for the purpose of more effectually providing for the national security and defense and prosecuting the war by establishing credits in the United States for foreign governments, the Secretary of the Treasury, with the approval of the President, is hereby authorized, on behalf of the United States, to purchase, at par, from such foreign governments then engaged in war with the enemies of the United States, their obligations hereafter issued, bearing the same rate of interest and containing in their essentials the same terms and conditions as those of the United States issued under authority of this Act; to enter into such arrangements as may be necessary or desirable for establishing such credits and for purchasing such obligations of foreign governments and for the subsequent payment thereof before maturity, but such arrangements shall provide that if any of the bonds of the United States issued and used for the purchase of such foreign obligations shall thereafter be converted into other bonds of the United States bearing a higher rate of interest than three and one-half per centum per annum under the provisions of section five of this Act, then and in that event the obligations of such foreign governments held by the United States shall be, by such foreign governments, converted in like manner and extent into obligations bearing the same rate of interest as the bonds of the United States issued under the provisions of section five of this Act. For the purposes of this section there is appropriated, out of any money in the Treasury not otherwise appropriated, the sum of $3,000,000,000, or so much thereof as may be necessary: *Provided,* That the authority granted by this section to the Secretary of the Treasury to purchase bonds from foreign governments, as aforesaid, shall cease upon the termination of the war between the United States and the Imperial German Government.

SEC. 3. That the Secretary of the Treasury, under such terms and conditions as he may prescribe, is hereby authorized to receive on or before maturity payment for any obligations of such foreign governments purchased on behalf of the

LIBERTY BOND ACTS

United States, and to sell at not less than the purchase price any of such obligations and to apply the proceeds thereof, and any payments made by foreign governments on account of their said obligations to the redemption or purchase at not more than par and accrued interest of any bonds of the United States issued under authority of this Act; and if such bonds are not available for this purpose the Secretary of the Treasury shall redeem or purchase any other outstanding interest-bearing obligations of the United States which may at such time be subject to call or which may be purchased at not more than par and accrued interest.

SEC. 4. That the Secretary of the Treasury, in his discretion, is hereby authorized to issue the bonds not already issued heretofore authorized by section thirty-nine of the Act approved August fifth, nineteen hundred and nine, entitled " An Act to provide revenue, equalize duties, and encourage the industries of the United States, and for other purposes "; section one hundred and twenty-four of the Act approved June third, nineteen hundred and sixteen, entitled " An Act for making further and more effectual provision for the national defense, and for other purposes "; section thirteen of the Act of September seventh, nineteen hundred and sixteen, entitled " An Act to establish a United States shipping board for the purpose of encouraging, developing, and creating a naval auxiliary and a naval reserve and a merchant marine to meet the requirements of the commerce of the United States with its Territories and possessions and with foreign countries, to regulate carriers by water engaged in the foreign and interstate commerce of the United States, and for other purposes "; section four hundred of the Act approved March third, nineteen hundred and seventeen, entitled " An Act to provide increased revenue to defray the expenses of the increased appropriations for the Army and Navy and the extensions of fortifications, and for other purposes "; and the public resolution approved March fourth, nineteen hundred and seventeen, entitled " Joint resolution to expedite the delivery of materials, equipment, and munitions and secure more expeditious construction of ships," in the manner and under the terms and conditions prescribed in section one of this Act.

That the Secretary of the Treasury is hereby authorized to

borrow on the credit of the United States from time to time, in addition to the sum authorized in section one of this Act, such additional amount, not exceeding $63,945,460 as may be necessary to redeem the three per cent. loan of nineteen hundred and eight to nineteen hundred and eighteen, maturing August first, nineteen hundred and eighteen, and to issue therefor bonds of the United States in the manner and under the terms and conditions prescribed in section one of this Act.

SEC. 5. That any series of bonds issued under authority of sections one and four of this Act may, under such terms and conditions as the Secretary of the Treasury may prescribe, be convertible into bonds bearing a higher rate of interest than the rate at which the same were issued if any subsequent series of bonds shall be issued at a higher rate of interest before the termination of the war between the United States and the Imperial German Government, the date of such termination to be fixed by a proclamation of the President of the United States.

SEC. 6. That in addition to the bonds authorized by sections one and four of this Act, the Secretary of the Treasury is authorized to borrow from time to time, on the credit of the United States, for the purposes of this Act and to meet public expenditures authorized by law, such sum or sums as, in his judgment, may be necessary, and to issue therefor certificates of indebtedness at not less than par in such form and subject to such terms and conditions and at such rate of interest, not exceeding three and one-half per centum per annum, as he may prescribe; and each certificate so issued shall be payable, with the interest accrued thereon, at such time, not exceeding one year from the date of its issue, as the Secretary of the Treasury may prescribe. Certificates of indebtedness herein authorized shall not bear the circulation privilege, and the sum of such certificates outstanding shall at no time exceed in the aggregate $2,000,000,000, and such certificates shall be exempt, both as to principal and interest, from all taxation, except estate or inheritance taxes, imposed by authority of the United States, or its possessions, or by any State or local taxing authority.

SEC. 7. That the Secretary of the Treasury, in his discretion, is hereby authorized to deposit in such banks and trust companies as he may designate the proceeds, or any part

LIBERTY BOND ACTS

thereof, arising from the sale of the bonds and certificates of indebtedness authorized by this Act, or the bonds previously authorized as described in section four of this Act, and such deposits may bear such rate of interest and be subject to such terms and conditions as the Secretary of the Treasury may prescribe: *Provided,* That the amount so deposited shall not in any case exceed the amount withdrawn from any such bank or trust company and invested in such bonds or certificates of indebtedness plus the amount so invested by such bank or trust company, and such deposits shall be secured in the manner required for other deposits by section fifty-one hundred and fifty-three, Revised Statutes, and amendments thereto: *Provided further,* That the provisions of section fifty-one hundred and ninety-one of the Revised Statutes, as amended by the Federal Reserve Act and the amendments thereof, with reference to the reserves required to be kept by national banking associations and other member banks of the Federal Reserve System, shall not apply to deposits of public moneys by the United States in designated depositaries.

SEC. 8. That in order to pay all necessary expenses, including rent, connected with any operations under this Act, a sum not exceeding one-tenth of one per centum of the amount of bonds and one-tenth of one per centum of the amount of certificates of indebtedness herein authorized is hereby appropriated, or as much thereof, as may be necessary, out of any money in the Treasury not otherwise appropriated, to be expended as the Secretary of the Treasury may direct: *Provided,* That, in addition to the reports now required by law, the Secretary of the Treasury shall, on the first Monday in December, nineteen hundred and seventeen, and annually thereafter, transmit to the Congress a detailed statement of all expenditures under this Act.

Approved, April 24, 1917.

WAR COSTS AND THEIR FINANCING

SECOND LIBERTY BOND ACT

AN ACT To authorize an additional issue of bonds to meet expenditures for the national security and defense, and, for the purpose of assisting in the prosecution of the war, to extend additional credit to foreign Governments, and for other purposes.

Be it enacted by the Senate and House of Representatives of the United States of America in Congress assembled, That the Secretary of the Treasury, with the approval of the President, is hereby authorized to borrow, from time to time, on the credit of the United States for the purposes of this Act, and to meet expenditures authorized for the national security and defense and other public purposes authorized by law, not exceeding in the aggregate $7,538,945,460, and to issue therefor bonds of the United States, in addition to the $2,000,000,000 bonds already issued or offered for subscription under authority of the Act approved April twenty-fourth, nineteen hundred and seventeen, entitled " An Act to authorize an issue of bonds to meet expenditures for the national security and defense, and, for the purpose of assisting in the prosecution of the war, to extend credit to foreign governments, and for other purposes"; *Provided,* That of this sum $3,063,945,460 shall be in lieu of that amount of the unissued bonds authorized by sections one and four of the Act approved April twenty-fourth, nineteen hundred and seventeen, $225,000,000 shall be in lieu of that amount of the unissued bonds authorized by section thirty-nine of the Act approved August fifth, nineteen hundred and nine, $150,000,000 shall be in lieu of the unissued bonds authorized by the joint resolution approved March fourth, nineteen hundred and seventeen, and $100,000,000 shall be in lieu of the unissued bonds authorized by section four hundred of the Act approved March third, nineteen hundred and seventeen.

The bonds herein authorized shall be in such form or forms and denomination or denominations and subject to such terms and conditions of issue, conversion, redemption, maturities, payment, and rate or rates of interest, not exceeding four per centum per annum, and time or times of payment of interest, as the Secretary of the Treasury from time to time at or before the issue thereof may prescribe. The principal

LIBERTY BOND ACTS

and interest thereof shall be payable in United States gold coin of the present standard of value.

The bonds herein authorized shall from time to time first be offered at not less than par as a popular loan, under such regulations, prescribed by the Secretary of the Treasury from time to time, as will in his opinion give the people of the United States as nearly as may be an equal opportunity to participate therein, but he may make allotment in full upon applications for smaller amounts of bonds in advance of any date which he may set for the closing of subscriptions and may reject or reduce allotments upon later applications and applications for larger amounts, and may reject or reduce allotments upon applications from incorporated banks and trust companies for their own account and make allotment in full or larger allotments to others, and may establish a graduated scale of allotments, and may from time to time adopt any or all of said methods, should any such action be deemed by him to be in the public interest: *Provided,* That such reduction or increase of allotments of such bonds shall be made under general rules to be prescribed by said Secretary and shall apply to all subscribers similarly situated. And any portion of the bonds so offered and not taken may be otherwise disposed of by the Secretary of the Treasury in such manner and at such price or prices, not less than par, as he may determine.

SEC. 2. That for the purpose of more effectually providing for the national security and defense and prosecuting the war, the Secretary of the Treasury, with the approval of the President, is hereby authorized, on behalf of the United States, to establish credits with the United States for any foreign governments then engaged in war with the enemies of the United States and, to the extent of the credits so established from time to time, the Secretary of the Treasury is hereby authorized to purchase, at par, from such foreign governments respectively their several obligations hereafter issued, bearing such rate or rates of interest, maturing at such date or dates, not later than the bonds of the United States then last issued under the authority of this Act, or of such Act approved April twenty-fourth, nineteen hundred and seventeen, and containing such terms and conditions as the Secretary of the Treasury may from time to time determine, or to make advances to or for the account of any such foreign governments and to receive such obligations at par for the amount of any such advances; but the rate or rates of interest borne by any such obligations shall not be less than the highest rate borne by any bonds of the United States which, at the time of the acquisition thereof, shall have been issued under authority of said Act approved April twenty-fourth, nineteen hundred and seventeen, or of this Act, and any such obligations shall contain such provisions as the Secretary of the Treasury may from time to time determine for the conversion of a proportionate part of such obligations into obligations bearing a higher rate of interest if bonds of the United States issued under authority of this Act shall be converted into other bonds of the United States bearing a higher rate of interest, but the rate of interest in such foreign obligations issued upon such conversion shall not be less than the highest rate of interest borne by such bonds of the United States; and the Secretary of the Treasury with the approval of the President, is hereby authorized to enter into such arrangements from time to time with any such foreign Governments as may be necessary or desirable for establishing such credits and for the payment of such obligations of foreign Governments before maturity. For the purposes of this section there is appropriated, out of any money in the Treasury not otherwise appropriated, the sum of $4,000,000,000, and in addition thereto the unexpended balance of the appropriations made by section two of said Act approved April twenty-fourth, nineteen hundred and seventeen, or so much thereof as may be necessary: *Provided,* That the authority granted by this section to the Secretary of the Treasury to establish credits for foreign Governments, as aforesaid, shall cease upon the termination of the war between the United States and the Imperial German Government.

SEC. 3. That the Secretary of the Treasury is hereby authorized, from time to time, to exercise in respect to any obligations of foreign governments acquired under authority of this Act or of said Act approved April twenty-fourth, nineteen hundred and seventeen, any privilege of conversion into obligations bearing interest at a higher rate provided for in or pursuant to this Act or said Act approved April twenty-fourth, nineteen hundred and seventeen, and to convert any

LIBERTY BOND ACTS

short time obligations of foreign governments which may have been purchased under the authority of this Act or of said Act approved April twenty-fourth, nineteen hundred and seventeen, into long time obligations of such foreign governments, respectively, maturing not later than the bonds of the United States then last issued under the authority of this Act or of said Act approved April twenty-fourth, nineteen hundred and seventeen, as the case may be, and in such form and terms as the Secretary of the Treasury may prescribe; but the rate or rates of interest borne by any such long-time obligations at the time of their acquisition shall not be less than the rate borne by the short time obligations so converted into such long time obligations; and, under such terms and conditions as he may from time to time prescribe, to receive payment, on or before maturity, of any obligations of such foreign governments acquired on behalf of the United States under authority of this Act or of said Act approved April twenty-fourth, nineteen hundred and seventeen, and, with the approval of the President, to sell any of such obligations (but not at less than the purchase price with accrued interest unless otherwise hereafter provided by law), and to apply the proceeds thereof, and any payments so received from foreign governments on account of the principal of their said obligations, to the redemption or purchase, at not more than par and accrued interest, of any bonds of the United States issued under authority of this Act or of said Act approved April twenty-fourth, nineteen hundred and seventeen, and if such bonds cannot be so redeemed or purchased the Secretary of the Treasury shall redeem or purchase any other outstanding interest-bearing obligations of the United States which may at such time be subject to redemption or which can be purchased at not more than par and accrued interest.

SEC. 4. That in connection with the issue of any series of bonds under the authority of section one of this Act the Secretary of the Treasury may determine that the bonds of such series shall be convertible as provided in or pursuant to this section, and, in any such case, he may make appropriate provision to that end in offering for subscription the bonds of such series (hereinafter called convertible bonds). In any case of the issue of a series of convertible bonds, if a subsequent series of bonds (not including United States certificates of indebtedness, war savings certificates, and other obligations maturing not more than five years from the issue of such obligations, respectively) bearing interest at a higher rate shall, under the authority of this or any other Act, be issued by the United States before the termination of the war between the United States and the Imperial German Government, then the holders of such convertible bonds shall have the privilege, at the option of the several holders, at any time within such period, after the public offering of bonds of such subsequent series, and under such rules and regulations as the Secretary of the Treasury shall have prescribed, of converting their bonds, at par, into bonds bearing such higher rate of interest at such price not less than par as the Secretary of the Treasury shall have prescribed. The bonds to be issued upon such conversion under this Act shall be substantially the same in form and terms as shall be prescribed by or pursuant to law with respect to the bonds of such subsequent series, not only as to interest rate but also as to convertibility (if future bonds be issued at a still higher rate of interest) or nonconvertibility, and as to exemption from taxation, if any, and in all other respects, except that the bonds issued upon such conversion shall have the same dates of maturity, of principal, and of interest, and be subject to the same terms of redemption before maturity, as the bonds converted; and such bonds shall be issued from time to time if and when to the extent that the privilege of conversion so conferred shall arise and shall be exercised. If the privilege of conversion so conferred under this Act shall once arise, and shall not be exercised with respect to any convertible bonds within the period so prescribed by the Secretary of the Treasury, then such privilege shall terminate as to such bonds and shall not arise again though again thereafter bonds be issued bearing interest at a higher rate or rates.

SEC. 5. That in addition to the bonds authorized by section one of this Act the Secretary of the Treasury is authorized to borrow from time to time, on the credit of the United States, for the purpose of this Act and to meet public expenditures authorized by law, such sum or sums as in his judgment may be necessary, and to issue therefor certificates of indebtedness of the United States at not less than par in such form or forms and subject to such terms and conditions

LIBERTY BOND ACTS

and at such rate or rates of interest as he may prescribe; and each certificate so issued shall be payable at such time not exceeding one year from the date of its issue, and may be redeemable before maturity upon such terms and conditions, and the interest accruing thereon shall be payable at such time or times as the Secretary of the Treasury may prescribe. The sum of such certificates outstanding hereunder and under section six of said Act approved April twenty-fourth, nineteen hundred and seventeen, shall not at any one time exceed in the aggregate $4,000,000,000.

SEC. 6. That in addition to the bonds authorized by section one of this Act and the certificates of indebtedness authorized by section five of this Act, the Secretary of the Treasury is authorized to borrow from time to time, on the credit of the United States, for the purposes of this Act and to meet public expenditures authorized by law, such sum or sums as in his judgment may be necessary, and to issue therefor, at such price or prices and upon such terms and conditions as he may determine, war-savings certificates of the United States on which interest to maturity may be discounted in advance at such rate or rates and computed in such manner as he may prescribe. Such war-savings certificates shall be in such form or forms and subject to such terms and conditions, and may have such provisions for payment thereof before maturity, as the Secretary of the Treasury may prescribe. Each war-saving certificate so issued shall be payable at such time, not exceeding five years from the date of its issue, and may be redeemable before maturity, upon such terms and conditions as the Secretary of the Treasury may prescribe. The sum of such war-savings certificates outstanding shall not at any one time exceed in the aggregate $2,000,000,000. The amount of war-savings certificates sold to any one person at any one time shall not exceed $100, and it shall not be lawful for any one person at any one time to hold war-savings certificates to an aggregate amount exceeding $1,000. The Secretary of the Treasury may, under such regulations and upon such terms and conditions as he may prescribe, issue, or cause to be issued, stamps to evidence payments for or on account of such certificates.

SEC. 7. That none of the bonds authorized by section one, nor of the certificates authorized by section five, or by section six, of this Act, shall bear the circulation privilege. All such bonds and certificates shall be exempt, both as to principal and interest from all taxation now or hereafter imposed by the United States, any State, or any of the possessions of the United States, or by any local taxing authority, except (a) estate or inheritance taxes, and (b) graduated additional income taxes, commonly known as surtaxes, and excess profits and war-profits taxes, now or hereafter imposed by the United States, upon the income or profits of individuals, partnerships, associations, or corporations. The interest on an amount of such bonds and certificates the principal of which does not exceed in the aggregate $5,000, owned by any individual, partnership, association, or corporation, shall be exempt from the taxes provided for in subdivision (b) of this section.

SEC. 8. That the Secretary of the Treasury, in his discretion is hereby authorized to deposit, in such incorporated banks and trust companies as he may designate, the proceeds, or any part thereof, arising from the sale of the bonds and certificates of indebtedness and war-savings certificates authorized by this Act, and such deposits shall bear such rate or rates of interest, and shall be secured in such manner, and shall be made upon and subject to such terms and conditions, as the Secretary of the Treasury may from time to time prescribe: *Provided*, That the provisions of section fifty-one hundred and ninety-one of the Revised Statutes, as amended by the Federal Reserve Act, and the amendments thereof, with reference to the reserves required to be kept by national banking associations and other member banks of the Federal Reserve System, shall not apply to deposits of public moneys by the United States in designated depositaries. The Secretary of the Treasury is hereby authorized to designate depositaries in foreign countries, with which shall be deposited all public money which it may be necessary or desirable to have on deposit in such countries to provide for current disbursements to the military and naval forces of the United States and to the diplomatic and consular and other representatives of the United States in and about such countries until six months after the termination of the war between the United States and the Imperial German Government, and to prescribe the terms and conditions of such deposits.

LIBERTY BOND ACTS

SEC. 9. That in connection with the operations of advertising, selling, and delivering any bonds, certificates of indebtedness, or war-savings certificates of the United States provided for in this Act, the Postmaster General, under such regulations as he may prescribe, shall require, at the request of the Secretary of the Treasury, the employees of the Post Office Department and of the Postal Service to perform such services as may be necessary, desirable, or practicable, without extra compensation.

SEC. 10. That in order to pay all necessary expenses, including rent, connected with any operations under this Act, except section twelve, a sum not exceeding one-fifth of one per centum of the amount of bonds and war-savings certificates and one-tenth of one per centum of the amount of certificates of indebtedness herein authorized is hereby appropriated, or as much thereof as may be necessary, out of any money in the Treasury not otherwise appropriated, to be expended as the Secretary of the Treasury may direct: *Provided,* That in addition to the reports now required by law, the Secretary of the Treasury shall, on the first Monday in December, nineteen hundred and eighteen, and annually thereafter, transmit to the Congress a detailed statement of all expenditures under this Act.

SEC. 11. That bonds shall not be issued under authority of sections one and four of said Act approved April twenty-fourth, nineteen hundred and seventeen, in addition to the $2,000,000,000 thereof heretofore issued or offered for subscription, but bonds shall be issued from time to time upon the interchange of such bonds of different denominations and of coupon and registered bonds and upon the transfer of registered bonds, under such rules and regulations as the Secretary of the Treasury shall prescribe, and, if to the extent that the privilege of conversion provided for in such bonds shall arise and shall be exercised, in accordance with such provision for such conversion. No bonds shall be issued under authority of the several sections of Acts and of the resolution mentioned in said section four of the Act approved April twenty-fourth, nineteen hundred and seventeen; but the proceeds of the bonds herein authorized may be used for purposes mentioned in said section four of the Act of April twenty-fourth, nineteen hundred and seventeen, and as set forth in the Acts therein enumerated.

WAR COSTS AND THEIR FINANCING

That section two of an Act of Congress approved February fourth, nineteen hundred and ten, entitled " An Act prescribing certain provisions and conditions under which bonds and certificates of indebtedness of the United States may be issued, and for other purposes," is hereby amended to read as follows:

" SEC. 2. That any certificates of indebtedness hereafter issued shall be exempt from all taxes or duties of the United States (but, in the case of certificates issued after September first, nineteen hundred and seventeen, only if and to the extent provided in connection with the issue thereof), as well as from taxation in any form by or under State, municipal, or local authority and that a sum not exceeding one-tenth of one per centum of the amount of any certificates of indebtedness issued is hereby appropriated, out of any money in the Treasury not otherwise appropriated, to pay the expenses of preparing, advertising, and issuing the same."

SEC. 12. That the Secretary of the Treasury is authorized during the war, whenever it shall appear that the public interests require that any of the accounts of the Military Establishment be audited at any place other than the seat of Government, to direct the Comptroller of the Treasury and the Auditor for the War Department to exercise, either in person or through assistants, the powers and perform the duties of their offices at any place or places away from the seat of Government in the manner that is or may be required by law at the seat of Government and in accordance with the provisions of this section.

(a) That when the Secretary of the Treasury shall exercise the authority herein referred to, the powers and duties of the said comptroller and auditor, under and pursuant to the provisions of the Act of July thirty-first, eighteen hundred and ninety-four, and all other laws conferring jurisdiction upon those officers, shall be exercised and performed in the same manner as nearly as practicable and with the same effect away from the seat of Government as they are now exercised and performed and have effect at the seat of Government, and decisions authorized by law to be rendered by the comptroller at the request of disbursing officers may be rendered with the same effect by such assistants as may be authorized by him to perform that duty.

(b) That when pursuant to this section the said comptroller

LIBERTY BOND ACTS

and auditor shall perform their duties at a place in a foreign country, the balances arising upon the settlement of accounts and claims of the Military Establishment shall be certified by the auditor to the Division of Bookkeeping and Warrants of the Treasury Department as now provided for the certification of balances by said auditor in Washington, and the balances so found due shall be final and conclusive upon all branches of the Government, except that any person whose account has been settled or the commanding officer of the Army abroad, or the comptroller may obtain a revision of such settlement by the comptroller upon application therefor within three months, the decision to be likewise final and conclusive and the differences arising upon such revision to be certified to and stated by the auditor as now provided by law: *Provided,* That certificates of balances due may be transmitted to and paid by the proper disbursing officer abroad instead of by warrant: *Provided further,* That any person whose account has been settled, or the Secretary of War, may obtain a reopening and review of any settlement made pursuant to this section upon application to the Comptroller of the Treasury in Washington within one year after the close of the war, and the action of the comptroller thereon shall be final and conclusive in the same manner as herein provided in the case of a balance found due by the auditor.

(c) That the comptroller and auditor shall preserve the accounts, and the vouchers and papers connected therewith, and the files of their offices in the foreign country and transmit them to Washington within six months after the close of the war and at such earlier time as may be directed by the Secretary of the Treasury as to any or all accounts, vouchers, papers, and files.

(d) That the Secretary of the Treasury is authorized to appoint an assistant comptroller and an assistant auditor and to fix their compensation, and to designate from among the persons to be employed hereunder one or more to act in the absence or disability of such assistant comptroller and assistant auditor. He shall also prescribe the number and maximum compensation to be paid to agents, accountants, clerks, translators, interpreters, and other persons who may be employed in the work under this section by the comptroller and auditor. The assistant comptroller and assistant auditor shall have full power to perform in a foreign country all the duties with reference to the settlement there of the accounts of the Military Establishment that the comptroller and auditor now have at the seat of Government and in foreign countries under the provisions of this section, and shall perform such duties in accordance with the instructions received from and rules and regulations made by the comptroller and auditor. Such persons as are residing in a foreign country when first employed hereunder shall not be required to take an oath of office or be required to be employed pursuant to the laws, rules, and regulations relating to the classified civil service, nor shall they be reimbursed for subsistence expenses at their post of duty or for expenses in traveling to or from the United States.

(e) That it shall be the duty of all contracting, purchasing, and disbursing officers to allow any representative of the comptroller or auditor to examine all books, records, and papers in any way connected with the receipt, disbursement, or disposal of public money, and to render such accounts and at such times as may be required by the comptroller. No administrative examination by the War Department shall be required of accounts rendered and settled abroad, and the time within which these accounts shall be rendered by disbursing officers shall be prescribed by the comptroller, who shall have power to waive any delinquency as to time or form in the rendition of these accounts. All contracts connected with accounts to be settled by the auditor abroad shall be filed in his office there.

(f) That any person appointed or employed under the provisions of this section who at the time is in the service of the United States shall, upon termination of his services hereunder, be restored to the position held by him at the time of such employment. No provision of existing law shall be construed to prevent the payment of money appropriated for the salary of any Government officer or employee at the seat of Government who may de detailed to perform duty under this section outside the District of Columbia, and such details are hereby authorized.

(g) That for the payment of the expenses in carrying into effect this section, including traveling expenses, per diem of $4 in lieu of subsistence for officers and employees absent

LIBERTY BOND ACTS

from Washington, rent, cablegrams and telegrams, printing, law books, books of reference, periodicals, stationery, office equipment and exchange thereof, supplies, and all other necessary expenses, there is hereby appropriated, out of any money in the Treasury not otherwise appropriated, for the fiscal year ending June thirtieth, nineteen hundred and eighteen, the sum of $300,000, of which not exceeding $25,000 may be expended at Washington for the purposes of this section, but no officer or employee shall receive for duty in Washington any compensation other than his regular salary.

(h) That the Secretary of the Treasury may designate not more than two persons employed hereunder to act as special disbursing agents of the appropriation herein, to serve under the direction of the comptroller, and their accounts shall be rendered to and settled by the accounting officers of the Treasury in Washington. All persons employed under this section shall perform such additional duties as the Secretary of the Treasury may direct.

(i) That the comptroller and the auditor, and such persons as may be authorized in writing by either of them, may administer oaths to American citizens in respect to any matter within the jurisdiction of either of said officers and certify the official character, when known, of any foreign officer whose jurat or certificate may be necessary on any paper to be filed with them.

(j) That persons engaged in work abroad under the provisions of this section may purchase from Army stores for cash and at cost price for their own use such articles or stores as may be sold to officers and enlisted men.

(k) That the authority granted under this section shall terminate six months after the close of the war or at such earlier date as the Secretary of the Treasury may direct, and it shall be the duty of the comptroller and auditor to make such reports as the Secretary of the Treasury may require of the expenditures made and work done pursuant to this section, and such reports shall be transmitted to the Congress at such time as he may decide to be compatible with the public interest.

(l) No officers, employees, or agents appointed or employed under this section shall receive more salary or compensation than like officers, employees, or agents of the Government now receive.

SEC. 13. That for the purposes of this Act the date of the termination of the war between the United States and the Imperial German Government shall be fixed by proclamation of the President of the United States.

Approved, September 24, 1917.

SUPPLEMENT TO SECOND LIBERTY BOND ACT

AN ACT To supplement the Second Liberty Bond Act, as amended, and for other purposes.

Be it enacted by the Senate and House of Representatives of the United States of America in Congress assembled, That until the expiration of two years after the date of the termination of the war between the United States and the Imperial German Government, as fixed by proclamation of the President —

(1) The interest on an amount of bonds of the Fourth Liberty Loan the principal of which does not exceed $30,000, owned by any individual, partnership, association, or corporation, shall be exempt from graduated additional income taxes, commonly known as surtaxes, and excess profits and war-profits taxes, now or hereafter imposed by the United States, upon the income or profits of individuals, partnerships, associations, or corporations;

(2) The interest received after January 1, 1918, on an amount of bonds of the First Liberty Loan Converted, dated either November 15, 1917, or May 9, 1918, the Second Liberty Loan, converted and unconverted, and the Third Liberty Loan, the principal of which does not exceed $45,000 in the aggregate, owned by any individual, partnership, association, or corporation, shall be exempt from such taxes: *Provided, however,* That no owner of such bonds shall be entitled to such exemption in respect to the interest on an aggregate principal amount of such bonds exceeding one and one-half times the principal amount of bonds of the Fourth Liberty Loan originally subscribed for by such owner and still owned by him at the date of his tax return; and

(3) The interest on amount of bonds, the principal of which does not exceed $30,000, owned by any individual,

LIBERTY BOND ACTS

partnership, association, or corporation, issued upon conversion of 3½ per centum bonds of the First Liberty Loan in the exercise of any privilege arising as a consequence of the issue of bonds of the Fourth Liberty Loan, shall be exempt from such taxes.

The exemptions provided in this section shall be in addition to the exemption provided in section 7 of the Second Liberty Bond Act in respect to the interest on an amount of bonds and certificates, authorized by such Act and amendments thereto, the principal of which does not exceed in the aggregate $5,000, and in addition to all other exemptions provided in the Second Liberty Bond Act.

SEC. 2. That section 6 of the Second Liberty Bond Act is hereby amended by striking out the figures " $2,000,000,000," and inserting in lieu thereof the figures " $4,000,000,000." Such section is further amended by striking out the words " The amount of war savings certificates sold to any one person at any one time shall not exceed $100, and it shall not be lawful for any one person at any one time to hold war savings certificates to an aggregate amount exceeding $1,000," and inserting in lieu thereof the words " It shall not be lawful for any one person at any one time to hold war savings certificates of any one series to an aggregate amount exceeding $1,000."

SEC. 3. That the provisions of section 8 of the Second Liberty Bond Act, as amended by the Third Liberty Bond Act, shall apply to the proceeds arising from the payment of war-profits taxes as well as income and excess profits taxes.

SEC. 4. That the Secretary of the Treasury may, during the war and for two years after its termination, make arrangements in or with foreign countries to stabilize the foreign exchanges and to obtain foreign currencies and credits in such currencies, and he may use any such credits and foreign currencies for the purpose of stabilizing or rectifying the foreign exchanges, and he may designate depositaries in foreign countries with which may be deposited as he may determine all or any part of the avails of any foreign credits or foreign currencies.

SEC. 5. That subdivision (b) of section 5 of the Trading with the Enemy Act be, and hereby is, amended to read as follows:

WAR COSTS AND THEIR FINANCING

"(b) That the President may investigate, regulate, or prohibit, under such rules and regulations as he may prescribe, by means of licenses or otherwise, any transactions in foreign exchange and the export, hoarding, melting, or earmarkings of gold or silver coin or bullion or currency, transfers of credit in any form (other than credits relating solely to transactions to be executed wholly within the United States), and transfers of evidences of indebtedness or of the ownership of property between the United States and any foreign country, whether enemy, ally of enemy, or otherwise, or between residents of one or more foreign countries, by any person within the United States and, for the purpose of strengthening, sustaining and broadening the market for bonds and certificates of indebtedness of the United States, of preventing frauds upon the holders thereof, and of protecting such holders, he may investigate and regulate, by means of licenses or otherwise (until the expiration of two years after the date of the termination of the present war with the Imperial German Government, as fixed by his proclamation), any transactions in such bonds or certificates by or between any person or persons: *Provided,* That nothing contained in this subdivision (b) shall be construed to confer any power to prohibit the purchase or sale for cash, or for notes eligible for discount at any Federal Reserve Bank, of bonds or certificates of indebtedness of the United States; and he may require any person engaged in any transaction referred to in this subdivision to furnish, under oath, complete information relative thereto, including the production of any books of account, contracts, letters or other papers, in connection therewith in the custody or control of such person, either before or after such transaction is completed."

SEC. 6. That section 5200 of the Revised Statutes, as amended, be, and hereby is, amended to read as follows:

" SEC. 5200. The total liabilities to any association, of any person, or of any company, corporation, or firm for money borrowed, including in the liabilities of a company or firm the liabilities of the several members thereof, shall at no time exceed 10 per centum of the amount of the capital stock of such association, actually paid in and unimpaired, and 10 per centum of its unimpaired surplus fund: *Provided, however,* That (1) the discount of bills of exchange drawn in good faith

LIBERTY BOND ACTS

against actually existing values, (2) the discount of commercial or business paper actually owned by the person, company, corporation, or firm, negotiating the same, and (3) the purchase or discount of any note or notes secured by not less than a like face amount of bonds of the United States issued since April 24, 1917, or certificates of indebtedness of the United States, shall not be considered as money borrowed within the meaning of this section; but the total liabilities to any association, of any person or of any company, corporation, or firm, upon any note or notes purchased or discounted by such association and secured by such bonds or certificates of indebtedness, shall not exceed (except to the extent permitted by rules and regulations prescribed by the Comptroller of the Currency, with the approval of the Secretary of the Treasury) 10 per centum of such capital stock and surplus fund of such association."

SEC. 7. That the short title of this Act shall be "Supplement to Second Liberty Bond Act."

Approved, September 24, 1918.

THIRD LIBERTY BOND ACT

AN ACT To amend an Act approved September twenty-fourth, nineteen hundred and seventeen, entitled "An Act to authorize an additional issue of bonds to meet expenditures for the national security and defense, and, for the purpose of assisting in the prosecution of the war, to extend additional credit to foreign governments, and for other purposes."

Be it enacted by the Senate and House of Representatives of the United States of America in Congress assembled, That the first section of the Act approved September twenty-fourth, nineteen hundred and seventeen, entitled "An Act to authorize an additional issue of bonds to meet expenditures for the national security and defense, and, for the purpose of assisting in the prosecution of the war, to extend additional credit to foreign governments, and for other purposes," be, and is hereby, amended to read as follows:

"That the Secretary of the Treasury, with the approval of the President, is hereby authorized to borrow from time to time, on the credit of the United States for the purposes of this Act, and to meet expenditures authorized for the national

WAR COSTS AND THEIR FINANCING

security and defense and other public purposes authorized by law, not exceeding in the aggregate $12,000,000,000, and to issue therefor bonds of the United States, in addition to the $2,000,000,000 bonds already issued or offered for subscription under authority of the Act approved April twenty-fourth, nineteen hundred and seventeen, entitled ' An Act to authorize an issue of bonds to meet expenditures for the national security and defense, and, for the purpose of assisting in the prosecution of the war, to extend credit to foreign governments, and for other purposes ': *Provided,* That of this sum $3,063,945,460 shall be in lieu of that amount of the unissued bonds authorized by sections one and four of the Act approved April twenty-fourth, nineteen hundred and seventeen, $225,000,000 shall be in lieu of that amount of the unissued bonds authorized by section thirty-nine of the Act approved August fifth, nineteen hundred and nine, $150,000,000 shall be in lieu of the unissued bonds authorized by the joint resolution approved March fourth, nineteen hundred and seventeen, and $100,000,000 shall be in lieu of the unissued bonds authorized by section four hundred of the Act approved March third, nineteen hundred and seventeen.

" The bonds herein authorized shall be in such form or forms and denomination or denominations and subject to such terms and conditions of issue, conversion, redemption, maturities, payment, and rate or rates of interest, not exceeding four and one-quarter per centum per annum, and time or times of payment of interest, as the Secretary of the Treasury from time to time at or before the issue thereof may prescribe. The principal and interest thereof shall be payable in United States gold coin of the present standard of value.

" The bonds herein authorized shall from time to time first be offered at not less than par as a popular loan, under such regulations, prescribed by the Secretary of the Treasury from time to time, as will in his opinion give the people of the United States as nearly as may be an equal opportunity to participate therein, but he may make allotment in full upon applications for smaller amounts of bonds in advance of any date which he may set for the closing of subscriptions and may reject or reduce allotments upon later applications and applications for larger amounts, and may reject or reduce allotments upon applications from incorporated banks and

LIBERTY BOND ACTS

trust companies for their own account and make allotment in full or larger allotments to others, and may establish a graduated scale of allotments, and may from time to time adopt any or all of said methods, should any such action be deemed by him to be in the public interest: *Provided,* That such reduction or increase of allotments of such bonds shall be made under general rules to be prescribed by said Secretary and shall apply to all subscribers similarly situated. And any portion of the bonds so offered and not taken may be otherwise disposed of by the Secretary of the Treasury in such manner and at such price or prices, not less than par, as he may determine. The Secretary may make special arrangements for subscriptions at not less than par from persons in the military or naval forces of the United States, but any bonds issued to such persons shall be in all respects the same as other bonds of the same issue."

SEC. 2. That the last sentence of section two of said Act approved September twenty-fourth, nineteen hundred and seventeen, be, and is hereby, amended to read as follows:

" For the purposes of this section there is appropriated, out of any money in the Treasury not otherwise appropriated, the sum of $5,500,000,000, and in addition thereto the unexpended balance of the appropriations made by section two of said act approved April twenty-fourth, nineteen hundred and seventeen, or so much thereof as may be necessary: *Provided,* That the authority granted by this section to the Secretary of the Treasury to establish credits for foreign Governments, as aforesaid, shall cease upon the termination of the war between the United States and the Imperial German Government."

SEC. 3. That section four of said Act approved September twenty-fourth, nineteen hundred and seventeen, is hereby amended by adding two new paragraphs, as follows:

" That holders of bonds bearing interest at a higher rate than four per centum per annum, whether issued (a) under section one, or (b) upon conversion of four per centum bonds issued under section one, or (c) upon conversion of three and one-half per centum bonds issued under said Act approved April twenty-fourth, nineteen hundred and seventeen, or (d) upon conversion of four per centum bonds issued upon conversion of such three and one-half per centum bonds, shall not be entitled to any privilege of conversion under or pursuant to this section or otherwise. The provisions of section seven shall extend to all such bonds.

"If bonds bearing interest at a higher rate than four per centum per annum shall be issued before July first, nineteen hundred and eighteen, then any bonds bearing interest at the rate of four per centum per annum which shall, after July first, nineteen hundred and eighteen, and before the expiration of the six months' conversion period prescribed by the Secretary of the Treasury, be presented for conversion into bonds bearing interest at such higher rate, shall, for the purpose of computing the amount of interest payable, be deemed to have been converted on the dates for the payment of the semiannual interest on the respective bonds so presented for conversion, last preceding the date of such presentation."

SEC. 4. That the last sentence of section five of said Act approved September twenty-fourth, nineteen hundred and seventeen, be, and is hereby, amended to read as follows:

"The sum of such certificates outstanding hereunder and under section six of said Act approved April twenty-fourth, nineteen hundred and seventeen, shall not at any one time exceed in the aggregate $8,000,000,000."

SEC. 5. That section eight of said Act approved September twenty-fourth, nineteen hundred and seventeen, be, and is hereby, amended to read as follows:

"SEC. 8. That the Secretary of the Treasury, in his discretion, is hereby authorized to deposit, in such incorporated banks and trust companies as he may designate, the proceeds, or any part thereof, arising from the sale of the bonds and certificates of indebtedness and war-savings certificates authorized by this Act, and arising from the payment of income and excess profits taxes, and such deposits shall bear such rate or rates of interest, and shall be secured in such manner, and shall be made upon and subject to such terms and conditions as the Secretary of the Treasury may from time to time prescribe: *Provided,* That the provisions of section fifty-one hundred and ninety-one of the Revised Statutes, as amended by the Federal Reserve Act, and the amendments thereof, with reference to the reserves required to be kept by national banking associations and other member banks of the

LIBERTY BOND ACTS

Federal Reserve System, shall not apply to deposits of public moneys by the United States in designated depositaries. The Secretary of the Treasury is hereby authorized to designate depositaries in foreign countries with which shall be deposited all public money which it may be necessary or desirable to have on deposit in such countries to provide for current disbursements to the military and naval forces of the United States and to the diplomatic and consular and other representatives of the United States in and about such countries until six months after the termination of the war between the United States and the Imperial German Government, and to prescribe the terms and conditions of such deposits."

SEC. 6. That said Act approved September twenty-fourth, nineteen hundred and seventeen, is hereby amended by adding four new sections, to read as follows:

" SEC. 14. That any bonds of the United States bearing interest at a higher rate than four per centum per annum (whether issued under section one of this Act or upon conversion of bonds issued under this Act or under said Act approved April twenty-fourth, nineteen hundred and seventeen), which have been owned by any person continuously for at least six months prior to the date of his death, and which upon such date constitute part of his estate, shall, under rules and regulations prescribed by the Secretary of the Treasury, be receivable by the United States at par and accrued interest in payment of any estate or inheritance taxes imposed by the United States, under or by virtue of any present or future law upon such estate or the inheritance thereof.

" SEC. 15. That the Secretary of the Treasury is authorized, from time to time, until the expiration of one year after the termination of the war, to purchase bonds issued under authority of this Act, including bonds issued upon conversion of bonds issued under this Act or said Act approved April twenty-fourth, nineteen hundred and seventeen, at such prices and upon such terms and conditions as he may prescribe The par amount of bonds of any such series which may be purchased in the twelve months' period beginning on the date of issue shall not exceed one-twentieth of the par amount of bonds of such series originally issued, and in each twelve months' period thereafter shall not exceed one-twentieth of the amount of the bonds of such series outstanding at the beginning of such twelve months' period. The average cost of the bonds of any series purchased in any such twelve months' period shall not exceed par and accrued interest.

"For the purposes of this section the Secretary of the Treasury shall set aside, out of any money in the Treasury not otherwise appropriated, a sum not exceeding one-twentieth of the amount of such bonds issued before April first, nineteen hundred and eighteen, and as and when any more such bonds are issued he shall set aside a sum not exceeding one-twentieth thereof. Whenever, by reason of purchases of bonds, as provided in this section, the amount so set aside falls below the sum which he deems necessary for the purposes of this section, the Secretary of the Treasury shall set aside such amount as he shall deem necessary, but not more than enough to bring the entire amount so set aside at such time up to one-twentieth of the amount of such bonds then outstanding. The amount so set aside by the Secretary of the Treasury is hereby appropriated for the purposes of this section, to be available until the expiration of one year after the termination of the war.

"The Secretary of the Treasury shall make to Congress at the beginning of each regular session a report including a detailed statement of the operations under this section.

"SEC. 16. That any of the bonds or certificates of indebtedness authorized by this Act may be issued by the Secretary of the Treasury payable, principal and interest, in any foreign money or foreign moneys, as expressed in such bonds or certificates, but not also in United States gold coin, and he may dispose of such bonds or certificates in such manner and at such prices, not less than par, as he may determine, without compliance with the provisions of the third paragraph of section one. In determining the amount of bonds and certificates issuable under this Act the dollar equivalent of this amount of any bonds or certificates payable in foreign money or foreign moneys shall be determined by the par of exchange at the date of issue thereof, as estimated by the Director of the Mint, and proclaimed by the Secretary of the Treasury, in pursuance of the provisions of section twenty-five of the Act · approved August twenty-seventh, eighteen hundred and ninety-four, entitled ' An Act to reduce taxation, to provide revenue for the Government, and for

LIBERTY BOND ACTS

other purposes.' The Secretary of the Treasury may designate depositaries in foreign countries, with which may be deposited as he may determine all or any part of the proceeds of any bonds or certificates authorized by this Act, payable in foreign money or foreign moneys.

" SEC. 17. That the short title of this Act shall be ' Second Liberty Bond Act.' "

SEC. 7. That the Act entitled " An Act to authorize an issue of bonds to meet expenditures for the national security and defense, and, for the purpose of assisting in the prosecution of the war, to extend credit to foreign governments, and for other purposes," approved April twenty-fourth, nineteen hundred and seventeen, is hereby amended by adding a new section to read as follows:

" SEC. 9. That the short title of this Act shall be ' First Liberty Bond Act.' "

SEC. 8. That the short title of this Act shall be " Third Liberty Bond Act."

Approved, April 4, 1918.

FOURTH LIBERTY BOND ACT

AN ACT To authorize an additional issue of bonds to meet expenditures for the national security and defense, and, for the purpose of assisting in the prosecution of the war, to extend additional credit to foreign Governments, and for other purposes.

Be it enacted by the Senate and House of Representatives of the United States of America in Congress assembled, That section one of the Second Liberty Bond Act, as amended by the Third Liberty Bond Act, is hereby further amended by striking out the figures " $12,000,000,000 " and inserting in lieu thereof the figures " $20,000,000,000."

SEC. 2. That section two of the Second Liberty Bond Act, as amended by the Third Liberty Bond Act, is hereby further amended by striking out the figures " $5,500,000,000 " and inserting in lieu thereof the figures " $7,000,000,000."

SEC. 3. That notwithstanding the provisions of the Second Liberty Bond Act, as amended by the Third Liberty Bond Act, or of the War Finance Corporation Act, bonds and certificates of indebtedness of the United States payable in any foreign money or foreign moneys, and bonds of the War Finance Corporation payable in any foreign money or foreign moneys exclusively or in the alternative, shall, if and to the extent expressed in such bonds at the time of their issue, with the approval of the Secretary of the Treasury, while beneficially owned by a nonresident alien individual, or by a foreign corporation, partnership, or association, not engaged in business in the United States, be exempt both as to principal and interest from any and all taxation now or hereafter imposed by the United States, any State, or any of the possessions of the United States, or by any local taxing authority.

SEC. 4. That any incorporated bank or trust company designated as a depositary by the Secretary of the Treasury under the authority conferred by section eight of the Second Liberty Bond Act, as amended by the Third Liberty Bond Act, which gives security for such deposits as, and to amounts, by him prescribed, may, upon and subject to such terms and conditions as the Secretary of the Treasury may prescribe, act as a fiscal agent of the United States in connection with the operations of selling and delivering any bonds, certificates of indebtedness or war savings certificates of the United States.

SEC. 5. That the short title of this Act shall be " Fourth Liberty Bond Act."

Approved, July 9, 1918.

VICTORY LIBERTY LOAN ACT

AN ACT To amend the Liberty Bond Acts and the War Finance Corporation Act, and for other purposes.

Be it enacted by the Senate and House of Representatives of the United States of America in Congress assembled, That the Second Liberty Bond Act is hereby amended by adding thereto a new section to read as follows:

" SEC. 18. (a) That in addition to the bonds and certificates of indebtedness and war-savings certificates authorized by this Act and amendments thereto, the Secretary of the Treasury, with the approval of the President, is authorized to borrow from time to time on the credit of the United States for the purposes of this Act, and to meet public expenditures

LIBERTY BOND ACTS

authorized by law, not exceeding in the aggregate $7,000,000,000, and to issue therefor notes of the United States at not less than par in such form or forms and denomination or denominations, containing such terms and conditions, and at such rate or rates of interest, as the Secretary of the Treasury may prescribe, and each series of notes so issued shall be payable at such time not less than one year nor more than five years from the date of its issue as he may prescribe, and may be redeemable before maturity (at the option of the United States) in whole or in part, upon not more than one year's nor less than four month's notice, and under such rules and regulations and during such period as he may prescribe.

"(b) The notes herein authorized may be issued in any one or more of the following series as the Secretary of the Treasury may prescribe in connection with the issue thereof:

"(1) Exempt, both as to principal and interest, from all taxation (except estate or inheritance taxes) now or hereafter imposed by the United States, any State, or any of the possessions of the United States, or by any local taxing authority;

"(2) Exempt, both as to principal and interest, from all taxation now or hereafter imposed by the United States, any State, or any of the possessions of the United States, or by any local taxing authority, except (a) estate or inheritance taxes, and (b) graduated additional income taxes, commonly known as surtaxes, and excess profits and war profits taxes, now or hereafter imposed by the United States, upon the income or profits of individuals, partnerships, associations, or corporations;

"(3) Exempt, both as to principal and interest, as provided in paragraph (2); and with an additional exemption from the taxes referred to in clause (b) of such paragraph, of the interest on an amount of such notes the principal of which does not exceed $30,000, owned by any individual, partnership, association, or corporation; or

"(4) Exempt, both as to principal and interest, from all taxation now or hereafter imposed by the United States, any State, or any of the possessions of the United States, or by any local taxing authority, except (a) estate or inheritance taxes, and (b) all income, excess profits, and war profits taxes, now or hereafter imposed by the United States, upon the income or profits of individuals, partnership, associations, or corporations.

"(c) If the notes authorized under this section are offered in more than one series bearing the same date of issue, the holder of notes of any such series shall (under such rules and regulations as may be prescribed by the Secretary of the Treasury) have the option of having such notes held by him converted at par into notes of any other such series offered bearing the same date of issue.

"(d) None of the notes authorized by this section shall bear the circulation privilege. The principal and interest thereof shall be payable in United States gold coin of the present standard of value. The word 'bond' or 'bonds' where it appears in sections 8, 9, 10, 14, and 15 of this Act as amended, and sections 3702, 3703, 3704, and 3705 of the Revised Statutes, and section 5200 of the Revised Statutes as amended, but in such sections only, shall be deemed to include notes issued under this section."

SEC. 2. (a) That until the expiration of five years after the date of the termination of the war between the United States and the German Government, as fixed by proclamation of the President, in addition to the exemptions provided in section 7 of the Second Liberty Bond Act in respect to the interest on an amount of bonds and certificates, authorized by such Act and amendments thereto, the principal of which does not exceed in the agregate $5,000, and in addition to all other exemptions provided in the Second Liberty Bond Act or the Supplement to Second Liberty Bond Act, the interest received on and after January 1, 1919, on an amount of bonds of the First Liberty Loan converted, dated November 15, 1917, May 9, 1918, or October 24, 1918, the Second Liberty Loan, converted and unconverted, the Third Liberty Loan, and the Fourth Liberty Loan, the principal of which does not exceed $30,000 in the aggregate, owned by any individual, partnership, association, or corporation, shall be exempt from graduated additional income taxes, commonly known as surtaxes, and excess profits and war profits taxes, now or hereafter imposed by the United States, upon the income or profits of individuals, partnerships, associations, or corporations.

(b) In addition to the exemption provided in subdivision (a), and in addition to the other exemptions therein referred

LIBERTY BOND ACTS

to, the interest received on and after January 1, 1919, on any amount of the bonds therein specified the principal of which does not exceed $20,000 in the aggregate, owned by any individual, partnership, association, or corporation, shall be exempt from the taxes therein specified; *Provided,* That no owner of such bonds shall be entitled to such exemption in respect to the interest on an aggregate principal amount of such bonds exceeding three times the principal amount of notes of the Victory Liberty Loan originally subscribed for by such owner and still owned by him at the date of his tax return.

SEC. 3. That section 5 of the Second Liberty Bond Act, as amended by section 4 of the Third Liberty Bond Act, is hereby further amended by striking out the figures " $8,000,000,000 " and inserting in lieu thereof the figures " $10,000,000,000."

SEC. 4. That section 3 of the Fourth Liberty Bond Act is hereby amended to read as follows:

" SEC. 3. That, notwithstanding the provisions of the Second Liberty Bond Act or of the War Finance Corporation Act or of any other Act, bonds, notes, and certificates of indebtedness of the United States and bonds of the War Finance Corporation shall, while beneficially owned by a nonresident alien individual, or a foreign corporation, partnership, or association, not engaged in business in the United States, be exempt both as to principal and interest from any and all taxation now or hereafter imposed by the United States, any State, or any of the possessions of the United States or by any local taxing authority."

SEC. 5. That the privilege of converting the 4 per centum bonds of the First Liberty Loan converted and 4 per centum bonds of the Second Liberty Loan into 4¼ per centum bonds, which privilege arose on May 9, 1918, and expired on November 9, 1918, may be extended by the Secretary of the Treasury for such period, upon such terms and conditions and subject to such rules and regulations, as he may prescribe. For the purpose of computing the amount of interest payable, bonds presented for conversion under any such extension shall be deemed to be converted on the dates for the payment of the semiannual interest on the respective bonds so presented for conversion next succeeding the date of such presentation.

WAR COSTS AND THEIR FINANCING

SEC. 6. (a) That there is hereby created in the Treasury a cumulative sinking fund for the retirement of bonds and notes issued under the First Liberty Bond Act, the Second Liberty Bond Act, the Third Liberty Bond Act, the Fourth Liberty Bond Act, or under this Act, and outstanding on July 1, 1920. The sinking fund and all additions thereto are hereby appropriated for the payment of such bonds and notes at maturity, or for the redemption or purchase thereof before maturity by the Secretary of the Treasury at such prices and upon such terms and conditions as he shall prescribe, and shall be available until all such bonds and notes are retired. The average cost of the bonds and notes purchased shall not exceed par and accrued interest. Bonds and notes purchased, redeemed, or paid out of the sinking fund shall be canceled and retired and shall not be reissued. For the fiscal year beginning July 1, 1920, and for each fiscal year thereafter until all such bonds and notes are retired there is hereby appropriated, out of any money in the Treasury not otherwise appropriated, for the purposes of such sinking fund, an amount equal to the sum of (1) $2\frac{1}{2}$ per centum of the aggregate amount of such bonds and notes outstanding on July 1, 1920, less an amount equal to the par amount of any obligations of foreign governments held by the United States on July 1, 1920, and (2) the interest which would have been payable during the fiscal year for which the appropriation is made on the bonds and notes purchased, redeemed, or paid out of the sinking fund during such year or in previous years.

The Secretary of the Treasury shall submit to Congress at the beginning of each regular session a separate annual report of the action taken under the authority contained in the section.

(b) Sections 3688, 3694, 3695, and 3696 of the Revised Statutes, and so much of section 3689 of the Revised 1 per centum of the entire debt of the United States to be set apart as a sinking fund, are hereby repealed.

SEC. 7. (a) That until the expiration of eighteen months after the termination of the war between the United States and the German Government, as fixed by proclamation of the President, the Secretary of the Treasury, with the approval of the President, is hereby authorized on behalf of the United

LIBERTY BOND ACTS

States to establish, in addition to the credits authorized by section 2 of the Second Liberty Bond Act, as amended, credits with the United States for any foreign Government now engaged in war with the enemies of the United States, for the purpose only of providing for purchases of any property owned directly or indirectly by the United States, not needed by the United States, or of any wheat the price of which has been or may be guaranteed by the United States. To the extent of the credits so established from time to time the Secretary of the Treasury is hereby authorized to make advances to or for the account of any such foreign government and to receive at par from such foreign government for the amount of any such advances its obligations hereafter issued bearing such rate or rates of interest, not less than 5 per centum per annum, maturing at such date or dates, not later than October 15, 1938, and containing such terms and conditions, as the Secretary of the Treasury may from time to time prescribe. The Secretary, with the approval of the President, is hereby authorized to enter into such arrangements from time to time with any such foreign government as may be necessary or desirable for establishing such credits and for the payment of such obligations before maturity.

(b) The Secretary of the Treasury is hereby authorized from time to time to convert any short time obligations of foreign governments which may be received under the authority of this section into long time obligations of such foreign governments, respectively, maturing not later than October 15, 1938, and in such form and terms as the Secretary of the Treasury may prescribe; but the rate or rates of interest borne by any such long time obligations at the time of their acquisition shall not be less than the rate borne by the short time obligations so converted into such long time obligations; and, under such terms and conditions as he may from time to time prescribe, to receive payment, on or before maturity, of any obligations of such foreign governments acquired on behalf of the United States under authority of this section, and, with the approval of the President, to sell any of such obligations (but not at less than par with accrued interest unless otherwise hereafter provided by law); and to apply the proceeds thereof, and any payments so received from foreign governments on account of the principal of such obligations, to the redemption or purchase, at not more than par and accrued interest, of any bonds of the United States issued under the authority of the First Liberty Bond Act or Second Liberty Bond Act as amended and supplemented, and if such bonds can not be so redeemed or purchased, the Secretary of the Treasury shall redeem or purchase any other outstanding interest-bearing obligations of the United States which may at such time be subject to redemption or which can be purchased at not more than par and accrued interest.

(c) For the purposes of this section there is appropriated the unexpended balance of the appropriations made by section 2 of the First Liberty Bond Act and by section 2 of the Second Liberty Bond Act as amended by the Third Liberty Bond Act and the Fourth Liberty Bond Act, but nothing in this section shall be deemed to prohibit the use of such unexpended balance of any part thereof for the purpose of section 2 of the Second Liberty Bond Act, as so amended, subject to the limitations therein contained.

SEC. 8. That the obligations of foreign governments acquired by the Secretary of the Treasury by virtue of the provisions of the First Liberty Bond Act and the Second Liberty Bond Act, and amendments and supplements thereto, shall mature at such dates as shall be determined by the Secretary of the Treasury: *Provided,* That such obligations acquired by virtue of the provisions of the First Liberty Bond Act, or through the conversion of short time obligations acquired under such act, shall mature not later than June 15, 1947, and all other such obligations of foreign governments shall mature not later than October 15, 1938.

SEC. 9. That the War Finance Corporation Act is hereby amended by adding to Title I thereof of a new section, to read as follows:

" SEC. 21. (a) That the corporation shall be empowered and authorized, in order to promote commerce with foreign nations through the extension of credits, to make advances upon such terms, not inconsistent with the provisions of this section, as it may prescribe, for periods not exceeding five years from the respective date of such advances:

"(1) To any person, firm, corporation, or association engaged in the business in the United States of exporting

LIBERTY BOND ACTS

therefrom domestic products to foreign countries, if such person, firm, corporation, or association is, in the opinion of the board of directors of the corporation, unable to obtain funds upon reasonable terms through banking channels. Any such advance shall be made only for the purpose of assisting in the exportation of such products, and shall be limited in amount to not more than the contract price therefor, including insurance and carrying or transportation charges to the foreign point of destination if and to the extent that such insurance carrying or transportation charges are payable in the United States by such exporter to domestic insurers and carriers. The rate of interest charged on any advance shall not be less than 1 per centum per annum in excess of the rate of discount for ninety-day commercial paper prevailing at the time of such advance at the Federal reserve bank of the district in which the borrower is located and

"(2) To any bank, banker, or trust company in the United States which after this section takes effect makes an advance to any such person, firm, corporation, or association for the purpose of assisting in the exportation of such products. Any such advance shall not exceed the amount remaining unpaid of the advances made by such bank, banker, or trust company to such person, firm, corporation, or association for such purpose.

"(b) The aggregate of the advances made by the corporation under this section remaining unpaid shall never at any time exceed the sum of $1,000,000,000.

"(c) Notwithstanding the limitation of section 1 the advances provided for by this section may be made until the expiration of one year after the termination of the war between the United States and the German Government as fixed by proclamation of the President. Any such advances made by the corporation shall be made upon the promissory note or notes of the borrower, with full and adequate security in each instance by indorsement, guaranty, or otherwise. The corporation shall retain power to require additional security at any time. The corporation in its discretion may upon like security extend the time of payments of any such advance through renewals, the substitution of new obligations, or otherwise, but the time for the payment of any such advance shall not be extended beyond five years from the date on which it was originally made."

SEC. 10. That section 15 of the War Finance Corporation Act is hereby amended to read as follows:

" SEC. 15. That all net earnings of the corporation not required for its operations shall be accumulated as a reserve fund until such time as the corporation liquidates under the terms of this title. Such reserve fund shall, upon the direction of the board of directors, with the approval of the Secretary of the Treasury, be invested in bonds and obligations of the United States, issued or converted after September 24, 1917, or upon like directions and approval may be deposited in member banks of the Federal Reserve System, or in any of the Federal Reserve Banks, or be used from time to time, as well as any other funds of the corporation, in the purchase or redemption of any bonds issued by the corporation. The Federal Reserve Banks are hereby authorized to act as depositaries for and as fiscal agents of the corporation in the general performance of the powers conferred by this title. Beginning twelve months after the termination of the war, the date of such termination to be fixed by a proclamation of the President of the United States, the directors of the corporation shall proceed to liquidate its assets and to wind up its affairs, but the directors of the corporation, in their discretion, may, from time to time, prior to such date, sell and dispose of any securities or other property acquired by the corporation. Any balance remaining after the payment of all its debts shall be paid into the Treasury of the United States as miscellaneous receipts, and thereupon the corporation shall be dissolved."

SEC. 11. That the short title of this act shall be " Victory Liberty Loan Act."

Approved March 3, 1919.

APPENDIX V

TAXATION IN THE UNITED STATES

INCOME TAXATION

A general review of the increase in the number of returns and income reported for the years since the inception of the present epoch of income taxation is given in the following comparative tables:

NET INCOME FROM PERSONAL RETURNS, CALENDAR YEARS
1913–1917

Year	Number of returns	Net income	Increase from year to year
1913.......	[1] 357,598	[2] $3,900,000,000	....
1914.......	[1] 357,515	[2] 4,000,000,000	$100,000,000
1915.......	[1] 336,652	[2] 4,600,000,000	600,000,000
1916.......	[1] 437,036	6,300,000,000	1,700,000,000
1917.......	[3] 3,472,890	13,700,000,000	7,400,000,000

[1] Returns reporting net incomes of $3,000 and over.
[2] Determined on the basis of the number of returns filed and the average net income in each class.
[3] Returns reporting net incomes of $1,000 and over.

INCOME TAX YIELD FROM PERSONAL RETURNS, CALENDAR YEARS
1913–1917

Year	Normal tax	Surtax	War excess-profits tax	Total tax
1913 [1]	$12,728,038	$15,525,497	....	$28,253,535
1914 [1]	16,559,493	24,486,669	....	41,046,162
1915 [1]	23,995,777	43,947,818	....	67,943,595
1916 [2]	51,440,558	121,946,136	....	173,386,694
1917 [3]	140,653,937	433,345,732	$101,249,781	675,249,450

[1] Annual reports of the Commissioner of Internal Revenue for the fiscal years ended June 30 immediately following the years shown above. Net incomes, $3,000 and over.
[2] Statistics of income, compiled from the returns filed for 1916. Net incomes, $3,000 and over.
[3] Net incomes, $2,000 and over.

WAR COSTS AND THEIR FINANCING

NUMBER OF PERSONAL RETURNS, CALENDAR YEARS 1914-1917, BY INCOME CLASSES [1]

Income Classes	1914	1915	1916	1917
$1,000 to $2,000........	....	....	....	1,640,758
$2,000 to $2,500........	....	....	....	480,486
$2,500 to $3,000........	....	....	....	358,221
$3,000 to $4,000........	82,754	69,045	85,122	374,958
$4,000 to $5,000........	66,525	58,949	72,027	185,805
$5,000 to $10,000.......	127,448	120,402	150,553	270,666
$10,000 to $15,000......	34,141	34,102	45,309	65,800
$15,000 to $20,000......	15,790	16,475	22,618	29,896
$20,000 to $25,000......	8,672	9,707	12,953	16,806
$25,000 to $30,000......	5,483	6,196	8,055	10,571
$30,000 to $40,000......	6,008	7,005	10,068	12,733
$40,000 to $50,000......	3,185	4,100	5,611	7,087
$50,000 to $100,000.....	5,161	6,847	10,452	12,439
$100,000 to $150,000....	1,189	1,793	2,900	3,302
$150,000 to $200,000....	406	724	1,234	1,302
$200,000 to $250,000....	233	386	726	703
$250,000 to $300,000....	130	216	427	342
$300,000 to $400,000....	147	254	469	380
$400,000 to $500,000....	69	122	245	179
$500,000 to $1,000,000..	114	209	376	315
$1,000,000 and over....	60	120	206	141
Married women making returns separate from husbands............	(2)	(2)	[2] 7,635	(2)
Total number of returns filed.......	357,515	336,652	437,036	3,472,890

[1] The returns for 1913 are omitted, as they pertain only to the last 10 months of that year.

[2] The net incomes reported on separate returns made by husband and wife in 1916 are combined and included as one return in the figures for the several classes. In 1914, 1915, and 1917 the returns of married women filed separately are included in their individual income classes independently of husband's income.

TAXATION IN THE UNITED STATES

INCOME TAX RATES
ACT OF 1913

Income	Normal	Surtax	Total
$4,000 and over.............	1	.....	1
$20,000–$50,000..................	1	1	2
$50,000–$75,000..................	1	2	3
$75,000–$100,000.................	1	3	4
$100,000–$250,000................	1	4	5
$250,000–$500,000................	1	5	6
$500,000 and over................	1	6	7

ACT OF 1916

Income	Normal	Surtax	Total
$4,000 and over....................	2	.....	2
$20,000–$40,000....................	2	1	3
$40,000–$60,000....................	2	2	4
$60,000–$80,000....................	2	3	5
$80,000–$100,000...................	2	4	6
$100,000–150,000...................	2	5	7
$150,000–$200,000..................	2	6	8
$200,000–$250,000..................	2	7	9
$250,000–$300,000..................	2	8	10
$300,000–$500,000..................	2	9	11
$500,000–$1,000,000................	2	10	12
$1,000,000–$1,500,000..............	2	11	13
$1,500,000–$2,000,000..............	2	12	14
$2,000,000 and over................	2	13	15

INCOME TAX RATES—*Continued*
ACT OF 1917

Income	Normal (Act of 1916)	Additional normal	Surtax (Act of 1916)	Additional surtax	Total
$2,000 and over.......	.....	2	....	....	2
$4,000 and over.......	2	2	....	....	4
$5,000–$7,500.........	2	2	....	1	5
$7,500–$10,000........	2	2	....	2	6
$10,000–$12,500.......	2	2	....	3	7
$12,500–$15,000.......	2	2	....	4	8
$15,000–$20,000.......	2	2	....	5	9
$20,000–$40,000.......	2	2	1	7	12
$40,000–$60,000.......	2	2	2	10	16
$60,000–$80,000.......	2	2	3	14	21
$80,000–$100,000......	2	2	4	18	26
$100,000–$150,000.....	2	2	5	22	31
$150,000–$200,000.....	2	2	6	25	35
$200,000–$250,000.....	2	2	7	30	41
$250,000–$300,000.....	2	2	8	34	46
$300,000–$500,000.....	2	2	9	37	50
$500,000–$750,000.....	2	2	10	40	54
$750,000–$1,000,000...	2	2	10	45	59
$1,000,000–$1,500,000..	2	2	11	50	65
$1,500,000–$2,000,000..	2	2	12	50	66
$2,000,000 and over...	2	2	13	50	67

ACT OF 1919

Income	Normal (1918)	Normal (1919 and after)	Surtax	Total (1918)	Total (1919 and after)
$2,000–$5,000........	6	4	....	6	4
$5,000–$6,000........	6	4	1	7	5
$6,000–$8,000........	12	8	2	14	10
$8,000–$10,000.......	12	8	3	15	11
$10,000–$12,000......	12	8	4	16	12
$12,000–$14,000......	12	8	5	17	13
$14,000–$16,000......	12	8	6	18	14
$16,000–$18,000......	12	8	7	19	15
$18,000–$20,000......	12	8	8	20	16
$20,000–$22,000......	12	8	9	21	17

TAXATION IN THE UNITED STATES

ACT OF 1919—*Continued*

Income	Normal (1918)	Normal (1919 and after)	Surtax	Total (1918)	Total (1919 and after)
$22,000–$24,000	12	8	10	22	18
$24,000–$26,000	12	8	11	23	19
$26,000–$28,000	12	8	12	24	20
$28,000–$30,000	12	8	13	25	21
$30,000–$32,000	12	8	14	26	22
$32,000–$34,000	12	8	15	27	23
$34,000–$36,000	12	8	16	28	24
$36,000–$38,000	12	8	17	29	25
$38,000–$40,000	12	8	18	30	26
$40,000–$42,000	12	8	19	31	27
$42,000–$44,000	12	8	20	32	28
$44,000–$46,000	12	8	21	33	29
$46,000–$48,000	12	8	22	34	30
$48,000–$50,000	12	8	23	35	31
$50,000–$52,000	12	8	24	36	32
$52,000–$54,000	12	8	25	37	33
$54,000–$56,000	12	8	26	38	34
$56,000–$58,000	12	8	27	39	35
$58,000–$60,000	12	8	28	40	36
$60,000–$62,000	12	8	29	41	37
$62,000–$64,000	12	8	30	42	38
$64,000–$66,000	12	8	31	43	39
$66,000–$68,000	12	8	32	44	40
$68,000–$70,000	12	8	33	45	41
$70,000–$72,000	12	8	34	46	42
$72,000–$74,000	12	8	35	47	43
$74,000–$76,000	12	8	36	48	44
$76,000–$78,000	12	8	37	49	45
$78,000–$80,000	12	8	38	50	46
$80,000–$82,000	12	8	39	51	47
$82,000–$84,000	12	8	40	52	48
$84,000–$86,000	12	8	41	53	49
$86,000–$88,000	12	8	42	54	50
$88,000–$90,000	12	8	43	55	51
$90,000–$92,000	12	8	44	56	52
$92,000–$94,000	12	8	45	57	53
$94,000–$96,000	12	8	46	58	54
$96,000–$98,000	12	8	47	59	55
$98,000–$100,000	12	8	48	60	56
$100,000–$150,000	12	8	52	64	60
$150,000–$200,000	12	8	56	68	64
$200,000–$300,000	12	8	60	72	68
$300,000–$500,000	12	8	63	75	71
$500,000–$1,000,000	12	8	64	76	72
$1,000,000 and over	12	8	65	77	73

WAR COSTS AND THEIR FINANCING

Estate Taxes Levied in the United States, 1916–1919

Net Estate	Act of 1916	Act of March 3, 1917	Act of October 3, 1917	Act of 1919
Not exceeding $50,000	1	1.5	2	1
$50,000–$150,000	2	3	4	2
$150,000–$250,000	3	4.5	6	3
$250,000–$450,000	4	6	8	4
$450,000–$750,000	5	7.5	10	6
$750,000–$1,000,000	5	7.5	10	8
$1,000,000–$1,500,000	6	9	12	10
$1,500,000–$2,000,000	6	9	12	12
$2,000,000–$3,000,000	7	10.5	14	14
$3,000,000–$4,000,000	8	12	16	16
$4,000,000–$5,000,000	9	13.5	18	18
$5,000,000–$8,000,000	10	15	20	20
$8,000,000–$10,000,000	10	15	22	22
In excess of $10,000,000	10	15	25	25

TAXATION IN THE UNITED STATES

Excise, Stamp, and Special Taxes Levied in the United States, 1914–1919

BEVERAGES

	Base	Rate in 1913	Act of 1914	Act of 1916	Act of 1917	Act of 1919
Distilled spirits:						
For beverage purposes...	gal.	$1.10	$1.10	$1.10	$3.20	$6.40
For non-beverage purposes...	gal.	1.10	1.10	1.10	2.20	2.20
Perfume...	gal.					1.10
Rectified spirits...	gal.				.15	.30
Floor tax on tax paid beverage...	gal.					3.20
Wines:						
Not over 14 per cent. alcohol...	gal.		.08	.04	.08	.16
14–21 per cent. alcohol...	gal.		.08	.10	.20	.40
21–24 per cent. alcohol...	gal.		.08	.25	.50	
Over 24 per cent alcohol...	gal.		.08	1.10	3.20	1.00
Imitation sparkling...	pint	.10	.10			6.40
Champagne or sparkling...	½ pint	.03	.03	.03	.06	.12
Grape brandy...	gal.		.05	.10	.20–.30	.30
Floor tax on grape brandy...	gal.					.30
Artificially carbonated waters...	½ pint		.015	.015	.03	.06
Liquors, cordials, etc...	½ pint		.015	.015	.03	.06
Sirups and extracts...	gal.				.05–.20	15%
Soft drinks...	gal.				.01	10%
Mineral waters...	gal.				.01	
Carbonic acid gas...	lb.				.05	.02
Fermented liquors...	bbl.	1.00	1.50	1.50	3.00	6.00

Excise, Stamp, and Special Taxes Levied in the United States, 1914–1919—*Continued*

TOBACCO

	Base	Rate in 1913	Act of 1914	Act of 1916	Act of 1917	Act of 1919
Cigars:						
3 lb. or less per 1000	1,000	$ .75	$ .75	$ .75	$1.00	$1.50
Over 3 lb. per 1,000	1,000	3.00	3.00	3.00		
Retailing, 4 cents or less	1,000				3.00	
5 cents or less	1,000					4.00
4–7 cents	1,000				4.00	
5–8 cents	1,000					6.00
7–15 cents	1,000				6.00	
8–15 cents	1,000					9.00
15–20 cents	1,000				8.00	12.00
Over 20 cents	1,000				10.00	15.00
Cigarettes:						
3 lb. or less per 1,000	1,000	1.25	1.25	1.25	2.05	3.00
Over 3 lb. per 1,000	1,000	3.60	3.60	3.60	4.80	7.20
Tobacco and snuff	lb.	.08	.08	.08	.13	.18
Cigarette paper or tubes	pkg.				.005–.02	.005–.03

TAXATION IN THE UNITED STATES

FACILITIES OF PUBLIC UTILITIES AND INSURANCE

	Base	Rate in 1913	Act of 1914	Act of 1916	Act of 1917	Act of 1919
Freight transportation	ad val.				3%	3%
Express transportation	per 20 cts.				.01	.01
Passenger fares	ad val.				8%	8%
Pullman tickets	ad val.		.01		10%	8%
Pipe line transportation	ad val.				5%	5%
Telegraph, telephone, radio:	per mess					
Over 15 cents			.01		.05	
15–50 cents						.05
Over 50 cents						.10
Leased wires, of price paid	ad val.					10%
Insurance:						
Life, on each $100	per $100				.08	.08
Under $500, of first premium	ad val.					40%
Fire, marine and casualty	per $1		.005		.01	.01

ADMISSIONS AND DUES

	Base	Rate in 1913	Act of 1914	Act of 1916	Act of 1917	Act of 1919
Admissions:						
Tickets sold by scalpers	per 10 cts.				.01	.01
Tickets sold at excess price	of excess					5–50%
Opera boxes, etc.	of excess of usual price					50%
Roof garden cabaret	per 10 cts. of food prchs.					10%
Where no admission charged	over $12					.015
Dues	over $10				10%	20%
						10%

WAR COSTS AND THEIR FINANCING

Excise, Stamp, and Special Taxes Levied in the United States, 1914–1919—Continued

EXCISES

	Base	Rate in 1913	Act of 1914	Act of 1916	Act of 1917	Act of 1919
Automobiles and motorcycles	sale price				3%	3%
Auto trucks and wagons	sale price					3%
Other autos and motorcycles	sale price					5%
Tires, tubes and accessories	sale price					5%
Musical instruments	sale price					5%
Sporting goods and games	sale price					10%
Chewing gum	sale price		4%		3%	3%
Cameras	sale price				3%	10%
Photo films, plates, etc	sale price					5%
Candy	sale price					5%
Fire arms	sale price					10%
Hunting and bowie knives	sale price					10%
Dirk knives, daggers, etc	sale price					100%
Portable electric fans	sale price					5%
Thermos containers	sale price					5%
Cigarette holders, humidors, etc	sale price					10%
Slot machines for vending	sale price					5%
Slot weighing machines	sale price					10%
Liveries and boots and hats	sale price					10%
Hunting and riding habits	sale price					10%
Articles made of fur	sale price					10%
Yachts, motor boats, canoes, etc	sale price					10%

TAXATION IN THE UNITED STATES

EXCISES—*Continued*

	Base	Rate in 1913	Act of 1914	Act of 1916	Act of 1917	Act of 1919
Pleasure boats, to user:						
Motor boats not over 5 tons	each				$5.00	$10.00
Not over 50 feet	each				.50	1.00
50–100 feet	each				1.00	2.00
Over 100 feet	each				2.00	4.00
Toilet soaps and powders	sale price					3%
Sculpture, paintings, etc.	sale price					10%
For following articles 10 per cent of amount in excess of specified price:						
Carpets and rugs	$5 per sq. yd.					10%
Picture frames	10.00					10%
Trunks	50.00					10%
Valises, bags, etc.	25.00					10%
Purses, shopping bags, etc.	7.50					10%
Portable lighting fixtures	25.00					10%
Umbrellas, parasols	4.00					10%
Fans	1.00					10%
House coats, lounging robes, etc.	7.50					10%
Fancy waistcoats	5.00					10%
Women's hats, bonnets	15.00					10%
Men's hats	5.00					10%
Men's caps	2.00					10%
Footwear	10.00					10%

Excise, Stamp, and Special Taxes Levied in the United States, 1914–1919—Continued

excises—Continued

	Base	Rate in 1913	Act of 1914	Act of 1916	Act of 1917	Act of 1919
For following articles 10 per cent of amount in excess of specified price—continued:						
Men's neckwear	$2.00					10%
Men's silk stockings	1.00					10%
Women's silk stockings	2.00					10%
Men's shirts	3.00					10%
Pajamas, nightgowns, etc.	5.00					10%
Kimonas, petticoats, and waists	15.00					10%
Jewelry	sale price				3%	5%
Moving picture films	per foot monthly rent.				.0025–.005	5%
Perfumes, toilet compounds, etc.	sale price		1/8–5/8 cts. per pkg.		2%	4%
Patent medicines	sale price				2%	4%

TAXATION IN THE UNITED STATES

STAMP

	Base	Rate in 1913	Act of 1914	Act of 1916	Act of 1917	Act of 1919
Bond and stock issues	per $100.00		$.05		$.05	$.05
Sales of stock	per $100.00		.02		.02	.02
Sales on produce exchanges	per $100.00		.01		.02	.02
Promissory notes	each		.02		.02	.02
Bills of lading	each		.01			
Bonds (except legal)	each		.50		.50	
Underwriting and surety bonds	each					
Certificates of profit	per $100.00		.02			
Certificates of damage	each		.25			
Other certificates	each		.10			
Brokers' notes	each		.10			
Conveyances	per $500.00		.50		.50	.50
Custom house entries	each		.25–1.00		.25–1.00	.25–1.00
Entry for withdrawal	each					.50
Powers of attorney	each		.10–.25		.25	.25
Protests	each		.25			
Cotton futures	per pound		.02a			
Proxies	each				.02	
Passage tickets	each		1.00–5.00		.10	.10
Playing cards	per pack				1.00–5.00	1.00–5.00
Parcel post packages	per 25 cts	.02			.07	.07
					.01	.01

(a) Imposed by Cotton Futures Act of August 18, 1914

Excise, Stamp, and Special Taxes Levied in the United States, 1914–1919—Continued

SPECIAL

	Base	Rate in 1913	Act of 1914	Act of 1916	Act of 1917	Act of 1919
Rectifiers, retail, wholesale	annual	$100, $200	(a)	(a)	(a)	(a)
Liquor dealers, retail, wholesale	annual	25, 100	(a)	(a)	(a)	(a)
Dealers in malt liquors, retail, wholesale	annual	20, 50	(a)	(a)	(a)	(a)
Manufacturers of stills	annual	50	(a)	(a)	(a)	(a)
Additional on each still	annual	20	(a)	(a)	(a)	(a)
Filled cheese, retail, wholesale, m'f't'rs	annual	12, 250, 400	(a)			
Adulterated butter or colored oleomargarine, retail, wholesale, m'f't'rs	annual	48, 480, 600	(a)	(a)	(a)	(a)
White oleomargarine, retail, wholesale, m'f't'rs	annual	6, 200, 600	(a)	(a)	(a)	(a)
Process or renovated butter, m'f't'rs	annual	50	(a)	(a)	(a)	(a)
Mixed flour, m'f't'rs and packers	annual	12	(a)	(a)	(a)	(a)
Opium, m'f't'rs and distributors	per 1,000 lb.	1	(a)			
Tobacco manufacturers						
annual sales, under 50,000 lbs	annual		6.00 and up to 2,496	3.00		$6.00
50,000–100,000	annual			6.00		12.00
100,000–200,000	annual			12.00		24.00
Over 200,000	annual			.08		.16
Over 1,000,000	annual					
Cigar manufacturers						
annual sales under 50,000	annual		3.00	2.00		4.00
50,000–100,000	annual					6.00

(a) No change made in rates existing in 1913.

486

TAXATION IN THE UNITED STATES

SPECIAL—Continued

	Base	Rate in 1913	Act of 1914	Act of 1916	Act of 1917	Act of 1919
Cigar manufacturers—continued:						
100,000–200,000	annual		and	12.00		12.00
200,000–400,000	annual		up			24.00
Over 400,000	per 1,000		to	.05		.10
Over 40,000,000	annual		2,496			
Cigarette manufacturers	per 10,000			.03		.06
annual sales under 1,000,000	annual		12.00			
Over 100,000,000	annual		to 2,496			
Dealers in leaf tobacco	annual		6.00–24.00			
Dealers in tobacco, sales over $200	annual		4.80			
Bankers	per $1,000		$1.00			
Brokers	annual		30.00	$30.00		$50.00
Stock exchange brokers	annual					100.–150.
Pawnbrokers	annual		50.00	50.00		100.00
Commercial brokers	annual		20.00			
Ship brokers	annual			20.00	$10.00	50.00
Custom house brokers	annual		10.00	10.00		50.00
Commission merchants	annual		20.00			
Corporations, on capital	per $1,000			.50		1.00
Proprietors of:						
Theatres, museums, music halls	annual		12.50–100.	12.50–100.		25.–200
Circuses	annual		100.00	100.00		100.00
Other exhibitions	annual		10.00	10.00		15.00
Street fair	annual					100.00
Bowling alleys and billiard rooms	per alley or table		5.00	5.00		10.00

Excise, Stamp and Special Taxes Levied in the United States, 1914–1919—*Continued*

SPECIAL—*Continued*

	Base	Rate in 1913	Act of 1914	Act of 1916	Act of 1917	Act of 1919
Proprietors of—*continued:*						
Shooting galleries	annual					20.00
Riding academies	annual					100.00
Auto hire, per car	annual					10.00–20.00
Brewers, distillers, liquor dealers, etc., in prohibition territory, additional (penal)	annual					1000.00
Proprietors of soft drinks and ice-cream parlors	each 10c. pch.					.01
Munitions manufacturers	on net profits			12%	10%	
MISCELLANEOUS						
Oleomargarine colored	per pound	.10				
white	per pound	.0025				
imported	per pound	.15				
Butter, adulterated	per pound	.10				
process	per pound	.0025				
Filled cheese, domestic	per pound	.01				
imported	per pound	.08				
Mixed flour	per barrel	.04				
Phosphorus matches	per 100	.02				
Opium	per pound	300.00				
Bank circulation	per month	.005				
State bank notes	all issued	10%				
Child labor (penal)	on net profits					10%

– No change made in previous taxes by subsequent legislation.

APPENDIX VI

PUBLIC DEBT OF THE UNITED STATES

The following is a summary of the public debt of the United States Government as it stood on June 30, 1919:

SUMMARY OF THE PUBLIC DEBT, JUNE 30, 1919

GROSS DEBT

Debt bearing no interest...................	$236,428,774.69
Debt on which interest has ceased..........	11,109,370.26
Interest-bearing debt.....................	25,234,496,273.54
Gross debt..........................	$25,482,034,418.49

NET DEBT

Gross debt..............................	$25,482,034,418.49
Deduct—	
Balance free of current obligations.....	1,002,732,042.00
Net debt............................	$24,479,302,376.49

In the following table are given the details as to the interest-bearing debt as it stood on June 30, 1919:

WAR COSTS AND THEIR FINANCING

INTEREST-BEARING DEBT,

DETAIL				
Title of loan	Rate, per cent	When issued	When redeemable or payable	Interest payable
Consols of 1930	2	1900	Payable after Apr. 1, 1930.	Jan., Apr., July, Oct.
Loan of 1925	4	1895–96	Payable after Feb. 1, 1925.	Feb., May, Aug., Nov
Panama Canal loan of 1916–1936.	2	1906	Redeemable after Aug. 1, 1916. Payable Aug. 1, 1936.	do
Panama Canal loan of 1918–1938.	..do....	1908	Redeemable after Nov. 1, 1918. Payable Nov. 1, 1938.	do
Panama Canal loan of 1961.	3	1911	Payable June 1, 1961.	Mar., June, Sept., Dec.
Conversion bonds	...do...	1916–17	Payable 30 years from date of issue.	Jan., Apr., July, Oct.
Certificates of indebtedness (various).	Various	1918–19	Various, not exceeding 1 year from date of issue.	At maturity or earlier.
Certificates of indebtedness.	2	1918–19	1 year from date of issue.	Jan., July.
First Liberty loan	3½	1917	Redeemable on or after June 15, 1932. Payable June 15, 1947.	June, Dec.
First Liberty loan converted.	4	1917	Redeemable on or after June 15, 1932. Payable June 15, 1947.	....do....
Do	4¼	1918	Redeemable on or after June 15, 1932. Payable June 15, 1947.	June, Dec.
First Liberty loan second converted.	...do...	1918	Redeemable on or after June 15, 1932. Payable June 15, 1947.	....do....
Second Liberty loan	4	1917	Redeemable on or after Nov. 15, 1927. Payable Nov. 15, 1942.	May, Nov.
Second Liberty loan, converted.	4¼	1918	Redeemable on or after Nov. 15, 1927. Payable Nov. 15, 1942.	May, Nov.
Third Liberty loan	...do...	1918	Payable Sept. 15, 1928.	Mar., Sept.
Fourth Liberty loan	...do...	1918	Redeemable on or after Oct. 15, 1933. Payable Oct. 15, 1938.	Apr., Oct.
Victory Liberty loan.	3¾ and 4¾	1919	Redeemable June 15, or Dec. 15, 1922. Payable May 20, 1923.	June, Dec.
War-savings and thrift stamps, series 1918–19.	4[3]	1917–1919	Payable Jan. 1, 1923, and Jan. 1, 1924.	At maturity[3]
Postal savings bonds (first to sixteenth series).	22	1911–1919	Redeemable after 1 year from date of issue. Payable 20 years from date of issue.	Jan., July
Aggregate of interest-bearing debt.				

[1] This amount represents receipts of the Treasurer of the United States on account of principal of bonds of the Fourth Liberty loan to June 30.
[2] This amount represents receipts of the Treasurer of the United States on account of principal of notes of the Victory Liberty loan to June 30
[3] The average issue price of war-savings stamps for the years 1918 and 1919 with interest at four per cent per annum compounded quarterly for the average

PUBLIC DEBT OF THE UNITED STATES

JUNE 30, 1919

Amount issued	OUTSTANDING JUNE 30, 1919		
	Registered	Coupon	Total
$646,250,150.00	$598,031,100.00	$1,692,950.00	$599,724,050.00
162,315,400.00	105,036,250.00	13,453,650.00	118,489,900.00
54,631,980.00	48,948,080.00	6,100.00	48,954,180.00
30,000,000.00	25,835,520.00	111,880.00	25,947,400.00
50,000,000.00	43,389,600.00	6,610,400.00	50,000,000.00
28,894,500.00	6,705,000.00	22,189,500.00	28,894,500.00
4,719,582,490.00	....	3,446,260,490.00	3,446,260,490.00
178,723,000.00	178,723,000.00	....	178,723,000.00
1,989,455,550.00	288,862,500.00	1,121,209,100.00	1,410,071,600.00
568,318,450.00	21,062,950.00	146,729,800.00	167,792,750.00
405,443,150.00	86,588,100.00	316,852,000.00	403,440,100.00
3,492,050.00	1,112,700.00	2,379,350.00	3,492,050.00
3,807,864,200.00	85,942,950.00	618,261,400.00	704,204,350.00
$3,034,609,850.00	$444,421,350.00	$2,417,830,900.00	$2,862,252,250.00
4,175,148,700.00	530,720,350.00	3,427,832,350.00	3,958,552,700.00
¹6,959,504,587.00	....	....	6,794,504,587.00
²3,467,844,971.77	....	....	3,467,844,971.77
³1,091,017,006.20	....	...953,997,434.77	953,997,434.77
11,349,960.00	10,676,000.00	673,960.00	11,349,960.00
$31,384,445,994.97	....	....	$25,234,496,273.54

period to maturity will amount to $5 on Jan. 1, 1923, and Jan. 1, 1924, respectively.
Thrift stamps do not bear interest.
⁴This amount represents receipts of the Treasurer of the United States on account of proceeds of sale of war-savings certificate stamps and United States thrift stamps.

INDEX

Acceptances, in Great Britain, 30, 108; in United States, 136, 139.
Adams, Henry Carter, 7, 234, 312, 315, 373, 391.
Adjustments from peace to war, of the various belligerents, 49–51; obstacles to, 51–53.
Admissions and dues, taxes on, in United States, 481.
Advances to Allies. *See* Loans, foreign.
Africa, foreign investments in, 16, 17; total war expenditures by, 105.
Aldrich-Vreeland notes, 58.
American Bankers' Association, 210.
American Economic Association, Committee on War Finance of, 219, 281, 356, 382.
American Expeditionary Force, 327.
American Foreign Securities Company, 68–69, 75, 171.
American Geographical and Statistical Society, 308.
Amsterdam, displaced by London as commercial center, 18; exchange in, 125.
Angell, Norman, 17.
Anglo-French loan, 66, 68, 162, 170, 396.
Annuities, 386.
Antwerp, sacking of, 18; stock exchange of, closed, 28.
Argentina, a borrowing nation, 12; foreign trade of, in 1913, 15; British investments in, 16; loans to, by United States, 65, 67; bonds of, as collateral, 69; exchange arrangements between United States and, 142; gold reserve in, 353; note issues in, 353; bank deposits in, 355.
Armistice, 224, 225, 286.
Australia, a borrowing country, 12; British investments in, 16; total war expenditures by, 105; direct issue of notes by, 130; straight-term bonds in, 149; bonds issued at par, 152, 386; number of subscribers to loans in, 157; war loans in, 184; imports from, into United States, 331, 386.
Austin, Oscar Phelps, 354.
Austria, expenditures of, 104; lowest denomination of bonds in, 156; number of subscribers to loans in, 157; loans by, 1914-1918, 196; revenues of, 1915-1918, 263; capital levy in, 380.
Austria-Hungary, manufactures in, 3; German investments in, 17; financial condition of, in 1914, 26; ultimatum of, to Serbia, 27; declaration of war by, 28; effect upon, of declaration of war, 33, 50; moratorium in, 37; loss of gold by, 42; increase of note issues in, 47; expenditures by, 102–104; national pre-war income of, 106; condition of Bank in, 1913–1917, 123; inflation in, 125; assistance to, by Bank, 126–128, 148; rate of interest unchanged by, 151; pre-war credit of, 151; lowest denomination of bonds in, 156; loans by, 194–195; war taxation in, 262–263; b u d g e t s, 1915–1918, 318; gold reserves and note issues, 352; distrust of paper money

493

INDEX

in, 366; pre-war population, 370; wealth, 370; income, 370; total debt, 370; interest charge, 371; capital levy in, 379.

Austro-Hungarian Bank, Imperial, gold reserves of, 40, 42, 123–124, 128, 352, 364; note issues of, 48, 123; run on, 122; condition of, 1913–1917, 123; deposits in, 123, 124; loans by, 126–128.

Bailey, W. W., 270.
Balkans, German investments in, 17.
Bank of Amsterdam, founding of, 6; gold reserves of, 353; note issues of, 353.
Bank of Algeria, 175.
Bank of England, establishment of, 6; head of credit system, 29; services of, upon outbreak of war, 31, 35, 108–110; suspension of Bank Act, 39; gold reserves of, 40, 352, 363; advances to Government, 160, 162, 166; note issues of, 352; deposits in, 355.
Bank of Finland, gold reserve of, 352; note issues of, 352; resumption of specie payments by, unlikely, 364.
Bank of France, establishment of, 6; discount of pre-moratorium bills of exchange, 37, 111; gold reserves of, 40, 41, 352, 363; note issues of, 45, 112, 352; advances to the state, 112, 168, 169, 171, 172, 389, 396; deposits in, 355; resumption of specie payments by, unlikely, 364.
Bank, Imperial, of Germany, gold reserves of, 23, 40, 352, 363; note issues of, 23, 117, 119–122, 352; loans of, upon outbreak of war, 38, 118; run on, 120; advances to government, 187; tax on, 260; deposits in, 355; resumption of specie payments by, unlikely, 364.
Bank of Hamburg, 6.
Bank of Italy, note issues of, 115, 352; advances to the government by, 183; gold reserves of, 352, 363; deposits in, 355; resumption of specie payments by, unlikely, 364.
Bank of Naples, 14.
Bank of Ottawa, shipment of gold to, from United States, 49; for Bank of England, 57.
Bank of Rumania, gold reserves of, 364.
Bank of Sicily, 114.
Bank of Sweden, founding of, 6; gold reserves of, 353; note issues of, 353; deposits in, 355.
Bank, Imperial, of Russia, gold reserves of, 26, 40, 41, 114, 352, 363; note issues of, 46, 113, 352; advances to government by, 113, 176, 177; resumption of specie payments by, unlikely, 364.
Bank of Turkey. See Imperial Ottoman Bank.
Bank of Venice, 6.
Bank deposits, in leading countries, 1913 and 1918, 355; in United States, 1913–1918, 357; reduction of, unlikely, 362.
Bank notes, usual conditions of issue, 351; issued by belligerents, 1914 and 1918, 352; by neutrals, 353; contraction of, will be slow, 362; begun in some countries, 365; limited circulation of, in Europe, 366–367.
Banking, functions of commercial, 5; deposit, 6; modern development of, 6; in

INDEX

Florence, 6; problem of, during war, 107, 351.
Bayley, N. A., 304.
Beer. *See* Liquor, malt.
Belgium, manufactures in, 3; a leading country, 12; foreign trade of, in 1913, 15; foreign investments of, 17; entered by German troops, 28; moratorium in, 37; total war expenditures by, 105; financial policy of war, 183; unable to pay war expenditures out of tax revenue, 316; acceptance credit granted to, 341; investment-trusts in, 343.
Berlin, stock exchange in, closed, 28; panic in, 33.
Bimetallism, 145.
Blaine, James G., 303.
Block, Maurice, 83.
Bogart, Ernest L., 103, 105, 106, 219, 250, 265, 293, 298, 325, 399, 417.
Bohemia, 366.
Bolivia, loans to, in United States, 67; exchange arrangements with, 142.
Bolles, A. S., 298, 299, 300, 304.
Bolshevik régime in Russia, 181, 253, 379.
Bons de la defense nationale, in France, 168, 171, 172, 174.
Bond-purchase fund, in United States, 218–220, 227, 389.
Bonds, serial, 386; straight-term, 387; optional or redeemable, 387; gold, 388. *See also* Loans, internal.
Bordeaux, municipal bonds of, sold in United States, 70.
Bourse, founding of, in Paris, 6.
Boy Scouts, 216.
Brazil, British investments in, 16.
British Dominions, war expenditures by, 105; war bonds made taxable, 153; loan policy of, 183; issued straight-term bonds, 387.
Brussels, stock exchange in, closed, 28.
Budget, effect of war upon, in Great Britain, 89–90; in France, 93–94; in Russia, 97, 254; in Germany, 99; in Austria-Hungary, 103; first war, in Great Britain, 236; second, 237; third, 238; fourth, 241; fifth, 243; in Germany, 259; summary of war, of leading belligerents, 317–318; since the armistice, 369; of 1920 in Great Britain, 394; of 1921, 395; of 1920 in France, 396; of 1920 in Germany, 402, 404.
Budapest, stock exchange in, closed, 28; prices in, 125.
Bulgaria, German investments in, 17; moratorium in, 37; total war expenditures by, 105; war loans in, 195; war costs of, defrayed largely by Germany, 198; unable to pay war expenditures out of tax revenues, 316.
Bullock, Charles J., 314.
Business as usual, prevented speedy adjustment to war organization, 52–53, 214; taxes on, in France, 249; future of, 409.

Canada a borrowing country, 12; British investments in, 14; foreign trade of, in 1913, 15; loans to, by United States, 65, 67; bonds of, as collateral, 69; total war expenditures by, 105; direct issue of notes by, 129; limitation on amount of loans in, 147; straight-term bonds in, 149; issue of bonds at par, 152, 386; lowest denomina-

INDEX

tion of bond in, 156; war loans in, 184; government support of price of bonds, 220; bank deposits in, 355; made bonds payable in gold, 388.

Capital, growth of, 25; demand for, 7; annual increase of, in United States, 77, 377; need of, 78; for reconstruction in Europe, 334–335; sources of available, 336; an available surplus in the United States, 337; how to be loaned to Europe, 338; investment by Americans in Germany, 345.

Capital Issues Committee, of Federal Reserve Board, 137, 217, 225.

Capital levy, proposed in Great Britain, 379; in France, 380; in Italy, 380, 400; in Switzerland, 380; in Czecho-Slovakia, 380; in Austria, 380; in Hungary, 380; in Germany, 381, 403; definition of, 381; arguments for, 382.

Certificates of indebtedness, of foreign governments, 206, 207, 230. *See also* Treasury bills; Treasury certificates of indebtedness.

Ceylon, British investments in, 16.

Chamber of Commerce of New York, 308.

Chamberlain, Austen, 166, 400.

Chase, Salmon P., 297, 298, 302, 303, 304, 305, 306, 307, 308, 309, 310, 311, 312, 313, 314, 316.

Chicago, centralization of banking in, 134; credit insurance in, 342.

Child labor, tax on, in United States, 295, 488.

Chile, a borrowing country, 12; bonds of, as collateral, 69.

China, a borrowing country, 12; foreign trade of, in 1913, 15; loans to, by United States, 65, 68.

Civil War in United States, financing of, 297–315.

Coal, government monopoly of, in Italy, 258; taxation of, in Germany, 260.

Collier, James W., 269.

Commerce. *See* Trade, foreign.

Constitutional budgetary procedure, breakdown of, in Great Britain, 89–90; in France, 93; in Germany, 101; in Austria-Hungary, 103.

Consumption taxes, 410.

Contraction, the remedy for inflation, 354, 361.

Cooke, Jay, 311.

Corporations, development of, 2; income tax on, 267, 271, 276, 288; excise tax on, 275; tax in Germany, 404.

Cost of World War, 1, 105; of nineteenth century wars, 85; of World War to United States, 87–88; to Great Britain, 90; to France, 90; to Russia, 98; to Italy, 98; to Germany, 100–101; to Austria-Hungary, 103, 104; to all belligerents, 105; of war, character of, 413–420; who pays, 413; not altered by bond issues, 414; extent to which borne by future generations, 415; indirect, to all belligerents, 417.

Cotton pool in United States, 57; buy a bale campaign, 58.

Crammond, Edgar, 52, 85.

Credit, conditions for the development of national, 1; of international, 10; organization of, in Great Britain, 29; breakdown of, as result of war, 34, 55; machinery for financing foreign trade, 80;

INDEX

use of, instruments in Germany, 120; needed by Europe during period of reconstruction, 340; acceptance, to B e l g i u m, 341; industrial, 341; guaranteed by governments, 342; granted by group export corporations, 342, 348; insurance, 342; interchange, system of National Association of Credit Men, 343; long term, 343; secured by first lien on government revenues, 347; short term, 348.

Creditor nation, the United States, a, 76, 200, 330, 348.

Crisp, Charles R., 270.

Cuba, loans to, in United States, 67.

Culbertson, W. S., 11.

Currency and Bank Note Act of August 6, 1914, in Great Britain, 43–44, 128.

Customs duties, in Great Britain, 239, 242, 244; in Russia, 250; in Italy, 257; in Germany, 262, 408; in United States, 269, 285, 295; during Civil War, 302, 306; future of, 411.

Czecho-Slovakia, difficulty of trade in, 366; capital levy in, 380; reduction in interest suggested in, 383.

Darlehenskassen. See Loan offices.

Davison, Henry P., 341.

Death duties. See Inheritance tax.

Debt, public, as an investment, 3; favoring conditions of, 7; growth of, 8; due to war, 8–9; floating, in Germany, 101, 194, 378; public, in Russia, 178; in Italy, 182, 399; in Germany, 193; amount of, of the European belligerents, 368–370; payment of, unlikely, 372; form of, 372; theory of perpetual, 373; assumed burdenlessness of domestic, 373; provision for payment of, in United States, 375; funding the floating, 375; of United States, 376; of Great Britain, 377; of Italy, 378; of Germany, 378; of Austria-Hungary, 379; form of, not adapted for payment, 385; kinds of, 386–388; willingness of belligerent nations to pay, 388; ability to pay, 389–390; payment of, not a loss, 416; statement of, in United States, 489–491.

Deficit, in United States, 393; in Great Britain, 394; in France, 396; in Italy, 400; in Germany, 402, 404.

Deflation. See Contraction.

Denmark, 353; bonds of, as collateral, 69; gold reserve in, 353; note issues in, 353.

Deposit banking, a development of nineteenth century, 6; increased during war, 355.

Deterioration of race through war, 418.

Dewey, Davis R., 314.

Direct tax of 1861 in United States, 302, 307; taxes, 277, 407.

Dix, John A., 298.

Dollar exchange, 336.

Door and window tax, in France, 249.

Edge Act, 344.

Education of American investor needed, 345–346.

Egypt, bonds of, as collateral, 69.

Embargo on gold, 39, 41, 141, 365.

Erzberger, Mathias, 402.

Estate tax. See Inheritance tax.

INDEX

Excess-profits tax in Great Britain, 239, 242, 243, 395, 407, 409; in France, 246, 247, 397, 409; in Russia, 251, 252; in Italy, 255, 256, 400, 409; in Germany, 259, 260, 261, 403; in United States, 274, 276, 280–282, 289–291, 407, 409.

Exchange, bills of, usually drawn on London, 19, 80; mechanism of foreign, in Great Britain, 29; movement of, after outbreak of war, 48, 56, 64; efforts to provide, in Great Britain, 109; pegging of, 141, 142; fall of, an obstacle to foreign trade, 336, 350; effect of inflation on, 359.

Exchequer bonds in Great Britain, 160, 162, 165.

Excise duties, in Great Britain, 239, 242, 395; in United States, 268, 275, 284, 285, 292; during Civil War, 302, 307, 308, 313; in France, 397; in Germany, 408; development of, 410; rates of, in United States, 479, 482.

Exemption from taxation, Liberty bonds, 208, 211–212, 215, 222, 226–227, 279; minimum of, under British income tax, 238; under French income tax, 248; under United States income tax, 266, 277, 279.

Expenditures for World War, 82–106; difficulties in estimating, 82; predictions as to, 83; effect on, of technical efficiency, 84; by United States, 86–89; by Great Britain, 89–93; extravagance of, 92; by France, 93–97; by Russia, 97–98; by Italy, 98; by Germany, 98–102; by Austria-Hungary, 102–104; by all belligerents, 105; compared with national incomes, 106; in United States since the armistice, 337, 392–393; extravagant plans for, in Europe, 340; growth of, probable, 374; in Great Britain, 393–395; in France, 396, 397; in Italy, 399; in Germany, 402, 404; comparison of, for five nations, 405–407.

Exports from United States, restricted to non-belligerent countries, 326; growth of during war, 327–329; value of, 328; destination, 328; future of, 331; by group export corporations, 342; for 1919, by months, 349.

Federal Reserve Act, 58, 80.

Federal reserve banks, 135; rediscounting by, 135; as fiscal agents of the government, 138–139, 206; preferential discounts by, 138; distributed Treasury certificates of indebtedness, 139, 203; note issues of, 139, 352; gold reserves of, 139, 140, 352, 363; discounts by, 139, 199; marketed Liberty loans, 206, 209; holdings of war paper, 213, 216–217, 224, 226; deposits in, 355. *See also* National banking system.

Federal Reserve Board, 70, 135, 323; capital issues committee of, 137, 217, 225; preferential discounts, 138; division of foreign exchange, 142; international gold clearance fund, 144.

Federal Reserve System, 132–140; centralization of reserves in, 135; asset currency, 136; gold settlement fund, 136; assistance in conduct of war, 137.

498

INDEX

Ferdinand, Archduke Franz, assassination of, 24, 27.
Fessenden, W. P., 314.
Fordney, Joseph W., 88.
Foreign Finance Corporation, 345.
Foreign Trade Corporation, 342.
Foreign trade. *See* Trade, foreign.
France, value of manufactures in, 3; value of property in, 5; a lending nation, 12; foreign trade of, in 1913, 15; foreign investments of, 16, 18, 25, 399; financial unpreparedness of, 25; pre-war loan of, 25; breakdown of credit in, 31–32; moratorium in, 36; methods to protect gold reserves, 41, 140; increase in note issues in, 45; effect of war upon, 50; loans to, in United States, 1915–1917, 67; mobilizes American securities, 74; war expenditures published by, 82; suspension of constitutional methods in, 93; credits voted in, 1914–1918, 94; expenditures by, 1914–1918, 95; classification of, 96; national pre-war income of, 106; utilization of services of Bank of France, 110–113, 148; limitation on amount of loan in, 147; short-term notes in, 148; issue of perpetual loans by, 149; pre-war credit of, 151; bonds issued below par, 152; pre-war debt converted by, 153; bond-purchase fund in, 154; loans to Allies by, 155; lowest denomination of bonds in, 156; number of subscribers to loans in, 157; loans by, 168–175; in 1914, 169; in 1915, 170; in 1916, 172; in 1917, 173; in 1919, 175; war taxation of, 245–250; revenues of, 1914–1918, 250; budgets of, 1914–1918, 317; financial situation in, 369, 396, 405; pre-war population of, 370; wealth, 370; income, 370; total debt, 370; interest charge, 371; floating debt in, 377; capital levy in, 380; taxes in, 396–398, 406, 408; tobacco monopoly in, 411; moratorium decrees of, 429–431.

Frederick, Leopold, 81.
Frederick the Great, 22.
Friday, David, 77.
Funding. *See* Debt.

Gerard, James W., 40.
Germany, value of manufactures in, 3; a lending nation, 12; foreign trade of, in 1913, 15; foreign investments of, 16, 17; ultimatum of, to France, 28; financial preparation for war, 33, 50; avoids a moratorium, 37; measures in, to safeguard gold reserves, 40; exchange of gold for notes in, 41, 140; currency measures in, 47; loan to, in United States, 67; mobilizes foreign securities, 75; expenditures by, 1914–1918, 99, 100; votes of credit, 1914–1918, 100; national pre-war income of, 106; assistance to, by banks, 115–122; note circulation in, 1914–1918, 119; inflation in, 120–122, 360; direct issue of notes by, 131; use of Treasury bills by, 148; issue of perpetual loans by, 149; date of issue, 150; rate of interest unchanged by, 151; pre-war credit of, 151; bond purchases by, 154; loans to Allies, 155; lowest denomination of bonds, 156; num-

INDEX

ber of subscribers to loans, 157; loans by, 183–194; in 1914–1918, 188, 194; financial policy of, 234, 258; war taxation in, 259–262; revenues of, 1915–1919, 262; budgets of, 1915–1919, 318; financial situation in, 369, 402–405; pre-war population, 370; wealth, 370; income, 370; total debt, 370, 378; interest charge, 371; floating debt in, 378; capital levy in, 381; reparations by, 385; taxes in, 402–404, 406, 408; act providing for loan offices in, 432–436.

Glass, Carter, 88, 392, 393.

Gold, withdrawal of, from banks in England, 31, 43; in Germany, 33; export forbidden in France, 41; in United States, 49, 141, 142, 365; in other countries, 141, 365; hoarding of, in England, 43; in France, 46; export of, from United States, 49, 56, 63, 142, 143, 365; pool in United States, 57; imports into United States, 64–65, 68, 141, 143; settlement fund under Federal Reserve System, 136; international clearance fund, 143; fall in price of, 144–145; production of, 145, 364; statistics of, 365.

Gold reserves, methods of safeguarding, 38; in principal central banks, 39, 140; increased by exchange of gold notes for bank notes by citizens, in Germany, 40–41; in France, 41, 363; in Russia, 41, 363; of Reichsbank, 122, 363; against currency notes in Great Britain, 129; against Dominion notes in Canada, 129; against Commonwealth notes in Australia, 130; in United States, 139, 140, 363; essential for support of credit, 143; of banks during Civil War, 305; of belligerents, 1914 and 1918, 352, 354; of neutrals, 353, 354; of leading banks in 1919, 363.

Great Britain, value of manufactures in, 3; value of property in, 5; a lending nation, 12; foreign investments of, 14, 16, 18, 24; foreign trade of, in 1913, 15; unpreparedness of, for war, 24; declares war on Germany, 28; breakdown of credit in, 29–30, 50; moratorium in, 35; currency measures in, 43; borrowings by, in United States, 1915–1917, 67; mobilizes American securities, 74; war expenditures published by, 82; appropriation system of, 89; expenditures of, 1914–1919, 90; by quarters, 91; extravagance in, 92; total war expenditures by, 105; national pre-war income of, 106, 370; use of paper money and bank credit by, 108–110; direct issue of notes by, 128; Treasury bills in, 148; continuous loan in, 149; pre-war credit of, 151; bonds issued at par, 152, 386; pre-war debt converted, 153; war bonds made taxable in, 153; bond purchase fund in, 154; loans to Allies by, 155; lowest denomination of bonds in, 156; number of subscribers to loans in, 157; loans by, 159–167; in 1915, 160; in 1916, 162; in 1917, 163; in 1918, 165; in 1919, 167; tax policy of, 234, 235; war taxes in, 235–245; revenues of, 1914–1919, 245; budgets of,

500

INDEX

1915–1919, 317; proportion of loans and taxes, 319; placed embargo on gold exports, 365; financial situation in, 369, 394, 405; pre-war population of, 370; wealth, 370; total debt, 371; interest charge, 371; floating debt in, 377; capital levy in, 379; reduction in debt of, 390; taxes in, 395, 406, 407; moratorium proclamations in, 423–428.

Greece, French loans to, 25; total war expenditures by, 105.

Guyot, Ives, 16.

Hart, A. B., 305, 310.
Havenstein, Rudolph, 120, 193.
Hay, John, 299.
Helfferich, Karl, 99, 183, 186, 189, 191, 234, 258, 259.
Hill, Ebenezer J., 271.
Hirst, F. W., 85, 151.
Hoarding of money, in England, 43; in France, 46; in Germany, 47, 120; in Austria-Hungary, 48, 123.
Hobson, C. K., 14, 16.
Holland, a lending country, 12; foreign trade of, in 1913, 15; bonds of, as collateral, 69; sale of foreign securities in, 75; French loans in, 171; gold reserves in, 353; capital levy in, 379.
Hollander, Jacob H., 205.
Hoover, Herbert C., on needs of Europe, 338–339.
Howe, Frederick C., 313.
Hull, Cordell, 265.
Hungary, expenditures of, 104; lowest denomination of bonds, 156; number of subscribers to loans, 157; war loans, 1914–1918, 196; revenues of, 1915–1918, 263; capital levy in, 380.
Hyndman, H. M., 26.

Imperial Ottoman Bank, decline of gold reserves of, 42, 364.
Imports into United States, of non-essentials curtailed, 326; growth of, during war, 327, 329–330; sources, 329; future of, 331, 332, 348; for 1919, by months, 349; restrictions upon, by Europe, 350.
Income, national, of principal belligerents, 106, 370; *per capita*, 371.
Income tax, in Great Britain, 236, 237, 242, 395, 407; in France, 246, 248, 250, 397, 398, 408; in Russia, 252; in Italy, 255, 257, 258, 400, 408; in Germany, 261, 403, 408; in Austria-Hungary, 263; in United States, 264–267, 271–273, 277–280, 287–289, 407; during Civil War, 302; statistics of, 1913–1917, 267, 473; personal returns of, 474; rates of, act of 1913, 475; act of 1916, 475; act of 1917, 476; act of 1919, 476.
Indemnity bonds, German, soon to be issued, 367; probable transfer of, 384; amount fixed by Treaty of Peace, 385; payment of, 397.
Independent Treasury Act of 1846, 304.
India, a borrowing country, 12; foreign trade of, in 1913, 15; British investments in, 16; total war expenditure by, 105; exchange arrangements between United States and, 142; issue of bonds at par, 152; number of subscribers to loans, 157; war loans in, 185; imports into United States from, 331.
Inflation, in Germany, 120–122; in Austria-Hungary, 124–126; effect on trade of, 126;

INDEX

in United States, 139, 200, 205, 323, 324; during Civil War, 313; must be avoided in extending credit to Europe, 347; a world phenomenon, 351; since the armistice, 354, 355; definition of, 356; effects of, upon prices, 356–358; upon wages, 356, 359; upon foreign exchange, 359; upon solvency of banks, 359; why permitted, 359; aided flotation of loans, 360; curtailed consumption of non-essentials, 360; evil effects of, upon the Treasury, 361; social cost of, 361; remedy for, 361; effect of new credits on, 367; persistence of, 368.

Inheritance tax, in Great Britain, 236, 407; in Germany, 261, 403, 409; in Austria-Hungary, 262; in United States, 273-274, 276, 283, 291, 407; in France, 397; in Italy, 401; use in post-war finance, 409; rates of, in United States, 478.

Insurance, rates of marine, 51; Bureau of War Risk, in United States, 58; taxation of, in United States, 481.

Intelligence of peoples in principal countries, 391–392.

Inter-Allied Purchasing Commission, 207, 232.

Interest charges on the public debt, of leading European belligerents, 369; *per capita*, 371; proposal to reduce, 383; on Allied debt postponed by United States Treasury Department, 384; of French debt, 396; German debt, 402, 404.

International Cotton Corporation, 342.

International High Commission, 144; proposes international gold clearance fund, 144.

Internationalism of trade, 20, 27.

Investment in undeveloped countries, 10–12; as a cause of war, 11, 12; effected by trade, 13, 15; of foreign capital in United States, 13; British, abroad, 14–16, 24; of French, 16–17, 25, 399; of German, 16–17; of Belgian, 17; of Dutch, 17; of Swiss, 17; widespread character of, 17; effect on international alliances of, 17–18; slight, by people of United States before the war, 65; during the war, 66–71, 346; larger profits from, at home, 81; permanent, in Europe called for by present situation, 343, 346; of American capital in Germany, 345; in foreign securities, 346.

Investment-trust, 343.

Italy, value of manufactures in, 3; German investments in, 17; refuses to make war in 1913, 23; moratorium in, 37; loans to, in United States, 1915–1917, 67; war expenditures published by, 82; expenditures by, 98, 106; national pre-war income of, 106; note circulation in, 1913–1918, 115; direct issue of notes by, 131; limitation on amount of loan in, 147; advances of banks to, 148; issue of perpetual loans by, 149; pre-war credit of, 151; lowest denomination of bonds in, 156; number of subscribers to loans in, 157; loans in, 181; debt in, 1914–1918, 182; loans, 1914–1918, 183; war taxation in, 254–258; revenues of, 1915–1919, 258;

INDEX

budgets of, 1915–1919, 318; financial situation in, 369, 399–401; pre-war population of, 370; wealth, 370; income, 370; total debt, 370; interest charge, 371; capital levy in, 380; taxes in, 400, 406, 408.

Japan, a borrowing country, 12; foreign trade of, in 1913, 15; loans to, in United States, 68; total war expenditures by, 105; loans to Allies by, 155; gold reserves in, 352; note issues in, 352; bank deposits in, 355.
Jastrow, J., 381.
Java, imports from, 331.
Jennings, H. H., 128.
Jèze, Gaston, 249.
Johnson, A. S., 111.
Jordan, David Starr, 418.
Jugo-Slavia, difficulties of exchange in, 367.

Kahn, Otto H., 211.
Keating, Edward, 270.
Kellogg, Vernon L., 418.
Kemmerer, Edwin W., 132.
Kent, F. I., 350.
Kenyon, William S., 384.
Kerensky, Alexander F., 253.
Keynes, John Maynard, 384.
Kinley, David, 311.
Kitchin, Claude, 202, 286.
Klotz, Louis, 380, 396.

Laughlin, J. Laurence, 30, 47, 429, 432.
Law, Andrew Bonar, 243.
League of Nations, 420.
Leffingwell, Russell C., 376.
Lenin, Nicholai, 253.
Liberty loans in United States, 199–233; marketed by banks, 138, 206; policy regarding, 201–202; characteristics of, 207; first, 208–210; second, 210–214; third, 214–220;

fourth, 220–225; fifth, 226–228; Bond Act, first, 437–441; second, 442–454; supplement to, 454–457; third, 457–463; fourth, 463–464; Victory Loan Act, 464–472.
Lindsay, Samuel McC., 89.
Liquor, distilled, taxation of, in Great Britain, 240, 244, 395; in France, 247, 397; in Russia, 251; in Italy, 255, 258; in Germany, 261; in United States, 284, 292, 294; during Civil War, 307; future of, 410; rates of, in United States, 479, 486.
Liquor, malt, taxation of, in Great Britain, 237, 240, 244, 395; in Russia, 251; in Italy, 255; in United States, 284; in France, 397; future of, 410; rates of, in United States, 479, 486.
Lloyd-George, David, 19, 35, 236, 237, 419.
Loan offices in Germany, 38, 47, 116, 189; act providing for, 432–436.
Loans, internal, of World War in Europe, 146–198; magnitude, 146; limitation of amount, 147; term, 148, 372; maturing and perpetual bonds, 149; period of subscription, 149; date of issue, 150; rate of interest, 150; before the war, 151; price of issue, 152; conversion privileges, 153; exemption from taxation, 153; collateral privileges, 153; bond-purchase funds, 154; internal or foreign, 154; methods of subscription and payment, 155; low denomination of bonds, 156; distribution and number of subscribers, 156–158; success, 158; war loans in Great Britain, 160–167; first,

INDEX

160; second, 161; third, 162–164; day-to-day borrowing, 164–166; fourth, 166; war loans in France, 168–175; pre-war loan, 168; first, 170; second, 171; third, 173; fourth, 174; war loans in Russia, 176–181; first, 176; second, 177; third, 177; fourth, 178; fifth, 179; sixth, 179; seventh, 180; Liberty loan, 180; war loans in Italy, 181–183; mobilization loan, 181; first to fourth, 183; war loans in Canada, 184; in Australia, 184; in New Zealand, 185; in India, 185; war loans in Germany, 183, 186–194; theory of war finance in, 186, 190, 316; first loan, 187, 189; second to eighth, 188; sale of bonds at nearly par, 192; ninth, 193; war loans in Austria-Hungary, 194–197; in Turkey, 195, 198; in Bulgaria, 195, 198; in United States, 199–233; during Civil War, 299, 303, 309, 313; policy of financing war by, 300, 307, 310, 312, 314.

Loans, foreign, by people of United States during the war, 66–71, 200; based on collateral, 69, 75; warning of Federal Reserve Board regarding, 70; by United States Government, to Great Britain, 164; to France, 173, 174; to Russia, 180; to Italy, 182; to Allies, 206, 208, 230–233, 319, 333; discontinued, 338; needed by Europe for reconstruction, 333–335; to Europe should be from private sources, 338; rationing of, 339; demand for, 340; proposal to cancel United States, 383.

Loans, proportion between, and taxes, 319–325; advantages of loans, 320; objections to heavy taxation, 321; desirability of heavy taxes, 322; evils of excessive loans, 323–325.

London, founding of stock exchange in, 6; closing of, 28; as a world center, 18–20, 29, 55; advantages of, 80; credit insurance in, 342.

Loree, L. F., 73.

Loria, Achille, 380.

Luxuries, taxation of, in Great Britain, 240, 241, 242, 244, 410; in France, 250, 398, 410; in Italy, 256, 401; in Germany, 261; in United States, 285, 293–294, 410, 483.

Lyons, municipal bonds of, sold in United States, 70.

McAdoo, William G., 202.
McCulloch, Hugh, 299, 300, 309, 314.
McKenna, Reginald, 161, 238, 241, 242.

Madrid, stock exchange in, closed, 28.

Manufactures, value of, in principal countries, 3.

Marseilles, municipal bonds of, sold in United States, 70.

Mexico, a borrowing country, 12; French investments in, 17, 399; loans to, in United States, 67.

Mill, John Stuart, 418.

Miller, Adolph C., 323.

Mitchell, Wesley C., 306.

Mobilization, of securities by British Government, 74; by French, 74; by German, 75; of financial resources of belligerents, 158.

Money, issue of, at outbreak of war, 42; paper money issued directly by British govern-

INDEX

ment, 43–45, 128; by chambers of commerce in France, 46; paper, and bank credit, 107–145; Dominion notes issued by Canada, 129; Commonwealth notes issued by Australia, 130; state notes in Italy, 131, 183; United States notes during Civil War, 308, 309, 310, 311, 313, 314; in circulation in United States, 1913–1918, 357; fiduciary, now in circulation, practically inconvertible, 358; reduction in total amount of, unlikely, 362; a beginning made in, 365; limited circulation of fiduciary, due to distrust, 366–367.

Monopolies, Government, revenue from, in Great Britain, 240, 244; in France, 247, 397; in Russia, 251; in Italy, 255, 257, 258; in Germany, 259; future of, 411.

Montreal, stock exchange in, closed, 28.

Moratorium, definition of, 34; in Great Britain, 35–36; in France, 36; in Russia, 37; in other countries, 37; in Germany, 37–38, 118; in Austria-Hungary, 122; British Proclamation of, August 2, 1914, 423; of August 6, 1914, 423; of August 12, 1914, 425; of September 3, 1914, 425; of September 30, 1914, 426; French Moratorium Decree, of August 9, 1914, 429; of September 27, 1914, 431.

Morgan, J. P., and Company, 69, 70, 341.

Morocco episode, 21.

Mulhall, M. G., 3.

Munitions tax, in Great Britain, 243; in United States 274, 488.

National Association of Credit Men, 342.

National banking system in United States, 132; decentralization, 133; inelasticity of note circulation, 133; cumbersome exchange methods, 134; lack of correlation, 134; act passed, 311. *See also* Federal Reserve banks.

Netherlands. *See* Holland.

Newfoundland, loans to, in United States, 67.

New York, founding of stock exchange in, 6; closing of, 28; debt owed by, in 1914, 55; as a world financial center, 76; conditions to be met, 77–81; centralization of banking in, 134; credit insurance in, 342.

New Zealand, total war expenditures by, 105; issue of bonds at par, 152, 386; number of subscribers to loans in, 157; war loans in, 185.

Nicholay, John G., 299.

Nitti, S., 399.

Norway, loans to, in United States, 67; bonds of, as collateral, 69; gold reserve in, 353; note issues in, 353.

Noyes, Alexander Dana, 24, 297.

Obligations de la defense nationale, in France, 169, 172, 174.

Owen, Robert L., 344.

Paish, Sir George, 13, 14, 91 384.

Panama, loans to, in United States, 67.

Panic, of July, 1914, on stock exchanges, 28–29; in Great Britain, 30–31; in France, 31–32; in Germany, 33, 121;

505

INDEX

in United States, 54; in Austria-Hungary, 1918, 126.
Paper money. *See* Money.
Paris, founding of Bourse in, 6; closing of Coulisse, 28; municipal bonds of, sold in United States, 70.
Peace Treaty, 396, 404.
Peru, loans to, in United States, 67; exchange arrangements with, 142.
Pethick-Lawrence, F. W., 382.
Petrograd, stock exchange in, closed, 28.
Pigou, A. C., 321, 382.
Plehn, Carl C., 8.
Poland, exchange difficulties in, 366.
Population, of leading nations, 370.
Prices, movement of, in United States, 1913–1918, 357; causes of high, 357–358; continuance of, 368.
Progressive taxation, 409. *See also* Excess profits tax; Income tax; Inheritance tax.
Prohibition in United States, 410.
Public utilities, taxation of, in United States, 481.

Rasin, Dr., 383.
Reconstruction of Europe, amount needed for, 333–334; must be supplied by loans, 335; sources from which available, 336–337; how to be made available, 338; must be largely by own efforts, 340; must be treated as a whole, 347.
Reichsbank. *See* Bank, Imperial, of Germany.
Reparations, 385.
Repudiation of debt in Russia, 379; in Hungary, 379.
Resources of leading belligerents, 391–392.

Revenue act, in United States, of October 3, 1913, 264; of October 22, 1914, 263; of September 8, 1916, 269–275; of March 3, 1917, 275–276; of October 3, 1917, 277–285; of February 24, 1919, 286; rates of all acts, 479–488.
Revenues, of leading European belligerents, 369, 405; of United States, 392–393; of Great Britain, 394–395; of France, 396, 397; of Germany, 402, 404.
Ribot, Alexandre F., 93, 249, 380, 396, 398.
Roedern, Count S. F. W. E. von, 261.
Rumania, French investments in, 17, 399; German investments in, 17; total war expenditures by, 105; financing the war in, 183.
Russia, value of manufactures in, 3; foreign trade of, in 1913, 15; French investments in, 16, 18, 25, 399; fiscal condition in, in 1914, 26; cereal crops of, 1910–1914, 26, 32; mobilization by, 28; effect of outbreak of war upon, 32–33, 50; moratorium in, 37; exchange of gold for notes in, 41, 140; increase of note issues in, 46; loans to, in United States, 1915–1917, 67; expenditures by, 1914–1917, 97, 98; national pre-war income of, 106, 370; use of Bank, 113–114, 148; pre-war credit of, 151; lowest denomination of bonds in, 156; number of subscribers to loans in, 157; loans in, 176–181; in 1914, 177; in 1915, 179; in 1916, 180, in 1917, 181; revolution in, 180, 252; Bolshevik régime, 181, 253; war taxation in, 250–

INDEX

254; revenues of, 1914–1917, 254; budgets of, 1914–1917, 317; financial situation in, 369; pre-war population, 370; wealth, 370; total debt, 370; interest charge, 370; alcohol monopoly in, 411.

St. Louis, centralization of banking in, 134.
Sales, tax on, in Germany, 259. *See also* Turnover, tax on.
Santo Domingo, loans to, in United States, 67.
Samuels, Herbert, 92.
Savings of American people, 77–78, 337.
Schanzer, Carlo, 380.
Schiffer, E., 100, 101, 262, 402.
Schuckers, J. W., 299.
Scotland, investment-trusts in, 343.
Securities, market for, 4; American, held abroad, 71, 73; resold to United States, 72–74; mobilization of, by British government, 74; by French, 74; by German, 75.
Seligman, E. R. A., 12, 84.
Serbia, French investments in, 25; ultimatum to, by Austria-Hungary, 27; war declared against, 28; total war expenditures by, 105; financing the war in, 183.
Sherman, John, 299.
Silver, in German war chest, 23; payment of, by Reichsbank, 47; exports of, from United States, 142; rise in price of, 145.
Simmons, F. McL., 265, 287.
Sinking fund, of Fifth Liberty Bond Act, 227, 375, 389; in Great Britain, 389.
Sixteenth Amendment of the Federal Constitution, 264.
Smith, George Otis, 22.
South America, closing of stock exchanges in, 28; foreign trade of United States with, 62.
Soviet. *See* Bolshevik.
Spain, manufactures in, 3; bonds of, as collateral, 69; exchange arrangements between United States and, 142; gold reserve in, 353; note issues in, 353; bank deposits in, 355.
Specie payments suspended, in Austria-Hungary, 34, 48, 122; by Bank of France, 39, 46; by Reichsbank, 39, 47; by Bank of Russia, 39, 46, 113; by Imperial Austro-Hungarian Bank, 39; nominally maintained by Bank of England, 39, 140; in Australia, 130; maintained in United States, 140; suspended during Civil War, 306; resumption of, unlikely in Europe, 362.
Stamp taxes in United States, 485.
Stock exchange, modern development of, 6; establishment of, in London, 6; in New York, 6; in Paris, 6; panic on, in 1914, 27–29; closed in European cities, 28; in New York, 28, 54.
Straits Settlements, imports from, 331.
Sugar, taxation of, in Great Britain, 239, 242; in Russia, 251, 252; in Italy, 255, 258; in United States during Civil War, 302, 307; in France, 397; future, in United States, 410.
Super- and surtax. *See* Income tax.
Sweden, bonds of, as collateral, 69.
Switzerland, a lending country, 12; foreign investments of,

INDEX

17; loans to, in United States, 67; bonds of, as collateral, 69; exchange arrangements between United States and, 142; gold reserve in, 353; note issues in, 353; bank deposits in, 355; capital levy in, 380; salt monopoly in, 411.

Taxation, in Europe, 234–264; in Great Britain, 235–245; in France, 245–250; in Russia, 250–254; in Italy, 254–258; in Germany, 258–262; in Austria-Hungary, 262–263; in United States, 264–296; during Civil War, 301; objections to heavy, 321; desirability of heavy, 322; after-war problems of, 391–412; in Great Britain, 395; in France, 397; in Italy, 400–401; in Germany, 402–404; probable development of, 407–412; direct, 407–409; of inheritances, 409; on business, 409; of articles of consumption, 410; customs, 411; by fiscal monopolies, 411. *See also* Revenue acts.

Tea, taxation of, in Great Britain, 236, 237, 239; in France, 247; in Italy, 258; in United States during Civil War, 302, 307; in the future, 410.

Thrift stamps, in United States, 229. *See also* War savings certificates.

Tobacco, taxation of, in Great Britain, 239, 243, 395; in France, 247, 397; in Russia, 251; in Italy, 257; in United States, 268, 275, 291, 294; during Civil War, 307; future of, 410; rates of, in United States, 480, 486–487.

Toronto, stock exchange in, closed, 28.

Trade, foreign, of principal lending and borrowing countries, 15; of United States, 59, 72; effect of war upon, 60–62; with Europe, 60–61; with South America, 62–63; regulated to help win war, 326–327; with Europe determined by reconstruction needs, 336. *See also* Exports; Imports.

Trade balance of United States, 13, 61, 64, 71, 72, 330, 349; of Great Britain, 25; of France, 25; result of self-denial, 332; will be paid by larger imports, 332.

Treasury bills, in Great Britain, bought by the banks, 110, 159; in Russia, 113–114; use of, in World War, 148; emissions of, in Great Britain, 160; in France, 168, 170; in Russia, 176, 179; in Italy, 181; in Germany, 187, 189, 192. *See also* Certificates of indebtedness.

Treasury certificates of indebtedness, of United States, 139, 202–205, 208.

Treasury notes, Imperial, in Germany, 22, 23, 131–132; in United States during Civil War, 298, 299, 303, 304.

Turkey, foreign trade of, in 1913, 15; French investments in, 17, 18, 25, 399; moratorium in, 37; loss of gold by, 42; total war expenditures by, 105; war loans in, 195.

Turnover, tax on, in France, 249, 398.

Ukraine, exchange difficulties in, 367.

Underwood, Oscar W., 265.

INDEX

United States, value of manufactures in, 3; value of property in, 5; a borrowing nation, 12; foreign investments in, 13; foreign trade of, in 1913, 15; exports of gold from, 49, 56, 143, 365; as a neutral, 54–81; debts owed by, 56; expansion of foreign trade, 59–63, 327–334, 349; imports of gold into, 63–65, 68, 141, 143; foreign loans floated in, 1915–1917, 65–71; annual payments owed by, 64, 71; exports and imports, 1910–1914, 72; repurchase by, of American securities, 73; financial position of, in 1916, 76; new securities issued in, 1910–1916, 78; as a lender of capital, 76–81; war expenditures published by, 82; monthly expenditures by, 1917–1918, 86; total, 1916–1919, 87; total war expenditures by, 105; national banking system in, 132–134; establishment of Federal Reserve System, 135; services to Government of, 136–140; as fiscal agents, 138–139; inflation in, 139–140, 200, 356–357, 361; control of gold exports by, 141; exports of silver from, 142; largest loan in, 147; limitations on amount of loans in, 147; use of Treasury bills by, 148; bonds issued at par, 152, 207, 386; war bonds made taxable, 153; bond purchase fund in, 154, 218; loans to Allies by, 155, 206, 230–233, 333; lowest denomination of bonds in, 156, 207; number of subscribers to loans in, 157; loans in, 199–233; war finance program, 201; issue of certificates of indebtedness by, 204; First Liberty Loan of, 208–210; Second, 210–213; Third, 214–219; Fourth, 220–224; Fifth, 226–228; sinking fund of, 227, 389; war savings certificates, 228–230; taxation in, 264–296; income tax, 264–267; act of October 22, 1914, 268; of September 8, 1916, 269–275; of March 3, 1917, 275; of October 3, 1917, 277–285; of February 24, 1919, 286–296; revenues of, 1914–1919, 295; proper proportion of loans and taxes in, 319; exports from, 1914–1919, 328; imports into, 1914–1919, 329; available capital in, 337; extension of credit to Europe by, 338–345; education of people of, in foreign investments, 346; financial situation in, 369, 392, 405; pre-war population, 370; wealth, 370; income, 370; total debt, 370; interest charge, 371; theory of debt payment in, 372; probable increase of expenditures, 374; floating debt in, 376; suggestion to cancel debt owed by Allies, 383; made bonds payable in gold, 388; reduction in debt of, 389; taxes in, 407, 410; First Liberty Bond Act, 437–441; Second, 442–454; Supplement to, 454–457; Third, 457–463; Fourth, 463–464; Fifth, 464–472; income tax statistics, 473, 474; rates of, 475–478; rates of excise, stamp, and special taxes, 1913–1919, 479–488; public debt of, 489–491.

Vanderlip, Frank A., 339, 343.
Vienna, stock exchange in, closed, 28; prices in, 125; panic in, 126.

INDEX

Votes of credit, in Great Britain, 90; in France, 93–94; in Germany, 100.

Wages, movement of, in United States, 1913–1918, 357.
War chest in Germany, 22.
War excess profits tax. *See* Excess profits tax.
War Finance Corporation, 137, 217, 227; amount of loans by, 338; suspended, 338; provisions of act relating to, 470.
War savings certificates, in United States, 228–230.
Wealth, of leading nations, 370; *per capita*, 371; redistribution of, by taxation, 412.
Wehrbeitrag, 22, 23.

Wells, David A., 309.
Whisky. *See* Liquor, distilled.
Wickersham, George W., 384.
Williams, John Sharp, 265.
Willoughby, Westel W., 89.
Willoughby, William F., 89, 137.
Wilson, Woodrow, 286, 294.
Wintermantel, Werner, 345.
Withers, Hartley, 44.
Wirth, G., 404.
World War, cost of, 1, 105; belief that it would be short, 51–52, 238, 245; expenditures for, 82–106; wastefulness of, 84; policy of financing, 315, 319–325; indirect costs of, 417; effect on racial vitality, 418; indirect benefits from, 419.

This volume from the
Cornell University Library's
print collections was scanned on an
APT BookScan and converted
to JPEG 2000 format
by Kirtas Technologies, Inc.,
Victor, New York.
Color images scanned as 300 dpi
(uninterpolated), 24 bit image capture
and grayscale/bitonal scanned
at 300 dpi 24 bit color images
and converted to 300 dpi
(uninterpolated), 8 bit image capture.
All titles scanned cover to
cover and pages may include
marks, notations and other
marginalia present in the
original volume.

The original volume was digitized
with the generous support of the
Microsoft Corporation
in cooperation with the
Cornell University Library.

Cover design by Lou Robinson,
Nightwood Design.

Printed in Great Britain
by Amazon